EFFECTIVE
BRIEF
THERAPIES

A CLINICIAN'S GUIDE

Effective Brief Therapies

A Clinician's Guide

Edited by

Michel Hersen and Maryka Biaggio

School of Professional Psychology
Pacific University
Forest Grove, Oregon

Academic Press
San Diego New York Boston
London Sydney Tokyo Toronto

Academic Press
a Harcourt Science and Technology Company
525 B Street, Suite 1900, San Diego, California 92101-4495
http://www.academicpress.com

Academic Press Limited
Harcourt Place, 32 Jamestown Road, London NW1 7BY, UK
http://www.hbuk.co.uk/ap/

Library of Congress Catalog Card Number: 00-103148

International Standard Book Number: 0-12-343530-7

PRINTED IN THE UNITED STATES OF AMERICA
00   01   02   03   04   05   MM   9   8   7   6   5   4   3   2   1

To Vicki

Michel Hersen

To Deb

Maryka Biaggio

Contents

Part III

Special Issues

Preface

Effective Brief Therapies: A Clinician's Guide emanates from our interactions with clinical students in practice, field placements, internships, and residencies over several decades. No matter how well prepared and trained in the theoretical aspects of our craft, nascent clinicians experience considerable anxiety in conceptualizing their cases and developing effective treatment regimens. Very often they are overwhelmed by clients who do not present as described in standard textbook fashion. Indeed, they find that inevitably there are concurrent diagnoses and treatments and numerous unanticipated treatment issues. Students also quickly learn in our era of accountability and managed care that time efficiency in dealing with clients is an imperative.

Our book, therefore, is devoted to facilitating clinicians' understanding of strategies for approaching cases, conducting viable assessments, and implementing contemporary therapies. The book is divided into three parts.

Part I (Introduction) includes one chapter that broadly considers assessment in effective brief therapy.

In Part II (Treatment of Specific Disorders) there are 18 chapters in which individuals with expertise for the specific disorders discuss the clinical approach to treatment. Most of the chapters in this part follow the following outline:

1. Case Description
2. Treatment Conceptualization
3. Assessment
4. Treatment Implementation
5. Concurrent Diagnoses and Treatment
6. Complications and Treatment Implications

7. Dealing with Managed Care and Accountability
8. Outcome and Follow-up
9. Dealing with Recidivism
10. Summary
11. References

In Part III (Special Issues), important issues frequently overlooked by some therapists are examined, including considerations for Gay and Lesbian Clients (Chapter 20), Clients with Marital Dysfunction (Chapter 21), Ethnically Diverse Clients (Chapter 22), and Older Adults (Chapter 23). Integral concern with diversity and cross-cultural issues should be a given in the contemporary clinician's daily activities. Chapters 20, 22, and 23 underscore these points.

Many individuals have contributed to the fruition of this book. First and foremost, we thank our eminent contributors for taking time out from their busy schedules to impart their erudite thinking about cases. Second, we thank Alexander Duncan, Carole L. Londerée, and Erika Qualls for their invaluable technical assistance. And, finally, but hardly least of all, we are most appreciative of Dr. George Zimmar's efforts as our editor at Academic Press. Indeed, when your editor is a psychologist himself you need to be on your toes. George's assistance, advice, and ideas have been of tremendous value to us.

Michel Hersen
Maryka Biaggio
Forest Grove, Oregon

Contributors

David O. Antonuccio, V.A. Medical Center, and University of Nevada School of Medicine, Reno

Ghazi Azaad, 20 Germantown Road, Danbury, Connecticut

Belinda E. Barnett, Arthur P. Noyes Clinical Research Foundation, The Norristown State Hospital, Norristown, Pennsylvania

Gary A. Birchler, Department of Psychiatry, University of California, San Diego, California

Deanna Zotter Bonifazi, Department of Psychology, West Chester University, West Chester, Pennsylvania

Claude Boutin, Université Laval, École de Psychologie, Québec, Canada

Sandra J. Coffman, University of Washington, Seattle

Michelle G. Craske, Department of Psychology, University of California, Los Angeles

William I. Dorfman, Center for Psychological Studies, Nova Southeastern University, Ft. Lauderdale, Florida

Barry A. Edelstein, Department of Psychology, West Virginia University, Morgantown

William Fals-Stewart, Department of Psychology, Old Dominion University, Norfolk, Virginia

Robin Ferguson, Mountain Employee Assistance Program, Reno, Nevada

Brian C. Goff, Dialectical Behavior Therapy Program, Portland, Oregon

Jeffrey L. Goodie, Department of Psychology, West Virginia University, Morgantown

G. Dorsey Green, University of Washington, Seattle

David C. Hodgins, Addiction Centre, Foothills Hospital, Calgary, Alberta, Canada

Sandra Y. Jenkins, School of Professional Psychology, Pacific University, Forest Grove, Oregon

Terence M. Keane, National Center for Posttraumatic Stress Disorder, V.A. Boston Healthcare System, Boston, Massachusetts

Robert D. Kerns, Yale University School of Medicine, V.A. Connecticut Healthcare System, New Haven, Connecticut

Soonie A. Kim, Dialectical Behavior Therapy Program, Portland, Oregon

Ronald A. Kleinknecht, Dean, College of Arts and Sciences, Western Washington University, Bellingham

Kathryn E. Korslund, Arthur P. Noyes Clinical Research Foundation, The Norristown State Hospital, Norristown, Pennsylvania

Robert Ladouceur, Université Laval, École de Psycholgie, Québec, Canada

James B. Lane, School of Professional Psychology, Pacific University, Forest Grove, Oregon

Steven B. Lawyer, Department of Psychology, Auburn University, Auburn, Alabama

Peter M. Lewinsohn, Oregon Research Institute, Eugene

Kenneth L. Lichstein, Department of Psychology, The University of Memphis, Memphis, Tennessee

M. Lowy, Department of Psychiatry, Prince of Wales Hospital, University of New South Wales, Sydney, Australia

Sherry G. MacGlashan, Department of Psychology, Loyola College in Maryland, Baltimore

Barry M. Maletzky, Department of Psychiatry, Oregon Health Sciences University, Portland

Charles S. Mansueto, Behavior Therapy Center of Greater Washington, Bowie State University, Bowie, Maryland

Ronald R. Martin, Department of Psychology, West Virginia University, Morgantown

Robin M. Masheb, Yale University School of Medicine, New Haven, Connecticut

Amanda McCombs-Thomas, Department of Psychology, Loyola College in Maryland, Baltimore

Nathaniel McConaghy, Department of Psychiatry, Prince of Wales Hospital, University of New South Wales, Sydney, Australia

F. Dudley McGlynn, Department of Psychology, Auburn University, Auburn, Alabama

Daniel M. McKitrick, School of Professional Psychology, Pacific University, Forest Grove, Oregon

J. Scott Mizes, Department of Psychology, West Chester University, West Chester, Pennsylvania

Michelle G. Newman, Department of Psychology, The Pennsylvania State University, University Park

Holly K. Orcutt, National Center for Posttraumatic Stress Disorder, V.A. Boston Healthcare System, Boston, Massachusetts

Melissa Piasecki, Department of Psychiatry, University of Nevada School of Medicine, Reno

Ruth M. T. Stemberger, Department of Psychology, Loyola College in Maryland, Baltimore

Amy E. Street, National Center for Posttraumatic Stress Disorder, V.A. Boston Healthcare System, Boston, Massachusetts

Carolyn Sylvain, Université Laval, École de Psychologie, Québec, Canada

Jennie C. I. Tsao, Department of Psychology, University of California, Los Angeles

Ralph M. Turner, Arthur P. Noyes Clinical Research Foundation, The Norristown State Hospital, Norristown, Pennsylvania

David L. Van Brunt, Department of Preventive Medicine, University of Tennessee College of Medicine, Memphis

PART

INTRODUCTION

CHAPTER

Overview of Assessment and Treatment Issues

James B. Lane
Pacific University
Forest Grove, Oregon

3

A basic principle of this Clinician's Guide is that assessment is an integral part of effective therapy, from diagnosis and treatment planning, through treatment implementation and monitoring progress toward treatment goals, to evaluation of outcomes. In keeping with this principle, subsequent chapters will include assessment considerations for specific disorders and special circumstances. This chapter considers general issues regarding the contribution of assessment to treatment planning, active intervention, and termination.

ASSESSMENT IN BRIEF TREATMENT

For pioneering developers of brief therapy interventions, formal assessment consisted largely of determining the suitability of clients for this approach (Vaillant, 1997). In the current climate of health care cost containment, brief interventions are the de facto treatments of choice for most clients. It would seem reasonable that the increased demand for efficiency and accountability in the provision of mental health services should lead to an increased emphasis on timely, effective assessment of clients as an integral aspect of treatment planning. However, two related trends contribute to decreased utilization of formal assessment in mental health treatment.

First, third-party payers are increasingly reluctant to pay for formal psychological assessment services. This is due, at least in part, to the historical development of assessment as a separate, and separately reimbursed, specialty service. A consultant or multidisciplinary team member not directly involved in treatment of the case often provide this service. Research documenting the cost-effectiveness of such formal assessment has lagged far behind research supporting the efficacy of interventions (Ollendick, 1999).

Second, current research and practices emphasize differential treatment selection based primarily on diagnosis. In current diagnostic practice, the clinician determines the presence or absence of facts that meet relatively explicit diagnostic criteria and then develops a descriptive, multiaxial diagnosis using the categories and language of the current diagnostic manual. Along with this straightforward, relatively noninferential diagnostic paradigm, the recent and long overdue emphasis on empirically supported interventions has contributed to overreliance on the clinical diagnosis for establishing treatment goals and selecting interventions. Assessment typically is limited to deriving a diagnosis, often without the aid of formal assessment techniques such as structured diagnostic interviews.

Diagnosis is an important step, but it is not sufficient for treatment planning. Meeting the criteria for a mental disorder documents that the client is experiencing significant distress or disability and justifies the clinician's intervention. For many disorders, the diagnosis also will direct the clinician to consider interventions with demonstrated efficacy. However, there are significant limitations to treatment selection based solely on matching diagnosis with empirically supported treatment.

Some limitations are practical. Empirically supported treatments have been documented for only a limited number of diagnoses. For many clients, an appropriate diagnosis will not have an associated treatment of established efficacy. In addition, the polythetic nature of some diagnoses means that there will be some heterogeneity of presentation in groups receiving the same diagnosis. For example, there are 105 combinations of symptoms that would meet the criteria for a major depressive episode in the current system (American Psychiatric Association, 1994). Unless we assume that these different presentations are due to the same underlying pathological process, a highly debatable assumption at best, then different presentations of the same disorder will require different treatment goals and interventions. Similarly, many clients seen in clinical practice are comorbid for two or more disorders. Such cases typically will require more complex treatment plans than those with uncomplicated disorders.

Other limitations are conceptual. Under our current diagnostic paradigm, the diagnosis of mental disorders, while potentially of high reliability, is of questionable validity for many specific diagnoses regarding their implications for etiology, course, and treatment response (Goodwin & Guze, 1996). It is troubling conceptually to select treatment based on a suspect criterion. In addition, the model of clinical practice that is implied by such a mechanical matching of treatment to diagnosis is one of a technician applying highly operationalized procedures. This model of practice as applied science (Peterson, 1991) is inconsistent with both the current development of our science and the actual practice of expert clinicians.

These comments are intended as an appeal for clinical practice to be as precise and scientific as our subject matter allows. In this regard, it can be useful to reframe the role of science in practice in a way that is consistent with contemporary developments in the philosophy of science. A positivist view of science interprets the empirically determined relationships between diagnoses and interventions as specific instances of more general basic principles, which it is science's role to discover. A more pragmatic, and more contemporary, view of our science would consider diagnoses and empirically supported treatments as potentially useful categories for collecting, organizing, and accessing practices that have produced their intended results (Fishman, 1999). Such information becomes part of the empirical base upon which expert clinicians draw in planning treatment.

Polkinghorne (1992) noted that novice practitioners tend to follow rules and procedures in a rather mechanical manner, as implied by the positivist applied science model of practice, while experts more often modify procedures in a flexible manner based on the requirements of particular situations. More recent authors have described this conceptually informed, empirically based model of professional activity as reflective practice (Schön, 1987), disciplined inquiry (Peterson, 1991), the local clinical scientist model (Trierweiler & Stricker, 1998), and the pragmatic paradigm (Fishman, 1999).

This discussion implies that the call to be more scientific in our practice requires a more flexible and complex response than a simple insistence on following the rules and procedures delineated in empirically supported treatment manuals. Such manuals are crucial for the advancement of our science and practice. Not only do they ensure adherence to procedure and repeatability in research, they are effective tools for teaching novice clinicians and add to the expert's empirical basis for conceptualizing and planning treatment for a specific case. However, they cannot by themselves tell us how to treat every client with the relevant diagnosis or the client for whom no such manual exists.

In this vein, Sanderson (1997) argues that clinicians must consider interventions that address the client's full range of symptoms and advocates a symptom-focused, rather than disorder-based approach to treatment planning. Similarly, Horowitz (1998) argues that clinicians should not rely exclusively on diagnosis in treatment planning. A more comprehensive formulation, a conceptualization of the client in his or her life context, is needed for appropriate selection of treatment goals and specific interventions for those goals.

Formulation is a key component in Peterson's (1991) description of practice as disciplined inquiry, which provides a useful framework for describing the role of assessment in brief therapy.

Professional activity as disciplined inquiry begins with the client, which can be an individual, a group, or some larger social unit. The client's problems and goals for change shape the professional task. The first step in the process is the initial assessment, and it is at this point that disciplined inquiry begins to diverge from the applied science model. As noted above, the current incarnation of applied science views assessment chiefly in terms of noninferential determination of descriptive diagnosis. In disciplined inquiry, the assessment process is shaped by the clinician's "guiding conception" of the phenomena under study (Peterson, 1991). This guiding conception includes the clinician's assumptions about epistemology, theory, and ethics, in addition to knowledge of relevant empirical research and personal knowledge of similar cases. The data collected by the assessment are then integrated into a formulation of the client's circumstances. The formulation represents the clinician's best understanding of this specific case, including the appropriate descriptive diagnosis in mental health practice, and may involve a reformulation of the client's initial presentation of problems and goals. The formulation points to a course of action, which is "either an intervention that offers the best available prospect of benefit to the client or a decision that will be useful to the client" (Peterson, 1991, p. 427). In many cases, this course of action will include an empirically supported intervention.

Clinician and client then evaluate the effectiveness of the action. If they agree that the changes or decisions are adequate to meet the client's goals or that further action is not likely to further those goals, the clinician completes the inquiry by conducting a concluding evaluation. However, if either party considers the outcome inadequate and both conclude that further action is likely to be beneficial, then "further cycles of reformulation, action, and evaluation may continue until an acceptable outcome is reached. Acceptable outcomes may include the decision by either or both parties that the attentions of the practitioner are of no use to the client" (Peterson, 1991, p. 427).

In an idealized applied science model, each case is an example of one or another general class, with class membership being the principal determinant of action. In contrast, in disciplined inquiry:

> Each case the practitioner studies adds to the store of knowledge he or she can bring to the next case. Usually the experience is assimilated within the body of comparable experiences the practitioner has accumulated previously. Occasionally, however, the outcomes or other characteristics of a case are so sharply inconsistent with the guiding conception the practitioner has followed until that time that an accommodating change in the conception is required. (Peterson, 1991, p. 427)

Each step of professional practice as disciplined inquiry is mediated by assessment data, either informal or standardized. Following are discussions of assessment in formulation and treatment planning, in monitoring evaluations, in the concluding evaluation, and in mediating change in the clinician's guiding conception.

ASSESSMENT AND FORMULATION

The formulation, as the clinician's best understanding of the case, can be thought of as a narrative about how the client came to manifest symptoms or distress at this time. It links the descriptive diagnosis and the client's personal and family history through hypotheses about functional relationships among personal, historical, and situational variables and the current problem situation. These functional relationships may be characterized as predisposing, precipitating, exacerbating, maintaining, or ameliorating various aspects of the diagnosed disorder or presenting complaint. An empirically grounded, comprehensive case formulation: (a) organizes the relevant facts of a case around the hypothesized functional relationships; (b) identifies those relationships that are accessible to direct intervention; (c) identifies treatment goals; and (d) prioritizes goals in terms of importance to the client and the feasibility of attaining them.

Empirically supported treatments are based on generalized formulations of the disorders they address. For example, cognitive therapy and interpersonal therapy for depression were developed to address hypothesized functional relationships between depression and cognitive and interpersonal variables, respectively. However, the demonstrated effectiveness of these interventions does not imply that either approach will be necessary or sufficient to address a given client's presentation of depression.

This point will be obvious to experienced clinicians, but in our experience as clinical supervisors it bears repeating. Treatment plans of novice clinicians often are variations on the following: "The client's problem of depression will be treated with weekly sessions of cognitive therapy with the goal of reducing his depressed mood, as indicated by self-ratings." Advanced students generally produce more specific and differentiated treatment plans, often targeting the symptoms they identified as meeting the diagnostic criteria for the disorder. However, unless the interventions address functional relationships with the disorder or target problem, they are unlikely to be beneficial.

This caricature does not do justice to the flexibility of empirically supported treatments in addressing the goals of individual clients. It does, however, point to the necessity of a careful formulation of the client over and above the generalized formulation of the disorder associated with a given intervention.

Formal assessment can play an important role in arriving at a timely and accurate formulation. Broad-bandwidth instruments, of which the Minnesota Multiphasic Personality Inventory (MMPI-2) is the most widely used, assess a wide range of client characteristics and provide several types of information relevant to the formulation in a time-efficient and cost-effective way (Maruish, 1999, offers an overview of several broad-bandwidth instruments). In addition, because they measure constructs that are not directly observable, they often provide information that cannot readily be obtained by direct inquiry of the client or significant others.

Such instruments can rapidly identify general categories of problems of which clients are unaware or that they do no recognize as relevant to their concerns. For example, clients rarely report that they have difficulty with impulse control; they may be unaware that impulsiveness contributes to their presenting complaint. Clinicians infer such problems on the basis of multiple indicators in the client's history and mental status, and psychometric indices of such characteristic assist in this process. Similarly, such measures provide information useful in making a diagnosis or ruling one out (Piedmont, 1998). At the very least, test results that are inconsistent with our diagnostic hypotheses should prompt us to consider alternative hypotheses carefully before rejecting them.

In addition to problem identification and diagnosis, broad-bandwidth instruments can be useful in clarifying the context of the client's difficulties. These instruments can be extremely useful in addressing the question of whether the client's difficulties are circumscribed or pervasive (Piedmont, 1998). Assessment instruments that address only a narrow range of symptoms or a narrow focus on the client's presenting complaint can lead to a premature, and inaccurate, formulation of a circumscribed symptom. It is not only the presence of a problem area that informs the selection of a specific treatment target, but the absence or comparative significance of problems in other areas as well. Broad-bandwidth assessment instruments provide a systematic and efficient way of characterizing the client's difficulties in this regard.

Similarly, broad-bandwidth instruments are useful in identifying client characteristics that are not construed as problematic in themselves but which may bear a functional relationship to the identified problem. For example, a depressed individual with a high level of introversion or social discomfort may not have ready access to the social supports that buffer life stresses. Such characteristics help identify additional targets for intervention or may catalyze reformulation of the client's difficulties, leading to a different treatment strategy.

In other cases, assessment will provide early indications of such client characteristics as interpersonal style, defenses, or motivation that may complicate treatment if they are not addressed early on. Conversely, assessment may identify characteristics on which the clinician can capitalize in establishing a collaborative relationship or developing interventions.

In summary, broad-bandwidth assessment instruments provide an efficient and cost-effective means to enhance the crucial formulation stage of treatment. Clinicians can avoid false starts and develop more effective brief interventions by including such instruments early in the contact with the client, rather than waiting until problems arise in treatment.

ASSESSMENT AND ACTIVE TREATMENT

The utility of assessment data does not end with the formulation. Such data can support a facilitative therapeutic relationship and enhance the effectiveness of treatment in progress.

Empathy and Rapport

Broad-bandwidth instruments provide a nuanced, contextual understanding of the client, including the motivational sources of problematic behavior (Piedmont, 1998). Such an understanding promotes a greater appreciation of the client's conflicts, struggles, and aspirations, which in turn enhances empathy and rapport. In addition, the clinician may share assessment data with the client, which, along with appropriate interpretation, can provide the client with direct, concrete evidence of the clinician's understanding. Such a sense of rapport supports progress toward treatment goals through its positive effect on client motivation and compliance.

Feedback and Self-Understanding

Discussing assessment data with the client also facilitates an exploration of problems, strengths, and motives that the client may be unable or unwilling to acknowledge (Piedmont, 1998). Addressing such issues early in brief therapy promotes agreement on treatment goals and strategies. In addition, hearing such feedback by itself is sometimes sufficient to lead to positive change. Indeed, Finn and Tonsager (1997) describe the use of personality assessment as a therapeutic intervention apart from its role in providing information to the clinician.

Establishing Baselines and Monitoring Progress

Once treatment targets have been identified, it is important to obtain baseline measures of the target symptoms or behaviors. Baseline measures characterize the client's functioning at the beginning of treatment and provide criteria against which to judge change over the course of treatment. It frequently is useful to express treatment goals in terms of change from baseline measures.

Broad-bandwidth measures are too unwieldy, imprecise, and inefficient to provide satisfactory baseline measures, since they measure higher-order constructs rather than specific symptoms or behaviors. For many observable behaviors, straightforward tallies of the frequency, duration, and/or intensity of occurrence are sufficient to establish a baseline and monitor progress. Similarly, the baseline for many covert phenomena such as of self-criticism may be established, and a change in their occurrence may be tallied in similar ways. In the case of both observable and covert phenomena, the client may need instruction and regular practice before becoming sufficiently proficient at self-observation to tally occurrences reliably.

In the case of more subjective phenomena, such as mood states, and in any case for which they are readily available, standardized measures are preferable to improvised measures. Such measures have established psychometric properties and provide consistency and comparability across occurrences and cases. Among the best known of such narrow-bandwidth instruments are the Beck inventories for depression, hopelessness, and anxiety, which have become standard instruments in clinical practice and research. However, there is a wide selection of commercially available and public-domain instruments that cover the symptoms and problem behaviors that most clinicians will encounter in their practices. It is beyond the scope of this chapter to review specific instruments. The reader is referred to Maruish (1999) and to subsequent chapters in this book for specific recommendations.

Whether the clinician establishes baselines and monitors progress by improvised or standardized measures, it is essential that such indices become part of the record of treatment. There is no other reliable way to establish whether the client is progressing toward treatment goals, that the goals have been achieved, or that more (or different) treatment is needed. Regular assessment with an appropriate measure provides data points that can provide a graphic representation of the course of treatment. Brief, narrow-bandwidth instruments can be administered weekly at little cost in time or money. The utility of the data they provide more than compensates for the expense.

The use of narrow-bandwidth instruments to establish baselines and to monitor treatment warrants a word of caution. It is easy to reify the scores on such measures as equivalent to the variable they are intended to measure. It is important to remember that such scores are only markers for what often are complex phenomena. Similar scores for two clients may reflect very different sets of functional relationships between the measured symptom and other client variables. Scores in themselves do not determine treatment strategy. Treatment strategy is mediated by the formulation.

Assessment and the Concluding Evaluation

If the clinician has used appropriate assessment instruments to establish baselines, to state treatment goals in terms of change from baseline, and to measure progress toward those goals, the concluding evaluation may consist of little more than reviewing the course of treatment with the client. However, especially in the case of clients with multiple or pervasive difficulties, it can be useful to revisit not only the agreed-upon goals of treatment but the presenting situation as well. A repeat administration of the broad-bandwidth instrument used in the initial assessment can provide a context for reviewing change in specific symptoms and behaviors. Such instruments can document consistency and change in domains of behavior and experience other than the specific treatment targets. In some cases, decreases in distress are accompanied by generalized improvement. For example, results for broad-bandwidth instruments are quite state dependent in individuals with bipolar disorder, with markedly different profiles produced during manic, depressive, and euthymic episodes (Lumry *et al.*, 1982). In other individuals, marked change from initial levels of distress occurs without accompanying change in measures of other important individual and interpersonal variables. Information of either sort can help facilitate adherence with maintenance strategies and relapse prevention, planning for continuing treatment, or laying the groundwork for additional treatment in the future. The concluding evaluation can provide both client and clinician with a vivid picture of how far the client has come, what remains to be done, and what pitfalls may lie along the way.

In addition to providing a summary and future directions for a clinician's work with a given client, assessment data also help to document the clinician's effectiveness. An established track record of effective treatment enhances the clinician's credibility, which is especially useful when seeking authorization for additional treatment for a client.

ASSESSMENT AND THE CLINICIAN'S GUIDING CONCEPTION

The discussion thus far has focused on the roles played by assessment data in formulation, treatment planning, treatment implementation, and evaluation of treatment outcome. In addition, however, assessment data can play an important role in the professional development of the clinician.

Cognitive psychology has shown that human beings are information processors of limited capacity. We make use of a variety of simplifying heuristics in organizing and processing the vast amount of information available in any given situation. Mental health clinicians are not immune to the biases in judgment to which such heuristics contribute. One task of the clinician-in-training is learning to delay arriving at diagnostic and other clinical decisions until all relevant data and viable alternative hypotheses are considered.

The value of formal assessment instruments in this learning process is twofold. First, standardized instruments provide information about a client that is unbiased by the clinician's information processing heuristics. Second, standardized assessment data have the capacity to surprise. While clinicians often take comfort when assessment data confirm their impressions of a client, such data are especially useful when their quantified representation of the client is discrepant with the clinician's impressions. Occasionally, such surprises represent a failure to consider all the relevant or competing hypotheses; that is, they reflect the role of assessment data in curtailing the impact of information-processing biases. In other cases, however, assessment surprises are instances in which the clinician is unable to assimilate the case at hand to his or her guiding conception and an accommodating change in the conception is required. Like diagnoses and empirically supported treatments, assessment data provide useful categories for collecting, organizing, and accessing information about clients, especially about clients who fail to conform to our expectations. Such clients enlarge and revise our guiding conceptions and thus increase our expertise and preparation for future clients.

FUTURE DIRECTIONS:
EMPIRICALLY SUPPORTED ASSESSMENT

Meehl (1959/1973) noted that, in order to demonstrate the utility of psy-chological assessment instruments, researchers needed to move beyond their psychometric properties to a consideration of their incremental valid-ity. Instruments with the highest level of incremental validity would pro-vide accurate information that either cannot be easily obtained from other available sources or provides it more rapidly than the other sources. In addition, this information facilitates more effective treatment of the client. As Ollendick (1999) pointed out, we have made little progress in this regard. Assessment researchers need to shift from a narrow focus on psy-chometric indices to include cost–benefit analyses of new and existing instruments. Such research is sorely needed if we are to move beyond logical arguments for the utility of formal assessment to demonstration of its contribution to effective practice.

SUMMARY

This chapter has presented assessment as an integral component of empiri-cally informed mental health practice. While it is not essential to use standardized instruments in all cases, such instruments do have the advan-tage of providing information that is quantified, consistent across cases, and relatively free of observer bias. Standardized instruments provide an efficient and economical way of expediting the disciplined inquiry that is at the heart of effective brief therapy. Assessment data play important roles in case formulation, treatment planning, treatment implementation, and evaluation of treatment outcome. This writer believes it is false economy for clinicians to eschew formal assessment on the basis of reimbursement policies of third-party payers. However, it is time to move beyond rational argument to research support for this position.

REFERENCES

American Psychiatric Association (1994). *Diagnostic and statistical manual of mental disorder* (4th ed.). Washington, DC: Author.
Finn, S. E., & Tonsager, M. E. (1997). Information-gathering and therapeutic models of assessment: Complementary paradigms. *Psychological Assessment, 9,* 374–385.

Fishman, D. B. (1999). *The case for pragmatic psychology.* New York: New York University Press.

Goodwin, D. W., & Guze, S. B. (1996). *Psychiatric diagnosis* (5th ed.). New York: Oxford University Press.

Horowitz, M. J. (1998). Personality disorder diagnoses. *American Journal of Psychiatry, 155,* 1464.

Lumry, A. E., Gottesman, I. I., & Tuason, V. B. (1982). MMPI state dependency during the course of bipolar psychosis. *Psychiatry Research, 7,* 59–67.

Maruish, M. E. (1999). *The use of psychological testing for treatment planning and outcomes assessment* (2nd ed.). Mahwah, NJ: Lawrence Erlbaum.

Meehl, P. E. (1959/1973). Some ruminations on the validation of clinical procedures. In P. E. Meehl, *Psychodiagnosis: Selected Papers.* Minneapolis: University of Minnesota Press.

Newmark, C. S. (Ed.). (1996). *Major psychological assessment instruments* (2nd ed.). Boston: Allyn & Bacon.

Ollendick, T. H. (1999). Empirically supported assessment for clinical practice: Is it possible? Is it desirable? *The Clinical Psychologist, 52,* 1–2.

Piedmont, R. L. (1998). *The Revised NEO Personality Inventory: Clinical and research applications.* New York: Plenum.

Peterson, D. R. (1991). Connection and disconnection of research and practice in the education of professional psychologists. *American Psychologist, 46,* 422–429.

Polkinghorne, D. E. (1992) Postmodern epistemology of practice. In S. Kvale (Ed.), *Psychology and postmodernism* (pp. 146-165). Newbury Park, CA: Sage.

Sanderson, W. C. (1997). Cognitive behavior therapy. *American Journal of Psychotherapy, 51,* 289–292.

Schön, D. A. (1987). *Educating the reflective practitioner: Toward a new design for teaching and learning in the professions.* San Francisco: Jossey-Bass.

Trierweiler, S. J., & Stricker, G. (1998). *The scientific practice of professional psychology.* New York: Plenum.

Vaillant, L. M. (1997). *Changing character: Short-term-anxiety-regulating psychotherapy for restructuring defenses, affects, and attachment.* New York, Basic Books.

PART

TREATMENT OF SPECIFIC DISORDERS (DSM-IV DIAGNOSES)

II

TREATMENT FOR MOOD DISORDERS (DSM-IV DIAGNOSES)

CHAPTER

Major Depressive Episode

David O. Antonuccio

Veterans Administration Medical Center
and
Univesity of Nevada School of Medicine
Reno, Nevada

Peter Lewinsohn

Oregon Research Institute
Eugene, Oregon

Melissa Piasecki

University of Nevada School of Medicine
Reno, Nevada

Robin Ferguson

Mountain Employee Assistance Program
Reno, Nevada

CASE DESCRIPTION

The following case description is based on a composite of several patients who were treated with the Coping with Depression Course. Patient names, identifying information, presenting symptoms, and other details of the cases have been altered to preserve confidentiality.

Roger is a 39-year-old caucasian male who presents to psychiatric triage because he is experiencing depressive symptoms. He worked until 2 years ago as a train engineer. He is married to his second wife and has 2 years of college. About 3 years ago, he was the engineer in a train that hit a car at a train crossing. All three occupants of the car were killed. Roger went back to work 7 days after the accident and started using alcohol daily after 3 years of sobriety. Several practitioners diagnosed him with posttraumatic stress disorder related to this incident. He dated his most recent depression symptoms to this incident. Roger presents with depressed mood, flat affect, anhedonia, social isolation, and psychomotor retardation.

He indicates that, although he "feels like dying," he does not currently have any suicidal intent and that he would not take his life because of his two children who are living with his ex-wife. On a list of target problems, the patient indicates that he would like to become less depressed, less anxious, and less worried, feel better about himself, get rid of suicidal thoughts, and become less withdrawn. He reports that "I've had no life for the past year. I feel dead inside." He reports feeling lethargic and apathetic, and talks about a loss of interest in activities and social relationships.

The patient reports a history of recurring depression. He reports that at the age of 16 he was so depressed he considered killing himself with a gun. He has some distress over the train accident, but he reported no anxiety, flashbacks, nightmares, or avoidance behavior over this event. He currently works part-time in a hardware store and spends most of his spare time watching TV and occasionally visiting his brother. He often feels resentful that others (i.e., his brother, children, and previous employer) are taking advantage of him.

Because of his recent history of alcohol dependence, treatment was made contingent on his continued sobriety and participation in an outpatient alcohol program.

TREATMENT CONCEPTUALIZATION

Although the patient has had a long history of depression, his problems were exacerbated several years ago when he was traumatized by the train accident. Subsequent to that event, he began avoiding his job and eventually left the railroad industry. He started drinking alcohol as a way of managing anxiety, loneliness, and depressive symptoms. Alcohol actually exacerbated his depressive symptoms, particularly dysphoria, social isolation, and interpersonal conflict. He gradually became more and more socially withdrawn. Although he had recently stopped drinking alcohol, he was left with residual social anxiety and a pessimism about the future.

ASSESSMENT

Consistent with the educational philosophy of the Coping with Depression (CWD) Course, contraindications have been minimal. This treatment is not recommended for those people who show evidence of mental retardation, dyslexia, serious visual or auditory impairment, bipolar disorder, schizophrenia, schizoaffective disorder, or acute substance abuse. Concurrent psychotherapy, counseling, or pharmacotherapy for depression or other problems is not an exclusion criterion, and typically 30%–50% of the course participants are also involved in some other form of treatment. Although a current episode of depression is not a prerequisite, approximately 80% of the participants meet DSM-IV criteria for a current diagnosis of unipolar depression.

In prior research (Steinmetz *et al.*, 1983), the single strongest predictor of posttreatment depression level (as measured by the Beck Depression Inventory [BDI]) is pretreatment depression level. Those who are the most depressed at the beginning are still, relatively, the most depressed at the end of treatment. Pretreatment BDI and seven other variables account for 56% of the variance in posttreatment BDI scores. The other seven variables are: (1) expected improvement (participants who expected to be the most symptom free at the end of treatment were actually the most improved); (2) satisfaction with major life roles (participants who had expressed more satisfaction were also the most improved); (3) concurrent treatment (participants who were not concurrently receiving additional treatment for depression were more improved); (4) perceived social support from family members (those with more perceived social support had better treatment outcome); (5) physical problems (patients who did not have a physical handicap, a disabling disease, or recent surgery were more improved); (6) suicide attempt (those who had a history of suicide attempts were less improved); and (7) perceived mastery (participants who felt they had achieved greater mastery were more improved). These predictors all have interesting clinical implications. For example, it may be beneficial to enhance treatment expectations, address major life roles, mobilize family support, address physical handicaps, and help patients to achieve mastery in at least one area in order to facilitate better outcome.

In the current case example, the patient's BDI score was +28, in the moderate range. He endorsed #1 on item 9 of the BDI, admitting to suicidal thoughts but affirming that he would not carry them out. On the Beck Anxiety Inventory (BAI), his score was +8, basically in the nonanxious range. These self-report inventories indicated that he was feeling much more depressed than anxious at the time of this evaluation. He was given a diagnosis of Major Depressive Disorder (recurrent, nonpsychotic)

TREATMENT IMPLEMENTATION

A classic behavioral model of unipolar depression (Lewinsohn *et al.*, 1979) postulates that depression can result from a stressor that disrupts important behavior patterns, causing a low rate of response-contingent positive reinforcement. Rate of reinforcement is functionally related to availability of reinforcing events in the patient's environment, personal competencies to act on the environment, or the impact (positive and negative) for the individual of certain types of events. If an individual cannot reverse the negative balance of reinforcement, a heightened state of self-awareness will follow that can lead to negative self-evaluation (Lewinsohn *et al.*, 1985). This model also suggests that family members and social networks may unwittingly reinforce "depressed" behavior (e.g., talking about suicide) when they show interest in the depressed individual. The resulting behavioral psychotherapy involves helping patients increase the frequency and quality of their engagement in pleasant activities. Consistent with this formulation, it has been found that depressed patients have low rates of pleasant activities and obtained pleasure, that mood covaries with rates of pleasant and aversive activities, and that mood improves with increases in pleasant activities. Also, depressed patients tend to lack social skills, at least during the depressed phase, which contributes to the depression.

The CWD course was derived from this theoretical perspective. The course was designed as a psychoeducational group or small seminar, teaching people techniques and strategies to cope with the problems that are assumed to be related to their depression. The course provides training in a "smorgasbord" of skills to deal with these problems, and people are encouraged to focus on those of most direct relevance to them. These strategies include improving social skills, addressing depressogenic thinking, increasing pleasant activities, and relaxation training.

The CWD course for adults consists of 12 2-hour sessions conducted over 8 weeks. Sessions are held twice weekly for the first 4 weeks. Groups typically consist of 6 to 10 adults, with a single group leader. One- and 6-month follow-up sessions ("class reunions") are held to encourage maintenance of treatment gains and to collect information on improvement or relapse. Booster sessions can be built in as needed to prevent relapse. All sessions are highly structured, and make use of the text *Control Your Depression* (Lewinsohn *et al.*, 1992) and a *Participant Workbook* (Brown & Lewinsohn, 1984b). In addition, an instructor's manual (Lewinsohn *et al.*, 1984) provides scripts, exercises, and guidelines. It has also been adapted and delivered in an individual format with outcome comparable to the group format (Brown & Lewinsohn, 1984b).

The acute and long-term efficacy of the CWD course has been demonstrated in several outcome studies with adults, adolescents, and elderly depressed patients, and in prevention efforts (Antonuccio, 1998). The CWD course has achieved comparable acute outcome and better long-term outcome than antidepressant medication (de Jong-Meyer & Hautzinger, 1996). Group format, individual treatment, and minimal phone contact have all fared equally well, providing therapists many convenient and cost-effective options that can be tailored to the needs of the patient.

CONCURRENT DIAGNOSES AND TREATMENT

The patient carried a concurrent diagnosis of alcohol dependence and peptic ulcer disease. There was no history of any street drug use or other addictions. The first and second sessions was devoted to getting the patient's history and presenting symptoms. They were also used to present the rationale and outline of the CWD course, which was delivered in an individual rather than group format. The cognitive behavioral model was highlighted and the cognitive–behavioral–feeling triad was introduced. It was made clear to the patient that for treatment to have any chance of working he would need to avoid alcohol because of its CNS-depressing properties. The patient was able to make this commitment and chose to attend weekly AA meetings for his outpatient sobriety program. He began monitoring his mood on a daily basis. Mood monitoring continued throughout treatment. He began his volunteer work the next week. He read the first two chapters in *Control Your Depression* (Lewinsohn *et al.*, 1992). Increasing pleasant activities was considered the highest priority for this patient, so modules related to Pleasant Activities were begun first. He made a commitment to volunteer at the Special Olympics office, helping to train athletes. He filled out the Pleasant Events Schedule (PES).

By the third session, the patient had already begun to feel much better. He volunteered 40 hours at the Special Olympics office and rode his bicycle a mile to and from work. He followed through on his commitment to attend AA meetings. His mood ratings were consistently between 4 and 6 on a 0–10 scale, with 0 representing to the most depressed he had ever felt and 10 the happiest he had ever felt. He noted that he felt some distance from his two adolescent sons, who were living with their mother. He had infrequent visits with them and believed they did not care about him. He was encouraged to schedule regular weekly contact with his boys as a way of establishing consistency in his relationship with them, something that had been lacking. He decided to schedule routine visits on Wednesday evenings and Saturday afternoons. Usually, he would share a favorite television program or go to a local park with his children. He discovered that he loved being with them, and they seemed to enjoy his company, but negative thoughts about the divorce had prevented him from seeing them regularly and left him resentful when he did not see them.

By the fourth session his mood was consistently between 5 and 7. He noticed that there were many highly pleasurable activities on the PES that he did not do very often. These included sports, outdoor activities, travel, and family and romantic relationships. He was given the assignment of taking his boys fishing, something they all enjoyed. A graph of his mood and pleasant activity did not reveal a strong correlation for this patient (see Figure 2.1). His mood was consistently around 6 with little variability, and total pleasant activities varied from 15 to 35 per day. He did notice that he felt best on days when he spent time with his boys.

Because of his interest in pursuing a romantic relationship, sessions 5 and 6 shifted to the social skill modules. He was interested in dating but had difficulty initiating social activities due to fear of rejection and humiliation. He enjoyed computers and was given the homework assignment of creating a photo personal ad on American Online. He was also given the assignment of signing up for an astronomy class, something he had always been interested in doing, at the local junior college.

The patient consistently rated his mood around 5 or 6. Although he was worrying less, he continued to feel guilty over a past event that occurred during a drunken episode when he poured sugar in his neighbors gas tank. He also had felt a great deal of guilt and responsibility over the breakup of his marriage and the impact on his children. For sessions 7 and 8, he worked on the constructive thinking modules and identified his nonconstructive thoughts (see Figure 2.2) that were contributing to the guilt feelings. He noticed having thoughts like "I shouldn't have been drinking alcohol." "I shouldn't have had an affair." "I've destroyed my children's future by causing them to come from a broken home." The therapist used a Socratic questioning approach to help the patient notice nonconstructive thoughts and ask himself, "Where's the evidence and what's another way to think about this situation?" He began examining the evidence in support of and against these thoughts. He countered these thoughts by telling himself that he had not understood at the time how severe his alcohol problems were and that now that he had been educated he could learn from his past mistakes. Based on the reading, the patient concluded that his most common nonconstructive thoughts were mind-reading, overgeneralization, disqualifying the positive, and all-or-nothing thinking. He worked on accepting and forgiving himself for having human fallibilities. He realized that many children from broken homes have turned out just fine. He told himself that he could not change the past but

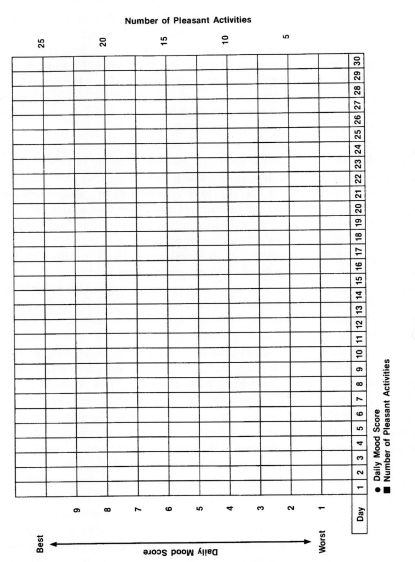

Figure 2.1.   Chart for recording daily pleasant activities and mood scores.

DAILY MONITORING

Date _____

A. **Activating Event**

(Briefly describe the situation or event that seemed to lead to your emotional upset at C).

B. **Beliefs or Self-Talk**

(List each of the things that you said to yourself about A.)

1.

2.

3.

4.

5.

(Now go back and place a checkmark beside each statement that is non-constructive or "irrational.")

C. **Emotional Consequences**

(Describe and rate how you felt when A happened.)

I felt: _____

_____

Rating (0 = mildly upset; 5 = extremely upset): _____

D. **Dispute of Self-Talk**

(For each checked statement in Section B, describe what you would ask or say to dispute your non-constructive self-talk).

Note: You should first complete Section C. Then go back and complete Section A and Section B. After the first week of self-monitoring, also complete Section D.

Figure 2.2. Daily monitoring form for identifying nonconstructive thoughts.

that he could have a powerful impact on his relationship with his children now.

The patient had a small setback prior to session 9. He felt down and upset that his sons had canceled their meeting with him due to a special soccer practice. The patient did not do his homework assignment that week of tracking anxiety-evoking situations. He expressed concern about failure. Interventions included reviewing improvement that had occurred over the past eight sessions, increasing the treatment alliance, and collaborating on treatment goals. The patient was taken through a progressive muscle relaxation exercise and rated his anxiety at a 2 on the 0–10 (very relaxed to very tense) scale. He estimated his anxiety at 8 to start the session. He was given a tape of the session and given the assignment of practicing relaxation at least 20 minutes at least every other day (see Figure 2.3).

The patient came to the next session indicating that he felt much better than he had at the beginning of treatment. A BDI score of 5 (item 9, the suicide item, had a score of 0, indicating no suicide risk) was consistent with his self-report. The patient practiced the relaxation on three occasions. He was much more active socially and had met a woman in his astronomy class whom he asked out to lunch. He also met someone on the internet with whom he was corresponding.

The process of termination was begun in the 10th session. The patient appeared bright, talkative, and smiled frequently. He expressed confidence that he had some skills he could draw on if he got depressed in the future. He reported feeling "symptom-free" and was happy about his newfound active social life. He also rediscovered an old pleasure, reading science fiction. His BDI score was 5 at termination and sustained at less than 10 at 1- and 6-month follow-ups.

COMPLICATIONS AND TREATMENT IMPLICATIONS

It was made clear that the CWD course was contingent on abstinence from alcohol and street drugs. The rationale for this contingency is that alcohol is a central nervous system depressant and works counter to efforts to help the patient overcome his depression. This was not meant as a punitive intervention for drinking but rather as a practical intervention to maximize the patient's potential for responding to the treatment. Basically, the patient was told that the CWD course was not likely to be effective if he continued to be dependent on alcohol.

DAILY MONITORING — RELAXATION

Relaxation Rating: 0 = Most relaxed you have ever been
10 = Most tense you have ever been

Date: _____ to _____

	Monday	Tuesday	Wednesday	Thursday	Friday	Saturday	Sunday	Average Score (add your scores and divide by 7)
Average Score for the Day								
Least Relaxed Time								
Score								
When								
Where								
Situation								
Most Relaxed Time								
Score								
When								
Where								
Situation								
Occurrence of Tension Symptoms								
H = Headache								
SA = Stomachache								
SP = Sleep problem								
Relaxation Practice								
When								
For how long								
Score before								
Score after								

Figure 2.3. Daily monitoring form related to relaxation.

Later in treatment, as the patient improved, he became less motivated to complete the assigned homework. Because he was feeling better, he had lost a sense of urgency. The therapist did not wish to make the homework a punishing experience, so the assignments were trimmed back to the minimum and emphasis was always placed on what the patient had accomplished, not what had been left undone.

DEALING WITH MANAGED CARE AND ACCOUNTABILITY

The CWD course is ideally suited to a managed care environment because it is time-limited with clearly defined goals. It can be delivered very cost-effectively in a group, individually, or even with minimal phone contact after an initial personal session (Brown & Lewinsohn, 1984a). Baseline data are gathered for each skill area, and the impact of acquired skills is systematically compared to the baseline data. Overall progress is systematically measured with daily mood monitoring and with periodic use of the Beck Depression Inventory. There are few treatments with more built in accountability.

OUTCOME AND FOLLOW-UP

The patient planned to periodically take the BDI to self-assess his overall depression symptoms. The patient continued to do well at 1- and 6-month follow-up, scoring 7 and 4, respectively, on the BDI.

DEALING WITH RECIDIVISM

Had this patient relapsed during the follow-up period, booster sessions could have been scheduled targeting specific skill areas identified by the patient. If the treatment had not been successful, the patient would have been given information about other treatment options, including antidepressant medication or other forms of psychotherapy, including interpersonal psychotherapy.

SUMMARY

The CWD course has been adapted to adolescents (CWD-A; Clarke *et al.*, 1990). In addition to the skill areas included in the adult CWD course, the CWD-A was expanded to incorporate the teaching of basic communication, negotiation, and conflict-resolution skills. A parallel course for the parents of depressed adolescents (Lewinsohn *et al.*, 1991) has also been developed.

The CWD course has also been modified for use with the elderly (Gallagher & Thompson, 1981), for frail or demented elderly persons and their caregivers, for prevention of depression in high-risk/low-income minority medical outpatients, for prevention in American Indians aged 45 and older, for prevention of more serious depression in mildly depressed adolescents, and for prevention of depression in smokers who are trying to quit cigarettes (see Antonuccio, 1998, for a complete list of references).

SYLLABUS FOR THE COPING WITH DEPRESSION COURSE

Session 1: Depression and Social Learning

Goals

This session presents an outline of the social learning view of depression. We see depression as being a learned phenomenon. Since you have learned to be depressed, you can also learn to become "undepressed." This course is intended to teach you the skills you will need in order to do this. The goals for this assignment are: (a) to become familiar with the social learning approach to depression, and (b) to understand what the implications of the social learning approach to depression are for you, and how this knowledge can help you to cope with depression.

Assignment

    a. Complete the Pleasant Events Schedule and return it as soon as possible.

    b. Read chapters 1, 2, and 3 of *Control Your Depression*. Do this only after completing the Pleasant Events Schedule.

    c. Begin to monitor your daily mood using the Daily Mood Rating form. See instructions in chapter 3, pages 38–40.

Session 2: How to Design a Self-Change Plan

Goals

This session focuses on the basic steps for designing a self-change plan. The goals for this assignment are: (a) to learn how to develop a systematic self-change plan, and (b) to learn how to apply these basic self-change methods in order to alleviate specific problems that you may be experiencing.

Assignment

    a. Continue to monitor your daily mood using the Daily Mood Rating form.

    b. Read chapter 4 of *Control Your Depression.*

    c. As you read chapter 4, identify some of the problems related to depression that seem to apply to you. Then create a personal plan to overcome depression by filling out Figure 4-1 on page 57. Read pages 55, 56, and 58 carefully and assign priorities to your problems. This is an important part of designing your self-change plan.

Session 3: Learning to Relax

Goals

This session teaches some basis relaxation skills. The goals for the assignment are: (a) to determine your current base level of relaxation, enabling you to evaluate your progress as you learn to relax more, and (b) to identify particular situations and/or times of day when you are most tense.

Assignment

    a. Continue to monitor your daily mood using the Daily Mood Rating form.

    b. Read chapter 5 of *Control Your Depression.*

    c. Complete the daily monitoring–relaxation form each day (see pages 60–64 for instructions).

Session 4: Relaxation in Everyday Situations

Goals

This session will focus on practicing relaxation skills and on using them in everyday situations when you experience stress or tension. The goals for this assignment are: (a) to learn to become more relaxed by practicing a relaxation technique, enabling you to feel more relaxed in general, and in specific situations when you experience stress and tension, and (b) to identify particular situations and/or times of day when you are most tense.

Assignment

a. Continue to monitor your daily mood using the Daily Mood Rating form.

b. Review chapter 5 of *Control Your Depression* if necessary.

c. Practice relaxation exercises each day (see pages 64–67 for instructions).

Session 5: Pleasant Activities and Depression

Goals

This session will focus on the relationship between engaging in pleasant activities and being depressed. The goals for this assignment are: (a) to determine your baseline level (current rate) of pleasant activities, and (b) to assess the degree to which your frequency of pleasant activities and the extent to which you are enjoying them may be contributing to your depression.

Assignment

a. Continue to monitor your daily mood using the Daily Mood Rating form.

b. Read chapter 6 of *Control Your Depression*.

c. Practice using relaxation in problem situations, and evaluate your progress by continuing to complete the Daily Monitoring–Relaxation in Problem Situations form each day.

    d. Construct your Activity Schedule (see pages 92–93, steps 1 and 2). Keep a tally of your rate of pleasant activities each day (see step 2) using this Activity Schedule

    e. Graph your daily mood score with your daily number of pleasant activities on the Chart for Recording Daily Pleasant Activities and Mood Scores (see pages 93–96 for instructions).

Session 6: Formulating a Pleasant Activities Plan

Goals

This session is intended to help you in planning to increase your rate of pleasant activities. The goals for this assignment are: (a) to become aware of the importance of specific activities that are especially related to your daily mood, and (b) to design and implement a self-change plan aimed at increasing pleasant activities. This involves setting a goal and pinpointing specific pleasant activities to be increased.

Assignment

    a. Continue to monitor your daily mood using the Daily Mood Rating form.

    b. Read chapter 9 of *Control Your Depression*. Review chapter 6 if necessary.

    c. Increase your daily rate of pleasant activities by writing a pleasant activities plan using the Weekly Plan form (see pages 98–103 for instructions). Be sure to fill out the Contract for Increasing Pleasant Activities that is included with the Weekly Plan form

    d. Begin to implement your pleasant activities plan and evaluate your progress (see pages 103–104) by continuing to monitor your daily pleasant activities using your Activity Schedule.

Session 7: Two Approaches to Constructive Thinking

Goals

This session is intended to familiarize you with two different approaches to constructive thinking. The goals of this assignment are: (a) to develop a working knowledge of two different approaches to more constructive thinking — the positive and negative thought method and the A–B–C method (also called RET), and (b) to make an informed choice as to which of these two approaches you will utilize to help you to think more constructively.

Assignment

a. Continue to monitor your daily mood using the Daily Mood Rating form.

b. Read chapter 10 of *Control Your Depression*.

c. Continue to implement your pleasant activities plan and evaluate your progress by monitoring your daily pleasant activities on your Activity Schedule.

d. Decide which of the two approaches to constructive thinking you wish to work with: the Positive and Negative Thought Method (chapter 9) or the A–B–C Method (chapter 10). Then do the exercises associated with the chapter you choose.

Session 8: Formulating a Plan for Constructive Thinking

Goals

This session is intended to help you to develop a plan to begin thinking more constructively. The goals for this assignment are: (a) to learn new ways to channel your thoughts in a more positive direction or new ways to think about problems so they are less upsetting, and (b) to become familiar with self-instructional techniques that will allow you to act on the ideas that you find useful (i.e., be your own coach).

Assignment

    a. Continue to monitor your daily mood using the Daily Mood Rating form.

    b. Read chapter 11 of *Control Your Depression*.

    c. Decide whether or not you wish to use self-instructional techniques (see pages 170–172). The use of self-instructional techniques is an optional section of the course.

    d. Depending upon the approach you have chosen, use your Positive and Negative Thought strategies or the A–B–C Method.

Session 9: The Ability to be Assertive

Goals

This session will focus on social skills and on how these skills affect your ability to get along with other people. The goals for this assignment are: (a) to identify any social skill problems that you may be experiencing, and (b) to monitor your performance in the problem social situations that you have identified.

Assignment

    a. Continue to monitor your daily mood using the Daily Mood Rating form.

    b. Read chapter 7 of *Control Your Depression*.

    c. Develop a Personal Problems List of situations that you would like to handle in a more assertive way (see pages 112–113 for instructions).

    d. Complete the self-monitoring of Assertiveness form each day (see pages 113–114 for instructions).

    e. Practice assertiveness imagery (see pages 114–118) for 15 minutes each day using two situations from your Personal Problems List.

Session 10: Using Your Social Skills

Goals

This session will focus on putting your social skills to work by engaging in more pleasant activities. The goals for this assignment are: (a) to assess your level of social participation (i.e., how often you engage in enjoyable activities involving other people), and (b) to develop and implement a plan to increase the number of pleasant social activities that you engage in.

Assignment

a. Continue to monitor your daily mood using the Daily Mood Rating form.

b. Read chapter 8 of *Control Your Depression.*

c. Practice assertiveness in real-life situations and evaluate your progress by continuing to complete the Self-Monitoring of Assertiveness form (see pages 113–114 and 118–119).

d. Complete the Social Activities Questionnaire (see pages 126–128).

e. Complete the Social Activities to Increase form (see pages 128–135).

f. Complete the Interferences: Activities to Decrease form (see pages 128–135).

g. Develop and carry out a plan to increase your pleasant social activities and evaluate your progress by completing the Social Activities to Increase form and the Interferences: Activities to Decrease form each day (see pages 132–138).

Session 11: Maintaining Your Gains

Goals

This session is intended to help you develop a plan for maintaining the gains that you have made during the course. The goals for this assignment are: (a) to assist you in integrating what you have learned, (b) to encourage you to monitor your depression level periodically so that you can recognize recurrences quickly, and (c) to alert you to certain stressful events that often cause depression.

Assignment

    a. Continue to monitor your daily mood using the Daily Mood Rating form.

    b. Read chapter 13 of *Control Your Depression.*

    c. Complete the Beck Depression Inventory (pages 13–17). Compare your current score with your score before the course started.

    d. Assign priorities to your problems and the methods for coping with them by completing ratings in the Integration section of chapter 12 (pages 178–180). Decide what you can do on a continuing basis to work on these problems.

    e. Develop an "emergency plan" that will allow you to anticipate and to deal with stressful situations when they occur in the future (see pages 181–184).

Session 12: Developing a Life Plan

Goals

This session is intended to help you develop a Life Plan to consolidate the gains you have made and to plan for prevention of future episodes of depression. The goals for this assignment are: (a) to assist you in actively planning your future, including consideration of your individual and interpersonal life goals, and B) to encourage you to think preventively and to make a plan for positive mental health.

Assignment

    a. Continue to monitor your daily mood using the Daily Mood Rating form.

    b. Read chapters 13 and 14 of *Control Your Depression.*

    c. Complete the Life Plan form. This involves consolidating your work from sessions 10 and 11 (particularly Parts II-D and 11-E from session 11). For information relevant to Part A of the Life Plan form ("Role Sketch") see pages 188–192. For information relevant to formulating a written statement of your individual and interpersonal goals (Part B of the Life Plan form) and philosophy of life (Part C of the Life Plan form), see pages 195–202.

REFERENCES

Antonuccio, D. O. (1998). The Coping with Depression Course: A behavioral treatment for depression. *The Clinical Psychologist, 51,* 3–5.

Brown, R. A., & Lewinsohn, P. M. (1984a). A psychoeducational approach to the treatment of depression: Comparison of group, individual, and minimal contact procedures. *Journal of Consulting and Clinical Psychology, 52,* 774–783.

Brown, M. A., & Lewinsohn, P. M. (1984b). *Participant workbook for the Coping with Depression Course.* Eugene, OR: Castalia Publishing.

Clarke, G. N., Lewinsohn, P. M., & Hops, H. (1990). *Adolescent Coping with Depression Course.* Eugene, OR: Castalia Publishing.

de Jong-Meyer, R., & Hautzinger, M. (1996). Results of two multicenter treatment studies among patients with endogenous and nonendogenous depression: Conclusions and prospects. *Zeitschrift für Linische Psychologie, 25*(2), 155–160.

Gallagher, D., & Thompson, L. W. (1981). *Depression in the elderly: A behavioral treatment manual.* Los Angeles: University of Southern California Press.

Lewinsohn, P. M., Youngren, M. A., & Grosscup, S. J. (1979). Reinforcement and depression. In R. A. Dupue (Ed.), *The psychobiology of depressive disorders: Implications for the effects of stress* (pp. 291–316). New York: Academic Press.

Lewinsohn, P. M., Antonuccio, D. O., Steinmetz-Breckenridge, J. L., & Teri, L. (1984). *The Coping with Depression Course: A psychoeducational intervention for unipolar depression.* Eugene, OR: Castalia Publishing.

Lewinsohn, P. M., Hoberman, H. M., Teri, L., & Hautzinger, M. (1985). An integrated theory of depression. In S. Reiss & R. Bootzin (Eds.), *Theoretical issues in behavior therapy* (pp. 331–359). New York: Academic Press.

Lewinsohn, P. M., Rhode, P., Hops H., & Clarke, G. N. (1991). *Leaders manual for parent groups: Adolescent Coping with Depression Course.* Unpublished.

Lewinsohn, P. M., Muñoz, R. F., Youngren, M. A., & Zeiss, A. M. (1992). *Control your depression* (2nd ed.). Englewood Cliffs, NJ: Prentice-Hall.

Steinmetz, J. L., Lewinsohn, P. M., & Antonuccio, D. O. (1983). Participant variables as predictors of outcome in a psychoeducational group treatment for depression. *Journal of Consulting and Clinical Psychology, 51*(3), 331–337.

CHAPTER

Alcohol Abuse

David C. Hodgins
Addiction Centre, Foothills Hospital
Calgary, Alberta, Canada

Effective Brief Therapies: A Clinician's Guide

CASE DESCRIPTION

Mrs. Sawchuk is a 68-year-old woman who was referred by her family physician for help with a significant alcohol problem. She has been married for more than 40 years and has three adult children. She had worked as a senior administrator at a local community college until her retirement at age 65. "They don't want you around after age 65," she reported. Since her retirement, she has been appointed to the board of the District Health Council, which is a prestigious and demanding volunteer appointment. She is also very involved with her three grandchildren, often providing child care.

Mrs. Sawchuk approached her physician about how to stop drinking "on her own." She had previously sought out information about the treatment resources available to her, including residential treatment, outpatient group treatment, and Alcoholics Anonymous (AA), but could not envision herself accessing any of them. Her physician suggested individual therapy as an alternative.

Mrs. Sawchuk described her drinking as heavy but nonproblematic until the last 3 years. She reported that her elder sister, who was living in a neighboring city, had become ill with cancer at that time. Mrs. Sawchuk spent 3 months living alone in her sister's apartment in order to visit her in the hospital. Mrs. Sawchuk would spend the afternoon at the hospital and then stop at a liquor store for a "mickey," a 12-oz bottle of vodka, on her way back to the apartment. She would then spend the evening reading and sipping vodka in order to relax and to be able to sleep. At the time her sister died, about 3 months later, she was consuming approximately six 12-oz bottles or 48 1.5-oz drinks per week. On returning home, she continued to purchase alcohol but now hid it from her husband. In order to consume a similar amount, she began to drink throughout the day. A number of months later, her first grandchild was born. At that point, her daughter-in-law approached her saying that she wanted Mrs. Sawchuk's close involvement with the baby, but that she would not allow her to take full charge of the child because of her drinking. Mrs. Sawchuk reacted with some surprise that her drinking was not as well hidden as she had hoped, but her reaction was mostly one of horror at the notion that she was viewed as incompetent to care for the baby. She immediately stopped drinking and was abstinent from alcohol for about 6 months.

Mrs. Sawchuk reported that she returned to drinking after the death of her father over a year ago. She started drinking secretly and very quickly resumed drinking about six bottles of vodka per week. Presently, she drinks throughout the day unless she has an engagement outside the home, in which case she delays having the first drink of the day. She drinks in social situations but limits herself to three glasses of wine. She experiences a bit of shakiness in her hands in the morning and her liver function tests showed moderate enzyme elevation.

TREATMENT CONCEPTUALIZATION: MOTIVATIONAL ENHANCEMENT THERAPY

A number of intervention models have received empirical support in the treatment of alcohol abuse and dependence. These approaches include relapse prevention, broad-spectrum skills training, marital and family therapies, cognitive–behavioral therapies, twelve-step facilitation, and motivational enhancement therapies (Miller *et al.*, 1995). Project Match, a large National Institute on Alcohol Abuse and Alcoholism–funded multisite outcome study, contrasted the effectiveness of the latter three of these approaches, and did not uncover large differences among them, finding them all to be generally effective (Project Match Research Group, 1997). One of these approaches, motivational enhancement therapy (MET), is distinguished by being particularly brief. In Project Match, MET consisted of 4 sessions compared with the 12 sessions required with the other two therapies.

MET can be viewed as a style of counseling as opposed to a distinct form of therapy. One assumption of MET is that a client has experience and resources to draw on in making the shift from problematic drinking to abstinence or nonproblematic drinking. What is offered is a "motivational nudge" of the client toward mobilizing and deploying these resources. The client is seen as ambivalent about making the necessary changes, and the therapist's task is to explore and help the client resolve this ambivalence. Issues concerning the etiology of the problem are not addressed. A full description of the model and practice of MET is provided by Miller and Rollnick (1991).

Mrs. Sawchuk is a good candidate for MET. She is reluctant to use the more public types of services such as self-help, group, and residential programs. She also has had some prior success at abstinence from alcohol, which suggests that she possesses at least some of the skills required. What she is lacking is confidence and sustained motivation.

THE ISSUE OF ABSTINENCE OR
CONTROLLED DRINKING

A great deal has been written about the appropriateness or lack of appropriateness of nonabstinent goals for people with alcohol problems (see Sobell & Sobell, 1993, for one discussion). This issue remains controversial in the United States, where the vast majority of alcohol treatment services insist on abstinence. Elsewhere in the world, more flexibility is allowed, in particular by providers of outpatient services.

Mrs. Sawchuk presented with a clear goal of abstinence, although she is ambivalent about tackling it. Research evidence suggests that individuals prefer to select their own goal and will tend to ignore goals imposed on them. Nonetheless, there are a number of contraindications for nonabstinence. These include indicators of greater alcohol dependence and greater severity of the problem (see below), medical conditions such as liver disease, pregnancy, and a belief on the part of the client or family members that abstinence is necessary.

ASSESSMENT

In MET, assessment and intervention are closely linked in two ways. First, assessment questions are asked in such a way as to elicit the client's own self-motivating statements. The client is encouraged to voice personal concerns about the impact, both positive and negative, of alcohol use and the benefits and costs of change. As the client makes these statements, the therapist uses reflective listening skills to encourage the client to restate and amplify the concerns. For example, self-motivating concerns include statements such as "My job will suffer if I continue to go on drinking like this," "I noticed that I am forgetting things," "I don't know what will happen if I get caught drinking and driving."

The therapist uses open-ended questions to elicit these statements: "I assume because you are here that you have had some worries about your drinking." "What have you noticed about your drinking that has concerned you?" "What reasons do you have for wanting to change your drinking?" and "What are the good and not-so-good things about drinking?" The therapist engages in a discussion about the client's perceptions of his or her alcohol use, inquiring about specific areas as convenient. Table 3.1 outlines the areas to cover, which include signs of alcohol dependence, quantity, consequences, treatment history, circumstances of drinking, and motivation.

TABLE 3.1

Assessment Domains for Alcohol Abusing Client

General dimension	Specific construct
Alcohol dependence	Tolerance Withdrawal Impaired control
Alcohol quantity	Lifetime history Daily amounts for past month
Consequences	Health (liver, hypertension, nutritional, gastrointestinal) Family Social Employment and financial Emotional (include comorbid conditions) Spiritual Legal
Treatment history	Programs started and completed Self-help group involvement Periods of abstinence and nonproblem drinking
Associations/circumstances of drinking	Functional analyses (antecedents, behaviors, consequences)
Motivation	Reasons to change Family and social support

The second way that assessment and intervention are linked in MET is that assessment results are fed back to the client in order to provide objective information to help enhance the "pros" of changing. Objective information is often received with less defensiveness than the "subjective" opinion of the therapist. Information is provided in a neutral and nonjudgmental fashion. A smaller or greater number of formal assessment instruments can be introduced into the therapy sessions depending on the setting and therapist preference. The MET protocol (Miller *et al.*, 1992) provides a comprehensive, multidimensional assessment package that incorporates a number of standardized instruments and a feedback format for clients. Areas include alcohol consumption, blood alcohol levels, negative consequences, liver function and other blood tests, and neuropsychological functioning. The emphasis is on comparing the client's functioning with normative data. For example, the client's weekly alcohol consumption is compared to American general population norms and neuropsychological function is compared with normative data. In this way, the client is provided with information that is as objective and neutral as possible. Alternatively, brief targeted instruments such as the Alcohol Use Disorders Identification Test (AUDIT, Saunders *et al.*, 1993) and the Alcohol Dependence Scale (ADS, Skinner & Horn, 1984) can be used in the same way. These instruments can also abbreviate the interview time in that essential assessment questions are incorporated within the scales. The AUDIT, for example, provides a total score that indicates level of severity of problem (low, medium, high, very high), but also asks about quantity and frequency of drinking, tolerance, impaired control, and so forth. The ADS provides a measure of dependence compared with a normative sample of individuals seeking treatment but specifically inquires about memory difficulties, blackouts, and so forth.

Finally, a number of comprehensive interview schedules exist, such as the Addiction Severity Index (McLellan *et al.*, 1990) and the Comprehensive Drinker Profile (Miller & Marlatt, 1984). These schedules are most helpful in a research context or setting, in which a substantial number of substance abusers are seen and a systematic assessment is desirable.[1]

Treatment Implementation

Phase 1: Building Motivation

MET comprises two phases: building of motivation to change and commitment to change (Miller *et al.*, 1992). The eliciting of motivational statements, described above, is part of the therapeutic task of phase 1. The other task is an exploration of ambivalence. The client is encouraged to discuss potential reasons for continuing to drink as well as reasons to stop or reduce drinking. This discussion allows the client to clarify his or her ambivalence, and, hopefully, to counter it. Completion of a Decisional Balance exercise can be helpful either during a session with the therapist or as homework. Mrs. Sawchuk completed this task, as described below (see Table 3.2). It involves the client identifying the pros and cons of

---

[1]Details about these and other alcohol assessment instruments is available at the NIAAA website (www.NIAAA.org).

TABLE 3.2

Example Decisional Balance Exercise for Mrs. Sawchuk

Pros of continuing to drink	Cons of continuing to drink
Easier to keep drinking Fills my time	Quality of life, depression Don't like myself
Pros of stopping	Cons of stopping
Can spend time with grandchildren Less depressed? More clear-thinking! Like myself better Live longer?	Too much time to fill Can't imagine life without alcohol

quitting and not quitting drinking. The therapist reflects back the client's responses and asks for elaboration of concerns.

Client resistance, reflecting ambivalence about change, is expected, and Miller and Rollnick (1991) recommend a number of therapist strategies for dealing with this resistance. Often, simply reflecting back to the client the concern about quitting is sufficient to evoke the opposite response. For example, T: "So you are feeling that you would lose all your friends if you didn't drink?" C: "Yes, but I have to stop drinking even if I have to figure out how to start some new relationships." A double-sided reflection can also be effective. The client's concern is reflected back, paired with some concerns that the client has previously expressed about continuing to drink. T: "You worry that you might lose your friends, on the one hand, but on the other hand, you are worried about your health, your family, and your financial situation." The therapist can also shift the focus away from the problematic issue. C: "I don't think I want to do this. My wife wants me to quit drinking. I don't see a problem." T: "Let's get back to your wife's concerns in a few minutes. Right now, I would like to hear what you would miss about not drinking." Finally, the therapist can "roll with the resistance, agreeing with the client in the hope that the agreement will evoke the opposite response." T: "You might decide that it is only your wife's problem and that it is too difficult for you to give up alcohol." The therapeutic task is to allow clients to share their ambivalence but also to sharpen their motivation to tackle their problem. Therapists should avoid increasing client resistance by attempting to convince the client that quitting drinking is necessary.

Session 1 with Mrs. Sawchuk: Example of Phase 1 Implementation

THERAPIST: I understand that you have some concerns about alcohol. Can you tell me about them? [open-ended elicitation of concerns]

MRS. SAWCHUK: Well, I requested that my doctor refer me to you. I feel that I have been drinking too much lately. I don't know if I am an alcoholic, but I have been concerned. I quit drinking for eight months once, so I know I can do it on my own. I wasn't interested in a treatment program.

THERAPIST: So, you aren't sure if you are an alcoholic but you have been concerned lately. What has made you concerned? [double-sided reflection]

MRS. SAWCHUK: Well, quantity, I guess. And the fact that I can't stop.

THERAPIST: Can you tell me more?

MRS. SAWCHUK: Well, I drink a mickey[2] of alcohol most days. I hate that word "mickey," but that is what it is. I decide almost every day that I won't do this, but I end up doing the same thing.

THERAPIST: So you decide to stop but then continue to drink?

MRS. SAWCHUK: Yes, I somehow decide to go to the liquor store and buy a bottle, and then I decide that I won't drink it and then I start with a sip . . . and then I drink the whole bottle. Not all at once of course. I don't ever get really drunk, just a little high. That's why I don't think I am an alcoholic.

THERAPIST: But it disturbs you that you don't stop? [therapist ignores the resistance to the alcoholic label and reflects back the feeling]

MRS. SAWCHUK: Yes.

THERAPIST: What other concerns have you had about your alcohol use? [more elicitation of concerns]

---

[2]A mickey of alcohol is a 12-ounce (340 ml) bottle that represents eight standard drinks.

MRS. SAWCHUK:	Well, I keep it fairly hidden. I don't drink in public. And I wouldn't drink and drive. But my daughter-in-law has commented. In fact, the reason I quit for eight months was because my daughter-in-law didn't trust me to care for my grandchild. I was mortified. I respect her for saying this, but it really hurt me.
THERAPIST:	So you feel your daughter-in-law was right to do this, although it was hard for you. What concerns did she have?
MRS. SAWCHUK:	Well, she didn't think it was safe, if I was drinking.
THERAPIST:	Hmm, so there are these concerns about safety on your daughter-in-law's part, and your own concerns about the quantity and drinking despite planning not to drink. What else?
MRS. SAWCHUK:	I know I would feel better if I stopped. I did the last time. I felt healthy and alive. A number of people commented.
THERAPIST:	Who noticed? [amplification]
MRS. SAWCHUK:	Well, my husband, who is a man of small words, didn't say much, but he did say it was nice that I quit. And one of my friends commented. That surprised me. And my children all said something.
THERAPIST:	So there were some clear positive effects of stopping. What was not so good about stopping? [shift to cons of quitting]
MRS. SAWCHUK:	Well. Nothing really. No, that's not true. I really missed it. I felt like something was missing.
THERAPIST:	Is that true now? Do you feel you would be missing something if you decide to stop?
MRS. SAWCHUK:	Oh, yes. I enjoy the taste.
THERAPIST:	What else is positive about alcohol for you?
MRS. SAWCHUK:	Hmm. I just like it. But it is so expensive.
THERAPIST:	Have you ever figured out how much you spend? [obtain objective information about the consequences of drinking; M and T calculated the cost of a mickey per day for a month]
THERAPIST:	So you like it, and would feel like something was missing if you quit, but also it is expensive, you worry about the quantity, and drinking more than you plan to, you know that other people have noticed, and you know you would feel better if you weren't drinking. Is there anything else? [double reflection and feedback]

MRS. SAWCHUK:	Well, the other thing that has bothered me is that I don't always remember what happens when I drink.
THERAPIST:	That can be upsetting. Can you tell me about the last time that happened?
MRS. SAWCHUK:	It doesn't happen very often. I just sometimes don't remember how much I ended up drinking. [possibly some resistance; therapist shifts focus]
THERAPIST:	Oh, so you don't always know how much you drink? And that bothers you. Let's just change direction here for a minute. What I have are a few questionnaires that we can use to compare your drinking to other people's. It is helpful to know where you stand. Does that make sense?

The interview continues until the basic assessment information is obtained and the client's ambivalence has surfaced and motivation is maximized. This may be achieved in one session or it may take two or more sessions. A challenge to the therapist is not to jump ahead before the client is ready to move to phase 2 and make a commitment to change. The therapist is typically ready for change before the client! At the end of this phase, the therapist provides an overall summary of the client's concerns.

Phase 2: Committing to a Change Plan

The change plan phase is initiated when the therapist senses that the client is "ready to change." This may occur during the first or a subsequent session. The client is ready to set a general goal and to make a plan for achieving this goal. The ambivalence about change has been attenuated and the client is explicitly or implicitly asking to move ahead with a plan to begin the change process. The client may request this directly ("So what can I do?"), or the therapist may need to raise the possibility that the client is ready ("So what are you thinking about all this?"). The therapist should encourage the client to take the lead. For example, "What do you make of all this?" or "So, given how you are feeling, what is your plan?" If the client has already expressed a goal of abstinence, then the therapist should reflect this back. Miller and Rollnick *et al.* (1991) describe this as "commending abstinence," not "prescribing it." For example, "So from what you have said, you are thinking of actually stopping drinking?" If the goal of quitting has not been expressed, then the therapist needs to raise the question ("Is your goal to stop drinking or is it to cut back?"). The next task is to establish some specific short-term goals and to explore the ambivalence about these goals. Again, the therapist encourages the client to take the lead, giving the message that it is the client's responsibility to change. For example, "Do you have specific ideas what you want to accomplish?" "What do you need to do to quit?" and "So what is the next step?" The therapist needs to be ready to provide information to the client that may be helpful in reaching a goal. For example, the client may express the desire to explore AA or may have concerns about the process of withdrawal from alcohol. The nonspecialist therapist may not be able to answer to all the questions and may need to consult with the client's physician or an addiction specialist. With each goal suggested by the client, the therapist should explore ambivalence by asking what would make this goal difficult to achieve and what would be the consequences if the client achieved the goal. For example, if a client suggested that he needed to stop going out to a bar with his work colleagues each evening, then issues for the therapist to query would include what the client will do with his time after work, whether he would feel lonely or bored, and what he might do about pressure from his work colleagues to join them. As illustrated below, through this discussion, the goal can be reformulated or specified to increase the chance of client success.

Session 1 Continued: Example of Phase 2 Implementation

THERAPIST: So from what you said, you are thinking that you need to quit drinking. That makes a lot of sense. Do you feel committed to do this? [commends abstinence goal and confirms readiness]

MRS. SAWCHUK: I have to do this. And I want to do this.

THERAPIST: So you feel ready to go on. Have you any thoughts about how to tackle this? [gives client the lead]

MRS. SAWCHUK: I don't know.

THERAPIST: What kinds of things did you do last time, when you quit for eight months? [begins to formulate a change plan]

MRS. SAWCHUK: Well, I just decided to quit. I completely stopped buying alcohol, and we didn't have any in the house.

THERAPIST: So you didn't buy any alcohol and removed alcohol from the house. Are you aware of what else you did to be successful?

MRS. SAWCHUK: Not really. Well, I kept myself busy. I babysat a lot for the new baby.

THERAPIST: How was that helpful?

MRS. SAWCHUK:	I just couldn't drink.
THERAPIST:	So a couple of the things you did last time were to stop buying alcohol, not having access to alcohol in the house, and keeping yourself busy. Are those things that would be helpful this time?
MRS. SAWCHUK:	Oh, yes.
THERAPIST:	So what would that look like? [begins discussion of specific goals]

The session continued with further specification of goals. Through discussion, Mrs. Sawchuk concluded that the latter part of the afternoon would likely be a problematic time for her and that she will plan a daily social activity for that time each day of the next week. Mrs. Sawchuk has expressed her embarrassment about her alcohol problem a number of times during the session. She did not, in fact, tell anyone about her appointment with the therapist. As shown below, the therapist gently suggested that she begin to tackle this.

THERAPIST:	From what you have said, a number of your family members quite quickly noticed that you weren't drinking the last time. How would it be helpful if you were to decide to tell them in advance this time?
MRS. SAWCHUK:	I can tell my husband, but I can't tell my kids.
THERAPIST:	How might telling Mr. Sawchuk be helpful? [ignores reluctance to tell children]
MRS. SAWCHUK:	He doesn't care whether we have alcohol in the house, but he usually keeps us well stocked. He will be supportive, but he won't say very much.
THERAPIST:	So in terms of telling other people you are comfortable with starting with your husband. And that will be helpful. [sets expectation that others will need to know]

The session then ends with a therapist summary of the general and specific goals. It is helpful with most clients to put this summary of the goals in writing. Again, the therapist provided Mrs. Sawchuk the opportunity to express her ambivalence, which she did. Finally, the therapist adds a cognitive–behavioral self-monitoring task with the goal of helping Mrs. Sawchuk identify high-risk drinking situations as well as coping strategies that she has available or may need to develop. This technique is not germane to MET but is a helpful adjunct (see below).

THERAPIST:	It appears you are ready to tackle this. That's great! To make sure I understand: you are planning to not drink between now and our next session, with the general goal of quitting all together. You recognize that you need to stop buying alcohol and will have your husband remove the alcohol from the house. And, you will tell him about coming here and your plans. You also predict that one difficult time staying away from alcohol will be toward the end of the afternoon — you will have a specific plan for each of the next 7 days to keep yourself busy. Is there anything else that I have missed? On a 10-point scale, how confident are you that you can achieve this, where 0 is not at all confident and 10 indicates extremely confident?
MRS. SAWCHUK:	Well, I am pretty confident . . . [hint of reluctance noted by therapist]
THERAPIST:	How would you rate your confidence?
MRS. SAWCHUK:	Overall, a 9. [another hint]
THERAPIST:	Any other problems you can foresee?
MRS. SAWCHUK:	Not a problem, but I should tell you. My anniversary is tomorrow, and Bill and I are going out for dinner. I plan to have a glass of wine. [therapist sidesteps the resistance and explores the feeling]
THERAPIST:	It is hard to imagine giving up alcohol completely?
MRS. SAWCHUK:	Yes.
THERAPIST:	I imagine that you will get to the point that you can choose not to drink in these types of special occasions. It will be interesting to see if it is difficult to limit yourself to just one glass. [therapist chooses to respect Mrs. Sawchuk's goal but encourages vigilance]
THERAPIST:	So we have a plan. Can I ask you to do one more bit of homework between now and next week? What I would like you to do is to keep track of what you do during the tricky times, times you really feel like drinking. We expect that these urges will occur, and it will be helpful to understand them, so you can plan how to deal with them. You should know that urges go away eventually. Some people think of them as waves — they can build to high levels but eventually they subside. What I would like you to do is to keep a daily record of the strong urges you feel. [Therapist provides a daily record form including the following columns: date/time, situation,

thoughts/feelings, intensity of urge (0–10), length of urge, and how client coped with urge. Therapist works through a plausible example.] This daily record will be helpful in a few ways. First, it will show which are your preferred ways of coping, of the strategies that you already use. It will also show what the high-risk situations might be in the future. You can then plan ways to avoid them or cope with them. I hope you are able to not drink in the coming week, except for that one glass of wine. If you are successful, then that is great. If you aren't completely successful, then you need to examine what happened. Sometimes we try to put it out of our mind instead of learning from it.

The final reason for the daily record is that the information might show whether there are situations or issues that you might think about beginning to address. Does all this make sense to you? Do you think it is a good idea? Do you think you can do this?

Good. Remember to bring this along for our next session so we can review it. Don't worry if it is not neat or if you have spelling mistakes. I won't be marking it! I don't even have to look at it, but the information is important. Any concerns?

Phase 3: Initiating and Maintaining Change

The third phase of MET involves monitoring the client's ability to follow through with the change plan. At each subsequent therapy session, progress toward the specific goals is reviewed and goals are renegotiated, and motivation and commitment are renewed as necessary. It is not expected that the path to recovery will necessarily be smooth (see section on "Dealing with Relapse" below). The therapist continues to use a nonjudgmental style and to encourage the client to take the lead. Progress is reinforced to enhance self-efficacy, and problem-solving around difficulties is encouraged and modeled by the therapist. Both the client and therapist will become increasingly aware of the strengths and limitations of the client's ability to successfully navigate through their weeks without drinking. The self-monitoring task described above will be a good source of information for review in the therapy session.

Integrating Techniques from Other Therapeutic Models

The MET model assumes that the client has a substantial number of resources on which to draw in quitting drinking. However, it becomes clear as therapy proceeds that some skills need sharpening. As such, techniques from other therapeutic models may be integrated as needed. Cognitive–behavioral and relapse prevention techniques, twelve-step support, and adjunctive medications fit nicely with the model. Often clients report that a benefit of heavy drinking is that it allows effective distancing from their feelings. Self-monitoring of situations and cognitions associated with particular feelings can be used to encourage greater client self-awareness. As clients are often unaware of the antecedents of lapses or relapses, wishing instead to put these negative experiences out of their minds, functional analysis of these situations and self-monitoring are helpful. Thus, the client is helped to identify thoughts, feelings, and circumstances before and after drinking. In this way, determinants of "high-risk" situations are predicted so that the client can learn to cope in ways other than drinking. Table 3.3 provides some of the standard cognitive–behavioral coping strategies helpful in dealing with high-risk situations.

TABLE 3.3

Cognitive–Behavioral Coping Strategies for Avoiding Alcohol Use

Avoiding cues to drink (antecedents)
Coping with urges to drink
— Distraction
— Recalling negative consequences
— Labeling the urge and letting it pass ("urge surfing")
— Using self-talk to challenge thoughts about drinking
— Seeking social support
Drink refusal skills
General problem-solving skills

Twelve-step programs such as AA are widely available in North America and many other places around the world. Self-help groups such as Women For Sobriety and Rational Recovery that are designed to be alternatives to AA also exist in some locations. The twelve-step model requires that individuals accept themselves as alcoholics and as "powerless" over alcohol. Because of this view, many individuals are reluctant to affiliate. This aspect of the model is also inconsistent with the personal self-control ideas that are central to MET (and, in fact, much of psychological therapy). Therapists are, therefore, often reluctant to encourage their clients to join AA, fearing that the inconsistencies will prove confusing. However, many clients happily attend both therapy and AA and report benefit from both. The inconsistencies in the models are usually of less concern to them than to their therapists. Moreover, a number of AA features can be important adjuncts to therapy. AA wisdom includes solid behavioral ("fake it until you make it," "one day at a time," stay out of bars), and cognitive advice (avoid "stinking thinking" that leads to relapse). AA, through frequent meetings and sponsors, is better able to offer timely crisis resolution than most therapists. AA also offers easy access to a social network of nondrinking individuals.

Clients should be asked as part of the assessment about prior twelve-step and other self-help group involvement and about their feelings about such experiences. It is helpful for therapists to become familiar with the AA principles. Therapists are able to attend open AA meetings, and AA literature is readily available.

A variety of pharmacological therapies have begun to emerge as potentially effective adjunct interventions. Most recently there is evidence that naltrexone (Revia®), an opioid antagonist, can reduce craving and drinking when offered as part of psychosocial treatment. Similar results have been found for acamprosate, a gamma-amnobutyric acid (GABA) agonist, available only in Europe. Research results for disulfiram (Antabuse"®") are mixed, but it may be helpful in preventing drinking when monitored by a client's spouse.

CONCURRENT DIAGNOSES AND TREATMENT

Treatment of comorbid substance use disorders has been the focus of much attention. Both epidemiological and clinical surveys reveal that rates are high and that the majority of people with alcohol problems suffer from at least one other lifetime psychiatric disorder. All disorders have shown a significant association with alcohol problems in at least one study, and stronger associations are typically found with alcohol dependence than with alcohol abuse. The most common comorbid disorders for men are antisocial personality disorder, other substance abuse, mood disorders, agoraphobia, and social phobia. In women, the most frequent associations are mood disorders, agoraphobia, and other substance disorders.

Diagnosis of comorbid disorders is challenging for a number of reasons. First, the physiological effects of heavy alcohol use and alcohol withdrawal can mimic psychiatric symptoms. Depressive symptoms, in particular, can be alcohol induced and anxiety symptoms are key features of alcohol withdrawal. Formal psychiatric diagnosis, as a consequence, should be delayed from 2 to 4 weeks after detoxification.

A second challenge in diagnosing comorbid disorders is that hazardous use of alcohol can occur as a symptom of the impulsive behavior associated with such psychiatric disorders as conduct disorder or the manic phase of bipolar disorders. An alcohol problem may not exist after the psychiatric disorder is effectively managed. Often, however, even when the alcohol use was initially symptomatic of another disorder, it evolves into an independent problem requiring specific treatment.

Finally, alcohol problems can be associated with major life disruptions, including significant social, family, and employment difficulties. Distress concerning these difficulties is expected and may represent appropriate emotional processing, as opposed to an independent comorbid disorder.

Comorbid disorders complicate the course and outcome of alcohol problems. It is generally found that the course is more challenging and there is greater need for more intensive treatment. However, others have argued that comorbid disorders can be a prime motivator for individuals with alcohol problems. Because of the associated life disruption, such individuals seek treatment earlier and have greater incentive to initiate and maintain recovery.

Until the mid-1990s, the common approach to comorbid disorders was to encourage the individual with a comorbid disorder to tackle the alcohol problem first and then, with stable abstinence, to tackle the remaining problem. There is wisdom in this approach given the quick resolution of some depressive and anxiety symptoms with abstinence from alcohol. An alternative model is to tackle the symptoms of both problems simultaneously. Certainly, a motivational interviewing and cognitive–behavioral approach can be adapted in this fashion to address a number of co-occurring symptoms.

Interventions that tackle the emotional disorder without addressing the alcohol use problem are not recommended. Many clients approach therapists with the hope that if the "underlying issue" is resolved then the alcohol problem will naturally, and effortlessly, dissipate. This is rarely the case.

In Mrs. Sawchuk's case, she presented with a number of symptoms of depression, including low mood, memory and concentration problems, poor appetite, and difficulty sleeping. She also reported some fleeting thoughts of suicide. A reasonable conceptualization of the etiology of her alcohol problem is that it developed as an attempt to self-medicate feelings of loss and depression associated with her retirement. The therapist chose to monitor these depressive symptoms as she became abstinent from alcohol and increased her activity level.

COMPLICATIONS AND TREATMENT IMPLICATIONS

Dealing with alcohol withdrawal is a specific issue facing the outpatient therapist dealing with alcohol abuse and dependence. Medical consultation is crucial. The severity of alcohol withdrawal varies from person to person and from one occasion to another for the same person. Generally, more severe withdrawal is associated with longer and heavier alcohol consumption. Mild reactions last for up to 48 hours and consist of insomnia, irritability, and tremor. In severe withdrawal, these symptoms may be followed by auditory, visual, or tactile hallucinations, seizures, and delirium (global confusion). The goal is to ensure the safety and comfort of the individual throughout the withdrawal process. Mild withdrawal can be accomplished through outpatient medical monitoring, typically by enlisting a family member to watch the individual. Severe withdrawal should be monitored in a formal detoxification program or hospital (Mayo-Smith, 1998).

A second potential concern for individuals with alcohol problems is the support of other people in their lives. Often family members and close friends are very concerned about the alcohol use and are fully supportive of the client's efforts to stop drinking. Alternatively, family and friends may themselves be heavy or problem drinkers and may feel threatened by the client's efforts to be abstinent. It can be helpful to request that close family and friends attend one or more therapy sessions. Family and friends can play an important role in strengthening the client's motivation and commitment. They may prove to be useful sources of feedback to the client and may provide valuable input into treatment goals. The therapist can provide some guidance concerning how to provide effective support to the client and can also make suggestions for seeking personal support from therapy or self-help groups such as Alanon.

DEALING WITH MANAGED CARE AND ACCOUNTABILITY

MET has been identified as the most highly cost-effective alcohol treatment with strong empirical support. As delivered in Project Match, it comprises four outpatient therapy sessions. Mrs. Sawchuk was seen for eight sessions. In comparison, alcohol treatment traditionally has been offered in 4-week hospital-based programs. The advent of managed care has encouraged greater use of day treatment and outpatient treatment. In the alcohol field, controlled research has not established superiority of intensive inpatient treatment over briefer outpatient treatment for individuals in general (Sobell & Sobell, 1993). Efforts to identify empirically robust matching factors, such as client characteristics that predict the optimal treatment approach, have not been successful (Miller *et al.*, 1995). Despite this, practice guidelines have become popular. Generally, these guidelines direct individuals with more severe problems to treatments of greater intensity. Alternatively, in a stepped-care approach, intensive treatment requires prior failure in a less intensive approach. Certainly, whatever the treatment options available, client involvement in the choice is highly desirable.

OUTCOME AND FOLLOW-UP

Mrs. Sawchuk was seen for a total of eight sessions over 12 weeks. She had planned to stop drinking after her wedding anniversary (before session 2) but continued to have small slips until she stopped her alcohol use completely at session 5. Sessions 2 to 5 were spent reviewing situations in which she had drank and those in which she had been successful in not drinking. She had obtained a prescription for Revia from her physician during this time to help with cravings but did not fill it. Sessions 6 and 7 were spent examining her feelings about retirement and aging. She continued to struggle with feelings of uselessness but had restructured her days to spend more social time with friends and was considering increasing her volunteer commitments. She had also begun to challenge her belief that her contributions were less valuable because she was not paid for her time. She no longer described herself as depressed and was cautiously optimistic about the future. The final session was spent reviewing her motivations, commitments, and progress to date. The possibility of relapse, which had been raised a number of times over the course of the other sessions, was again discussed. Mrs. Sawchuk agreed to call for a follow-up appointment if she felt at risk for drinking or if she did, in fact, resume drinking.

DEALING WITH RELAPSE

There is a high risk of relapse in individuals with addictive disorders. Rates of alcohol relapse range from 30 to 90% in the first year, depending on the study and the definition of relapse. Individuals are expected to make an average of four to six solid attempts at quitting before they become completely stable in their abstinence. That is not to imply that alcohol treatment is ineffective. Instead, this pattern is the reason that much of treatment is focused on preventing relapse and minimizing relapses if they occur.

Clients should be provided with this information in a way that will encourage them to recommit to abstinence quickly if they do drink again. It is often suggested that individuals learn strategies from each attempt to quit that they make and, in fact, get better at quitting with each try. It can be helpful to point out similarities with quitting smoking. Some people are successful the first time they quit; most will quit a few times before they become nonsmokers. Each attempt is important. Starting to smoke again does not need to lead to a lengthy period of regular smoking before another attempt is made.

SUMMARY

We have a wide variety of interventions for individuals suffering alcohol problems, many with solid empirical support (Miller *et al.*, 1995). Many of these interventions are brief and easily offered on an outpatient basis. Among these, motivational enhancement therapy is among the most cost-effective. MET provides the individual with a motivational nudge to mobilize his or her own resources in tackling a challenging problem. A client-directed and therapist-aided process is undertaken. MET meshes nicely with other models of intervention since it allows clients to benefit from coping skills training, twelve-step support, pharmacological agents, and other strategies as necessary. Mrs. Sawchuk is typical of clients who choose an outpatient approach to battle their problem. She wished for privacy and believed that she could be successful in outpatient therapy. Her path to recovery was challenging, but she achieved her goals in a timely and resource-efficient manner.

REFERENCES

Mayo-Smith, M. (1998). Management of alcohol intoxication and withdrawal. In A. W. Graham & T. K. Schultz (Eds.), *Principles of addiction medicine* (2nd ed., pp. 431–440). Chevy Chase, MD: American Society of Addiction Medicine.

McLellan or McLennan, A. T., Parikh, G., Braff, A., Cacciola, J., Fureman, B., & Incmikoski, R. (1990). *Addiction Severity Index, administration manual* (5th ed.). Philadelphia: Pennsylvania Veterans Administration Center for Studies of Addiction.

Miller, W. R., & Marlatt, G. A. (1984). *Manual for the Comprehensive Drinker Profile.* Odessa, FL: Psychological Assessment Resources.

Miller, W. R., & Rollnick, S. (1991). *Motivational interviewing: Preparing people to change addictive behavior.* New York: Guilford Press.

Miller, W. R., Zweben, A., DiClemente, C., & Rychtarik, R. (1992). *Motivational Enhancement Therapy manual: A clinical research guide for therapists treating individuals with alcohol abuse and dependence.* Washington, DC: Project Match Monograph Series, Vol. 2, DHHS 92-1893.

Miller, W. R., Brown, J. M., Simpson, T. L., Handamaker, N. S., Bien, T. H., Luckie, L. F., Montgomery, H. A., Hester, R. K., & Tonigan, J. S. (1995). What works? A methodological analysis of the alcohol treatment outcome literature. In R. K. Hester & W. R. Miller (1995). *Handbook of alcoholism treatment approaches: Effective alternatives* (2nd ed.). Boston: Allyn and Bacon.

Project Match Research Group (1997). Matching alcoholism treatments to client heterogeneity: Project Match posttreatment drinking outcomes. *Journal of Studies on Alcohol, 58,* 7–29.

Saunders, J.B., Aasland, O.G., Babor, T. F., De La Fuente, J. R., & Grant, M. (1993). Development of the alcohol use disorders identification test (AUDIT): WHO collaborative project on early detection of persons with harmful alcohol consumption-II, *Addiction, 88,* 791–804.

Skinner, H. A., & Horn, J. L. (1984). *Alcohol Dependence Scale (ADS) users guide.* Toronto: Addiction Research Foundation.

Sobell, M. B., & Sobell, L. C. (1993). *Problem drinkers. Guided self-change to treatment.* New York: Guilford Press.

CHAPTER

Panic Disorder

Jennie C. I. Tsao

Department of Psychology,
University of California, Los Angeles

Michelle G. Craske

Department of Psychology,
University of California, Los Angeles

Case Description
Treatment Conceptualization
Assessment
Treatment Implementation
Concurrent Diagnoses and Treatment
Complications and Treatment Implications
Dealing with Managed Care and Accountability
Outcome and Follow-up
Dealing with Recidivism
Summary
References

Send reprint requests to Jennie C. I. Tsao, Anxiety Disorders Behavioral Research Program, University of California, Los Angeles, Department of Psychology, 405 Hilgard Ave., Los Angeles, CA 90095-1563, (310) 206-9191, jtsao@ucla.edu

Effective Brief Therapies: A Clinician's Guide

CASE DESCRIPTION

Jeff was a 48-year-old divorced man who was working as a freelance landscape designer. He had experienced his first panic attack 4 years earlier while hiking up a mountain on a hot sunny day. At that time, Jeff's symptoms included severe chest pain, heart palpitations, shortness of breath, dizziness, and a fear of dying. His symptoms forced him to end the hike and return to his car, where he sat with friends who drove him to the emergency room. At the hospital, Jeff was given a sedative and discharged home after a series of tests revealed no medical cause for his symptoms.

Following this first attack, Jeff experienced an average of four full-blown and 10 to 15 limited symptom attacks each month. Prior to the initial episode, Jeff was experiencing financial difficulties, as well as marital problems with his wife of 15 years — they eventually divorced. Most episodes began with Jeff noticing a feeling of tightness in his chest and were likely to occur when exercising, in crowded places, and while driving long distances. Jeff noted that he often felt panicky when working outside on a hot day, or when "stressed out" by his job or financial obligations. The attacks were interfering significantly with his life, as he had given up most activities he had formerly enjoyed, including hiking, traveling, and all aerobic exercise. In addition, Jeff found it increasingly difficult to perform at his job, as he would have to leave early when he experienced a particularly bad attack. Jeff expressed severe apprehension over having his "next" attack (i.e., the idea of experiencing an attack was frequently on his mind and he was unable to plan activities without considering how he would escape or cope with an attack). During panic episodes he would immediately stop all activity, which he felt "aggravated" the situation, return home and lie down. Jeff had been prescribed Klonopin® (1.5 mg a day) and was taking this drug when he entered cognitive–behavioral treatment for panic. Despite the medication, Jeff continued to panic, worry about panic, and avoid situations due to anticipation of panic.

Jeff received 16-session group treatment for Panic Disorder and Agoraphobia. Treatment focused initially on education about the nature of panic and anxiety, helping Jeff understand that his symptoms were part of the normal anxiety response and not dangerous. He was then taught a breathing technique that helped him relax and control his symptoms. This technique is called *breathing retraining*. Treatment then focused on identifying and systematically challenging thoughts about the dangerousness of his symptoms (cognitive restructuring), for example, jumping to the conclusion that chest pain was a sign of a heart attack. Jeff was instructed to keep careful records of his thoughts, describing the situations in which they occurred, the probability of the feared event (e.g., heart attack), coun-tercognitions based on examination of the evidence and a search for alter-natives, and rerating of the realistic probability of the event. Next, Jeff repeatedly practiced a series of exercises to induce the bodily sensations he feared (interoceptive exposure), thereby learning that the sensations are harmless. For example, because Jeff was particularly fearful of experienc-ing cardiac symptoms while "overheated," he was instructed to practice running and up and down the stairs at home wearing heavy clothes. Finally, Jeff was instructed to gradually confront the situations he feared (e.g., hiking on a hot day, driving by himself on the highway) using the cognitive and breathing techniques learned during treatment to manage his symptoms.

TREATMENT CONCEPTUALIZATION

Panic attacks are discrete episodes of intense fear or discomfort accompa-nied by four or more of 13 physical and cognitive symptoms, including heart palpitations, chest pain/discomfort, shortness of breath, dizziness, depersonalization, and fears of death or loss of control. The symptoms begin abruptly and reach peak intensity within 10 minutes (DSM-IV, American Psychiatric Association, 1994). Panic attacks may occur in the context of a variety of anxiety disorders, and the diagnosis of Panic Disor-der (PD) is only given in the presence of recurring, unexpected panic attacks followed by at least 1 month of persistent worry or concern about having the attacks, or a significant behavioral change as a result of the attacks. Panic attacks are considered "unexpected" if they are not associ-ated with any situational triggers, that is, they occur "out of the blue." PD individuals may also experience "situationally predisposed" panic attacks that are likely to (but do not always) occur on exposure to situational triggers, or "situationally bound" panic attacks that almost always occur on exposure to situational triggers.

Panic Disorder may occur with or without agoraphobia (PDA and PD, respectively). Agoraphobia refers to anxiety about being in situations or places from which escape may be difficult (or embarrassing), or in which help may not be available in the event of an unexpected panic attack, or panic-like symptoms; these situations are avoided or endured with dread (DSM-IV; APA, 1994). Agoraphobic situations include crowds, malls, movie theaters, waiting in line, traveling by car/public transportation, and being outside the home alone. Agoraphobic avoidance ranges from mild to moderate to severe, depending on degree of impairment in functioning.

The mildly agoraphobic individual may, for example, avoid driving long distances alone, but manages to drive to and from work, feels uncomfortable in crowds, and sits in the aisle seat in movie theaters. A person with moderate agoraphobia may limit driving to within a 5-mile radius from home, may drive only if accompanied, and may avoid malls and large supermarkets. Severe agoraphobia refers to the more housebound individual.

Cognitive–behavioral treatment (CBT) for PD/PDA was largely developed during the late 1980s and early 1990s, based on the biopsychosocial model of panic (e.g., Barlow, 1988). In this model, the initial panic attack is conceived of as a "false alarm," or misfiring of the fear system, in biologically and psychologically vulnerable individuals during a period of stress. These individuals are believed to possess an inherited tendency towards neurobiological overreactivity to stressful life events such as death of a loved one and job or school-related stress. This physiological overreactivity interacts with a psychological vulnerability conceptualized as a set of danger-laden beliefs about bodily sensations (e.g., "Heart palpitations mean I could be having a heart attack"), and about the world in general (e.g., "I have no control over what happens to me"). These concepts of anxiety sensitivity (Reiss et al., 1986) and uncontrollability (Barlow, 1988), respectively, are central to the cognitive schemata in PD/PDA.

In this model, the experience of an unexpected false alarm in vulnerable individuals leads to learned associations between internal and external cues present during the attack. For example, in the case illustration, Jeff experienced a racing heart during the initial panic; reexperiencing a racing heart while exercising led Jeff to think he was having a panic attack. As a result, heart-rate elevations, as well as harmless exercise, become conditioned cues or "learned alarms" for panic. Following the initial panic, vulnerable individuals develop hypervigilance for internal sensations, becoming highly sensitive to any somatic response or change. External cues present at the time of the attack may also become associated with having a panic, leading to agoraphobic avoidance. Jeff, for example, avoided hiking and being out in the sun following his initial attack. Both internal and external cues may generalize over time so that the range of triggering sensations/situations becomes increasingly broad.

Most importantly, vulnerable individuals develop anxious apprehension over the possibility of having future panic attacks. As mentioned earlier, these individuals possess a tendency to view anxiety-related bodily sensations as dangerous (anxiety sensitivity). Thus, unexpected autonomic arousal generates fear, which in turn intensifies the feared sensations (because fear produces more autonomic arousal), resulting in more fear, and so on — the "fear-of-fear" cycle. Because the initiating cues (i.e., bodily sensations) may not be immediately obvious, individuals perceive the attacks as unexpected or "out of the blue" (Barlow, 1988). These interoceptive cues and resulting panic attacks are therefore unpredictable and relatively uncontrollable (i.e., they are difficult to escape) (see Craske, 1999), resulting in elevated levels of chronic anxious apprehension (Barlow, 1988), which in turn increases the likelihood of panic.

CBT entails several components addressing the physiological and cognitive aspects of PD, and agoraphobic avoidance in PDA. The treatment is brief (8–12 weeks) and highly effective: approximately 75% of patients are panic-free at the end of treatment (see Craske, 1999). A CBT protocol has been developed to treat nocturnal panic attacks, that is, awakening from sleep in a state of panic in the absence of nightmares, loud noises, or other interruptions. Nocturnal attacks are symptomatically similar to daytime panic attacks and are experienced by approximately 40% of individuals with PD/PDA. Treatment for nocturnal panic is described below.

ASSESSMENT

Appropriate treatment selection for CBT is dependent on a thorough and reliable assessment. Moreover, continued assessment during and after treatment allows monitoring of progress and evaluation of treatment effectiveness.

Initial diagnosis of PD/PDA is often determined through clinical interview. The Anxiety Disorders Interview Schedule for DSM-IV (ADIS-IV; Brown et al., 1994) is one of the most widely used clinical interviews and was designed specifically for assessment of the anxiety disorders. This semistructured instrument contains questions pertaining to DSM-IV diagnoses for anxiety disorders and takes approximately 1.5 to 2.5 hours to administer, depending on the severity of symptoms and the experience of the interviewer. The ADIS-IV provides a reliable means of determining diagnoses of PD/PDA, as well as providing information about comorbid conditions.

Ongoing self-monitoring is another important aspect of assessment and treatment. Using portable panic attack records, Jeff, for example, recorded the frequency, duration, situational context, and symptoms as soon as possible after each attack, beginning 2 weeks prior to the start of treatment and continuing throughout. He also rated items such as average and maximum levels of anxiety during the day, preoccupation with panicking, percentage chance of panicking the next day, average depression, and medication use. Jeff recorded these ratings upon retiring each night on a Weekly Record of Anxiety and Depression. He also monitored activities by logging daily excursions in a diary and checking off activities completed on an agoraphobic checklist.

Self-report inventories are used to provide information for treatment planning, as well as to assess therapeutic change. Jeff completed a series of inventories assessing factors such as degree of avoidance of common agoraphobic situations, degree to which specific bodily sensations are feared, and frequency/severity of anxiety symptoms over the past week. Information from these instruments was used to construct exposure hierarchies for both *in vivo* and interoceptive practices.

Behavioral tests provide an objective measure of avoidance of specific situations that may differ from the individual's subjective impressions of what they can and cannot do. Thus, although these tests traditionally are the province of research scientists, they can also provide clinically useful information. Tests may be standardized or individually tailored. Standardized behavioral tests typically involve walking/driving an established route (e.g., a 1-mile loop around the clinic). Anxiety levels are rated at regular intervals, and the actual distance traveled is recorded. Standardized tests may also be administered to assess fear of bodily sensations. Tasks such as spinning in a chair, breathing through a tube, and hyperventilation are attempted; anxiety levels before and after each task and task duration are recorded. For individually tailored behavioral tests, individuals attempt three to five situational tasks identified as being somewhat to extremely difficult. For Jeff, these tasks included driving a set distance on a highway, sitting in the middle seat in an auditorium, and shopping in a crowded supermarket. Maximum levels of anxiety and extent of approach (i.e., attempted but escaped, refused, or completed) were recorded for each task.

TREATMENT IMPLEMENTATION

The major components of CBT for PD/PDA target cognitive distortions and problematic behaviors (e.g., avoidance of internal sensations and/or external situations) of PD/PDA. Treatment may be administered in a group format (four to six participants and two cotherapists in our clinic) or individually. Sessions are highly structured and focus on current symptoms and thoughts associated with recent or ongoing panic attacks. Homework assignments are given regularly throughout treatment, and practices are carefully monitored. Collaboration between patients and therapist(s) is emphasized; patients are encouraged to become their own personal scientists.

Treatment begins with education about the nature of panic and anxiety. Individuals are informed that fear is a natural response, part of the body's "fight or flight" system that is triggered in reaction to an actual or perceived threat. The physiological basis of panic symptoms is explained in detail (e.g., racing heart is a means of getting blood to the limbs for quick escape) and myths about panic (e.g., too much anxiety "wears out" the nerves) are discussed and debunked. The adaptive nature of the fear system is emphasized — that is, a highly reactive "fight or flight" system was necessary for survival in prehistoric times. The goal of treatment is, thus, not to eliminate all anxiety, but rather to learn effective ways of managing extreme, inappropriate anxiety. Also presented is the "three systems model" of anxiety — that is, the experience of panic can be delineated into what "one thinks," "one does," and "one feels." The interaction of these three systems in eliciting and ameliorating anxiety is explained.

A model of panic is presented emphasizing the role of cognition and behavior in the development and maintenance of panic. Anxiety is presented as a response that may be triggered at inappropriate times, leading to the experience of uncomfortable yet harmless symptoms. When no external stimulus is readily available to explain the cause of such symptoms, the tendency is to search internally. For individuals predisposed towards anxiety such as Jeff, some malignant internal cause (e.g., heart attack, stroke) is often deemed the source of these symptoms. This misappraisal results in an intensification of the symptoms, which in turn confirms the initial misappraisal, leading to an urgency to escape. This urgency to flee in turn contributes to accelerating arousal, and so on. The notion that anxiety symptoms are normal and time-limited in nature is discussed and represents an initial step towards correcting misappraisals that are more formally targeted via cognitive restructuring (discussed below).

Breathing retraining (BRT) is then introduced as a method of symptom control. To illustrate the similarity between hyperventilatory and panic symptoms, an in-session demonstration of hyperventilation is conducted. Jeff was instructed to stand and breathe deeply and rapidly for 90 seconds; the sensations elicited and their similarity to his typical panic symptoms were noted. Hyperventilation is presented as a process that may occur subtly, without conscious awareness, and that occurs naturally when anxious/stressed, as the body attempts to increase its energy intake in the form of oxygen. The physiological processes of hyperventilation are presented in detail — for example, if more oxygen is taken in than can be used by the body, the resultant imbalance between oxygen and carbon dioxide in the blood leads to constriction of the blood vessels and reduced oxygen to the tissues; this reduction leads to sensations of dizziness, lightheadedness, and tingling in the extremities. The harmless nature of these sensations is emphasized.

BRT is taught as an antidote to overbreathing. Jeff was instructed to breathe slowly and deeply from his diaphragm, rather than the chest, because shallow chest breathing contributes to hyperventilation. A meditational component is added in which Jeff concentrated on counting (e.g., "one, two, . . .") during the inhalation, and on the word "relax" on exhalation, proceeding up to 10 and back down to 1 in a continuous cycle. BRT is practiced in-session and patients are instructed to practice BRT at least twice a day for 10 minutes. Jeff was instructed to begin practicing in a quiet, undisturbed place, but to gradually introduce distractions to facilitate implementation of BRT in a broader range of settings. He was eventually encouraged to use BRT as a control strategy whenever he experienced anxiety or panic.

Cognitive restructuring targets misappraisals of bodily sensations as being threatening or dangerous. Panic-inducing thoughts may be automatic, that is, they occur habitually and outside of conscious awareness. Examples include: immediately scanning for "safe" seats in an auditorium; assuming that dizziness inevitably leads to fainting; or constantly monitoring for physiological changes, as Jeff did, without full awareness of so doing. Thoughts may also be discrete, that is, they may shift depending on the situation. Thus, for Jeff, fears of death predominated when he was alone whereas fears of embarrassment prevailed in social situations. Identification of the specific cognitions associated with a particular panic episode therefore requires detailed and careful questioning by therapists.

Once specific thoughts are identified, they are categorized as probability overestimations (i.e., inflating the likelihood of a negative outcome) and/or catastrophizations (i.e., blowing events out of proportion, or viewing them as disastrous and unmanageable). Following categorization, thoughts are questioned using an empirical, hypothesis-testing approach (i.e., "What is the evidence for. . . ?"). Using socratic methods, therapists assist patients in examining realistic probabilities (e.g., "What is the actual likelihood of having a stroke?"), gathering data (e.g., medical status), exploring alternative explanations (e.g., attributing lightheadedness to a skipped meal), and examining realistic consequences and concrete strategies for dealing with events should they occur (e.g., "How bad would it really be if I fainted? How would I actually cope if it happened?").

Interoceptive exposure is introduced to weaken or disrupt the associations between specific internal cues and panic reactions. Jeff practiced a series of exercises in-session to identify those that reliably induced sensations that mimicked his panic symptoms. Exercises included hyperventilation, spinning, and holding one's breath. Relevant exercises were ranked according to anxiety levels elicited and, starting with the least anxiety-provoking, the exercises were repeated until anxiety decreased to a mild level. During each exposure, Jeff was instructed to experience the sensations to the fullest, and to tolerate the sensations for a period of time before ending the exercise. In this way, he learned that feared outcomes did not occur (e.g., fainting, losing control, or dying). Cognitive and breathing strategies were applied *after*, not during, each exposure. Jeff was instructed to conduct interoceptive exposures daily between sessions. After habituating to these exercises, Jeff identified naturalistic activities (e.g., drinking coffee, exercising, watching thriller movies), which were ranked in a hierarchy. He was then instructed to practice these exercises repeatedly at least three times a week.

For patients with agoraphobic avoidance such as Jeff, *in vivo* exposure is conducted after the above interventions. A hierarchy of relevant agoraphobic situations was generated and exposure was graduated, beginning with the least anxiety-provoking situation; Jeff was instructed to practice at least three times per week. An interoceptive component may be introduced to increase task demand — for example, Jeff practiced driving with the heater on. During exposures, negative cognitions are identified and challenged; BRT is applied as needed. Maladaptive coping strategies are also addressed — for example, use of safety signals (e.g., cell phones, medications), distraction (e.g., thinking about something else), and unnecessary precautions (e.g., keeping a tight grip on the steering wheel so as not to lose control of the car). Exposures are planned and rehearsed (i.e., negative cognitions are anticipated and countered) in advance; practices from the previous week are reviewed and modified. When possible, *in vivo* exposures are conducted in-session with therapist encouragement and feedback.

CBT for nocturnal panic incorporates all of the above components with appropriate modifications for treatment of nighttime attacks. The model of panic is expanded to include explanations of how autonomic arousal during sleep as a result of anxiety or stress experienced during the day, natural physiological changes during sleep, inefficient breathing during sleep, and anticipatory anxiety before sleep may induce sensations that cause awakening. Misappraisal of sensations then leads to fear, heightened sensations, and panic. Since sleep deprivation may contribute to anxiety, sleep hygiene guidelines (e.g., establishing a regular routine) are instituted. Cognitive strategies target fears related to the dangers of panicking, or experiencing panic-like symptoms during sleep (i.e., the person may believe that it is more dangerous for them to have an elevated heart rate during sleep than during the day because cardiac arrests are more common during sleep). BRT is practiced immediately prior to sleep and upon waking throughout the night. Interoceptive exposure includes meditative relaxation (a state that is often fear-provoking for persons with nocturnal panic), as well as deliberate startles from sleep to overcome fear reactions to elevated arousal from a sleeping state.

CONCURRENT DIAGNOSES AND TREATMENT

Concurrent diagnoses (comorbidity) in individuals with principal diagnoses of PD/PDA is common. (A principal diagnosis is defined as the most severe or interfering disorder, without reference to chronology, whereas a primary diagnosis chronologically precedes other conditions that are secondary to the earlier disorder.) Two recent studies found high rates of comorbidity in principal PD/PDA. Brown et al. (1995) reported that 51% of 126 principal PD/PDA patients had at least one additional diagnosis of clinical severity prior to the start of treatment. Similarly, we (Tsao et al., 1998) found that 64% of 33 patients with principal PD/PDA presented with one or more concurrent diagnoses at pretreatment. Both studies used the ADIS-R (DiNardo & Barlow, 1988) to determine diagnostic status. ADIS-R interviewers assigned a severity rating, ranging from 0 (none) to 8 (very severe) for each diagnosis to indicate the level of distress and/or impairment — a rating of 4 (moderate) or more indicated clinical severity, whereas a rating of less than 4 indicated subclinical severity.

Both the Brown et al. (1995) and our own (Tsao et al., 1998) study reported that the most common concurrent diagnoses in principal PD/PDA were generalized anxiety disorder (GAD), social phobia, and depression (including major depression and dysthymia). Both studies also found specific phobia to be the most frequent subclinical comorbid condition, followed by social phobia in the Brown et al. study, and GAD and posttraumatic stress disorder (PTSD) equally in our study.

Clinicians are understandably concerned that individuals with concurrent diagnoses may constitute a different population than those without additional diagnoses and that treatment outcome may be adversely affected by the presence of comorbidity. Although many studies, including

Brown *et al.* (1995), found that individuals with comorbid conditions were more severely afflicted at pretreatment, we (Tsao *et al.*, 1998) did not find any differences in ADIS-R severity ratings for PD/PDA between individuals with and without additional diagnoses prior to treatment. Regarding the impact of comorbidity on treatment outcome, both studies (Brown *et al.*, 1995; Tsao *et al.*, 1998) reported that comorbidity did not predict poorer response to CBT.

In sum, CBT has been shown to be effective in the treatment of PD/PDA despite the presence of concurrent diagnoses. Moreover, it appears that CBT for principal PD/PDA results in substantial and clinically meaningful reductions in the frequency and severity of concurrent diagnoses that are not the focus of treatment (Tsao *et al.*, 1998), although whether these gains are maintained over the long term remains unclear (see Brown *et al.*, 1995). These findings suggest that the most efficient and effective use of clinical resources involves treating the principal disorder (PD/PDA) first and then judging what remaining symptoms require further treatment, rather than targeting all presenting syndromes at once. We are currently evaluating this recommendation empirically. Although a full behavioral analysis of all conditions requiring amelioration should be conducted, treatment should begin with the most disabling condition first, followed by reassessment at the end of treatment before proceeding with additional interventions.

COMPLICATIONS AND TREATMENT IMPLICATIONS

Despite findings that CBT for principal PD/PDA appears to be effective in the presence of concurrent diagnoses, complications may arise during treatment in the event PD/PDA ceases to be the most disturbing/disabling disorder and another condition becomes predominant. Clinicians must carefully judge whether such patients should be continued in treatment. In the case of concurrent depression, for example, lack of motivation and difficulty concentrating, as seen in mild to moderate depression, may retard progress but do not necessarily indicate additional treatment. The presence of severe symptoms such as extreme hopelessness and suicidality, however, indicates discontinuation of CBT for PD/PDA and institution of treatment for depression.

An issue not addressed in the previous section is the presence of axis II disorders in principal PD/PDA. The presence of personality disturbances is not a contraindication for CBT because several investigations have shown that such individuals still benefit, although perhaps at a slower rate. However, personality disorders may complicate treatment if, for example, the individual is particularly demanding. In a group setting, such individuals may "take over" by speaking at length about their particular problems, or by engaging the therapist in side conversations. Such behavior is disruptive to the group and, because extra time is devoted to meeting the demands of one individual, treatment may be compromised for other group members. Setting firm limits within the group and privately reminding the individual that treatment is for all group members can help the situation. In other instances, individuals with personality disturbances may make unreasonable demands on the therapist that run counter to treatment goals (e.g., paging or calling the therapist every time a panic attack occurs). The therapist should encourage the patient to attempt to use skills learned in-session rather than rely on the therapist in the event of a panic.

Medications may also potentially interfere with administration of CBT. Some medications diminish physical symptoms, resulting in a decrease in the effectiveness of exercises designed to expose individuals to feared physical sensations. Patients may also attribute improvements to medication, rather than their own efforts. The lack of perceived self-efficacy engendered by these attributions may result in increased risk of relapse when medication is withdrawn or, alternatively, continued use of medication due to patient's belief that he or she would not be able to function without it. Some medications have sedating or soothing effects that may lower motivation, thereby reducing the time and effort dedicated to behavioral practices.

Noncompliance with treatment procedures is commonplace and may interfere with treatment goals. Lack of compliance may arise for several reasons. Those individuals who remain intensely fearful may be less compliant. For such patients, exposures should be conducted in a more graduated fashion; additional discussion of cognitive restructuring skills may also prove helpful. Others may not comply due to the treatment's perceived lack of credibility. For example, patients may believe they are different from others with panic because of certain symptoms they experience, and that treatment will therefore not be helpful. These beliefs may be explored through cognitive work. Finally, it may be that a lack of social support reduces motivation and compliance with treatment. Group treatment may prove helpful in this instance.

Dealing with Managed Care
and Accountability

Treatment of PD/PDA is increasingly being conducted in the context of managed care. It is now recognized that the majority of individuals who suffer from PD/PDA are initially seen by primary care physicians, rather than mental health professionals. The high prevalence rate of PD/PDA in primary care settings indicates a need for effective treatments such as CBT. Data from numerous sources indicate PD/PDA causes substantial economic burden — individuals with PD/PDA evidence high rates of unemployment and disability; they also use primary care services at a higher rate than most other patients. Alleviating this burden requires that treatment be administered in a cost-effective, efficient manner.

Rapaport and Cantor (1997) describe specific strategies for dealing with managed care in treating PD/PDA. In order to work effectively within managed care, the clinician who contracts with a managed care plan must first understand the benefit plan structure. Important aspects to consider are whether the plan is capitated, whether the mental health benefits are well defined, who is the "gatekeeper" for the mental health portion of the plan, and what criteria are used for evaluating treatments. The authors suggest that clinicians meet personally with the professionals who administer the plan, for example, the primary care providers and administrators overseeing delivery of care. These personal contacts may facilitate referrals and increase the possibility of influencing future decisions regarding benefits and care delivery.

In addition to meeting with managed care professionals, Rapaport and Cantor (1997) advocate establishing a role as a consultant within the plan. As consultants, clinicians can educate other professionals about the social and economic cost of PD/PDA, and how effective treatments can reduce patient use of medical services, as well as increase patient satisfaction and quality of life. Information regarding diagnosis and treatment should be relayed to professionals and patients alike. Given the social stigma attached to mental conditions, clinicians should strive to educate patients regarding the benefits of treatment in terms of both symptom relief and overall quality of life. "Frontline" professionals (e.g., primary care physicians, nurses) should be educated to screen for PD/PDA and not to dismiss patient complaints.

Given the effectiveness and brevity of CBT for PD/PDA, the treatment is highly appropriate for implementation within managed care. Wider dissemination of information regarding PD/PDA (e.g., course, prognosis, treatment options), educating managed care members on how treatment can lower overall costs (e.g., by reducing use of services), providing quantifiable data regarding treatment outcome, and developing well-defined algorithms for care delivery are all important strategies for dealing with managed care (Rapaport & Cantor, 1997).

OUTCOME AND FOLLOW-UP

The clinical significance of treatment outcome remains an important consideration for researchers and clinicians alike. Outcome is typically assessed by examining changes in measures administered during pre-, post-treatment, and follow-up. Changes may be examined across an entire sample or by individual; measures may also be examined individually or combined into composite variables (e.g., high end-state functioning).

Among the most important outcome variables are frequency and severity of panic attacks, and extent of agoraphobic avoidance (if relevant). Consideration of interference (i.e., levels of functioning) and degree of apprehension are also important in assessing clinically significant improvement. The ADIS-IV (Brown *et al.*, 1994) provides information on these and other variables; the interviewer assigns new severity ratings at post-treatment and follow-up that are compared to ratings at pretreatment. Performance on behavioral tests and self-report inventories are used to round out the clinical picture.

Returning to the case of Jeff, his ADIS severity rating decreased from a 6 (severe) for PD with moderate to severe agoraphobia, to a 2 (mild) with none to mild agoraphobia at post. Frequency of panic declined from four full-blown panics per month to only one limited symptom episode during the last month of treatment. Jeff reported only occasional worry about his next attack, compared to frequent worry at pretreatment; notably, the panics no longer interfered with his life by the end of treatment. He was able to do almost everything he wished, including hiking and exercising, as well as traveling out of town by car. In addition, he no longer felt apprehension at work since he had not left early due to an attack for a number of weeks. These gains were maintained at 6-month follow-up.

DEALING WITH RECIDIVISM

Despite the effectiveness of CBT, there is increasing recognition that recidivism remains a problem for a portion of patients. Findings from 20 independently conducted and controlled studies suggest that patients receiving CBT either maintain their treatment gains or continue to improve over the follow-up period (up to 2 years) (see Craske, 1999). However, one study found that when individuals were tracked over time, more than a third who had been classified as panic-free 24 months after treatment had experienced a panic attack in the preceding year (Brown & Barlow, 1995).

One approach that may reduce recidivism is lengthening the period over which treatment is administered, without increasing the number of sessions. Rather than use a traditional once-a-week schedule, it may be beneficial to space sessions such that the time interval between them gradually lengthens. In a 13-session protocol for nocturnal panic described above, the first three sessions are administered over a 10-day period; Sessions 4 to 9 are held weekly, and sessions 10 and 11 biweekly. Review sessions are held 3 and 6 months after the 11th session. Based on cognitive models of memory, spacing sessions in this manner may facilitate learning and protect against attrition and recidivism (see Craske, 1999). Evaluation of this intervention is ongoing.

Other ways to combat recidivism include maintaining regular phone contacts with patients and administering booster sessions. Instructing patients to initiate contact in the event of anticipated or unexpected stress or as soon as minor symptoms recur may also help. Patients should be encouraged to keep and review session materials at regular intervals. Continued practice of homework assignments, including monitoring of cognitions and *in vivo* exposure to problematic situations, is also recommended.

SUMMARY

Cognitive–behavioral treatment for Panic Disorder with or without Agoraphobia is a highly effective intervention — roughly 75% of individuals are panic-free by the end of treatment (see Craske, 1999). In addition, CBT is brief in duration (8–12 weeks) and its effects are long-lasting (see Craske, 1999). Treatment is based on the biopsychosocial model of Panic Disorder (see, e.g., Barlow, 1998) in which neurobiological overreactivity to stress interacts with psychological vulnerability characterized by the tendency to view anxiety-related bodily sensations as dangerous, and the world as threatening and uncontrollable. An initial misfiring of the fear system (panic attack) in vulnerable individuals leads to a learned set of associations resulting in a continuing cycle of fear and apprehension concerning bodily sensations (panic disorder).

Treatment focuses on targeting cognitive distortions (i.e., the misappraisal of bodily sensations as dangerous) and behavioral aspects, including fear and avoidance of bodily sensations and agoraphobic situations. Treatment includes: (1) education about the nature of panic and anxiety; (2) breathing retraining; (3) cognitive restructuring; (4) interoceptive exposure; and (5) *in vivo* exposure. Treatment for nocturnal panic involves these components adapted for treatment of nighttime attacks.

CBT for panic remains effective despite the presence of concurrent diagnoses (Brown *et al.*, 1995). Numerous complications however, may arise in the event of coexisting axis II disorders, severe depression, medication use, and noncompliance with treatment procedures. Given its effectiveness and brevity, CBT for PD/PDA is gaining popularity in managed care settings. Clinicians should strive to educate managed care providers about the social and economic costs of PD/PDA while disseminating information regarding diagnosis and treatment. Recidivism remains a problem despite outcome data suggesting that most patients maintain their gains or continue to improve following treatment. Strategies for dealing with recidivism include lengthening the period over which treatment is administered, maintaining regular phone contacts, and giving booster sessions.

REFERENCES

American Psychiatric Association (1994). *Diagnostic and statistical manual of mental disorders* (4th ed.). Washington, DC: Author.

Barlow, D. H. (1988). *Anxiety and its disorders: The nature and treatment of anxiety and panic.* New York: Guilford.

Brown, T. A., & Barlow, D. H. (1995). Long-term outcome in cognitive–behavioral treatment of panic disorder: Clinical predictors and alternative strategies for assessment. *Journal of Consulting and Clinical Psychology, 63,* 754–765.

Brown, T. A., DiNardo, P. A., & Barlow, D. H. (1994). *Anxiety Disorders Interview Schedule for DSM-IV (ADIS-IV).* Albany, NY: Graywind.

Brown, T. A., Antony, M. M., & Barlow, D. H. (1995). Diagnostic comorbidity in panic disorder: Effect on treatment outcome and course of comorbid diagnoses following treatment. *Journal of Consulting and Clinical Psychology, 63,* 408–418.

Craske, M. G. (1999). *Anxiety disorders: Psychological approaches to theory and treatment.* Boulder, CO: Westview Press.

DiNardo P. A., & Barlow, D. H. (1988). *Anxiety Disorders Interview Schedule — revised (ADIS-R).* Albany, NY: Graywind.

Rapaport, M. H., & Cantor, J. J. (1997). Panic disorder in a managed care environment. *Journal of Clinical Psychiatry, 58*(Suppl. 2), 51–55.

Reiss, S., Peterson, R., Gursky, D. M., & McNally, R. J. (1986). Anxiety sensitivity, anxiety frequency and the prediction of fearfulness. *Behaviour Research and Therapy, 24,* 1–8.

Tsao, J. C. I., Lewin, M. R., & Craske, M. G. (1998). The effects of cognitive–behavioral therapy for panic disorder on comorbid conditions. *Journal of Anxiety Disorders, 12,* 357–371.

CHAPTER

Specific Phobia

F. Dudley McGlynn and Steven R. Lawyer
Department of Psychology
Auburn University
Auburn, Alabama

Effective Brief Therapies: A Clinician's Guide

CASE DESCRIPTION

Jessica is a female African American college student 24 years of age. One presenting complaint was failure to tolerate a nuclear magnetic resonance imaging (MRI) examination that would have required being inserted into a small, tunnel-like space and remaining for 40 minutes without movement. Jessica described her failed MRI trial as "terrifying" and as "like being put into a casket." She reported also that she was breathless during the failed insertion, that she feared the machine would be left unattended with her inside, and that she would be unable to get out and might die. Jessica sought treatment that would enable her to tolerate MRI assessment because the diagnostic information was deemed important by her physician. Another presenting complaint was anxiety and avoidance in relation to crowds of any kind (e.g., movies, athletic contests, malls, and supermarkets).

Jessica has developed a pattern of avoiding and escaping crowded elevators, and of avoiding air travel. She reported having used over-the-counter medicines in order to endure necessary airplane flights, and that her anxiety was related to confinement, not to fear of crashing. Jessica has developed a habit of shopping early in the day and very late at night so as to avoid crowds. She was particularly frustrated during the Olympic Games in Atlanta. She endured the large crowds without escaping, but strong feelings of impending doom detracted significantly from her enjoyment of the Olympic experience. Jessica believes that her fears began to develop at 5 or 6 years of age when a brother locked her in a closet that contained a frightening, large poster of a frog.

TREATMENT CONCEPTUALIZATION

Five Approaches to Behavior Therapy for Fear

At least five identifiable approaches to behavior therapy for fear have evolved during the 35-year course of the behavior-therapy movement. Orthodox behavior therapy (e.g., Wolpe, 1990) rests on the twofold assumption that fear behaviors mirror sympathetic activation, and that stimulus control over sympathetic activation reflects a history of either aversive Pavlovian conditioning or exposure to (mis)information. Sympathetic activation is construed as fundamental, but misconceptions in thinking sometimes are deemed important. During assessment, emphasis is placed on identifying the cue-stimuli for sympathetic activation and on delineating precisely their elements, dimensions, or abstract themes that influence the likelihood and vigor of sympathetic responses. Treatment emphasizes deconditioning or decoupling the sympathetic responses from their controlling stimuli via systematic desensitization, flooding, or correcting misconceptions.

Cognitive therapy (e.g., Beck & Emery, 1985) rests on the assumption that the basic problem in maladaptive fear is incorrect thinking. The themes of incorrect thinking are related to the uncontrollability of events in the feared situation, to the likelihood and consequences of deficit performances in the feared situation, and the like. During assessment, emphasis is placed on delineating the themes of incorrect thinking. Treatment emphasizes cognitive alteration.

Social learning approaches within behavior therapy (e.g., Bandura, 1986) also place emphasis on the role of incorrect thinking in fear behavior. In this case, expectations of deficit performance and/or expectations of adverse performance outcomes produce fear in the form of behavioral inhibition. Treatment is geared to enhancing self-efficacy expectations and reducing adverse performance–outcome expectations via personal mastery experiences such as those engendered by participant modeling. Assessment related to the self-efficacy construct is central because the strength of self-efficacy predicts the vigor and persistence of self-change efforts.

A "prescriptive treatment" approach is emerging within behavior therapy, that is, "the prescription of a highly specified, thoroughly evaluated treatment regimen in order to ameliorate a highly specified, thoroughly assessed complaint" (Acierno et al., 1994, p. 3). Assessment within a prescriptive approach attends to the problem behaviors themselves, to discriminative stimuli and contingencies that influence the problem behaviors, to psychological ontogenies mirrored by the problem behaviors, and to clinically germane characteristics of the persons who exhibit problem behaviors. In general, the prescribed treatment involves some form of exposure technology (see below) and/or cognitive therapy and/or pharmacotherapy.

Despite the successes of the behavioral fear therapies just described, the dominant contemporary approach is identified with terms such as *in vivo* exposure, guided exposure, and exposure technology (see Marks, 1975). Exposure-based treatment does not derive from assumptions about the nature of fear or about mechanisms of fear reduction. Rather, it derives from the post hoc assertion (Marks, 1975) that exposure is the common element of successful approaches such as orthodox behavior therapy and social learning approaches. The only guiding principle of exposure-based treatment is that fear can be overcome by arranging for *in vivo* exposure to fear-cue stimuli until the fear inevitably subsides. Assessment in exposure-based approaches typically entails periodically recording behavioral and/or self-reported indices of diminishing fear as treatment proceeds. Treatment typically entails exposing patients to representative subsets of the fear-cue stimuli that pose adaptive hazards in the natural environment.

The Approach to Treating Jessica

Two initial treatment targets were selected from among Jessica's complaints. One target was MRI avoidance, chosen due to the seemingly pressing need for diagnostic images from the procedure. Another target was shopping at Jessica's preferred supermarket during busy times of day. Tolerating the crowded supermarket was chosen both because grocery shopping is necessary and because shopping only at uncrowded times was intruding on other preferred activities.

Jessica's treatment was an amalgam of several of the approaches to behavioral fear therapy just described. *In vivo* exposure constituted the basic approach because it is clearly the empirical treatment of choice for phobic and other fear-related conditions. However, the details of exposure were influenced by results from a pretreatment assessment protocol that went well beyond the limited assessment seen customarily in association with exposure therapy. In general our assessment of Jessica derives from orthodox behavior therapy (see above).

Many questions arise routinely in planning for exposure-based treatment. How long should the exposure trials be? Should exposure trials be massed or distributed? Should exposure be graduated in fearsomeness or be maximally fearsome from the outset? Should the patient be in charge of events during exposure or should the therapist be in control? Is there room for adjunctive treatment components such as preexposure medication or preexposure relaxation training? Is there a place for cognitive intervention before, during, or after exposure experiences? Questions such as these are difficult to answer confidently because there is no consensually endorsed theory of how exposure reduces fear, no theory that guides exposure treatment step-by-step. Questions such as those above are also difficult to answer because the relevant literature sometimes provides contradictory answers to procedural questions.

Finally, the details of the exposure-based treatment used here were influenced by the differential diagnosis. The common thread that bound

Jessica's problems together appeared to be "claustrophobia," and specific claustrophobia turned out to be the main diagnosis. Claustrophobic escape/avoidance of an MRI device and/or a crowded supermarket could, however, have reflected a variation of panic disorder (i.e., Jessica was afraid of having a panic attack during the procedure and/or at the store) or a variation of social phobia (i.e., Jessica was afraid of performing poorly, of looking foolish, etc.). Fear of panic and fear of looking foolish would have guided the cognitive aspects of treatment in somewhat different directions, and both would have been different from specific phobia. The following narrative describes our assessment and treatment of MRI refusal and fearful avoidance of the crowded supermarket as variations of specific phobia.

ASSESSMENT

The assessment and treatment described herein are idealized for didactic reasons. This report should not be taken as providing evidence of treatment efficacy. The original sources for most of the various assessment materials described below are provided elsewhere (McGlynn & Rose, 1998).

The Goals of Pretreatment Assessment

The initial goal of assessment was arriving at one or more correct diagnoses based on the DSM-IV (American Psychiatric Association, 1994) categories. A DSM diagnosis rarely provides sufficient information for treatment planning. However, a differential diagnosis within the phobic disorders is important for the reasons noted above and is mandated more or less by the economic context of clinical practice. A more important goal was to provide pictures of Jessica's problems that were sufficiently detailed to provide templates for planning behavior therapy. The latter goal amounted to developing conceptualizations of the objective and/or thematic features of the MRI and supermarket experiences that served to cue Jessica's fear, and to fleshing out a description of her fear in terms of its cognitive, physiological, and behavioral aspects (see McGlynn & Rose, 1998).

Pretreatment Structured Interviewing

Jessica was initially interviewed according to the structure of the Anxiety Disorders Interview Schedule for DSM-IV (ADIS-IV). Using the ADIS-IV affords diagnosis within the anxiety disorders domain and prompts clinicians to systematically acquire information about the history of the anxiety problem(s), about situational and cognitive factors that influence the anxiety problem(s), and about ongoing symptoms in the areas of depression, psychosis, substance use, and neurological impairment. The ADIS-IV renders diagnoses demonstrably reliable across raters, especially for disorders with clear behavioral referents. The ADIS-based interview with Jessica initially produced a diagnosis of specific phobia (claustrophobia) with possible comorbid diagnoses of both panic disorder and generalized anxiety disorder. As the interview proceeded, however, a picture developed provisionally in which the apparent panic symptoms were aspects of claustrophobia. Generalized anxiety disorder remained as a possible comorbid diagnosis.

Pretreatment Behavioral Assessment

Motor behavior vis-à-vis feared circumstances can be assessed in contrived or in naturalistic settings. In clinical work, naturalistic assessment is preferred because naturalistic measurement avoids potential problems in the domain of external validity. Accordingly, naturalistic behavioral assessment was used to develop a picture of Jessica's fear of the crowded supermarket. For practical reasons, however, a contrived behavioral test was used to assess Jessica's response to the MRI procedure.

The basis of assessing Jessica's reaction to crowded supermarkets was a 15-item behavioral checklist that described, in an increasingly fearsome sequence, some major events in driving to the supermarket and shopping for groceries in a crowd. Some checklist items were (#1) "drive to Publix and park"; (#4) "guide a shopping cart down the crowded aisle next to the fresh fruits and vegetables"; (#7) "stand and wait while several rude college students (or others) block an aisle while chatting"; (#8) "say please excuse me and guide a shopping cart through some chatting college students (or others blocking the aisle)"; (#13) "stand quietly in checkout line with people in front of you and behind you"; (#15) "guide a full shopping cart through the front doors and across the lane of slow traffic to your car." During the naturalistic assessment a graduate-student cotherapist met Jessica at her home, followed her to the supermarket, and observed her in the supermarket at some distance. Jessica herself used the checklist; she was unable to go past item 7, and left the store after 9 minutes, voicing anxiety and frustration.

Wood and McGlynn (in press) have described a mock MRI apparatus that has the dimensions of a General Electric machine. It is research equipment built so as to permit either self-controlled insertion or externally controlled insertion, and to record in inches the distances into the machine traveled by subjects during each insertion. Jessica was tested vis-à-vis this apparatus. First, she was positioned on her back with her head toward the mock MRI tube. Then there was a 10-minute rest/anticipatory period (see below) during which Jessica was laying on the conveyor surface still outside the tube. Subsequently, she was told that the therapist would insert her into the mock device slowly, that she was to signal to the therapist if and when she wished to exit the tube, and that she would be removed immediately if she signaled. Jessica was inserted 44 inches into the tube by the therapist. She then signaled to indicate her desire to exit and was promptly removed by reversing the conveyor.

Pretreatment Psychophysiological Assessment

Computer-based recording of heart beats in real time was ongoing during the contrived behavioral test with the mock MRI apparatus. Periods of heart monitoring were used to generate 15-second averages for heart rate in beats-per-minute values. Jessica's mean heart rate during the 10th minute of the rest/anticipatory period was 82. The mean heart rate from the time the top of her head entered the tube until the time of her exit signal was 113.

Pretreatment Self-Report Assessment

Subjective Units of Distress (SUDs). A Subjective Units of Discomfort (SUDs) scale was explained to Jessica as having a range from 0 for "absolute calm" to 100 for "terror." Four ratings based on the scale were acquired. Jessica was instructed to rate her ongoing fear just before going into the supermarket and during the 8th minute of the rest/anticipatory period before the mock MRI exposure. Her ratings were 50 and 30, respectively. Jessica was also instructed to rate the most fear she experienced while in the supermarket and while in the mock imaging apparatus. Both ratings were 100.

State–Trait Anxiety Inventory — State Form. Jessica completed this 20-item scale ($R = 20 - 80$) before the rest/anticipatory period of the mock MRI assessment was begun and after the test was completed. Ratings of state anxiety were intended to supplement the SUDs ratings (above). Her scores successively were 29 and 78. Thus, she was calm 15 minutes or so before the behavioral testing was begun and quite anxious just after testing was finished.

Self-Efficacy Ratings. A 0–100 point scale was used to anchor ratings of Jessica's sense of self-efficacy (confidence) regarding completion of both the 15-item supermarket checklist and the MRI assessment, that is, full insertion for 30 minutes. In both cases, she was instructed simply to rate her confidence orally on a 0 (not confident at all) to 100 (totally confident) scale. Both self-efficacy ratings were 0.

Fear Survey Schedule. One of several omnibus fear-rating questionnaires was administered as part of the attempt to develop a comprehensive picture of Jessica's problems. Not surprisingly, she described her response to suffocation and to closed-in places as one of "terror." In addition, she endorsed "terror" in relation to dead bodies, snakes, crowded places, dark places, heights, and swimming alone. There was no unifying theme for these additional "terror" responses.

Claustrophobia Questionnaire. This is a 30-item questionnaire that contains two subscales. The separate subscales serve to quantify fear of suffocation and fear of restriction, the two dominant and somewhat separate themes of claustrophobic catastrophizing. Use of the Claustrophobia Questionnaire was prompted, in part, by the themes of suffocation and restriction that emerged during Jessica's descriptions of her crowd avoidance and her MRI failure. Her subtest scores indicated clearly that her fear of restriction was more pronounced than her fear of suffocation.

Anxiety Sensitivity Index. The anxiety-sensitivity construct summarizes a person's habitual tendency to think catastrophically about the presence of particular bodily sensations. Anxiety sensitivity is quantified with the 16-item Anxiety Sensitivity Index or ASI. Ordinarily, anxiety sensitivity is of interest in evaluating panic disorder. The ASI was used here because claustrophobia sometimes shares features with panic disorder (see Craske & Sipsas, 1992), and because there were suggestions of panic disorder based on the ADIS-IV interview. The ASI has a range of 0 to 64. Jessica's score on the ASI was 21. That score failed to identify anxiety sensitivity as a relevant clinical concern.

State–Trait Anxiety Inventory — Trait Form. The Trait Form of the State–Trait Anxiety Inventory ($R = 20 – 80$) was administered along with the State–Trait Anxiety — State Form prior to the rest/anticipatory period before the mock MRI test. Jessica's score was 42. As noted, there were indications of generalized anxiety disorder during the ADIS-IV interview. The score of 42 was not diagnostic.

Penn State Worry Questionnaire. Because generalized anxiety disorder was potentially a comorbid diagnosis, we attempted to quantify Jessica's worry behavior as well as her trait anxiety (see above). The Penn State Worry Questionnaire is an increasingly popular instrument for that purpose. Despite having only 16 items, it has a good psychometric record in terms of temporal stability, discriminant validity, and the like. Jessica's responses to the Penn State Worry Questionnaire provided no evidence of worry that was a criterion of generalized anxiety disorder. That result along with the score for trait anxiety (see above) caused us to abandon the comorbid diagnosis of Generalized Anxiety Disorder.

Agoraphobia Cognitions/Body Sensations Questionnaires. These questionnaires contain 14 items about cognitive themes and 17 items about somatic experiences associated with fear and anxiety. They were administered, as was the ASI, because of the possible relationship between claustrophobia and panic disorder. There is not sufficient normative data to permit use of them routinely in clinical decision-making, but the scores they yield can suggest directions for continued assessment. Jessica's score for agoraphobic cognitions was in the average range; her score for body sensations was low. As with the results of the ASI, the data from these instruments did not implicate panic-like phenomena as features in Jessica's problem.

The Results of Pretreatment Assessment

Jessica's fearful escape/avoidance of the MRI procedure and of the crowded supermarket were diagnosed as specific phobia (claustrophobia). There were no significant indications that Jessica could be described as having social phobia. A diagnosis of generalized anxiety disorder was ultimately discarded. The main cognitive theme of Jessica's claustrophobia was fear of restriction (not fear of suffocation). Her fears did not seem to be based on catastrophic misinterpretation of usually benign bodily sensations, as is seen in panic disorder. Jessica was able, for awhile, to allow insertion nearly four feet into the mock MRI device, before requesting that she be withdrawn. She entered the supermarket alone and was able to tolerate a small group of people blocking an aisle she was trying to negotiate with her cart. Her heart rate was significantly elevated during the mock MRI trial; just afterward she endorsed "terror" as describing her experience. She also endorsed "terror" as describing her greatest fear while in the supermarket.

Treatment Implementation

Based on the picture portrayed above, we decided to treat both of Jessica's problems with *in vivo* exposure. The details of the two regimens of exposure treatment were different as dictated by the objective features of the two feared environments. The treatment of MRI avoidance turned out to be more arduous than was treatment for fear of the crowded supermarket.

Treatment of MRI Fear

The basic protocol for treating Jessica's MRI avoidance included multiple exposure trials (insertions into the mock MRI apparatus) separated by 5-minute rest periods, and preceded by self-efficacy ratings regarding successful completion. Jessica was to control the distances and durations of the early insertions; the therapist was to control insertion durations later on. The initial protocol also included feedback about trial durations and praise contingent on trial-to-trial improvement in distance and/or duration. Finally, some trials were preceded by instructions (reminders) to covertly rehearse as needed: "They're right outside and will not leave me in here," and "I can leave whenever I want under my own power."

Exposure (Insertion) Session 1. Jessica was experiencing flu symptoms and had just self-medicated when she arrived, but we decided to proceed with the session. Based on her pretreatment behavioral test, we anticipated that she would accomplish full insertion. Problematically, Jessica traveled an average of only 39 inches into the tube during the first three trials. After the third trial, she was very discouraged and fearful. Apparently, her flu symptoms were contributing to a sense of breathlessness during the exposures. Jessica reported thinking "I'm going to die," "I'm going to suffocate," and "I won't be able to get out" during each of the first three trials. After the third trial, we brought a radio into the room with the intent of distracting her during the remaining exposures. Jessica improved by 13 inches on the fourth trial, nearly accomplishing full insertion. However, she said she was too ill to continue and was dismissed with an instruction to bring a favored audiotape cassette to the next session.

Exposure (Insertion) Session 2. We telephoned the radiology clinic and learned that distraction via music during an actual MRI session was not feasible due to noise from the moving magnets of the imager. Due to the apparent improvement on the fourth trial of the first session (with the presumably distracting music), we decided to use Jessica's preferred music anyhow, but to use it early on and then fade the music out as she overcame her fear. We also realized that the noise of the magnets was a potentially important feature of the MRI experience. Therefore, we went to the radiology clinic and made an audiotape of the running imager. The plan was to introduce recorded magnet sounds at some point and to increase their loudness gradually over the final trials of exposure.

Jessica brought her favorite recordings to the session. She reported some optimism that the music would be helpful. Jessica inserted herself fully into the mock MRI device and was withdrawn at her signal after 35 seconds. Afterwards she showed a stable trend of increasing durations at full insertion. As dictated by the protocol, there was feedback of cumulative times at full insertion along with praise for trial-to-trial improvement. Jessica also voiced pretrial self-efficacy ratings that increased over the session. On the other hand, she continued to report concerns with suffocation. By the end of the session, she tolerated 14 minutes of full insertion.

Exposure (Insertion) Session 3. On arrival, Jessica reported strong self-efficacy for the initial trial of the session. She then proceeded to remain in the mock MRI tube for a full 30 minutes at full insertion. An additional trial was conducted after a 5-minute interval. Again there was a strong pretrial self-efficacy judgment and 30 minutes at full insertion. At the end of the session, the therapist told Jessica that a recording of mechanical noises would replace the music at the next session, that the therapist would control her insertion at the next session, and that the therapist was confident that Jessica could make the transition smoothly. Jessica told the therapist she was confident of overcoming the problem because "if something bad was going to happen it would have happened by now."

Exposure (Insertion) Sessions 4–8. Nothing remarkable occurred during any of the remaining exposure sessions. In each Jessica was inserted fully by the therapist after having been told to remain if possible for 45 minutes, and after having been reminded that she would be withdrawn as needed at her signal. Her pretrial self-efficacy ratings increased from 75 to 100. During the fourth session there was no music; the recording of magnet sounds was played at increasing loudness so that during the last 10 minutes it was at maximum volume. During the remaining sessions, it was played at maximum loudness throughout the 45 minutes of exposure. Jessica remained in the tube for 45 minutes each time. By the end of the seventh session, she had overcome her fear to the point that she complained of boredom.

Exposure (Insertion) Session 9. One week after the final treatment session, Jessica's problem behaviors were assessed using the same behavioral testing procedures and some of the paper-and-pencil tests employed during the pretreatment behavioral assessment (described earlier). Of course, performance during a clinical MRI is a criterion of success; none-theless, measures were taken of Jessica's posttreatment responses to our mock MRI. Jessica inserted herself completely into the tube without hesi-tation or pause, and remained for 45 minutes. Jessica's mean heart rate during the 10th minute of the 10-minute rest/anticipatory period was 79; her mean heart rate from the time her head entered the tube until it cleared the tube was 86. Jessica's rating of subjective units of discomfort during the 8th minute of the rest/anticipatory period was 0; her retrospective rating of the maximum fear experienced during her 45-minute exposure was 25. Her corresponding scores on the State–Trait Anxiety — State Form were 24 and 38. Jessica reported a self-efficacy rating of 90 for completing the clinical MRI and voiced her intention to contact her physician promptly to arrange for the procedure.

Treatment of Supermarket Fear

Jessica was able to drive to the supermarket, park, and enter even when the parking area showed it to be crowded. Hence, each treatment trial began after she had entered the store (with Jessica's approval, the store manager was told about the nature of her visits). The protocol was simpler than that used for the MRI problem. There were no self-efficacy ratings about upcoming performances and no instructions for cognitive rehearsal while in the store. Jessica and her cotherapist were instructed to seek out and remain close to crowded conditions whenever possible (narrow aisles facilitated compliance with this instruction). The cotherapist timed each trial duration from the moment he and Jessica entered the supermarket until the time she voiced a compelling desire to leave.

Exposure Session 1. Initially, the cotherapist accompanied Jessica throughout the supermarket. The cotherapist kept records on the same 15-item behavioral checklist used for assessment. On the first trial for the session, Jessica completed checklist items through 8, in which she said "please excuse me" in order to prompt another shopper to make room by moving her cart to the side of the aisle. Shortly thereafter, she voiced a desire to leave. The trial had lasted just over 9 minutes. After a 10-minute rest in the parking lot, Jessica and cotherapist reentered the supermarket and retrieved the partially filled grocery cart. This time the store environ-ment did not afford opportunities to complete some checklist items; they were bypassed. Jessica was able to complete checklist item 13 ("Stand quietly in checkout line with people in front of you and behind you"). She abruptly voiced a desire to leave and withdrew from the line to go outside.

The trial had lasted 15½ minutes. The cotherapist tried to get Jessica to reenter the supermarket for a third trial, if only to retrieve her groceries, but she refused politely, citing fatigue (there were lingering flu symptoms) and frustration as reasons.

Exposure Session 2. During the first exposure session (see above), the cotherapist met Jessica in the parking lot and accompanied her into the store. Beginning with the second session, the cotherapist instructed Jessica to find him inside, then entered the supermarket first and positioned himself so as to see (and begin timing) when Jessica entered. After observing Jessica's entry, the cotherapist placed himself in the most crowded shopping area possible. After Jessica joined him there, they shopped "together" for the next 30 minutes; the cotherapist was discretely positioned behind Jessica but remained in view. Jessica actually purchased her groceries. The purchase included checklist item 14 ("get out your checkbook and pen, write the check with people looking on").

The original plan included more trials in which Jessica began by entering the store alone and then finding the cotherapist inside. After the first trial of that kind, Jessica announced that another would not be needed; that she felt confident she could handle the supermarket "from now on." The cotherapist prevailed on Jessica to endure one more exposure session within a week, planned so as to occur when the store was most crowded.

Exposure Session 3. The third exposure session took place after the workday on a Friday, when, according to the store management, it was typically the most crowded. According to the original plan, the cotherapist was to stand around the entrance while Jessica shopped without the behavioral checklist. At the beginning of the third exposure session, she indicated that the cotherapist could just stay in the parking lot. Therefore, the cotherapist provided Jessica with a small list of specific items to purchase and remained outside. Jessica reappeared in 20 minutes carrying the listed items saying, "it was a piece of cake." The cotherapist then told Jessica that he was going back to his office, and would not be in the parking lot when she entered the store on the next trial. He then gave Jessica a longer list of items and instructed her to bring them to the office. (These were items the cotherapist needed, so he provided the money for them.) The cotherapist also told Jessica to take her time shopping and to spend at least 40 minutes in the supermarket. Just over an hour later, Jessica appeared at the therapist's office with the listed items.

After this session, Jessica was alerted that fears sometimes returned, and that it should not be thought of as a failure if her fear of the crowded supermarket bothered her again. She was instructed to never give in to her fear if possible, and was reassured that "booster treatment" was available as needed and that very probably her treatment would ultimately be a complete success.

CONCURRENT DIAGNOSES AND TREATMENT

Several investigators have used careful diagnoses based on ADIS interviews to study comorbidity among specific phobics. The results suggest that half the persons diagnosed with specific phobia will receive at least one additional diagnosis, and that additional diagnoses will include panic disorder, social phobia, generalized anxiety disorder, and various depressive syndromes. There is likewise little doubt that specific phobias sometimes overlap with somatoform disorders and with some personality disorders.

In the case of claustrophobia in particular, there is good reason to expect that panic disorder will stand out among the comorbid diagnoses; both disorders have significant origins in catastrophic reactions to normally benign bodily signals. There was no evidence for panic disorder in the present case and, as noted earlier, a potential diagnosis of generalized anxiety disorder was ultimately discarded. Whether the GAD diagnosis was applicable never became really clear. There were interview data that suggested the presence of chronic, mild to moderate anxiety that was sufficient to meet the DSM-IV criteria for GAD. However, chronic, needless worry about two or more identifiable themes is a criterion for the diagnosis as well. Jessica did report frequently worrying about the status of her marriage, the health of her parents, money, and her performance in school. Problematically, at least some of these worries were realistic. Furthermore, her score on the Penn State Worry Questionnaire placed her low on the worry dimension. Nonetheless, Jessica has been encouraged to contact the therapist as needed should her worries mount and/or a sense of dread or related mood be experienced.

Just after completing the demanding series of mock MRI exposures, Jessica was not motivated to tackle problems such as fear of flying and of really large crowds. The therapist told her that she could return for help in overcoming her aversion to airplanes and large crowds if and when she was motivated to do so.

The common theme of Jessica's MRI, airplane, and crowd avoidance is fear of restriction. Airplane and large-crowd experiences are difficult to arrange. Therefore, we would probably approach treatment of the latter two problems with some variety of imagery-based systematic desensitization based on relaxation (e.g., Wolpe, 1990). In systematic desensitization, the patient is first taught the skill of muscle relaxation using some format of progressive relaxation training. Then the patient is instructed to visualize each item from an increasingly fearsome hierarchy of scenarios in which he or she encounters feared circumstances. Care is taken to accomplish relaxed visualization of each scenario before proceeding to the next. Finally, the patient is encouraged to arrange for real-life practice of the calmly visualized scenarios when practice is feasible, and to allow the real-life practice to lag a few items behind successful visualization.

In one approach to systematic desensitization, the to-be-visualized hierarchy of fearsome scenarios is organized thematically. The behaviors depicted in the scenes vary topographically but are organized according to a common principle. Jessica might be a candidate for systematic desensitization using a thematic hierarchy involving increasing restriction. Such a hierarchy could include "booster" MRI-related scenarios as well as those involving airplane travel and very large crowds. Further assessment of Jessica's psychophysiological responsivity during fearsome imagery would be needed to establish her as a candidate for systematic desensitization, but the method has appeal because, as noted above, real-life practice with airplanes and very large crowds is difficult to arrange. In addition, the training in relaxation she would receive in the context of systematic desensitization would be applicable if, at some point, a decision was made to treat her for generalized anxiety disorder.

COMPLICATIONS AND TREATMENT IMPLICATIONS

MRI Avoidance

Claustrophobia is not the only reason for MRI refusal; MRI refusal is sometimes motivated by a denial-coping strategy (i.e., some medical patients do not want to know what is wrong with them). The pattern of excessive concern and coping by denial that motivates MRI avoidance is related to hypochondriasis (i.e., preoccupation with the idea that one has a serious illness). Treatment of claustrophobia in such a case would be misdirected; cognitive therapy for hypochondriacal rumination is indicated.

Given the ages and medical conditions of many who are referred for MRI evaluation, pain during the procedure is a common complication. Lying flat on a hard surface without movement for prolonged periods is difficult for people in pain and can serve to motivate MRI refusal. Again, treatment of MRI avoidance as claustrophobia is misdirected when pain

avoidance is the issue. Other medical conditions can also pose unanticipated difficulties in exposure approaches to treatment; for example, Jessica's flu and associated breathlessness.

The nature of the MRI-related treatment here was opportunistic: a
mock MRI machine built for research was available, so it was used as the
basis of *in vivo* exposure treatment. While mock MRI exposure was convenient given our circumstances, actual nonoperating MRI exposures in
the radiology clinic would be preferable because they would overcome the
generalization decrement associated with moving from one environment
to another (i.e., transfer of training is affected negatively by personnel
changes, context changes, etc.).

Supermarket Fear

There were no complications in treating Jessica's supermarket fear via
guided rehearsals with a cotherapist providing "safety." Arrangements
had to be made with the supermarket management. There was some risk
of interpersonal friction during crowded periods with narrow aisles and
hurried customers. Fortunately, nothing untoward happened. Difficulties
along these lines could, in principle, be treated with narrow-band social
skills training.

DEALING WITH MANAGED CARE
AND ACCOUNTABILITY

Behaviorally oriented providers are positioned advantageously in the
arena of managed care because relatively careful assessment of outcomes
has always been part and parcel of behavior therapy. Providers who treat
people classified as having anxiety disorders are particularly well-positioned because of the ready availability of assessment tools that are both
economical and trustworthy (see McGlynn & Rose, 1998).

The prescriptive clinical approach mentioned earlier incorporates
means for arguing accountability. Part of the approach is comprehensive
initial assessment, which includes describing the problem behaviors themselves, conceptualizing the etiology of the behaviors and their maintaining
conditions, and delineating relevant personal characteristics and history.
Another part of the approach is continuing assessment as intervention
proceeds. A third aspect of the prescriptive approach is using clinical
interventions that enjoy demonstrable scientific support in the peer re-

viewed literature. In brief, accountability is argued on the basis of developing a complete understanding of the patient's problems and of how to assess them, and on the basis of using a demonstrably effective intervention for them.

Our assessment and treatment of Jessica probably fell short of the prescriptive treatment ideal. However, we did measure her problem behavior with some exactitude. We did determine that her MRI and supermarket avoidance were related to claustrophobia and not to some other factor (such as denial by avoidance of diagnostic knowledge). We did bring to bear a contemporary conceptualization of claustrophobia by evaluating Jessica separately for fear of suffocation and fear of restriction. We did evaluate the possible connection between claustrophobia and panic. We did assess the degree to which heart-rate acceleration due to MRI exposure constituted a potential problem to treat, etc.

In the case described here, the economic benefit from timely treatment is easily argued. Proceeding clinically without the information provided by MRI assessment would probably add to the ultimate cost of care. Delaying MRI assessment of some ongoing disease process would likewise be relatively costly in the long run.

OUTCOME AND FOLLOW-UP

The clinical assessment of MRI avoidance is described in the intervention narrative above. A week after treatment, Jessica was able to remain inside the mock MRI tube for 45 minutes, her heart rate was relatively low, and her self-reported fear levels were tolerable. For reasons related to her medical management, the needed MRI evaluation was canceled not long after we ended the series of mock exposures. Insofar as the success of behavior therapy is judged by naturalistic performance of adjustively problematic behaviors, therefore, the efficacy of our treatment of Jessica's MRI avoidance was left unknown. However, we did request that Jessica return for a mock MRI assessment 6 weeks after treatment, 2 weeks after the decision was made to cancel her real MRI evaluation. At the follow-up evaluation, Jessica's self-efficacy rating for completing a 45-minute exposure was 95. Her (0–100) Subjective Units of Discomfort rating during the 8th minute of the rest/anticipatory period was 10; her rating of the highest discomfort experienced during the mock procedure was 25. Jessica's mean heart rate during the 10th minute of the rest/anticipatory period was 79; her heart rate while in the device was 101.

There was no formal attempt to assess the long-term efficacy of our treatment for Jessica's fear of the crowded supermarket. Jessica was telephoned routinely 1 and 3 months after treatment ended. She reported no difficulties regarding grocery shopping. During the second telephone conversation, Jessica wanted reassurance that help was available, if needed, during the upcoming college football season, when she hoped to tolerate crowds of 80,000 to 90,000 fans well enough to enjoy the games with her husband.

SUMMARY

Jessica presented with fearful avoidance of an MRI examination and of her preferred supermarket when it was crowded. Five identifiable approaches to therapy for fear have evolved during the 35-year course of the behavior-therapy movement. Jessica was treated in a way that recognized several of the approaches, but that emphasized *in vivo* exposure as the main vehicle of change. One goal of pretreatment assessment was to establish a differential diagnosis among the several diagnoses that were consistent with her presenting complaints. Another goal of assessment was to identify the objective and/or thematic features of the MRI and supermarket settings that served to cue Jessica's fear and avoidance. A final goal of assessment was to describe Jessica's fearful avoidance in terms of its cognitive, physiological, and behavioral features. These assessment goals were accomplished with several approaches, including a structured interview, behavioral testing vis-à-vis feared circumstances or approximations to them, assessment of heart rate in some of those circumstances, and psychometric assessment of fear and of potentially relevant constructs such as claustrophobia and anxiety sensitivity.

Treatment of Jessica's fearful avoidance of the MRI setting entailed a series of *in vivo* exposures to a mock MRI device. There were eight exposure sessions tailored to the details of Jessica's situation; they included cognitive instructions and self-control over the exposures, both intended to ameliorate Jessica's fear. Treatment of Jessica's fearful avoidance of the supermarket entailed three escorted visits to the supermarket along with instructions to the therapist to be present at first then to fade out of the context as treatment progressed.

Behavior therapy for fear and avoidance is well-positioned in the age of almost mandatory accountability. Empirical support for assessment and intervention practices has long been part of a behavioral approach to clinical problems. Prescriptive assessment and treatment is particularly well-positioned in the age of cost alertness ushered in by managed care. The benefit of timely treatment of MRI fear and avoidance is especially easy to argue. Owing to a medical decision, Jessica was never tested in an actual MRI apparatus but did perform well in a follow-up assessment with the mock MRI apparatus 6 weeks after treatment. Jessica reported no enduring problems with grocery shopping after the escorted exposure treatment.

REFERENCES

Acierno, R., Hersen, M., & Ammerman, R. T. (1994). Overview of the issues in prescriptive treatments. In M. Hersen & R. T. Ammerman (Eds.), *Handbook of prescriptive treatments for adults* (pp. 3–27). New York: Plenum.

American Psychiatric Association (1994). *Diagnostic and statistical manual of mental disorders* (4th ed.). Washington, DC: Author.

Bandura, A. (1986). *Social foundations of thought and action: A social-cognitive perspective*. Englewood Cliffs, NJ: Prentice-Hall.

Beck, A. T., & Emery, G. (1985). *Anxiety disorders and phobias: A cognitive perspective*. New York: Basic Books.

Craske, M. G., & Sipsas, A. (1992). Animal phobias versus claustrophobias: Exteroceptive versus interoceptive cues. *Behaviour Research and Therapy, 30,* 569–581.

Marks, I. M. (1975). Behavioral treatments of phobic and obsessive-compulsive disorders: A critical appraisal. In M. Hersen, Eisler, R. M., & Miller, P. M. (Eds.). *Progress in behavior modification* (Vol. 1, pp. 66–143). New York: Academic Press.

McGlynn, F. D., & Rose, M. P. (1998). Assessment of anxiety and fear. In M. Hersen & A. S. Bellack (Eds.). *Behavioral assessment: A practical handbook* (4th ed, pp. 179–209). New York: Allyn & Bacon.

Wolpe, J. (1990). *The practice of behavior therapy*, 4th ed. New York: Pergamon Press.

Wood, B. A., & McGlynn, F. D. (in press). Research on post-treatment return of claustrophobic fear, arousal, and avoidance using mock diagnostic imaging. *Behavior Modification.*

CHAPTER

Social Phobia

Ronald A. Kleinknecht

Dean, College of Arts & Sciences
Western Washington University
Bellingham, Washington

Please address all correspondances to Ronald A. Kleinkencht, PhD, Department of
Psychology, Western Washington University, Bellingham, WA 98225; Tel: (360) 650-3763;
Fax: (360) 650-6809; Email: Ronald.Kleinknecht@cc.wwu.edu

CASE DESCRIPTION

Clinical Description

James was among the one in eight U.S. adults whose social, emotional, or occupational functioning is adversely affected by social phobia (Kessler *et al.*, 1998). The anxiety that brought James to therapy at age 36 centered on his fear of using public restrooms. He especially feared using them when others were present or when he believed that others might walk in while he was relieving himself. If someone was either already there or walked in on him, he would tense, his face would become flushed, he was unable to speak, his knees went weak, his head felt light, and his heart raced. With this general tensing, his sphincter muscles would tighten up so that he was unable to urinate. Standing at the urinal, he worried about what others might think since he was unable to speak, and he just stood there. This reaction was present although somewhat diminished when he was alone or in an anonymous situation.

Diagnostic Considerations

People like James who experience social phobia fear that others will observe them, scrutinize their person or behavior, and negatively evaluate them (American Psychiatric Association [APA], 1994). They tend to worry to the point of experiencing a panic attack about what others might think of them and about embarrassing themselves. They fear exposing themselves to public scrutiny and are unable to control their cognitive rumination and negative self-talk: "I don't want to make a fool of myself," or "People will think there is something wrong with me." Rather than subject themselves to felt humiliation, social phobics avoid their feared situation, often at great personal and professional cost. If they do not avoid feared situations, their anxiety can become so great that it is likely to impair their performance and lead them to embarrass themselves, just as they feared. Other commonly feared social situations include speaking in public, writing while being observed, speaking to authorities or to members of the opposite sex, and meeting strangers. Fear of using public restrooms is one of the more prevalent types of social phobia, affecting approximately 2.3% of the general adult population (Kessler *et al.*, 1998). This type of social Phobia is more common among male than female social phobics (Turk *et al.*, 1998).

Social fear such as that of James, in which there is a single and highly specific focus of fear, is diagnosed as Circumscribed Social Phobia. Generalized Social Phobia, diagnosed when the person fears most or all social situations, is considerably more restricting.

As a social phobia type, fear of using restrooms is differentiated from, for example, fear of touching a public toilet seat and thereby contracting a disease. This latter situation would be classified as a Specific Phobia since the feared stimulus would be a specific object or situation rather than fear of embarrassing oneself in social situations (APA, 1994).

Onset

James's Social Phobia began during his adolescent years, as do most social phobias — the median age of onset is 16 years (Magee *et al.*, 1996). As a teenager, James was slower to mature physically than his classmates and was very self-conscious about his lack of pubertal development. In junior high school, he would not use the school lavatories at all and was highly anxious when required to shower after physical education classes. He suffered similarly through high school and, although feeling badly about himself for having this fear, he managed to find ways to avoid exposure or endure his embarrassment.

Impairment

As an adult, James graduated from college, married, had two children, and was employed in a middle-management position in a bank. Although he was professionally successful, his fear limited his social activities and was a major source of stress at work. He hesitated to go to bars with friends, coworkers, or business clients for fear that after drinking a beer he would have to use the restroom. On the few occasions in which he did go out, the enjoyment was diminished due to his nagging fear that he might have to go to the restroom. At work, he restricted his coffee intake and kept track of when each employee had used the restroom. He could then plan his own trip down the hall when it was least likely that others would be there or would walk in on him. After more than 20 years of living with this fear and keeping it to himself, he sought treatment.

TREATMENT CONCEPTUALIZATION

Social phobia is often conceptualized as a disorder of self-focused attention and of social comparison. When in social situations, social phobic patients focus a great deal of their attention on how they behave, look, and feel. They are sure that others will see them as they fear they appear due to their self-focused attention. Social phobics' fears are based on the assumption that they will behave poorly or ineptly in their feared situation and that they will be humiliated and lose status in the eyes of those who see them. In this sense, these maladaptive cognitive processes associated with self-focused attention maintain social phobia. The fear is driven by the belief that others focus a great deal of attention on them, so that they will become the center of attention.

When in a social situation, the attention of social phobics narrows to an internal self-focus on how they are feeling. They focus on their heart racing, sweating, shaky knees, and related bodily sensations, that is, they tend to focus on their anxiety while believing that others can see what they are feeling. They equate the "feeling" that they are the center of attention with their "being" the center of attention (Clark & Wells, 1995). For example, when James was in a restroom, he focused on how nervous he was, how tense his legs were, and how his face felt flushed. He felt conspicuous even when no one was there. When someone would come in, he immediately felt as if he had become the center of attention and that all eyes were on him. Worse, he felt that the intruder saw all of this and evaluated him negatively because of his strange behavior.

Social comparison is closely related to self-focused attention. Social phobic patients also will typically compare themselves to others and assume that others are similarly comparing them. Again they equate "feeling different" with "being different." In James's case, this social comparison probably dates back to adolescence, when he was late in his physical development and was indeed different from his teenaged peers. Although those differences had long since disappeared, the concerns over comparison to his peers have persisted.

James recalled no specific incident or incidents that he could point to as constituting the onset of his phobia. However, many cases of social phobia do begin as a result of either a direct or vicarious conditioning situation that leads to the experience or observation of personal humiliation or embarrassment. Following such incidents, social phobics subsequently avoid similar situations and become severely distressed if forced into them. However, James's social phobia appeared to result from the accumulation of years of social comparison coupled with the resulting self-focused attention and negative self-evaluation.

Because social phobics maintain such intense internal focus, of necessity they are unable to attend fully to external events. Being inattentive to what is actually occurring around them prevents them from being able to interact normally and prevents them from being able to evaluate the accuracy of their assumptions. Since James was so focused on his internal symptoms, on being the center of attention, and on his perceived inadequacy, he did not have enough cognitive resources left to evaluate whether he was actually the center of attention. In all likelihood, others coming into the restroom were unconcerned with his presence and did not give his behavior a second thought. However, due to his self-focused attention he was unable to appraise the situation objectively and get accurate and corrective feedback.

An additional factor contributing to maintenance of social phobia is the use of "safety behaviors." Often patients will engage in some behavior in an attempt to forestall committing a potentially embarrassing behavior. However, enacting safety behaviors may actually serve to maintain the problem. For example, James's safety behaviors included tensing his body while standing at a urinal to prevent himself from shaking. This very act of holding himself tense increased his self-focus and decreased external observations that might disconfirm his beliefs. Further, it probably made matters worse by making his face turn red and tightening up the sphincter muscles, thereby making it more difficult to urinate. Thus, the safety behaviors intended to prevent the feared scenario from occurring can actually set up a self-fulfilling prophecy, making the phobic become the center of attention as feared.

Given this cognitive conceptualization of Social Phobia maintenance, there are several specific treatment implications. For most phobias, exposure is widely agreed upon as the treatment of choice. Exposure to the feared stimulus situations should be arranged so that it is: (1) graduated in terms of their fear-evoking power, (2) prolonged until anxiety diminishes, and (3) repeated (Butler & Wells, 1995). Although these guidelines are relatively easily adapted to most Specific Phobia and agoraphobic situations, they are not so readily adaptable for social phobias. In contrast to the animal phobic being exposed to a small animal in a cage, or the agoraphobic being exposed to a shopping mall for an extended period, many social phobic situations are time-limited, such as saying "hello" to a stranger or, in the current case, using a public restroom. Further, a strict exposure to the stressor might be counterproductive, as the increased anxiety experienced is likely to heighten self-focused attention and impair the person's social performance. Finally, for the treatment to be successful, the cognitive element that contributes to maintaining the phobia must be addressed directly, and exposure alone cannot do that. Combining elements from both cognitive and behavioral treatments seems to provide an effective treatment for most social phobic situations and will be described in greater detail in the Treatment Implementation section. In short, directing efforts at restructuring the cognitive processes that maintain the fear behavior, such as self-focused attention while being exposed to graduated situations, provides a framework that is often highly efficacious in treating social phobia (Heimberg *et al.*, 1998).

ASSESSMENT

Assessment of Social Phobia is critically important for treatment planning and involves identifying the severity of the fears and the variety of circumstances that are feared and avoided. As such, assessment provides detailed information on the cognitive processes that maintain the phobia. Thorough assessment will also provide a benchmark against which to gauge treatment success. In the present case, I used several procedures to assess James's Phobia in addition to obtaining background, family, social, and occupational information.

Anxiety Disorders Interview Schedule–IV (ADIS–IV)

The ADIS-IV (Brown *et al.*, 1994) is a structured interview that allows the clinician to obtain detailed information necessary for differential diagnoses of anxiety and common comorbid disorders, as well as to obtain specific cognitive and behavioral information needed for developing a treatment program.

The social phobia section of ADIS-IV provides a list of situations commonly feared by social phobics, including "using public restrooms." Patients respond by rating, on a 0-to-8 scale, how much fear and avoidance they experience to several typical social phobic situations. On this particular item, James responded with a 6 to the fear part and a 7 to the avoidance part. Thus, he reported his fear of using public restrooms as "severe" and his avoidance of them between "often" and "always."

Another pertinent question from the ADIS-IV is, "What are you concerned will happen in these situations?" James replied that he feared that if others came into the restroom and said anything to him he would be unable to respond, his face would turn red, and he would not be able to urinate. Further, he feared that people would think something was wrong with him for standing at the urinal or being in a booth for such an extended period of time. This inability to respond would seriously humiliate him in front of his colleagues. Other ADIS-IV questions concern the various situations avoided due to fears and how the fear has interfered with one's social life, occupational performance, and educational attainment. Based on James's responses to the ADIS-IV, the diagnosis of Social Phobia, Circumscribed, was clearly indicated.

Social Phobia Scale (SPS) and the Social Interaction Anxiety Scale (SIAS)

James also completed the SPS, which is a commonly used self-report scale focusing on fear of being observed by others, and its companion scale, the SIAS, which assesses one's anxiety level while interacting with others, such as in situations involving speaking to authorities (Mattick & Clarke, 1998). James's score of 35 on the SPS was just above the mean for male social phobics. On the SIAS he scored a 40, about 3 points below the male phobic mean. This latter scale did not focus directly on fear of speaking to others while in a restroom and suggests that, although James was more anxious than the average nonpatient, he did not fear such situations as much as do most social phobics, that is, his social phobia is likely to be more circumscribed and focused primarily on one situation.

Behavioral Assessment

To examine more directly the behavioral component of this phobia, James and I devised a behavioral avoidance test (BAT). Although BATs are often difficult to contrive in clinical situations, we were able to approximate such a test. We set up a small hierarchy of situations pertaining to his use of the clinic restroom. The behavioral steps included:

1. He enters alone.

2. He enters with me standing just outside the door.

3. We enter together but I stay by the door with my back to him and not speaking.

4. He enters and I am there already.

5. He goes in and I am there and begin speaking to him as he enters.

We anticipated that these items would not be nearly as difficult as they would be at work or in some other setting, since the clinician is a doctor and therefore a "safe person." Nonetheless, if any anxiety were present under such relatively safe circumstances, then we would anticipate much greater anxiety elsewhere. Further, to the extent that he could achieve any of these steps, this accomplishment could provide hope for him that he could also accomplish them outside of our office after some coaching. It would provide a successful starting point to build on.

James was able to achieve steps 1, 2, and 3 in the hierarchy with only modest anxiety on a Subjective Units of Distress (SUDs) test, rating 4 on a 1-to-10 scale. However, he was unable to enter while I was already in the restroom. This was consistent with his verbal report of indicating that walking in on someone was very difficult for him. Similarly, step 5, having someone walk in on him, was even more anxiety provoking.

TREATMENT IMPLEMENTATION

James's treatment plan consisted of three basic components: (1) First, he had to learn to control his bodily reactions from his sympathetic nervous system arousal and his muscle tension. To achieve this we instituted Progressive Muscle Relaxation training. This skill was used initially to prepare him for entering into an anxiety-provoking situation and to enable him to use imagery exposure to restroom scenes. He would later use it with live exposure to restrooms. (2) We closely examined the cognitive processes described above that appeared to initiate and maintain his fear. To detail these, James was encouraged to record all thoughts associated with either going to the restroom or thinking about going. The purpose was for him to see how his thoughts led to his anticipatory anxiety before he even entered a restroom. For example, "I hope no one comes in" or "I hope I don't panic." These cognitions were used to develop a program of cognitive retraining, such as using coping self-statements to modify maintaining cognitive processes. For example, instead of saying "I hope no one comes in," he would substitute "Just relax and finish what you are doing; no need to panic." (3) The third element consisted of repeated exposure to multiple restroom situations while using all the preparatory skills of relaxation and cognitive processes learned in steps 1 and 2 (Meichenbaum, 1977). In practice, rather than implementing these steps in a lockstep fashion, we began weaving them together early on by introducing simple steps and building up to more challenging steps as his coping skills progressed.

Our first session consisted of assessment including history-taking, administration of questionnaires such as the ADIS-IV, and identification of fear-eliciting situations and associated cognitive processes. We mapped out the treatment plan noted above so that he would have an overall context for understanding the components and their rationale as they were introduced.

Session 2 began with progressive muscle relaxation training in which I instructed James to alternately tense and relax muscle groups. This process provided practice in relaxing and gave James conscious, deliberate control over his state of bodily tension. While relaxing, I asked him to attend to the rate and depth of his breathing and to coordinate deep diaphragmatic breath exhalations while letting his muscles relax. Also, as the muscles were allowed to relax, he was encouraged to say to himself, "just relax." James was encouraged to practice this process twice each day for periods of 15 to 20 minutes. Additionally, he was encouraged to attend to his state of tension–relaxation periodically throughout the day. If he found himself more tense than he wanted to be, he was to institute the relaxation and breathing procedure. This allowed him to begin using relaxation skills in a variety of situations encountered daily.

James reported an incident during the week in which, on one of the rare occasions that he went to a bar with friends, he had to go to the restroom. On his first attempt, he was unable to urinate. He went back into the bar, drank more beer, and returned to the restroom. This time he was successful. This incident was then discussed in terms of using his own relaxation skills rather than beer to assist in relaxation to the point that he could successfully go. The next week's homework plan included: (1) practicing relaxation while urinating at home and in other safe places until it felt natural, (2) recording all of this restroom-related cognitions during the week, and (3) continuing twice-daily relaxation practice.

At session 3, James reported a couple of incidents and associated cognitions. At work, he had to go, and as he was beginning to relax himself in preparation and rehearsing how he would proceed, someone else went into the restroom ahead of him. He decided not to go, but chided himself for being "silly." He labeled the incident a failure. However, that fact that he began to take preparatory steps to deal with the problem, even though these steps were not used in this instance should be labeled a successful step after only two sessions. We then did a 20-minute relaxation session and instituted visualization of him at the office taking his preparatory steps to use the restroom. After several imaginal exposures to this scene, he reported a SUDs rating of 0 and no physical tension. He was then encouraged to seek out restroom settings in which to practice relaxation and visualization of others walking in on him. Also in preparation for *in vivo* practice, at our next session I encouraged him to drink several cups of coffee prior to our next appointment.

Session 4 was devoted to reviewing the previous week's practice and using the office restroom as exposure practice. James had explored several restrooms within walking distance of his office and had used them successfully. He felt that they were not good tests or practice settings because they were vacant and therefore did not challenge him a great deal. Nonetheless, he had taken the initiative and exposed himself to several restrooms, each of which had the possibility of having others present or of having others walk in on him. We then practiced exposure using the situational hierarchy that we developed in the behavioral assessment phase. Having preloaded his bladder with water and coffee prior to coming in, James was eager to test his new skills with me present. Since he had successfully completed step 3 in our earlier test, we decided to begin exposure at step 4 with me being in the restroom when he entered. He was able to enter, go to the urinal, and, after a while, urinate. Although it took him a little while longer than if he were alone, he was successful and reported a SUDs rating of only 3. To continue the exposure, we remained in the restroom for several minutes longer, talking to illustrate that he could do what he had feared and that, as anxiety came over him, he was able to pause and reduce it. In short, he found that he was able to control his state of tension and his thinking processes, focusing on what he was doing rather than on who was present and what they might be thinking of him. At this point, he felt very good about what he had accomplished. He was instructed to continue to seek out and practice using restrooms around town over the next 2 weeks before the next session.

Session 5 revealed that he had again sought out several restrooms in which to practice and was able to urinate while experiencing a manageable amount of anxiety. We then repeated the exposure practice in our office restroom, and again he was successful. However, he had not yet practiced sufficiently using the restroom at work. Although he had made good progress in using a variety of restrooms, the restroom at work remained the final hurdle. We decided to focus the next 2 weeks on achieving this goal. A specific plan was laid out in detail in which James would specifically prepare himself for using his office restroom. His task was to practice relaxation while imagining himself going into the restroom and finding specific colleagues already there. He would rehearse what he would say to them and how he would control his physical reactions. He also practiced imagining himself urinating while talking to these colleagues. Further, James would find "safe" times at work when he would go into the restroom and actively rehearse speaking to colleagues as he imagined them coming in, using his relaxation and coping self-statements. Additionally, he was to maintain an understanding that there were no real consequences to someone walking in and that conversation in the restroom should be no different from that out in the hallway. Further, he was to practice thinking about the fact that he was not the center of others' attention when they were in the restroom. (They came in to use the restroom, not to speak to him.) Although he could accept this logically, he still needed practice thinking this way when others were present.

By session 6, James had again tried several restrooms. However, he indicated that he felt he had not worked as hard as he should have and that he had actually done little work in the office restroom. Further, he revealed that he had considered his efforts a failure since, even though he was now able to urinate, he still experienced anxiety. We then discussed the incremental nature of resolving this problem and that each step along the way was an accomplishment. He should strive for achieving successive increments that would build to the final goal. Again we rehearsed the scenarios that were likely to occur in his office restroom and laid out the plan to be worked on over the next couple of weeks.

At this point, we also instituted a self-reinforcement program to facilitate more sustained efforts at exposure to the restroom at work and to decrease avoidance. Collaboratively, we designed a contingent self-reinforcement program with varying steps that James felt were realistic to achieve and that provided ample reinforcement on completion:

> **Behavioral goal**: After preparing himself,'he would go to any restroom on four different occasions per week when someone else was there.

> **Interim reinforcements**: With four trials in a given week, he could choose either to play golf, buy a piece of pecan pie, or take his wife to dinner (none of the above were allowed until the criterion was met).

> **Terminal reinforcer**: If he achieved this interim goal twice within a four-week period, he would schedule a weekend vacation with his wife. To ensure social support and accountability, he would tell is wife of the contingencies and discuss progress with her each day before taking credit for achieving a step.

At session 7, James reported having successfully used a variety of restrooms with minimal anxiety (SUDs rating from 2–3). He had successfully used the office restroom, and, although it took longer than normal, he reported that he had no "heart-pounding knee-shaking fear." We considered it a successful start at what was to be his last step in this process. He achieved one reinforcer by ultimately using the restroom on four occasions over the 2-week period between appointments. (He played golf this time.)

Session 8 found some additional progress in that he had used the office restroom on four more occasions during the week. (He took his wife to dinner this time.) This being his second interim reinforcement, he and his wife planned a weekend trip. He now felt confident that he could accomplish his goal of regular use of the office restroom whether others were there or not. He felt that he was on track and knew what he had to do to complete his program. He scheduled a follow-up appointment in 1 month to check out his progress and to troubleshoot as needed.

CONCURRENT DIAGNOSES AND TREATMENT

In assessing Social Phobia, it is important to screen for additional diagnoses, particularly other anxiety disorders, since comorbid conditions are common accompaniments (Magee *et al.*, 1996). First, social fear should be broadly assessed so that all possible fears can be identified. For example, speech anxiety is a common complaint of most social phobics (Kessler *et al.*, 1998). James reported some anxiety about public speaking and giving business presentations. He also reported always having been somewhat shy when meeting new people. However, he felt that these issues were not significant problems for him and he was not interested in focusing treatment on those fears. He was aware that the same procedures used in treating his fear of restrooms could be applied to overcome his fears of public speaking and of meeting strangers.

A broad-based assessment should also assess for panic disorder and agoraphobia. Social phobic-like avoidance of situations where others are present can be a part of a larger picture of panic disorder with agoraphobia, and this picture can significantly complicate treatment (APA, 1994; Magee *et al.*, 1996).

Major Depressive Disorder and its more chronic course, Dysthymia, are additional diagnoses often found to be comorbid with Social Phobia. Either of these mood disorders might require separate treatments and, if present, could complicate treatment of social phobia. When comorbid conditions exist, the overall severity and functional impairment are typically more pronounced (Magee *et al.*, 1996). One of the reasons that James's treatment progressed relatively smoothly was that, although his phobia had been chronic, it was not complicated by other disorders.

COMPLICATIONS AND TREATMENT IMPLICATIONS

Adhering to Homework

One of the common complicating factors in treating phobias is that it is difficult for patients to initiate and maintain homework practice on their own. This is not surprising since their homework usually involves exposure to the very situation that they fear most. This fear-motivated avoidance of contact was seen in that James frequently mentioned that he felt he had not devoted sufficient time to his homework tasks and that he felt badly for not doing so. Some patients terminate therapy because they feel they are not upholding their responsibilities in the treatment program.

There are several things that can be done to facilitate adherence to the treatment plan. First, it is important to ensure before the patient leaves the therapy session that the tasks and procedures are clear and that the patient knows exactly what he or she is to do and why. Second, it is important that the tasks be challenging but not so difficult that they overly tax the patient and are therefore avoided. This can be addressed and rehearsed in session.

Third, it is important to have another person readily available between sessions with whom the patient can discuss the tasks. A spouse or friend should be enlisted to work with the patient, or at least to be a sounding board for report and discussion of how practice went. In James's case, his wife was enlisted. Her involvement was particularly important here since James had not told anyone, including her, that he had this problem. By sharing the information with her, he was able to share some of the load he felt and, for the first time, did not have to harbor his secret. Further, she was able to discuss his practice with him and provide an additional source of motivation in the form of someone to check with or answer to. Since James continued to feel that he was not following through on his homework as he should, in the sixth session we set up a self-reinforcement system in an attempt to strengthen his adherence to the program.

Finding Exposure Situations

A second complicating factor is that in social phobias it is often difficult to find exposure situations that are predictably graduated, prolonged, and repetitious. We were able to construct some graduated situations by using the office restroom under varying circumstances of me present or not and then with varying degrees of interaction. Prolonged exposure posed somewhat more of a challenge in that one can only urinate for so long and with a limited frequency. Further, loitering in restrooms might indeed appear a bit odd. Nonetheless, with some ingenuity, situations can usually be constructed that approximate the necessary conditions even though they might not be ideal. Imaginal exposure is always an option as well.

Complications of Exposure

Treatment with exposure only for Social Phobia might not be as effective as for other phobias, since raising patients' anxiety levels also increases their self-focused attention, which in turn might preclude effective social interaction. Thus, if this is an issue, then cognitive interventions must be incorporated (Butler & Wells, 1995; Meichenbaum, 1977). Further, it is important to keep the exposure situations sufficiently graded so that they are not too draconian and inhibit treatment progress.

Discounting Accomplishment

An additional difficulty often seen is that the patient, having achieved some initial success, will discount the importance of accomplishing that step. This discounting is a deterrent to progress, as it diminishes the potential reinforcing value of accomplishing a step, and thereby reduces motivation. To minimize this discounting of accomplishment, it is important to have steps laid out clearly at the outset of treatment. Then these steps should be reviewed along the way to keep patients aware of what they could not previously do and of where they currently are in terms of increased mobility and behavioral approach to their feared situations.

DEALING WITH MANAGED CARE AND ACCOUNTABILITY

Although managed care has received some well-deserved bad press in recent years, the experience in the present case did not meet the stereotype. In many cases, the accountability requirements that come with managed care might work to maintain a well-structured treatment plan and keep it on track. Because many gatekeepers of the system have some discretion in what they allow (e.g., number of sessions), it is important that the provider establish a good working relationship with those in the managed care system. The most important component of this relationship is a well-documented and responsible performance record.

In the present case, James was allowed a total of eight sessions. If sessions beyond that were required, they would have to have been requested along with a justification report for review by the management group.

Most managed care systems require thorough documentation of an intake and diagnostic assessment and a proposed treatment plan. They also require that the treatment plan be discussed with the patient and signed off on, with all risks and benefits explained. After that, complete records of each session must be kept along with a session-by-session assessment of progress on each of the presenting complaints. Treatment plans following each session need to be documented as well.

Although much of this record-keeping and reporting appears arduous, it is also good practice — that is, it is good practice to conduct a thorough assessment, use standardized assessment procedures such as those used with James, develop and discuss the treatment plan with the patient, and keep regular assessments of progress.

Such systematic record-keeping focuses the clinician and the patient on specific goals. Finally, in keeping with cognitive and behavioral approaches, this is goal-oriented therapy. You know when you get to where you wanted to go since you had clear goals and a road map to follow.

OUTCOME AND FOLLOW-UP

The present case appeared to have a relatively successful outcome in that James met most of his goals by the time treatment terminated. He was able to comfortably use a variety of restrooms around town and was able to handle each of the five situations of the behavioral assessment hierarchy. Having accomplished this, he reflected back to his first attempts at those hierarchy steps, and it was apparent to him that he had accomplished a great deal. I used the term "relatively successful" because, although James had met part of his goal of using the restroom at work, he still experienced some anxiety and still had a desire to avoid using it. Ideally, a few more booster sessions would have been useful to ensure that he had continued to make progress on this final goal. However, one additional accomplishment suggested that he was continuing to progress. In a letter written 6 weeks after our final session, James reported having been out in the woods evaluating a tract of land on which his bank was considering a loan. He had to urinate and excused himself from his colleagues (the same ones he feared seeing in the restroom at work), walked off into the bushes, and successfully relieved himself. He reported that he had always wanted to do that, and this was the first time in his life he had been able to. He also reported another occasion while golfing with friends. He had to go while on the course, wandered off into the trees, and successfully urinated. The ability to do this made him feel "normal."

DEALING WITH RECIDIVISM

Perhaps the best time to deal with recidivism is before terminating therapy. Proper preparation might prevent or forestall relapse. I routinely prepare my patients at termination for the possibility that they might experience setbacks or recurrences of their symptoms. Such recurrences are not uncommon, but seldom do they relapse to the level that brought them to therapy in the first place. In other words, they typically retain significant treatment gains.

Preparation for relapse begins with a warning that, as managing their anxiety becomes more automatic and less effortful, there is a tendency to slack off on their maintenance program. They might forget or consciously decide not to practice relaxation or to prepare themselves for entering stressful situations. Under particularly high-stress conditions they can be caught off guard and reexperience their phobic-level anxiety.

In those cases in which relapse does occur, they have been warned and given a routine to follow. They are instructed to attempt to identify what they did differently, what they should or could have done to prevent the relapse, and then to get back on the program. They are told that a relapse does not mean that they are back to their pretreatment state since they had learned and still retain a number of skills. They simply need to put those skills back to work for them. I also invite them to return for a "booster" session or two to troubleshoot, identify what happened, and assist in reinstituting the treatment program. It is common for former patients to take advantage of this offer, and it typically only takes a couple of sessions to assist patients to get back on track and functioning at the level they had at termination.

In this case, James was scheduled for a 1-month follow-up. He wrote a note indicating that he had been doing very well and did not feel the need to return but said that he would call 3 months later. He did not call then, but that is often a good sign that a patient is doing well. In my experience, when patients relapse and are unable to get their program going again, they eventually return since treatment worked the first time — they hope that it can help again.

SUMMARY

Treatment of James's Social Phobia was generally successful, as is often the case with Circumscribed Social Phobia uncomplicated by comorbid conditions. However, as often is the case in clinical practice, the clinician does not always get good long-term follow-up information. Nonetheless, it appeared here that James's program of cognitive and behavioral treatment was successful in that he was able to routinely use a variety of restrooms, including the one at work that he had so long feared and avoided. He was also able to do some of the things he feared since his teens, such as urinating in the woods. Further, he learned the value of various techniques of relaxation, of cognitive preparation, of how thoughts can lead to avoidance, and of how those thoughts can be challenged and changed to work for him. He also learned that these skills could be generalized and applied to other fear and anxiety situations. Should relapse occur, he will be prepared to put these skills back into practice.

Some of the difficulties encountered during therapy have been described, such as maintaining patient motivation to carry out treatment plans. Procedures such as self-reinforcement programs and means for enlisting family and friends to assist can be designed to minimize lapses in treatment adherence. Knowing ahead of time what might occur enables the clinician to prepare the patient to minimize these relapses.

ACKNOWLEDGMENTS

I would like to thank Drs. Julie Major and Erica Kleinknecht for their helpful comments on an earlier draft of this manuscript.

REFERENCES

American Psychiatric Association (1994). *Diagnostic and statistical manual of mental disorders* (4th ed.) Washington DC: Author.
Brown, T. A., DiNardo, P., & Barlow, D. H. (1994). *Anxiety Disorders Interview Schedule for DSM-IV*. Albany, NY: Graywind.

Butler, G. and Wells, A. (1995). Cognitive behavioral treatment: Clinical applications. In R. Heimberg, M. Liebowitz, D. Hope, & F. Schiener (Eds.), *Social phobia: Diagnosis, assessment, and treatment* (pp. 310–333). New York: Guilford.

Clark, D. M., & Wells, A. (1995). A cognitive model of social phobia. In R. Heimberg, M. Liebowitz, D. Hope, & F. Schiener (Eds.), *Social phobia: Diagnosis, assessment, and treatment* (pp. 69–93). New York: Guilford.

Heimberg, R., Liebowitz, M., Hope, D., Schiener, R., Holt, C. S., Welkowitz, L. A., Juster, H. R., Campeas, R., Bruch, M. A., Cloite, M., Fallon, B., & Klein, D. (1998). Cognitive behavioral group therapy vs. phenelzine therapy for social phobia: 12-week outcome. *Archives of General Psychiatry, 72,* 1133–1141.

Kessler, R. C., Stein, M. B., & Berglund, P., (1998). Social phobia subtypes in the National Comorbidity Study. *American Journal of Psychiatry, 155,* 613–619.

Magee, W. J., Eaton, W. W., Wittchen, H.-U., McGonagle, K. A., & Kessler, R. C. (1996). Agoraphobia, Simple Phobia, and Social Phobia in the National Comorbidity Survey. *Archives of General Psychiatry, 53,* 159–168.

Mattick, R. P., & Clarke, J. C. (1998). Development and validation of measures of social phobia scrutiny fear and social interaction anxiety. *Behaviour Research and Therapy, 36,* 455–470.

Meichenbaum, D. (1977). *Cognitive-behavior modification: An integrative approach.* New York: Plenum.

Turk, C. L, Heimberg, R. G., Orsillo, S. M., Holt, C. S., Gitow, A., Street, L. L., Schneier, F. R., & Liebowitz, M. R. (1998). An investigation of gender differences in social phobia. *Journal of Anxiety Disorders, 12,* 209–223.

CHAPTER

Obsessive-Compulsive Disorder

Ralph M. Turner, Belinda E. Barnett, and Kathryn E. Korslund
Arthur P. Noyes Clinical Research Foundation
The Norristown State Hospital
Norristown, Pennsylvania

Address requests for information to: Ralph M. Turner, PhD, 416 Lincoln Woods, Lafayette Hill, PA 19144; (610) 313-1127; Fax: (610) 313-5753; Email: MACTURNER@AOL.COM

CASE DESCRIPTION

Jake is a 34-year-old married man plagued with persistent obsessive ruminations and intrusive worrisome thoughts for the past several years. Jake came to our clinic after being encouraged by his wife to seek help. He was experiencing problems in both his workplace and his marriage due to the fact that he was constantly late. While driving to and from work, he stated that he would frequently fear that he had caused an accident, and would have to return to the suspected scene several times to be certain that no one was injured. Often, this would consume 2 to 3 hours, as he repeatedly drove back to check for evidence of a car wreck or an accident scene. Consequently, he was put on probation at work for constant tardiness. As a result, he now leaves his house at 4:30 am to compensate for the time needed to engage in this checking behavior. In the evenings, he often did not arrive home until 9:00 pm. His wife worried constantly about his safety and grew increasingly irritated at the amount of time he spent away from home. Recently, she informed Jake that if he did not seek help for his problematic behavior, she felt that she would have to divorce him. Jake was initially reluctant to talk about his experiences, stating, "I'm afraid you're going to think I'm totally crazy. I'm afraid I am totally crazy."

Jake's core problem is the repetitive, distressing thoughts that he has caused harm to other people. These thoughts center around the idea that he has gravely offended, angered, or injured someone through his words or actions, and he feels that he must be constantly on guard. He states that these thoughts encompass about 75% of his time, and often keep him from speaking to other people or leaving the house. Situations in which he interacts with people he does not know well or in potentially dangerous situations seem to cue the ruminations. His compulsions include repetitive checking of door locks, and hoarding newspapers and old magazines, in addition to the driving ritual.

He traced indecisiveness and fear of harming others to his childhood. His mother, who was an alcoholic, was aggressive and abusive toward him and his brothers. His father abandoned the family when Jake was 5 because of the mother's abusive behavior. Throughout his adolescence, Jake got into verbal and physical fights with his mother in order to protect his two younger brothers from her abuse. On two occasions, he caused her physical injury — one time breaking her arm. It was during this time that he began to fantasize that he had caused her harm when he had not.

Jake first entered psychiatric treatment several years ago when he was expelled from college. Dismissal was a result of his consistent failure to complete term papers and projects that require a high degree of organi zation and prolonged duration of work. The difficulty stemmed from intrusive, obsessive ruminations and ritualistic behaviors that interfered with his ability to concentrate and work effectively. The resulting anxiety and depression caused him to seek treatment. Before this, he had not experienced any depressed feelings.

Driving a car is the most troublesome situation for Jake. He becomes fearful that while driving he will anger or otherwise cause another driver to lose control of the vehicle and have a fatal accident. He will then feel compelled to return repeatedly to where he had last seen the driver, to assure himself that there had not been an accident. This sometimes results in his driving great distances, several times a day. He is embarrassed to let other people ride in the car with him, because he believes that they will think he is "crazy" for repeatedly returning to the imagined accident site. However, the very idea of refraining from driving past the location is extremely anxiety provoking. He therefore does not allow other people in the car when he drives so that he can perform the repetitive checking behavior.

When Jake came into the clinic, he was taking 40 mg of fluoxetine daily for depression, and 1 mg of lorazepam as needed for panic attacks. He stated that these medications helped control his emotional distress but that they did not stop the obsessions or compulsions.

TREATMENT CONCEPTUALIZATION

Early behavioral case conceptualizations of obsessive-compulsive disorder originated in Mower's (1960) two-factor theory of avoidance learning, which specifies that avoidance responses are acquired in two stages. In the first stage, a neutral stimulus that does not evoke anxiety is paired with an unconditioned stimulus that innately elicits anxiety or distress. Through classical conditioning, the neutral stimulus becomes a conditioned stimulus that triggers anxiety and a fear response. Through higher-order conditioning, other images, thoughts, and words may also begin to evoke anxiety. Over time, the anxiety is experienced as increasingly distressing. In the second stage of the two-factor theory, a response is developed to decrease or escape the anxiety caused by the conditioned stimuli. Such responses are termed avoidance or escape responses. For patients with OCD, these responses often result in ritualistic or compulsive behavior. Reduction in anxiety and emotional discomfort that results from engaging in these behaviors serves to reinforce the continued pattern of obsessional and ritualistic behavior. Thus, compulsions serve as active avoidance patterns to reduce anxiety to a tolerable level.

Based on this conceptualization, treatment involves exposing patients to the fear-eliciting stimuli (obsessions) for extended periods of time and preventing them from performing their avoidance and escape responses (compulsions). Over successive exposures, habituation to the obsessional stimuli occurs, resulting in decreased discomfort and a reduction in the anxiety associated with not performing the ritual. The philosophy behind the treatment is that compensating rituals will not be necessary if obsessions no longer cause distress.

There is compelling evidence that the exposure and response prevention treatment model produces a dramatic and sustained improvement in obsessive-compulsive symptoms (Steketee, 1993). Approximately 70% of patients treated with exposure and response prevention show marked improvement.

Despite its heuristic success, the two-factor model has not received sustained empirical support as a valid theory for the development of obsessive-compulsive symptoms or as an explanation of why prolonged exposure and response prevention works. Consequently, newer, cognitively oriented conceptualizations have been developed. Foa and Kozak (1986) have developed one of the more interesting models, conceptualizing anxiety disorders as specific impairments in affective memory networks. Following this model, anxiety reactions are characterized by: (1) inflated estimates of threat, (2) high emotional reactivity to events perceived as threatening, (3) prolonged reaction to perceived threat, and (4) disconnected affective–cognitive schema structures that are difficult to retrieve in a cohesive fashion.

According to this model, no single type of fear structure is common to all individuals with obsessive-compulsive disorder. Most OCD sufferers base their beliefs about level of threat on the absence of information indicating that safety is assured. Thus, situations are viewed as dangerous unless evidence proves them to be safe. Sufferers fail to develop a sense of safety, despite exposure to feared situations in which no harm results. Therefore, anxiety-reducing behaviors are performed and must be repeated, despite the fact that they can never truly guarantee safety. According to Foa and Kozak (1986), the unremitting fears among OCD clients is attributed to a failure to access their fear network due to absence of a cohesive schematic structure. This could be due either to structural deficits related to the fear network, or to active avoidance of situations that spontaneously evoke anxiety in everyday life. Due to mechanistic factors such as cognitive defenses or heightened arousal, anxiety may persist. Additionally, faulty belief systems that interfere with the information-processing requisite for altering the problematic fear structure may impede reduction of anxiety.

According to this model, prolonged exposure and response prevention works by changing patients' attitudes, beliefs, and schema about the world as a dangerous place in general, and the dangerousness of their specific obsessions in particular. In addition, prolonged exposure and response prevention provides sufficient time and focus for the cognitive–emotional fear structures to be reorganized into a structure that can be modified through habituation.

Salkovskis (1985) has formulated an alternative cognitive model of OCD, suggesting that intrusive thoughts, images, and impulses lead to distress when they are associated with negative automatic thoughts and constitute personal significance for the individual. According to this model, the experience of anxiety is generated from beliefs about causing harm to others or self. The resulting self-condemnation compels OCD sufferers to take actions to absolve themselves of blame and guilt. The problem lies not in the intrusions themselves, but rather in the processing of automatic thoughts and beliefs. Efforts at neutralization are directed at reducing anxiety generated by fear of the consequences. Ritualizing thus becomes the prevalent method of coping, and is maintained via negative reinforcement.

Unquestionably, these newer cognitive models have created new insights into our understanding of obsessive-compulsive disorder and the mechanism whereby exposure and response prevention works. However, the treatment implications are the same. Exposure plus response prevention is the treatment of choice for obsessive-compulsive disorder. These newer cognitive models suggest that there are advantages to adding cognitive treatment components to the exposure and response prevention treatment. Cognitive techniques can be used to persuade patients to risk engaging in behavioral experiments, render the obsessions more ego dystonic and consequently more amenable to behavioral intervention, to improve compliance, and to modify dysfunctional attitudes and core belief schemata.

ASSESSMENT

The purpose of assessment is to understand OCD symptoms in the context in which they occur so that an appropriate treatment plan can be formulated. In our short-term behavioral treatment approach, we limit assessment to two 3-hour sessions. Typically, assessment sessions are scheduled 10 days apart to allow sufficient time for patients to gather self-monitoring data on the frequency and duration of the obsessions and compulsions. Assessment involves: (1) obtaining a background and developmental history, (2) determining DSM-IV axis I and II diagnoses, (3) specification of types of obsessive-compulsive symptoms and their severity, (4) determination of the extent to which the symptoms are disrupting patients' daily lives, and (5) development of the exposure hierarchy. The assessment phase of treatment also involves educating patients about the treatment and developing a treatment contract that specifies the activities and roles of the patient and clinician in carrying out the plan. These last two agenda items are actually transitional; they help prepare patients for moving into the second stage of treatment, the exposure and response prevention phase of treatment.

Obtaining the personal and psychiatric history can be conducted in the clinicians' usual manner. Information about the history and onset of obsessive-compulsive symptoms does not necessarily aid in designing an effective treatment program.

The accuracy of diagnosis is critical for designing an effective treatment plan. Thus, patients need to be evaluated to determine if they meet criteria for Obsessive-Compulsive Disorder, as well as for any comorbid axis I disorders or personality disorders. Structured interviews such as the SCID I (Spitzer & Williams, 1985) to assess axis I psychopathology and the SCID II (Spitzer *et al.*, 1987) to assess axis II psychopathology are excellent for this purpose. The presence of comorbid diagnoses, such as major depression, alcohol or substance dependence, or a severe personality disturbance, will most certainly suggest modifications to the exposure and response prevention treatment plan, or suggest that exposure and response prevention is not an appropriate treatment.

The next task of the assessment procedure is to specify patients' specific types of obsessive-compulsive symptoms, measure their severity and the extent to which they disrupt patients' daily functioning, and then use this information to develop the exposure hierarchy. The Yale–Brown Obsessive Compulsive Scale (YBOCS) (Goodman *et al.*, 1989) is a commonly used symptom checklist for this task. It inquires about current and past symptoms over a wide range of obsessions and compulsions. A second component of the YBOCS is the 10-item severity scale assessing the severity of OCD symptoms in a standardized fashion that is independent of the nature of the obsessions and compulsions. Using this component of the YBOCS, the patient and clinician select the three most debilitating obsessions, compulsions, and target behaviors to be the focus of treatment.

The list of obsessions and compulsions is arranged hierarchically based on the amount of distress reported by the patient. Jake's score on the core section of the YBOCS indicated a high level of obsessive-compulsive symptoms. The exposure hierarchy developed for Jake is depicted in Table 7.1.

TABLE 7.1

Jake's Fear Hierarchy

Situation	Discomfort level
Locking car door and walking away	40
Locking car door and driving	50
Being criticized (by mother, wife, etc.)	80
Driving in traffic and causing an accident	100

Critical to an understanding of OCD symptoms is assessment of both external and internal cues for obsessions and compulsions. External cues are directly observable in the real world, whereas internal cues consist of thoughts, images, and impulses. These cues pertain to fear triggers and avoidance behaviors, as well as worries about feared consequences of not performing compulsive rituals. Subjective distress and discomfort associated with obsessions should be indexed in a quantitative fashion. Indexing discomfort is readily accomplished using the zero (complete relaxation) to 100 (extremely upset) Subjective Units of Discomfort (SUDs) Scale. This provides a metric for the therapist to evaluate the patient's anxiety responses during therapy. Assessment for compulsions should include evaluation of mental rituals and passive-avoidance associated with obsessional ruminations, as well as readily apparent overt repetitive behaviors. There are several published clinical interviews, behavioral observations, and patient and family questionnaires to facilitate accurate diagnosis and assessment of OCD. Steketee (1993) lists some of the more prevalently used instruments.

In order to assess the specific content and nature of Jake's obsessions and compulsions, Steketee (1993) suggests asking patients to describe a typical day, focusing specifically on symptomatic situations. Asking patients to focus on compulsions and compulsive behaviors is often preferable, as these are often observable events. Once these behaviors are described, identifying the underlying obsessive thoughts and fears is more easily accomplished. The following is Jake's report of a typical day.

I'll be driving along, listening to the radio. Usually the traffic will be pretty heavy, because of rush hour. I listen to the radio, because sometimes that helps me not to get upset— My thoughts don't start to race if there's something to keep my mind occupied. And then I'll come up to a light that's turning yellow, and I won't think its safe to go— So I'll stop, and the person behind me will ride right up on my bumper, and start flashing his lights and honking like I should have gone. So then, when the light turns green, I'll purposefully drive really slowly, and I'll sort of weave back and forth, so he can't pass me. When I think he's had enough, I'll speed up a little and start driving normally again, but I'll keep an eye on the guy in my rear-view mirror. Sometimes, he'll go screeching past me, but the worst is when I look back and he's just gone. He just disappears from my mirror, and I don't know what happened. I don't know if he turned off, or if he fell back behind another car, or if I caused him to loose control, and he's lying dead in a ditch. So then I start worrying. I think, he's had a wreck, he's hurt, maybe he's even dead . . . and it's my fault, because I made him angry, and that made him loose control. Then I get really scared, so I have to go back — even if I'm almost home. I'll go back to check to see if there was an accident. There never is, so I'll turn around and start back home. But then I think, maybe I didn't go back far enough . . . and I'll have to go back, and check again. And again, there will be nothing. So I'll start home again, but then I think that maybe it was so serious that the paramedics have already come to get him, so I'll drive back, and get out of my car and look on the side of the road for evidence of a car wreck, or blood, or some sign of an accident. I can never find anything, so I'll start home again. But then I start thinking, this time, I really did it — I really hurt this guy, maybe even killed him — and I've got to go help. I know that nothing really happened. I know that, but I don't feel it— I feel like I have to go back and check, just one more time. And so I will.

At the end of the first assessment session, we gave Jake daily self-monitoring forms and taught him how to record the occurrence of obsessions and compulsions on a daily basis. He was taught to use the SUDs scale to rate the severity of discomfort of the events.

A final important area of assessment is overvalued ideation. This refers to the degree to which the patient actually believes the obsessional thought. Insight into the reality of the feared outcome is considered a predictor for treatment success and a feature that distinguishes obsessive rumination from psychotic ideation. Patients who present with overvalued ideation regarding the actual likelihood of the situation have a poorer prognosis than those who do not. Jake's statements reflect that he "knows" that an accident did not occur, indicating the absence of an overvalued ideation.

TREATMENT IMPLEMENTATION

Exposure and response prevention treatment consists of *in vivo* and imaginal techniques and is intensive and short term in nature. Four to five meetings a week are scheduled for a 3-week period, each session lasting 2 to 3 hours. The format for the sessions is as follows: (1) homework review, (2) modification of treatment target hierarchy (if necessary) as determined by homework review, (3) imaginal exposure and response prevention (as appropriate), (4) *in vivo* exposure and response prevention, and (5) assignment of new homework. Homework practice involves having patients engage in an additional 2 hours of exposure to the anxiety-provoking stimuli and response prevention of the compulsion that they worked on during that day's therapy session.

The nature of exposure therapy is collaborative and progressive. Before beginning treatment, it is very important for clinicians to take time to orient clients to the cognitive-behavioral–based approach. During the second assessment session, Jake was taught the rationale for exposure and response prevention treatment. He was told that the treatment would not be pleasant or easy:

> In this treatment program, we are going to focus on your obsessional thoughts and compulsive behaviors. We've already talked a little about how treatment will proceed, by exposing you to your feared situations and not allowing you to engage in the rituals, thoughts, or behavior that alleviates your anxiety. We've also talked about the fact that while the obsessive ruminations and the urge to ritualize are unpleasant experiences, it is the time and energy that the compulsion takes that is actually causing your true problems in your life. The reason for this is that by confronting the situations which make you anxious, instead of avoiding them or "undoing" the worry by compensating with ritualistic behaviors, you will learn that the situations do not result in the catastrophic outcome you imagine. Over time, you will see that your anxiety and discomfort will go down naturally and that your rituals are unnecessary. Of course, this will not be

easy or pleasant, because when you do not engage in the rituals, your anxiety might go up. It will probably continue to go up for awhile, and that's going to be very unpleasant. But, one thing we know is that it's physiologically impossible for intense anxiety to last more than about twenty minutes, so if you stick with it, and the discomfort will start to go down. If, however, you do not keep yourself in the feared situation, your conditioned response to ritualize will grow stronger.

Although hesitant, Jake agreed to the therapy, stating, "nothing could be worse than what I'm feeling now." He then signed a therapeutic contract, agreeing to remain in therapy for 3 weeks, with 12 scheduled meetings lasting approximately 2 hours each. He also agreed to return for follow-up sessions in order to check on the progress of his independent exposure sessions, the degree of symptom reduction, and the development of new coping strategies to help prevent relapse. These follow-up sessions were scheduled for a minimum of once a week for 4 weeks. Additionally, booster sessions were scheduled for 1-month, 3-month, and 6-month post-treatment intervals.

During the final assessment session, we discussed with Jake the importance of involving his wife in treatment, and asked him to have her accompany him to the first treatment session. Involvement of a family member or close friend can be a critical component of therapy for many reasons. First, significant others often become entangled in patients' ritualistic behavior. This involvement can take the form of unintentional encouragement, of involvement in managing patients' life tasks and duties, or high levels of interpersonal conflict and fighting. Intervention to modify the entanglement will take different routes depending on the type of expressed emotion shown. Regardless of the valence of the expressed emotion and education about the disorder, the necessary components of treatment to alleviate the symptoms and the roles significant others play in maintaining the symptoms are paramount. When the interpersonal situation permits, the most important role the significant other plays in therapy is as a homework response prevention guide. That is, the therapist teaches significant others the rationale of treatment and has them guide patients through the homework. This provides a support system for patients as they do homework and helps to reinforce for significant others what has to be done to break the obsessive-compulsive symptom complex. It also helps to steer the significant other away from their former interactional pattern and toward a healthy and logical response pattern for the future. This will become especially helpful at times of relapse.

Session 1

Jake and his wife, Molly, both came to the first session. The initial part of the session focused on teaching Molly about the nature of obsessive-compulsive disorder and the role that she could play in treatment. Molly related that she did reinforce Jake's checking behavior by responding to his requests for reassurance that he had not caused an accident. She would console him from the time he arrived at home until the time he went to bed, repeatedly assuring him that his actions had not resulted in any harm. In addition, she got up early in the morning to fix breakfast for Jake, so that he could leave by his appointed hour of 4:30 am. We explained to Molly how she was reinforcing Jake to continue his checking behavior. We assured her that it was very common for spouses of individuals suffering from OCD to unknowingly reinforce the behaviors, and that her responses were natural and expected. As a part of treatment, Molly agreed to stop discussing Jake's obsessions and ritualistic behavior with him. She and Jake agreed that she would no longer help him to get ready for work in the early morning. They both agreed that Molly would aid Jake in his homework by encouraging him to engage in the exposure and not engage in the rituals. We emphasized to both of them that this would likely be difficult, as this had been part of their behavior patterns for a long time. When Jake requested reassurance, the plan involved Molly saying, "I understand why you are asking me that, but I want to help you get better so I can't answer you. Remember that I do love you and support you." In order for Molly to understand how the homework assignments should be handled, she stayed in the treatment session to learn through modeling.

The next step in the initial session was to use imaginal exposure to tackle the first situation on Jake's hierarchy: checking the door locks on his car. There were two scenes used in this procedure. First, he was asked to imagine arriving home from work, getting out of his car, locking the door, turning away from the car, and walking into the house without checking the locks. Second, he was told to imagine getting into his car, locking the door, turning on the engine, and driving to work without checking the lock. During the imaginal exposures, the clinician verbally directed Jake to not check the locks and to imagine going about his tasks without returning to check. For both of these imaginal exposures, Jake's SUDs ratings peaked at 60 after 10 minutes and returned to 20 after 25 minutes.

The next step in this session involved *in vivo* exposure. Jake, Molly, and the therapist went to Jake's car. Jake was instructed to get into the car, drive around the block, and return to the parking lot. Then he got out of the car, locked the door, and everyone proceeded back into the therapist's office. He was not permitted to look back at the car or to return to check the lock. His anxiety peaked at a SUDs level of 30. Such a low level of anxiety was due to the reassurance he felt by the presence of Molly and the therapist. For homework that evening, Jake was assigned to not check the lock when he and Molly got home, and to drive around the block that evening, park, lock the door, and not check the lock. He was to then go into the house and monitor his SUDs level for the next hour.

Session 2

Jake reported that he had successfully completed the homework. His SUDs had gone to 50 but dropped off to 25 within an hour. The remainder of session 2 was spent on repeating the same imaginal exposure and *in vivo* exposure scenes used on day 1. The homework was the same.

Session 3

Jake had success with the homework; his SUDs level had gone up to only 30. The remainder of the session followed the previous format.

Session 4

During the previous evening's homework, Jake's SUDs level did not go above 20. During both the imaginal and *in vivo* exposure his SUDs level did not go above 10. It was decided to move on to the second situation on his hierarchy, eyelash and eyebrow pulling, at the next session. Jake was instructed to continue engaging in this homework for the remainder of treatment.

Session 5

Jake's homework again went well. Imaginal exposure focused on having Jake picture himself speaking with his mother on the telephone. She told him that he was crazy, stupid, and lazy, and that he would never amount to anything. He then was to imagine he was sitting at home, experiencing a strong urge to pull at his eyelashes and eyebrows. However, he was to refrain from moving his hands from his lap and just experience the urge, as well as the anxiety. Jake's SUDs level went to 80 at its peak; it diminished to 30 after 70 minutes.

Then the therapist and Jake role-played the previously imagined scenario, with the therapist playing the role of Jake's mother. Jake was then asked to sit in the office chair and refrain from pulling his eyebrows and eyelashes. His homework involved two steps. First, he was to refrain from touching his face at all except for bathing and shaving for the next 2 weeks. Second, Molly would spend 30 minutes criticizing that evening, and he would sit quietly for 90 minutes and experience the urge and anxiety associated with the situation.

Sessions 6 through 8

Sessions 6 through 8 continued with a format of imaginal exposure followed by in-session role-play. With Molly's help, Jake was able to successfully complete the homework. Over these three sessions Jake's peak anxiety habituated from a SUDs level of 80 to one of only 15.

Session 7 through 15

At session 7, the accident-checking situation was introduced. This situation involved an embedded hierarchy, as shown in Table 7.2. Both imaginal and *in vivo* exposure began with the least feared situation, working upwards through the hierarchy to the most feared. Homework assignments were made to coincide with the in-session exposures.

*   *   *

The first several sessions with Jake went well. With the therapist's encouragement, he was able to successfully prevent himself from checking for accidents in many of his feared situations. He described the anxiety as "almost overwhelming," and the urge to check as "intense." However, he was able to allow himself to experience the anxiety as it peaked and declined.

Jake's first real challenge came when he reached his second most feared situation, that of being tailgated by a car and not seeing the car turn away in his rear-view mirror. While the therapist accompanied Jake in his car, we arranged for a confederate to "tailgate" Jake at a close but safe distance for approximately 5 minutes. Then, while the therapist attempted to keep Jake's attention focused on the road in front of him, the confederate

TABLE 7.2

Jake's Exposure Hierarchy: Automobile Accident Checking Behavior

Situation	Discomfort level
Driving in light traffic	40
Driving in moderate traffic	50
Driving in rush hour traffic	60
Being tailgated in the daytime, and having the other car back off to a safe distance	65
Being tailgated in the daytime, and seeing the other car turn off in the rear-view mirror	70
Being tailgated at nighttime, and seeing the other car's headlights turn off in the mirror	80
Being tailgated in the daytime, and not seeing the other car turn off in the rear-view mirror	95
Being tailgated at nighttime, and *not* seeing the other car's headlights turn off in the mirror	100

Feared Consequences

Caused someone to lose control of their car, they had a wreck, and died
Caused someone to lose control of their car, they had a wreck, and were seriously injured
Caused someone to lose control of their car, they had a wreck
Caused someone to get so angry that they veered off the road and did minor damage to their car
Caused someone to get so angry that they had a close call with another car
Caused someone to get so angry that they turned off the road and took another route

---

driver turned off onto a side road, out of view of Jake's rear-view mirror. Jake's anxiety level immediately increased:

> I know . . . I know that nothing happened just now. I mean, we would have heard something, right? But I have to go back . . . I just have to. I know nothing happened, especially since you know the person who was driving that car. But I just feel like something did. What if they're wrecked on the side of the road? What if they're dead? I know they're not, but I still feel like I have to go check.

Jake reported that his heart was "pounding" and that he felt short of breath. The therapist encouraged Jake to keep driving as he described what he called "irresistible" urges to return to the last place he remembered seeing the car, as well as the feeling that he "didn't know what would happen" if he did not. The therapist instructed Jake to simply allow himself to experience his feelings. During the exposures to the accident-checking situation, Jake's urges and anxiety levels peaked at a SUDs level of 100. However, both within and across sessions his SUDs level reduced. By the 15th session, Jake was reporting a peak SUDs level of only 20.

He was instructed to continue the accident-checking homework for 2 more weeks. During the once-per-week sessions that followed, he reported zero frequencies of the compulsive behaviors on his self-monitoring log.

CONCURRENT DIAGNOSES AND TREATMENT

The results of the diagnostic assessment showed Jake had concurrent diagnoses of Generalized Anxiety Disorder and Major Depression (in partial remission). Most patients are quite anxious before the start of treatment. However, their distress is usually related to their OCD fears and decreases during exposure therapy. Patients like Jake, however, who present with a concurrent diagnosis of GAD, often have a low threshold for arousal and demonstrate high reactivity during exposure sessions. These individuals may benefit from serotonergic pharmacotherapy as an adjunct to behavior therapy. It is important to note that such patients are generally less optimistic about their ability to succeed with the exposure and response prevention sessions and are more prone to manifest negative effects of life stresses. Thus, throughout treatment, we were especially supportive and encouraging of Jake, as we knew he would be less likely to take credit for his successes.

Jake reports that his depression is well controlled with his current medication regime. He states that, while he was originally given this prescription by a psychiatrist, he now sees a general practitioner for his medications. We elected to assess Jake's level of depression using the Beck Depression Inventory (BDI). Jake's score at the beginning of treatment was 12, indicating a mild but not clinically significant level of depression. We continued to administer the BDI biweekly to monitor Jake's mood each week. His depression level remained subclinical and stable throughout treatment; thus, we felt that no additional intervention was warranted in regards to this diagnosis. There is also good evidence to suggest that as OCD symptoms improve with cognitive behavioral therapy, so does affect.

COMPLICATIONS AND TREATMENT IMPLICATIONS

Successful treatment of OCD requires patients to habituate to anxiety-producing stimuli. Failure to achieve a reduction in anxiety or discomfort over successive exposure sessions may indicate a problem in one or more aspects of treatment. It is important for the therapist to identify the source of the patient's difficulty in therapy. Careful observation during exposure sessions and discussion of the patient's thoughts, feelings, and reactions to therapy can help clarify the source of the problem.

One potential problem the therapist should consider is the patient's threshold for emotional or somatic arousal. Low threshold and overarousal are common problems among individuals suffering form severe depression, anxiety disorders, and personality disorders. These problems can be addressed by beginning with stimuli very low on the fear hierarchy list and, as previously mentioned, including adjunct pharmacotherapy. Further, the clinician should anticipate a longer course of therapy with more frequent exposure sessions.

In the case presented here, the additional diagnosis of GAD contributed to a low threshold for stimulation and high reactivity, which lead to overarousal during exposure sessions. Jake's heightened baseline level of anxiety interfered in the habituation process both during and between sessions. This resulted in Jake progressing more slowly than anticipated through his fear hierarchy. His anxiety did not abate as readily as individuals with uncomplicated OCD.

Problems maintaining attention to the exposure situation can also result in failure to habituate. Distraction from the feared stimuli interferes with cognitive processing important for fear reduction. Alternatively, habituation may fail to occur if patients engage in intermittent rituals during the exposure, thereby failing to expose themselves completely to the feared situation.

Rituals that are mental in nature can be particularly difficult for both therapist and patient to detect. The therapist should help the patient to develop strategies for focusing attention on the content of the exposure session and to avoid the neutralizing effects of such rituals. Clients reporting obsessions with no identifiable, overt rituals are often more difficult to treat than are individuals with distinct rituals. In these cases, it is very important to get a detailed account of the mental ritual, such that therapy can proceed with exposure to the obsession and instruction to prevent the associated mental response. It is important to determine whether the patient's distraction or use of rituals during exposure is due to extraneous environmental factors or is due to deliberate, self-protective avoidance of the feared stimuli.

Resistance to therapy must also be considered as a possible source of poor recovery. Cognitive and behavioral avoidance problems frequently stem from skepticism about the effectiveness of therapy, secondary gain of

OCD, faulty belief systems, and concerns about the safety or social appropriateness of the exposure situation. To achieve progress in therapy, it may be necessary to challenge the patient's belief systems and increase flexibility in thinking. Additionally, it may be helpful to review the treatment rationale and contract.

Obsessions and rituals accompanying excessive religious devotion can be particularly difficult to treat. While excessively strict religious and moral beliefs may be necessary targets for modification during treatment, the clinician may wish to collaborate with the appropriate religious leaders to ensure proper representation of religious doctrine. Duration of symptoms does not appear to impact treatment outcome.

DEALING WITH MANAGED CARE AND ACCOUNTABILITY

Provision of the best clinical care is the utmost goal for any clinician. With the advent of managed care, however, provision of quality care may be limited by benefit schedules and plan requirements. Clinical practice decisions such as therapeutic approach and the frequency and duration of therapy may now be subject to the approval of managed care organizations. This introduces a new dynamic into the traditional patient–therapist relationship in which therapists must balance the economic and administrative demands of the health plan while providing good-quality care for their patients.

Increasingly, managed health care companies are adopting short-term–oriented therapies designed to ameliorate specific problematic behaviors that interfere with an individual's routine adjustment and functioning. Fortunately for the cognitive-behavioral therapist, exposure and response prevention therapy is often touted as the treatment of choice for OCD by many managed care plans.

Before beginning treatment, prospective patients should be told to familiarize themselves with the reimbursement policies of their health plan and be informed of the clinician's payment policies and any insurance network participation. Further, patients should be advised that authorization for treatment may be terminated before treatment objectives are achieved. Options for continuing treatment should be discussed, including early termination, fee-for-service arrangements, and referral to less expensive practitioners. Treatment providers should discuss the limits of confidentiality with their patients, respective of the managed care arena: patients should be informed that their insurance carriers might require therapists to release sensitive information such as a clinical diagnosis, treatment plan, and progress notes as a condition of reimbursement.

One of the ways we have dealt with this problem is to prepare a short educational document that outlines the success rate for short-term exposure and response prevention treatment for obsessive-compulsive disorder, and the cost savings to insurance companies for approving this intensive treatment. The document provides a concise one-page overview of the exposure and response prevention treatment plan. It provides a table with the studies supporting the effectiveness of this treatment in eliminating obsessive-compulsive disorder symptoms, and documents the success rate at 70% for patients who are motivated and appropriate for the treatment. Also, the document shows that the relapse rate is about 20% over a 12-year period. We have been careful to include a list of the predictors of treatment failure, such as initial severe depression, late age of symptom onset, the presence of overvalued ideation, and excessively high levels of pretreatment anxiety. We then compare the cost savings between our treatment plan and several other treatment scenarios. For the type of treatment we provide Jake, we charge a flat fee of $5,000. We then contrast this to the $12,600 cost for a 3-week hospitalization in our area and to the $7,200 cost of 2 years of weekly traditional therapy at $75 per hour.

We routinely submit this document with our initial treatment plan for patients and request pretreatment authorization. Then we follow this with telephone calls to the insurance carrier, or we make visits to their local office to explain the rationale of the treatment, the success rate, the absence of success for alternative treatments, and how we will show accountability for our treatment. Thus far, we have found this strategy to be successful in obtaining pretreatment authorization at full cost. In Jake's case, his insurance company, realizing that they had spent $9,000 on previous care for him over the past 3 years, readily agreed to authorize pretreatment approval and payment.

OUTCOME AND FOLLOW-UP

By the end of the active phase of treatment, Jake's symptoms had decreased significantly. He was completely able to resist checking car door locks and pulling his eyebrows and eyelashes. He was able to arrive at work and at home in a timely fashion, and no longer needed to restrict driving to off-peak hours. He experienced no urge to check for accidents during daylight; however, he reported that he still felt urges to check at nighttime and during bad weather, when visibility was low. Nevertheless, he engaged in no accident checking.

At 6-month follow-up, Jake was experiencing only very mild urges to accident-check even at night. In addition, the desire to check his car door locks was completely gone. However, the urge to pull his eyebrows and eyelashes had increased to a SUDs level of 50. He had relapsed on two brief occasions. This was caused by stress associated with starting a new job. The clinician instructed Jake to engage in self-controlled exposure and response prevention homework for 1 week and scheduled an extra session the next week to check on his progress. At that time, Jake's anxiety and urges were back to a controllable level. Importantly, his recent job ratings have improved markedly; he has not been late for work, and Jake and Molly report that the degree of satisfaction with their marriage has improved considerably.

Dealing with Recidivism

Relapse occurs in approximately 20% of patients treated with prolonged exposure and response prevention (O'Sullivan and Marks, 1990). However, even patients who relapse maintain their treatment benefits up to 12 years before relapsing. When relapse occurs, it is typically associated with adverse life events and major depressive episodes.

The best strategy for relapse prevention that we have found is to educate patients about these facts and train them to learn to predict and identify the onset of stressors that are likely to lead to a reoccurrence of symptoms. Patients then can be taught to reassert self-controlled exposure and response prevention interventions at the onset of these stressful periods. In addition, it is critical to teach patients that returning to therapy for short booster sessions, when needed, does not constitute treatment failure. If clinicians develop a plan whereby patients make once-yearly post-therapy telephone check in contacts, this can help to reduce patients' resistance to coming in for booster sessions if a relapse occurs.

Summary

Exposure and response prevention therapy has been shown to be successful in alleviating the suffering of most people with OCD, including those with long-standing and severe symptoms. Approximately 70% of patients show an 80% reduction in symptoms. Treatment refusal and dropout, due to the harshness of the procedure, are complicating factors. Over extended periods of follow-up, only about 20% of treated patients relapse.

The exposure component of treatment can consist of both *in vivo* and imaginal techniques, or *in vivo* techniques only. *In vivo* exposure requires patients to come into direct contact with their feared stimuli. This technique is successfully used with individuals who have obsessional fears about contamination. Imaginal exposure involves asking the patient to confront feared situations or images in their mind. In general, *in vivo* exposure is preferable over imaginal exposure when possible. However, for patients like Jake, who fear a specific catastrophe, imaginal exposure may be the only tool available for creating exposure situations.

The response prevention component of treatment consists of assisting patients to refrain from engaging in the compulsive activities. Response prevention can often be controlled by patients. For severe situations, where the urge to engage in the compulsion is incapacitating, it is usually necessary for the therapist or a family member to keep patients from making the compulsive response. In Jake's case, he was able to successfully use self-controlled response prevention to refrain from checking his car door locks. However, for the eyebrow-pulling behavior and the automobile accident-checking behavior it was necessary to use therapist-guided response prevention during sessions and to have his wife assist with response prevention during homework assignment. When therapist-assisted response prevention is used, clinicians try to reduce patients' need for their help, and encourage the patient to become increasingly responsible for engaging independently in exposure and response prevention exercises.

Finally, it is important to mention one of the most important aspects of exposure and response prevention treatment: the development of a warm, empathetic, and trusting therapeutic relationship with patients. Often, patients enter treatment emotionally upset because of the toll the symptoms have been taking on their lives. Usually, such patients have struggled with the disorder for many years. Because of this, family and other interpersonal relationships are disrupted, work functioning is greatly impaired or devastated entirely, self-confidence is weak, and pessimism dominates patients' expectations about the future. Individuals with obsessive-compulsive disorder believe that the world is a dangerous place, and that they are not competent to effectively cope with daily life problems. In addition, their trust in the ability of others to help them is low. Clinicians must be prepared to listen empathetically and supportively to patients' presentations. It is critical that the clinician expresses empathy for the emotional torture the patient has been baring. From the beginning of therapy, it is essential to provide patients with a basis of caring so that trust can be developed. In order to get patients to initiate exposure and response prevention treatment and persevere through the anxiety-provoking situations, clinicians must demonstrate a caring and optimistic attitude. Patients' trust in the clinician will be absolutely necessary to counteract the harshness of the treatment and insure success.

REFERENCES

Foa, E. B., & Kozak, M. (1986) Emotional processing of fear: Exposure to corrective information. *Psychological Bulletin, 44,* 99, 20–35.

Goodman, W. K., Price, L. H., Rasmussen, S. A., Masure, C., Fleischmann, C., Hill, C., Heninger, G., & Charney, D. (1989). The Yale Brown Obsessive-Compulsive Scale (Y-BOCS) I: Development, use, and reliability. *Archives of General Psychiatry, 46,* 1006–1011.

Mower, O. H. (1960). *Learning Theory and Behavior.* New York: Wiley.

O'Sullivan, G., & Marks, I. M. (1990). The treatment of anxiety. In M. Roth (Ed.) *Handbook of anxiety* (pp. 327–340). New York: Elsevier.

Salkovskis, P. M. (1985). Obsessional-compulsive problems: A cognitive-behavioural analysis. *Behaviour Research and Therapy, 23,* 571–583.

Spitzer, R. L., & Williams, J. B. W. (1985). *Structured Clinical Interview for DSM-III — Psychotic Disorders Version.* New York: Biometrics Research Department, New York State Psychiatric Institute.

Spitzer, R. L., Williams, J. B., & Gibbs, W. R. (1987). *Structured Clinical Interview for DSM-III Personality Disorders (SCID-II).* New York: New York State Psychiatric Institute.

Steketee, G. S. (1993). *Treatment of Obsessive Compulsive Disorder.* New York: Guilford.

CHAPTER

Posttraumatic Stress Disorder

Terence M. Keane, Amy E. Street, and Holly K. Orcutt
National Center for Posttraumatic Stress Disorder
V.A. Boston Healthcare System
Boston, Massachusetts

Case Description
Treatment Conceptualization
Assessment
Treatment Implementation
Concurrent Diagnoses and Treatment
Complications and Treatment Implications
Dealing with Managed Care and Accountability
Outcome and Follow-Up
Dealing with Recidivism
Summary
References

Effective Brief Therapies: A Clinician's Guide

CASE DESCRIPTION: THE CASE OF MR. G.

A 58 year-old African-American male, Mr. G. was the married father of three children who worked successfully for 28 years as a janitorial staff member for a railway system in the Northeastern United States. His three children were adults, professionally trained, and living on their own. Often working the late night shift, Mr. G. was confronted one night by a stranger who entered a train car that he was cleaning. Following a short conversational exchange, the young man left the car. About 20 minutes later, Mr. G. finished that car and was proceeding to break for his evening meal when the stranger appeared from a dark corner bearing a knife and demanding money. Mr. G. panicked, handed over his wallet, and attempted to run from his assailant. He was overtaken a few moments later, thrown to the ground, stabbed repeatedly, and left for dead. As he lay on the ground, Mr. G. felt his life ebbing away, and he thought he was going to die alone and in a cold dark place.

Some days later, Mr. G. awakened following extensive life-saving surgery. His physical recovery was slow and painful, and he required several subsequent surgical procedures to correct features of his wounds. Ten weeks later he attempted to return to his work site. He felt anxious and fearful, and approached his work with a sense of dread. During his first night, he felt panicky and was preoccupied with fears of another attack. He went home early in his shift and that night began to drink extensively in order to relax. He returned to work the next evening and could only stay a short time due to overwhelming feelings of anxiety. His disability grew over time, and he felt incapacitated and unable to work. This pattern continued, and he eventually decided he could no longer hold his job.

Approximately a year following the event, Mr. G's daughter sought psychological assistance for her father. The initial examination was conducted in his home, after several appointments were broken due to his inability to travel. On examination, it was clear that Mr. G. met criteria for diagnoses of posttraumatic stress disorder (PTSD), major depressive disorder, and alcohol abuse. He reported nightmares recapitulating the attack, a preoccupation with the assault and how it had affected every phase of his life, a lack of interest in anything and anyone, alienation from his wife and family, difficulties concentrating, avoidance of television and news media due to the presence of violence, unsuccessful efforts to avoid thoughts and images of the event, and disruption of his sleep and sexual functioning. Further, he reported being irritable and short-tempered with others, personality and behavioral features that emerged only after the attack and about which he felt tremendous guilt.

TREATMENT CONCEPTUALIZATION

An information processing framework, which grows out of Lang's (1979) bio-informational theory of emotion, has been widely used to understand the development of anxiety disorders. Lang's theory focuses on the role of fear in the development and maintenance of these disorders. He has suggested that emotions, including fear, are represented in memory in network form. These "fear networks" store memory representations of anxiety-provoking events. Fear networks contain three important elements: (1) information about the feared stimuli, or elements of the feared situation; (2) information about the person's response to the feared stimuli or feared situation; and (3) information about the meaning of the feared stimuli and the consequent response. In the case of Mr. G, the fear network that stores the representation of his assault includes information about the feared stimuli (young man, knife, robbery, threatening gestures and words, the workplace), the consequent response (I froze, I gave him my money, I panicked) and meaning elements (I'm going to die, I'll never see my wife again, I'm weak and helpless). Anxiety disorders develop when fear networks become pathological. While a nonpathological fear network consists of realistic connections between elements, a pathological fear network consists of erroneous connections that do not truly represent the state of the world or that overstate associations or probabilities. For example, in the case of Mr. G, a realistic association exists between the stimulus ("stranger holding a knife in a threatening manner") and the meaning element ("I'm in danger"). In reality, a threatening stranger wielding a large knife does indicate danger. However, Mr. G's fear network also contains several erroneous associations. For example, his pathological fear network consists of erroneous connections between the stimulus ("the place where I work") and the meaning element ("I'm in danger"). In reality, this part of the stimulus is not directly relevant to the dangerousness of the situation. Other pathological connections exist between stimulus elements (e.g., "young man" and "knife") and between response and meaning elements (e.g., "I panicked and ran," and "I'm weak and helpless"). The fear network can be activated by relevant stimulus, response, or meaning elements (or by a degraded match of one of the elements — e.g., seeing a man whose appearance is similar to that of the assailant). The fear network is more easily and frequently activated when it consists of many erroneous connections among stimulus, response, and meaning elements.

Expanding Lang's bio-informational theory of emotion specifically to the study of PTSD, Foa and Kozak (1986) have posited that the fear networks of traumatized individuals differ both quantitatively and qualitatively from the fear networks of individuals with other anxiety disorders. These authors suggest that for traumatized individuals the size of the fear network is larger (the network contains a greater number of erroneous connections), the network is more easily activated, and the affective and physiological response elements of the network are more intense. Most PTSD symptoms can be conceptualized as excessive response elements. Stimuli reminiscent of the traumatic experience activate the fear network and prompt states of high sympathetic arousal (e.g., increased heart rate, blood pressure, sweating, generalized muscle tension) and intense feelings of fear and anxiety. Fear-related behavioral acts like avoidance/escape behaviors and hypervigilance can also be conceptualized as excessive response elements. Reexperiencing symptoms can be understood by examining state-dependent memory effects. Specifically, the autonomic arousal that accompanies mood is related to how memories are stored. This primes retrieval of affective memory: when individuals are afraid, they are more likely to recall fear-associated memories.

These pathological fear networks, and the related behavioral, cognitive, and affective symptoms, disrupt normal emotional processing of the trauma, as well as disrupting mood, interpersonal relationships, and occupational functioning. Exposure-based treatments are designed to facilitate emotional processing of the traumatic experience, thereby reducing PTSD symptomatology. Processing the traumatic experience requires two conditions. First, the traumatized individual must have access to the emotional material. That is, they must respond in a way that is affectively similar to the way they responded during the feared situation. Second, while in this state, the individual must be exposed to corrective (nonfear) information. If both of these conditions are met, exposure-based treatments reduce PTSD symptoms in a number of different ways. First, these treatments decrease avoidance behaviors. Over time, the traumatized individual learns that escape and avoidance are not the only way to manage the negative affectivity associated with memories of the experience. After several exposure sessions, during which escape from aversive stimuli is prevented, the individual begins to habituate to the emotionally laden material. Memories of the experience diminish in their capacity to create distress. Finally, the pathological fear network is fundamentally altered. That is, connections between elements that should not be connected are modified and new connections and associations are made. Exposure treatments provide a corrective learning experience, allowing traumatized individuals to reinterpret the meaning of a negative situation. This more cognitive change is frequently a function of the patient's own efforts, but occasionally it is the result of a synthesis created by the patient–therapist interactions.

ASSESSMENT

Mr. G. was assessed using multiple methods: a semistructured clinical interview to evaluate the presence and absence of axis I and II disorders, a structured clinical interview developed specifically to assess PTSD, self-report questionnaires for PTSD and comorbid conditions, a clinical interview with Mr. G's spouse, and a review of his medical records. In complicated cases in which the diagnosis is unclear, psychophysiological assessment and additional information from collateral sources may prove valuable. The use of multiple methods to assess PTSD has several benefits. Individuals may respond differently to different methods. For example, some individuals may disclose more distress on a self-report questionnaire, while others may feel more comfortable in the context of an interview and so provide more accurate information. The use of multiple methods increases the likelihood of capitalizing on the best method to obtain information from any given individual. In addition, each assessment method has strengths and weaknesses. Clinical interviews rely more heavily on clinician judgment than self-report measures (a disadvantage of clinical interviews) but allow more flexibility in follow-up and clarification (an advantage of clinical interviews). The use of multiple methods aids in balancing the relative strengths and weaknesses of each method.

A clinical interview in the context of an assessment for PTSD focuses on pretrauma functioning, information about the traumatic event(s), and posttraumatic functioning. Functioning prior to the trauma is critical in order to determine posttrauma changes in functioning. Areas of pretrauma functioning to assess include family composition and relationship with family members, family history of psychopathology/substance use, pretrauma stressors and their impacts (e.g., deaths, injuries, accidents, and abuse), and educational, occupational, relationship (i.e., peers and dating), legal, substance use, medical, and sexual histories.

When obtaining information about the client's trauma history, the clinician is advised to proceed slowly and create a safe interpersonal context for discussing sensitive material. A general framework for conducting a clinical history containing traumatic material would focus on the pretrauma period, the details of the traumatic event, and the impact that the event had on the individual across multiple domains of functioning. Specifically, assessment of the traumatic experience involves gathering information about events immediately preceding the trauma, the traumatic event itself (i.e., Criterion A event in DSM-IV), the person's response to the event (what was seen, heard, and felt, as well as the cognitions, motor behavior, and physiological responses that accompanied the experience), a description of events immediately following the trauma (e.g., responses of self and others), and the meaning of the trauma for the survivor.

Assessment of posttrauma functioning includes information about presenting complaints and PTSD symptomatology, comorbid diagnoses (especially substance abuse, depression, panic disorder, borderline personality disorder, and antisocial personality disorder), additional stressors since the index trauma and subsequent coping behaviors, previous treatment history, sources of support and client strengths, lethality (risk to self as well as others), and changes in functioning following the trauma in a number of areas (e.g., occupational/educational/social, legal status, medical status, and sexual behavior). Assessment of pre- and posttrauma history may be significantly more difficult, and perhaps even arbitrary, for individuals with a history of multiple traumas. In these cases, a thorough trauma history and assessment of symptomatology and functioning throughout the life-span would prove useful.

Although structured assessment strategies (e.g., structured clinical interviews, self-report questionnaires) are extremely useful in the assessment of PTSD, a review of such strategies and their psychometric properties is beyond the scope of this chapter. Newman *et al.* (1997) provide a comprehensive review of these methods and their psychometric properties.

TREATMENT IMPLEMENTATION

A structured diagnostic assessment comprised the first phase of treatment. This consisted of a clinical history, a diagnostic interview, and psychological questionnaires accompanied by a meeting with his spouse. Treatment for Mr. G. began with a contract to restrict all alcohol use as a requirement for treatment. He and his wife agreed to notify the therapist in the event that drinking continued to be a problem. A period of psychoeducation about the impact of traumatic events and PTSD ensued. We emphasized the psychological, interpersonal, and biological effects of PTSD. Mr. G. was deeply impressed by the simple fact that other people had experienced these symptoms, that there was a name for the condition, and that there were treatments specifically available for PTSD.

He was then taught progressive muscle relaxation and diaphragmatic breathing. It took several sessions for him to master these skills, even with the use of daily homework sessions accompanied by an audiotape of the relaxation exercises. Following this, six sessions of imaginal desensitization containing key elements of the traumatic event were conducted. These sessions specified the details of the experience, the patient's real-time emotional and behavioral reactions to the event, and his thoughts about the experience and its aftermath.

The next phase of the treatment was *in-vivo* exposure whereby he and the therapist went to the railway yard, sat across from the station on a bench, and processed his emotional reactions to being at the scene of the traumatic event. As he described the experience and verbalized his reactions, he was initially overcome with anxiety and emotion, crying visibly. The second session showed marked improvement in his reactions and he proceeded to walk the therapist to the site of the assault. Successive sessions revealed that a different perspective on the event was developing and that he was coping and managing his fear, dread, and stress in fundamentally different ways. His cognitive appraisals of the assailant changed, as did his view of himself. No longer did he feel decimated as the victim of an uncaring criminal, but rather he felt that he was a survivor.

CONCURRENT DIAGNOSES AND TREATMENT

PTSD, a condition that is highly comorbid with a number of diagnoses, has been strongly associated with disorders such as Substance-Related Disorders, Panic Disorder, Major Depressive Disorder, and Borderline Personality Disorder (see Keane & Kaloupek, 1997, for a review of the comorbidity in PTSD literature). Thus, treatment of PTSD will often involve decisions about the treatment of other axis I and II disorders. Specifically, clinicians must decide if the ancillary disorders are best treated concurrently or if treatment should proceed sequentially. For instance, in the case of Mr. G., substance abuse and depression coexisted with PTSD. Moreover, Mr. G. had panic symptoms that restricted him to his home at the beginning of treatment. Decisions about the interdependence of these conditions needed to be made. Did these disorders precede, follow, or develop concomitantly with the PTSD? The clinical history implied that they certainly developed after the traumatic incident, and it was likely that the PTSD preceded the development of these other conditions. We concluded that these disorders were secondary to the PTSD and decided to treat PTSD first.

A concurrent diagnosis of substance abuse raises a number of challenging issues in the treatment of PTSD. Because of the complex interaction that exists between these disorders, there is no clear consensus about how to proceed in treating PTSD and comorbid substance abuse. Because exposure therapy frequently results in temporarily increased urges to use substances, it can be argued that treatment for PTSD should not proceed until sobriety is firmly established. It is also the case, however, that substance use may follow directly from PTSD symptomatology as a means of coping (i.e., self-medication), and a decrease in substance use may not occur until the patient experiences a decrease in PTSD symptomatology.

Treatment planning with comorbid substance abuse and PTSD requires consideration of multiple factors. It is critical to assess the patient's level of motivation to stop using/maintaining sobriety as controversy exists about conducting exposure therapy with individuals who are actively using substances. It is important to understand the relationship between substance use and PTSD symptomatology, specifically whether substances are used to cope with PTSD symptomatology and whether PTSD symptomatology has triggered relapses for the patient. If one chooses to begin the clinical interventions with the treatment of PTSD, careful monitoring of any changes in alcohol and drug use is essential. Receiving this feedback on a session-by-session basis informs the clinician of the impact of treatment on this critical comorbid problem. Initiating treatment with a behavioral contract limiting the use of substances during treatment is strongly recommended. In addition, patients with longstanding substance abuse problems might well be encouraged to make frequent use of community resources (e.g., AA/NA) as part of treatment planning. It may also be necessary to establish a separate provider to treat substance abuse; this treatment might actually precede the PTSD treatment and be a condition for future work on the effects of traumatic experiences. Finally, if patients are deemed too "high risk" for exposure treatment due to relapse risk, it is recommended that nontrauma-focused treatments, such as stress management, anger management, and other current-focused coping methods, be provided to lay the groundwork for exposure-based treatment.

Panic disorder or panic attacks also occur concurrently with PTSD. When this is the case, exposure-based treatments may be augmented with muscle relaxation and breathing retraining, two essential skills in the treatment of panic attacks. When conducting exposure therapy with patients who have panic attacks, it is important to prepare the patient for the possibility that exposure exercises could lead to the occurrence of a panic attack. Preparing them for this possibility by instructing them in the use of various coping strategies to utilize during a session will aid in prevention of panic attacks or in a reduction of the severity of in-session reactions. At the conclusion of exposure treatment, clinicians are encouraged to reassess panic symptomatology and make decisions about the need for additional treatment focused on panic symptoms. Some therapists actually incorporate components of panic control interoceptive training in order to prepare PTSD patients for the reactions attendant with the use of prolonged exposure. Efforts to improve the personal control that a patient feels during the exposure phase of treatment are welcome and will undoubtedly enhance the ability of the patient to emotionally process the traumatic experience.

Individuals with PTSD often report a number of depressive symptoms. In addition, there is some overlap in the criteria for PTSD and Major Depression, (e.g., anhedonia, concentration problems, and sleep disturbance). Treatment of PTSD may be effective in alleviating depressive cognitions and affect related to the trauma. Following successful PTSD treatment, however, it may be necessary to treat any remaining depressive features. Special attention to depressive symptoms may be fundamental to the maintenance of any treatment gains secondary to the PTSD treatment; cognitive–behavioral treatments, interpersonal psychotherapy, and psychopharmacological treatments all have considerable empirical support for improving depression.

Borderline Personality Disorder is also associated with PTSD, primarily because of the role of early childhood trauma in the development of both disorders. Clinical decisions about treating PTSD in the context of Borderline Personality Disorder involve careful assessment of current and past parasuicidal behavior. Exposure therapy may not be the best choice for some patients due to the risk of increased parasuicidal behavior. When treatment of parasuicidal behaviors are a priority, an approach such as Linehan's (1993) Dialectical Behavior Therapy might be considered, as it first targets reduction of parasuicidal behavior before processing of traumatic material.

In terms of our case example, Mr. G. met criteria for Alcohol Abuse and Major Depression, both of which developed following his assault. Treatment of his alcohol abuse was initiated by the use of a behavioral contract among the therapist, the patient, and his wife. A rationale for remaining sober was highlighted in the first sessions. In particular, Mr. G. was forewarned of the temptation to resume drinking as we attempted to help him master the memories of the traumatic event. Drinking was viewed as an escape or avoidance behavior that simply made his situation worse, as it did not permit appropriate emotional processing of the experience and his reactions to it. Further, drinking itself created new problems for him emotionally, maritally, interpersonally, and physically. While he admitted the urge to resume drinking during the early parts of treatment, Mr. G recognized the problems associated with his heavy alcohol consumption and was compliant with the contract.

COMPLICATIONS AND TREATMENT IMPLICATIONS

Returning to the scene of a traumatic experience, whether *in vivo* or imaginally, is an intense and difficult experience for a patient with PTSD. Reexperiencing, avoidance/numbing, and hyperarousal, the defining symptoms of PTSD, engender behaviors that interfere with facing the trauma directly. The feelings of intense anxiety that often accompany exposure exercises make treatment difficult, and can increase the patient's level of distress, suicidal ideation, and maladaptive coping behaviors, such as substance abuse. Given the possibility that PTSD symptomatology and distress will get worse before they get better, it is important that the clinician ensure that the patient is relatively stable and safe prior to beginning exposure treatment. Second, a clear and convincing rationale with examples is key to educating the patient regarding the goals, objectives, and benefits of this treatment. Facing the trauma directly can be such a painful process for patients that it requires special effort on the part of the clinician to ensure treatment compliance and prevent dropout. The clinician must approach treatment flexibly, carefully monitoring what the patient can tolerate and at what pace to proceed. Titrating the dose of exposure and the patient's capacity to tolerate that exposure is one of the requisite skills for treating PTSD, as it is for treating many other anxiety-mediated conditions.

Many of the difficulties inherent in exposure treatment can be avoided by maintaining a collaborative therapeutic relationship and allowing the patient a sense of control over the process of treatment. Important psychoeducational groundwork is critical to the success of exposure treatment. For example, the clinician should provide the patient with a sound treatment rationale, particularly regarding the role of avoidance in maintaining PTSD symptomatology. In addition, predicting a brief symptom increase, and assuring the patient that this is an expected part of treatment, may help to decrease the patient's feelings of distress. Greater treatment compliance can be gained by beginning with imaginal exposure exercises, which are often perceived as less threatening by the patient, and then moving on to *in-vivo* exposure exercises. Validation and encouragement from the therapist during exposure exercises is also extremely important (e.g., "I know that was really hard but you stuck with it; that's great"). The intense distress associated with exposure exercises can also be decreased by teaching the patient anxiety management skills, such as muscle relaxation and deep breathing techniques, prior to beginning exposure treatment. These skills will not only help to manage the patient's intense anxiety but will also provide the patient with an important coping strategy and a greater sense of control. While anxiolytic medication can also be prescribed to help control the symptoms of anxiety, such medications can interfere with exposure exercises. If these medications must be used, they should be avoided immediately before and after exposure exercises so that the medications do not disrupt the natural process of extinction to anxiety-provoking stimuli. Further, if a patient is prescribed a psychoactive medication, it is valuable for the clinician to assist the patient in making appropriate attributions for the success of behavioral exercises. Attributing success to the medications undermines the future progress of an individual, as the changes are ascribed to an external agent rather than to the individual.

Emotional numbing, which is often conceptualized as an extreme form of avoidance, can interfere with a patient's ability to access emotional reactions to the traumatic material, an important condition of the exposure exercise. Prior to beginning exposure, the clinician may wish to help those patients who are disconnected from their emotions learn to identify and label their emotional reactions. Emotional numbing may be particularly problematic during imaginal exposure exercises when patients have a greater ability to defend against the emotional material by distancing themselves from the memory. The intensity of the emotional experience can be increased by having the patient close his eyes, speak in the first-person present tense, and provide a great deal of sensory detail. In these cases, the clinician should query specifically for emotional content during the exposure exercise.

In addition to the difficulties related to the intensity of the treatment, the clinician often experiences logistical problems during exposure treatment. In some cases, such as that of a Vietnam combat veteran, it may be difficult or impossible to return to the scene of the trauma for an *in-vivo* exposure exercise. This treatment requires creativity in designing exposures as well as flexibility regarding session location and session length. The therapist must plan on allowing time for the patient's anxiety and fear to decrease before the session ends. While exposure therapy is almost always an intense experience for patients, it can also be a very intense experience for clinicians. The clinician may be reluctant to enter a treatment that generates such intense emotions and that requires repeatedly listening to stories that can be quite horrific. Appropriate supervision/consultation and frequent debriefings are a necessity in helping clinicians to cope with their own reactions to trauma-related therapy.

DEALING WITH MANAGED CARE AND ACCOUNTABILITY

We now live in an age of managed care. The managed care reality affects many (if not most) clinicians and holds significant implications for clinical practice. The virtue of the managed care environment is that it requires that patients be provided with treatment services that are known to be effective (i.e., empirically validated treatments). Additionally, this environment requires that patients not be kept in treatment longer than necessary. Therefore, it is important that clinicians be competent in brief or time-limited therapy and for them to engage in ongoing assessment of a patient's status. The demands of managed care also require that a specified treatment result in improvement for a particular patient within a reasonable period of time or the treatment must be changed. In the age of managed care, more than ever before, clinicians are required to demonstrate quality services that are also cost-effective. Clinicians must justify that their services are effective and that these services enhance clinical outcomes. A priority is placed on effective treatments that can be provided in an efficient manner with high levels of patient satisfaction.

Exposure-based treatments meet many of the demands of managed care. These treatments have been empirically validated and shown to be effective in reducing PTSD symptoms, as well as symptoms of many other psychological disorders (see Keane, 1998, for a review). The empirically validated nature of the treatment appeals to managed care companies and can aid clinicians in defending their treatment decisions. Additionally, the orientation of most exposure-based treatments is brief, symptom-focused, and designed to improve functioning. These treatments can be effective within the constraints of the time-limited therapy model required by managed care companies. Lange *et al.* (1988) reported that 63% of health maintenance organizations (HMOs) have a 20-visit maximum for outpatient mental health services. In most cases of noncomplicated PTSD, 20 visits should be sufficient to complete a program of exposure therapy. We believe that effective assessment and treatment of PTSD requires 12 sessions at a minimum. However, many patients will begin to exhibit improvements in symptomatology and functioning after a few exposure sessions, providing important data that clinicians can use to justify continued treatment, if necessary.

In addition to finding brief, effective models for behavior change, the demands of managed care programs require that clinicians be more accountable for their services than at any time in the past. While the requirements for time-limited treatment may generate pressure for a quick diagnosis, clinicians are encouraged to still complete a thorough assessment. Using well-validated measures for assessment and follow-up of PTSD symptomatology (see Newman *et al.*, 1997, for a thorough review) provides an opportunity to demonstrate that the patient has made broad-based progress in symptoms and functioning. Including measures that assess depressive symptomatology and substance use/abuse can also be beneficial, as these symptoms may also show improvement following exposure-based treatments for PTSD. Progress reports, generally required by HMOs, demand a well-considered treatment plan including operationalized goals that are concrete, specific, and focused on symptom improvement. Treatment goals for exposure-based treatments might highlight the ways in which PTSD symptomatology interferes with performance in multiple areas, including occupational and social functioning, and physical health status. In addition to these progress reports, session content needs to be well-documented, as some HMOs can and will demand treatment records to ensure that clinicians are following treatment guidelines. With regard to exposure treatment, session notes could include the patient's ongoing report of their "Subjective Units of Distress (SUDs) level" in response to exposure material or the use of a self-report measure of PTSD symptoms such as the PTSD Checklist in order to document improvement in level of distress within and across sessions.

OUTCOME AND FOLLOW-UP

Mr. G. improved on measures of PTSD, depression, and anxiety after treatment. The combination of anxiety management training with imaginal and *in-vivo* exposure resulted in improved functioning in his marriage and interpersonal relationships. Moreover, he kept his contract to not use alcohol throughout the intensive phases of treatment. At posttesting, he did not meet diagnostic criteria for PTSD, depression, or alcohol abuse. These changes were maintained over a 1-year period.

Vocationally, Mr. G was ready to return to work in some capacity. He was clear that he did not wish to return to the same shift and the same duties, as he felt these placed him at risk for another assault. There was a labor disagreement that ultimately led him to opt for retirement. Thus, he never did return to his usual work. Rather, he acquired numerous odd jobs in his neighborhood that occupied his time and supplemented his income. This provided some job-related satisfaction.

His wife and children all felt that he had significantly recovered and that he was now able to contribute to the family in ways that he had not done since the assault. Mr. G himself felt much better about his ability to be with his family and friends and, most importantly, to be with his grandchildren. While he could not yet forgive his assailant for what he had done, Mr. G. accepted that violence is something that occurs in the lives of many people and that he needed to put this behind him and not allow it to govern the remainder of his life.

DEALING WITH RECIDIVISM

For a significant minority of individuals, PTSD is best described as a chronic condition (see Keane *et al.*, in press, for a review of the literature on the course of PTSD). Even among those for whom it is a chronic condition, PTSD symptomatology often charts a dynamic course, waxing and waning over time. Both the potential chronicity of PTSD and the fluctuating symptom picture can make it difficult to clearly define recidivism and, similarly, to distinguish between remission and recovery. Symptom resurgence may be seen in reaction to anniversaries of the traumatic event or the occurrence of nontrauma-related stressors such as medical illness, death of a loved one, unemployment, and relationship losses. Controversy exists as to whether or not episodes of increased symptomatology represent new discrete episodes of PTSD or an end to a period of remission.

Given the possibility of symptom resurgence, we recommend that relapse prevention strategies be incorporated into the treatment of PTSD. When possible, clinicians should schedule booster sessions, particularly at the time of anniversaries of traumatic events. In addition, it may be helpful to educate patients about warning signs that treatment should be reestablished (e.g., periods of nightmares, increased urge to use substances, episodes of anger). Because PTSD symptoms often interact in a multiplicative fashion (e.g., increased flashbacks may lead to avoidant behavior), early treatment of new or increased symptomatology may prove beneficial in limiting the extent of a relapse.

The nature of a new treatment episode for PTSD will depend on the patient's presentation and reasons for reestablishing treatment. Has the patient experienced additional traumatic experiences that could benefit from exposure therapy? If additional exposure therapy is not warranted, the patient may require assistance in coping with day-to-day symptoms of stress that may be exacerbating symptoms. Over time the symptom picture for PTSD tends to shift (i.e., reexperiencing symptoms become less dominant as emotional detachment and estrangement symptoms become more dominant; McFarlane & Yehuda, 1997), and effective intervention strategies will be those that can address the patient's dominant symptoms at any given time.

SUMMARY

Some estimate the prevalence of PTSD in the United States at 6% of males and 12% of females (Kessler *et al.*, 1995). Exposure to traumatic events is much higher: often estimated to be as high as 70% of the adult population (Norris, 1992). These findings place trauma and PTSD among the most frequent of psychological disorders, ranking behind substance abuse and depression. Thus, the development of methods to assess and treat PTSD is a high priority among those concerned with public health issues. Unfortunately, there are no reliable estimates of PTSD in developing countries, yet several authorities suggest that the prevalence of PTSD may well be higher in these countries due to the frequency of traumatic events and the absence of resources to buffer their effects (de Girolamo & McFarlane, 1997).

Treatment outcome studies for PTSD are beginning to appear regularly in the scientific literature (Keane, 1998). Generally, these studies examine the effects of anxiety management interventions, exposure therapy, cognitive therapy, and psychopharmacological treatments. More recently, combination therapies such as eye movement desensitization and reprocessing (EMDR) have been tested, with some positive results. It is clear from these studies that interventions that directly address the symptoms of the disorder yield positive outcomes. Moreover, these outcomes transcend the level of symptom improvement and include functional domains as well.

In the case of Mr. G., treatment included multiple phases. After a comprehensive assessment that utilized structured diagnostic interviews for assessing PTSD and other axis I and II disorders and psychological tests, treatment proceeded with a major psychoeducational intervention. This psychoeducation involved teaching Mr. G. about trauma and its impact on individuals, as well as its effects on work, marriage, and interpersonal relationships. Teaching specific anxiety management skills like breathing retraining and progressive muscle relaxation provided Mr. G with coping skills that he could use once the exposure treatments began.

Given the extent of his symptomatology, we found it reasonable to approach the exposure phase of treatment with Mr. G. by the initial use of imaginal techniques. While Mr. G. found this aspect of treatment difficult, it did prepare him for the even more trying phase of returning to the site of his victimization. With the successful completion of each phase, he did gain a sense of mastery and efficacy that communicated to him that he could indeed overcome the fears and frightening images of his assault. These changes were accompanied by improvements in his substance abuse, depression, and his marital and interpersonal relationships. Further, Mr. G. was himself satisfied with the course of treatment that he received.

REFERENCES

de Girolamo, G., & McFarlane, A. C. (1997). The epidemiology of PTSD: A comprehensive review of the international literature. In A. J. Marsella, M. J. Friedman, E. T. Gerrity, & R. M. Scurfield (Eds.), *Ethnocultural aspects of posttraumatic stress disorder: Issues, research and clinical applications* (pp. 33–86). Washington DC: American Psychological Association.

Foa, E. B., & Kozak, M. J. (1986). Emotional processing of fear: Exposure to corrective information. *Psychological Bulletin, 99*, 20–35.

Keane, T. M. (1998). Psychological and behavioral treatments of post-traumatic stress disorder. In P. E. Nathan & J. M. Gorman (Eds.), *A guide to treatments that work* (pp. 398–407). New York: Oxford University Press.

Keane, T. M., & Kaloupek, D. G. (1997). Comorbid psychiatric disorders in PTSD: Implications for research. In R. Yehuda & A. C. McFarlane (Eds.), *Psychobiology of posttraumatic stress disorder. Annals of the New York Academy of Sciences* (Vol. 821, pp. 24–34). New York: New York Academy of Sciences.

Keane, T. M., Zimering, R. T., & Kaloupek, D. G. (in press). Posttraumatic stress disorder. In A. Bellack & M. Hersen (Eds.), *Psychopathology in adulthood: An advanced text*. Boston: Allyn & Bacon.

Kessler, R. C., Sonnega, A., Bromet, E., Hughes, M., & Nelson, C. B. (1995). Post-traumatic stress disorder in the National Comorbidity Survey. *Archives of General Psychiatry, 52*, 1048–1060.

Lang, P. J. (1979). A bio-informational theory of emotional imagery. *Psychophysiology, 16*, 495–512.

Lange, M., Chandler-Guy, C., Forti, R., Foster-Moore, P., & Rohman, M. (1988). Providers' views of HMO mental health services. *Psychotherapy, 25*, 455–462.

Linehan, M. M. (1993). *Cognitive-behavioral treatment of borderline personality disorder*. New York: Guilford.

McFarlane, A. C., & Yehuda, R. (1997). Resilience, vulnerability, and the course of posttraumatic reactions. In B. Van der Kolk, A. McFarlane, & L. Weisaeth, (Eds.), *Traumatic stress: The effects of overwhelming experience on the mind, body, and society.* New York: Guilford.

Newman, E., Kaloupek, D. G., & Keane, T. M. (1997). Assessment of posttraumatic stress disorder in clinical and research settings. In B. Van der Kolk, A. McFarlane, & L. Weisaeth (Eds.), *Traumatic stress: The effects of overwhelming experience on the mind, body, and society.* New York: Guilford.

Norris, F. H. (1992). Epidemiology of trauma: Frequency and impact of different potentially traumatic events on different demographic groups. *Journal of Consulting and Clinical Psychology, 60,* 409–418.

CHAPTER

Generalized Anxiety Disorder

Michelle G. Newman
The Pennsylvania State University
University Park, Pennsylvania

Case Description
Treatment Conceptualization
Assessment
Treatment Implementation
 Treatment Rationale
 Early Cue Detection
 Relaxation Training
 Cognitive Therapy
 Imagery Exposure
Concurrent Diagnoses and Treatment
Complications and Treatment Implications
Dealing with Managed Care and Accountability
Outcome and Follow-Up
Dealing with Recidivism
Summary
References

Generalized anxiety disorder (GAD) is a common and disabling problem that has a lifetime prevalence rate of about 5% (American Psychiatric Association, 1994). The goal of this chapter is to present a description of Cognitive Behavioral Therapy (CBT) for GAD. Despite strong empirical support for the efficacy of CBT (Chambless *et al.*, 1996), this chapter also addresses some limitations of the treatment.

CASE DESCRIPTION

M. is a 28-year-old married Jewish white female graduate student who presented with the problem of chronic worrying. She reported that her worrying felt excessive and uncontrollable once it started, and that it was currently leading to chronic distress. She also reported that her current worrying and the symptoms associated with it severely interfered with her life. As a result of her worrying, she avoided situations where she might have to talk about anything that might trigger worry; she experienced frequent crying spells, had difficulty sleeping, and was chronically anxious. She further reported that she had decreased confidence, that her school performance was suffering, and that she was so preoccupied with the reactions of other people that she was unable to "be herself" when with others.

When asked about precipitants to the current series of symptoms, M. explained that although she had always been a worrier, she noticed an exacerbation of her symptoms during the time that she was anticipating a geographical separation between herself and her husband. This separation was necessary for her husband to complete his graduate studies while M. completed her Masters degree in the sciences. However, the consequence of the separation was to place a great deal of stress on their marriage.

M. indicated that she worried about a number of topics. For example, she worried about the consequences of living apart from her husband and was concerned that the financial burden of this separation would plunge them deeply into debt. She also indicated that she felt responsible for her husband's well-being and worried about potential negative consequences of daily choices that he made without her guidance. She explained that her husband was unassertive and that she was constantly on edge that he would do the wrong thing. As a result of this worry, she reported that during their daily phone conversations she would avoid asking him how his day went for fear that his response would trigger her anxiety and worry.

Another topic that M. frequently worried about was her safety and health. She indicated that since she had begun living alone she was frequently worried about an intruder. In addition, she worried about contamination from food-borne illnesses, doorknobs, and toilets as well as contamination from the pathogens of others. In addition to worrying about her own health, M. indicated that she worried about the health of her mother-in-law, who had had recurrent bouts of leukemia, as well as the health of her own mother. Moreover, M. worried about the health of any children she might have in the future. Asked when health worries had become a problem, M. indicated that she had always been this way and that her mother had raised her to be concerned about such things.

M. was diagnosed with GAD and, as with most GAD clients, generally viewed the world as a dangerous place. To be safe, M. tried to avoid and control negative outcomes by persistently anticipating all potential past, present, or future dangers. The continual scanning of her environment and of her internal experiences for danger was thought to have developed into a habitual, rigid, and maladaptive response pattern to internal and external cues. Such responses appeared to include interactions among cognitions (e.g., "What if I become contaminated from the raw chicken that I touched?"), behaviors (e.g., active avoidance of worry triggers, such as avoiding touching raw meat), and physical sensations (e.g., feeling keyed up, full of muscle tension). Each response tended to feed on the prior one, as the responses interacted and regularly resulted in the spiraling intensification of her anxiety.

Worrying had become M.'s primary coping strategy to avoid threat. However, each time the anticipated danger did not occur, the relief sensation negatively reinforced the perception of the initial threat as accurate as well as the view that worry was an efficacious way to cope. In this way, worrying had become self-reinforcing. For example, M. was concerned that her husband would make a decision that would lead to a catastrophic outcome. She then worried about this for a day. When the catastrophic outcome did not occur, M. felt relieved, but rather than make the attribution that "I worried for nothing," she felt that her husband avoided the catastrophic outcome *because* she worried. Therefore, the worry process had become a kind of superstitious behavior, with the idea that if she did not worry something bad would happen.

TREATMENT CONCEPTUALIZATION

The treatment conceptualization of M. was based on a CBT model that primarily views worry as the spiraling interaction among cognitive, behavioral, and physiological cues for anxiety. Because of the spiraling nature of worry, the first goal of the therapy was to teach M. to intervene in response to early anxiety cues. This allowed M. to learn how to cut off the anxiety spiral before it reached a high level of intensity. The earlier M. could identify initial cues for anxiety, the earlier she could intervene. Moreover, if M. intervened at a point when her anxiety level was not as intense, she was told that the intervention was more likely to be successful.

Early intervention with an anxiety-reducing strategy was theorized to have several effects. First, cues that had previously elicited a conditioned anxiety response would become repeatedly paired with a response that decreased M.'s anxiety. Therefore, through the process of counterconditioning, M. would begin to break herself of the habit of allowing certain internal and external cues to automatically trigger worry. At the same time, M. would develop the new habit of cutting off the anxiety spiral by using a positive coping strategy, and the cue that initially elicited anxiety would come to habitually elicit a positive coping response.

Based on the CBT model of GAD, the anxiety-reducing interventions included cognitive restructuring, multiple relaxation techniques, and self-control desensitization to target cognitions, sensations, and behaviors that were contributing to M.'s worry patterns. The cognitive therapy (CT) intervention was based on the idea that the way that M. interpreted situations influenced her emotional reactions to them. GAD clients are particularly prone to making negative interpretations of and predictions from ambiguous situations. The main goal of CT for GAD was to help M. create more balanced perspectives and to view the world more accurately. However, it is important to note that like many GAD clients, M. often believed that worrisome negative interpretations helped her. Commonly held GAD beliefs include "worry helps motivate me," "worrying helps keep me vigilant toward potential dangers," "worry allows me to foresee problems and work out advance solutions," and "it is wise to predict the worst possible outcome to ensure that I am prepared for it." Because many GAD clients often have a strong belief in the benefits of worrying, cognitive therapy must directly address such a view as well as any other inaccurate views that maintain the worrying.

In addition to intervening at the cognitive level, M. was trained in multiple interventions that targeted her physiological responses. These physiologically targeted interventions were administered to help M. cut off her worry spiral, as well as to develop flexible autonomic nervous system responses in place of the restricted autonomic variability characteristic of most GAD clients. Relaxation techniques included diaphragmatic breathing, progressive muscle relaxation, pleasant imagery, and daily application of applied relaxation. Experimenting with a variety of these techniques allowed M. to determine which methods were most effective for her.

Another technique that was implemented was self-control desensitization (SCD). SCD is an imagery exposure technique that is particularly helpful for anxiety problems such as GAD, for which the phobic stimuli are not discrete (Goldfried, 1971). Instead of targeting a discrete phobic stimulus (i.e., a dog for a dog phobic), clients imaginally expose themselves to situations that are representative of those associated with anxiety and worry (i.e., a work situation representative of a trigger for time pressure). For every representative situation, clients expose themselves to physiological (e.g., muscle tension), cognitive (e.g., "What if I don't get this done on time?"), and behavioral cues (e.g., rushing around) as well as external triggers (e.g., computers) for associated anxiety. Clients can begin with mildly anxiety-provoking situations, and as they become more proficient with the technique they can move to situations rated as moderate and later as severe. The goal is for clients to initially learn to relax in response to images of worry triggers and then to eventually learn to apply this response to the worry triggers in everyday life.

Although overt avoidance is less common with GAD clients than persons with other anxiety disorders, the treatment also included exposure instruction whenever subtle avoidance was detected. The clear and consistent message was that it was important for M. not to deal with her anxiety with avoidance but to approach and cope with her anxiety triggers at all times. For example, M. noted that watching the news had become a trigger for her anxiety. Her solution to this dilemma was to stop watching the news. However, she was told that she should instead work on watching the news and view it as an opportunity to use a coping strategy such as cognitive restructuring. She was told that it was not the news that triggered her anxiety but how she experienced the news that triggered anxiety.

In addition to directly targeting the overt symptoms of GAD, other secondary effects of GAD symptomatology were targeted. First, M., like most GAD clients, had come to habitually operate from a perspective of negative reinforcement. That is, she focused so much of her energy and attention on evading danger that her primary emotional experiences were numbness, anxiety, or relief. Thus, she failed to actively pursue the gratification of some of her needs and did not attend to the positive outcomes that did occur. As a result, a component of the treatment was centered on teaching her to behaviorally pursue and cognitively process positive outcomes.

Worrying also prevented M. from living in and enjoying the moment. M. was often distracted by thoughts about the past or future. The irony was that such inattention kept her from gaining corrective evidence that could help her to prevent future worrying. Therefore, another component of the treatment was to direct M. to spend time being present-moment focused. A part of living in the moment was to generally focus on "process" rather than on "outcome" and "intrinsic" rather than "extrinsic" reward. For example, when M. had a weekend with her husband, she was directed to actively enjoy each moment spent with him, rather than to spend time anticipating the sadness she would feel when he had to leave. Similarly, she was directed to focus on the intrinsic pleasure she gained from tasks associated with her graduate work, rather than to focus on the ultimate grade that she would receive. The idea is that clients have control over the process but not the outcome and a focus on the outcome detracts from their ability to fully enjoy the process and ultimately to enjoy the moment.

ASSESSMENT

The fourth edition of the *Diagnostic and Statistical Manual* (DSM-IV; American Psychiatric Association, 1994) defines Generalized Anxiety Disorder (GAD) as excessive and uncontrollable worry about a number of events or activities. Diagnosis requires that the person has worried more days than not for at least 6 months and that the worry has been associated with significant distress or impaired functioning. In addition, the person's symptoms cannot be due to a drug, a general medical condition, or another axis I condition. Moreover, while the person is worrying, he or she must be typically experiencing three of six symptoms (restless/keyed-up/on-edge, easily fatigued, difficulty concentrating, irritability, muscle tension, and sleep disturbance).

Confirming a GAD diagnosis can sometimes be difficult. Compared to other anxiety disorders, GAD has the lowest interrater agreement (Barlow & DiNardo, 1991). The low reliability of this diagnosis may result from its chronic nature. Like M., many persons with GAD report that they have been worriers their whole lives. As a result, they may fail to fully process the negative impact of their current worry-related symptoms. For example, GAD clients often initially deny that worrying impairs their functioning. Such clients are so used to worrying that they are able to function fairly well and are able to accomplish various tasks throughout their day. Therefore, when assessing impaired functioning, it is often helpful to ask about the impact of specific GAD symptoms such as sleep disturbance, diminished concentration, and feeling tired all the time on ability to function. Such a focus often reminds clients that they could probably function much better in the absence of these symptoms. Another feature that may contribute to low diagnostic reliability is a desire to be perfect, which is common in persons with GAD. Such a desire may lead these individuals to inconsistently report or underreport the severity of their symptoms.

The battery of devices used to assess and diagnose M. included the Anxiety Disorders Interview Schedule-IV (ADIS-IV, Brown *et al.*, 1994a), The Penn State Worry Questionnaire (Meyer *et al.*, 1990), and the Generalized Anxiety Questionnaire-IV (GADQ-IV; Newman *et al.*, 1997). The former measure is a structured interview specifically developed for the assessment of anxiety disorders, and the latter two measures are helpful GAD screening devices that can also be used to gauge improvement during the course of therapy. According to these measures, M.'s initial primary diagnosis was generalized anxiety disorder with a severity rating of 7 (between severe and very severe) on an 8-point scale. She also met criteria for a specific phobia of contracting an illness from particular foods such as raw meat.

In addition to completing diagnostic measures, M. completed a daily diary measure throughout therapy. Such a diary was used to help M. detect the patterns of her anxiety levels as well as internal and external cues that triggered anxiety shifts. She started using the daily diary for 2 weeks before she began treatment to establish a record of her initial level of functioning. In this way, she and the therapist were able to track positive changes during the course of therapy. As part of this assessment, M. was asked to begin to check in with herself on an ongoing basis and to become aware of even minor shifts in her anxiety levels. When such shifts were noted, she was asked to record the date and time, the circumstances, and her anxiety levels. She was also asked to note any external anxiety triggers (e.g., subtle comment or gesture made by another person, unexpected financial or work demands, events in which she lacked information) or internal cues that triggered her anxiety (e.g., thoughts, images, bodily sensations, emotions, behaviors). In addition, she recorded her anxiety level at regular intervals (e.g., when she first awoke, at the end of the morning, at the end of the afternoon, and at bedtime). Such an ongoing record helped her become aware that her anxiety levels fluctuated more than she had realized.

Another assessment device that can help clients begin to identify their patterns of subtle avoidance is a diary of interpersonal interactions. The goal of such a diary is to help the client begin to identify and eventually eliminate three types of problematic avoidance: (1) self-defeating avoidance of emotional experience, expression and vulnerability toward others, (2) avoidance of awareness as to how they may be directly contributing to negative responses from others, and (3) avoidance of interpersonal behavior change. In their use of this diary, clients are asked to keep a record of positive and negative interactions with others. This diary includes information about the circumstances between themselves and another person, the response from the other person that they had hoped to get, what they were afraid would happen, what they actually did, and what the person did in response to what they did. This helps the client begin to see how they tend to act on their fears (via avoidance), rather than in pursuit of their needs, and the ultimate consequences of this pattern.

TREATMENT IMPLEMENTATION

Treatment Rationale

At the very beginning of treatment, the therapist presented a comprehensive rationale for the combined physiological, cognitive, and behavioral view of anxiety. Some clients may not immediately endorse the rationale for the differing techniques. Nonetheless, in such instances the therapist can accept this view as legitimate, but can suggest that such a perspective can be tested by proceeding with treatment on an experimental basis (i.e., "Let's see what happens"). A similar approach can be adopted during the course of treatment whenever the client has reservations about a particular approach or therapeutic technique. However, in order for therapy to succeed, clients must actively participate and agree to carry out homework assignments. One important component of the rationale is that anxiety is useful at moderate levels on a sporadic basis. It only becomes problematic when it occurs too frequently or at excessive levels. Therefore, the goal of the treatment is not to remove the client's anxiety entirely but rather to help clients learn to cope with anxiety and bring it down to a more moderate level.

CBT for GAD is based on the supposition that most therapeutic change results from frequent practice and application of CBT techniques between sessions. Therefore, the therapist must ensure that clients fully understand the rationale and method of application for each technique as well as the importance of regular practice. Clients are told that worry is not a personality trait, but instead results from past habits over which they have control. The therapy, on the other hand, is focused on teaching new skills. As with all skills, therapy techniques cannot be mastered without frequent practice. Frequent practice can help clients ultimately replace maladaptive habitual responses with more adaptive responses.

Early Cue Detection

The first step in therapy is for the client to begin to self-monitor for early anxiety cues. As noted earlier, clients are encouraged to routinely check in with themselves on a regular basis and note any shifts from a lower to higher level of anxiety as well as what triggered this shift. For example, by monitoring her early anxiety cues, M. became aware that certain questions by others (e.g., "What is it like to live apart from your husband?" "When are you going to graduate?") were common anxiety triggers.

Once M. had begun to identify early anxiety cues, she was trained in a series of cognitive and behavioral strategies. Whenever a new strategy was introduced in therapy, the therapist demonstrated its impact by practicing it with her. Such a demonstration ensured that she was properly applying each technique and helped to inspire confidence that the technique could successfully lower her anxiety.

Relaxation Training

M. was trained to use several relaxation techniques to cut off her worry spiral. The first relaxation technique was diaphragmatic breathing. The rationale for this technique is that people with anxiety get into the habit of breathing quickly from their chest. However, rapid chest breathing physiologically induces anxiety, whereas breathing slowly from the diaphragm induces relaxation. It can be helpful if the therapist demonstrates the difference between these two types of breathing by asking clients to breathe rapidly from their chest until they feel anxious. Next, the therapist can ask clients to breathe slowly from their diaphragm to lower their anxiety. This exercise can help clients note the impact of their breathing rate on their anxiety level. Such diaphragmatic breathing can be applied each time the client notices early anxiety or tension.

The second relaxation technique introduced to M. was progressive muscle relaxation (PMR), which entails systematic production and subsequent release of tension in various muscle groups. When she first learned PMR, M. was asked to tense and release 16 separate muscle groups. These muscle groups included the right hand and lower arm, left hand and lower arm, right biceps, left biceps, upper face, central face, lower face, neck, chest, shoulders and upper back, abdomen, right thigh, left thigh, right calf, left calf, right foot, and left foot. However, after M. mastered the 16-muscle group PMR, she was trained to tense and relax her muscle groups in larger combinations. Therefore, she moved from 16 muscle groups to seven combined muscle groups, and then to four groups. Once she had mastered tensing and releasing four muscle groups, she was taught how to relax her muscles without tensing them by remembering the feelings associated with relaxation of each muscle group. The latter technique is called "relaxation-by-recall."

An important component of PMR training is the notion of "letting go" of anxiety. The idea is that at the time clients are releasing physical tension from their muscle groups, they attempt to actively let go of anxious thoughts, images, and emotions. Then whenever they notice a thought, image, or emotion that is distracting, they do not force it away but, rather, imagine it floating out of their head as though it were a balloon filled with helium. After mastering the process of "letting go" during PMR practice, clients can regularly apply it in response to their everyday anxiety and worry. For example, when clients notice a shift in their anxiety related to a worrisome image, they might try to immediately let go of the image and any associated anxiety and physical tension. This is called applied relaxation.

M. was also trained in the use of pleasant imagery. This is a relaxation technique in which she was invited to imagine herself in a place (e.g., the beach) she associated with serenity, peace, and/or comfort. She began by practicing this technique at the end of each PMR session, at which time she would use an associated cue word to prompt her to vividly imagine all of the sights, sounds, smells, and tactical sensations that would be present in her identified place. She later applied this technique whenever she felt anxious, using the cue word to prompt the associated sensations.

Cognitive Therapy

In addition to learning relaxation techniques, M. was trained in several cognitive therapy (CT) techniques to cut off her anxiety spiral. The first step in the implementation of CT was to help M. become aware of the link between her thoughts and her anxiety. The connection between thoughts and anxiety became elucidated as M. began to note the self-statements that she was making at times when she was also experiencing anxiety and worry. M. was told that each time she worried about catastrophes in the future (e.g., "What if I get sick?") or the past (e.g., "What if my husband made a bad decision?"), she created an emotional illusion. Even though the feared outcomes had not actually happened, worrying about them caused her body to react as though they had. In this way, she was creating her own anxiety reaction simply by thinking worrisome thoughts or imagining catastrophic images.

A central goal of CT was to identify recurrent, underlying themes that reflected core beliefs held by M. Asking her to describe a rule that she had for herself related to a particular worry often helped her to identify such a core belief. For example, the therapist asked M. if she had any rules regarding the benefits of worrying. Such rules had to be identified and directly addressed before she was willing to practice CT as a means to reduce her worrisome thoughts. M. was able to identify two such rules. The first rule was, "Expect the worst, and then you will be prepared." The second rule was, "If I allow myself to relax when I am supposed to be worrying about something, I am putting myself in a vulnerable state." These rules were addressed in the same way as other inaccurate beliefs. Therefore, to challenge the belief that one should expect the worst, the therapist conducted a cost–benefit analysis. M. had been so invested in the benefits of worrying that she had been inattentive to the costs, which included sleeplessness, chronic anxiety, chronic fatigue, depressed mood, and inability to concentrate. In addition, when M. actually tested the belief by expecting the worst and tracking the outcome, she discovered that most situations never really turned out exactly as predicted; it was therefore not possible to prepare for them. Moreover, by testing this rule and tracking the actual outcome, M. discovered that even in instances when she accurately predicted the outcome she had not successfully prevented distressed feelings in response to it. Instead, she had prolonged her distress. In this way, she spent more time feeling distressed without gaining any real advantage.

To address M.'s second rule, the therapist asked her to give him an example of a situation in which not worrying would place her in a vulnerable state. M. selected her belief that worrying about illness motivated her to take precautions that kept her vigilant about all the potential dangers. She used the analogy of radar and indicated that when she stopped worrying her radar would be off. The therapist then pointed out that it was inaccurate to think that worrying enhanced her capacity to attend to or focus on things, and in fact the research showed that worrying actually diminished one's attention, energy, and concentration level. The therapist also suggested that M. do a behavioral experiment to test her theory by letting down her guard and then determining whether she became ill. M. retorted that she could remember two times when she had not worried and she had gotten sick. However, when the therapist asked her whether those were the only two times she had gotten sick, M. began to laugh because she realized she had been sick many times despite having worried.

CT for GAD should be approached as a flexible thinking skill that the therapist teaches the client rather than as an exercise for the therapist to prove that the client's belief is inaccurate. Therefore, it is important for the therapist to outline the steps that the client can follow each time he or she identifies an anxiety-provoking thought, image, prediction, interpretation, or belief. First, M. was told to treat her thoughts like hypotheses rather than facts and, as a scientist would, to systematically gather evidence to support and refute her thoughts. As a component of the evidence, M. was asked to estimate the probability that her feared outcome would come about. The likelihood of a future occurrence was gauged by examining the number of times the event had happened in M.'s personal history. Another approach was to ask M. to imagine a friend who had the same worry and try to logically analyze the worry for her friend. After M. and the therapist had listed all the evidence, M. was told to weigh the data in support and in refutation of her belief to determine which was most convincing. M. was then asked to try to generate a list of nonanxiety-provoking alternative self-statements. The goal was for M. to come up with self-statements that she believed to be accurate, that helped her view the situation in a way that felt less anxiety-provoking, and that were specific to her fear. Once she had devised the list, M. was instructed to choose the most believable and least anxiety-provoking self-statement and then substitute if for the original fear-producing one. In instances when no alternative self-statement seemed believable to M., she was directed to test out various perspectives by conducting experiments during her daily life. For example, to test out the belief that worrying helped her, M. was asked to actively not worry for a period of time to see whether she functioned any worse. This helped M. track the actual outcomes and gather the evidence needed.

One common misconception that clients sometimes take away from CT training is that they can generate one or two nonspecific reassuring self-statements (e.g., "It is going to be okay" and "I can cope with this situation") that are applied to all anxiety-provoking situations. Such nonspecific self-statements are not nearly as anxiety-reducing or believable to the client as self-statements derived from an effortful attempt to generate multiple alternative interpretations specific to each situation.

Imagery Exposure

As noted earlier, M. was trained to use the imagery exposure technique called SCD. Implementation of SCD required several steps. In the first step, M. formally practiced PMR until she was fully relaxed. Next, she pictured herself in a circumstance that commonly elicited anxiety. For example, M. pictured herself encountering a fellow student who asked her what it was like to be living apart from her husband. She was directed to continue to imagine herself in this circumstance until she felt anxious. Once her anxiety was elicited (which was signaled to the therapist during in-session practice by raising her finger), she was directed to relax it away as she pictured herself letting go of and relaxing away the anxiety. After she no longer noticed any anxiety cues (signaled by lowering her finger), she continued to imagine herself relaxed and coping effectively with the situation (for about another 20 seconds). Finally, she was directed to stop imagining the situation and return to focusing solely on the process of relaxation (about 20 seconds).

CONCURRENT DIAGNOSES AND TREATMENT

GAD is one of the most common secondary conditions when other anxiety and mood disorders are primary (Brown & Barlow, 1992). In fact, some researchers believe that its early onset, chronicity, and resistance to change provide evidence that GAD may be the basic anxiety disorder out of which additional anxiety disorders commonly arise (Brown et al., 1994b). Therefore, knowledge of how to effectively treat GAD may have significant implications for treatment and/or prevention of other disorders.

As a primary diagnosis, GAD has a high rate of concurrence with axis I and II conditions. The most common comorbid axis I conditions are social phobia, simple phobia, panic disorder, major depression, dysthymia, and somatoform disorders (Brown & Barlow, 1992; Rogers et al., 1996). The most common comorbid axis II conditions occur in clusters B and C (Mancuso et al., 1993).

Only two studies have examined the relationship between axis I comorbidity and CBT treatment success. One of these studies found that GAD treatment was more likely to fail when axis I comorbid conditions were present (Durham et al., 1997). However, another study found that when GAD symptoms were successfully treated comorbid axis I conditions were also dramatically reduced (Borkovec et al., 1995).

The minimal research on comorbid axis II conditions is even less optimistic than data on axis I conditions. Although it appears that CBT can successfully address anxiety symptoms in some clients with comorbid personality disorders, it is also clear that GAD treatment is less successful when personality disorders/interpersonal problems are present. One study found that cognitive therapy led to successful reduction of GAD anxiety symptoms in 9 out of 16 personality-disordered participants (Sanderson *et al.*, 1994). However, this study also reported that personality-disordered clients were more likely to drop out of therapy. Additional research (Borkovec *et al.*, 2000) showed that the greater the degree of interpersonal problem, the less likely that clients would achieve clinically significant change in GAD symptomatology. Moreover, at follow-up assessment points, interpersonal problems were especially associated with failure to maintain any therapeutic gains that had been evidenced at post therapy.

In addition to reducing the effectiveness of CBT therapy for GAD, the data show that interpersonal problem symptoms are unlikely to be successfully addressed, even when the GAD has been successfully treated. For example, Borkovec and colleagues (2000) found that standard CBT for GAD failed to address two of the three interpersonal problem clusters that had been found to characterize GAD subjects (the Domineering/Overly Nurturant, and Intrusive scales).

As a result of the data on interpersonal problems lowering the success rate of CBT for GAD, our research group (Newman *et al.*, 1999b) is currently conducting a clinical trial to determine whether adding interpersonally oriented therapy techniques to the current empirically supported CBT treatment for GAD will better address both GAD and interpersonal symptoms.

COMPLICATIONS AND TREATMENT IMPLICATIONS

There are several potential complications that therapists should be aware of in order to successfully address them in treatment for GAD. A common complication is related to noncompliance with self-monitoring and practice of CBT techniques. Many GAD clients seek treatment because they feel extremely stressed out and time pressured. When the therapist then assigns multiple structured homework exercises, a common first reaction is for clients to feel quite resentful that a therapist who is supposed to lower their anxiety is actually contributing to its increase. One helpful means to address this problem is to tell clients that they should view the homework time as an investment. The cost of lowering their anxiety and feeling better is to comply with these exercises. However, if the exercises successfully reduce their anxiety, such reduction will ultimately lead to a saving in time. People with lower anxiety function more efficiently and therefore can get more things accomplished due to increased energy and ability to concentrate.

Another common problem is that clients may sometimes forget to do their homework. To address this, the therapist can work with them to generate ways to create reminders in their daily environment. For example, to remind clients to regularly work to identify early anxiety cues, the therapist can suggest that the client place post-it notes in places that they will see frequently (e.g., telephone, television, computer, datebook). Then whenever they notice anxiety cues, they can apply a coping strategy. The important thing is to establish numerous prompts that can repeatedly remind clients to notice their internal processes and then to intervene. Eventually, this should lead to the development of a habitual adaptive response.

Similar to common problems with homework compliance, there are several common complications related to successful application of cognitive restructuring. One common CT problem is difficulty generating flexible alternative ways of thinking about anxiety-provoking events. GAD clients tend to have longstanding habitual schemas related to themselves, the world, and the future, and it is sometimes hard for them to think about particular situations differently. However, the therapist can tell them that if they generate numerous perspectives, they have more options than when their perspectives are determined by habit. As a means to learn to think flexibly, the client may find it easier at first to practice using neutral topics. For example, clients can try to generate a list of the advantages and disadvantages of a sunny day, or of getting older. Practicing on a neutral topic can be the first step in preparing clients to think flexibly about an anxiety-provoking topic.

Another common CT complication is that even though GAD clients can generate alternative self-statements that make sense logically, no alternatives feel as true as the old perspective does. For example, M. initially reported that no alternative self-statement felt as true as her belief that worrying helped her to avoid germs and to prevent illness. The therapist provided a logical explanation for this. GAD clients have imagined catastrophic outcomes so many times that they become real. Similarly, they have had so few images of positive outcomes, that such images feel foreign. To help the alternative perspective feel more real to M., she was directed to try integrating it into the SCD procedure. In this way, she paired the image of herself coping successfully with a nonanxiety-provoking thought. Using the above SCD example, M. was directed to imagine herself touching raw chicken, feeling relaxed, and at the same time using the self-statement "As long as I take reasonable precautions (i.e., washing my hands), I will not get sick."

Another common CT difficulty is that GAD clients are extremely good at countering logic and evidence. Such clients have become so practiced in anticipating every possible negative outcome that they are able to provide infinite detailed reasons as to why the world is a dangerous place and why they may not be able to cope. As a result, therapists can frequently find themselves in a nonvictorious debate with their clients when they are trying to demonstrate the application of CT based on the client's specific worries. The solution is for the therapist to work toward the goal of helping the client see that there are numerous ways to interpret the same situation. This goal is preferable to trying to get the client to accept a particular alternative perspective for each example. Then, for each example, the therapist can observe whether any of the alternative perspectives are helpful to the client and in those instances suggest the client apply the alternative.

In addition to common complications during CT training, there is another common complication called relaxation-induced anxiety (RIA). This term refers to the fact that for some GAD clients letting go of tension to attain a fully relaxed state may, in itself, generate anxiety that can interfere with obtaining the goal. The therapist can address RIA in the same way that they would address graduated exposure to any feared situation. This can be accomplished by suggesting that clients gradually expose themselves to increasingly deeper levels of relaxation.

DEALING WITH MANAGED CARE AND ACCOUNTABILITY

CBT can create a paradox when dealing with managed care. On the one hand, it is the only empirically supported therapy for GAD and is highly successful with some clients. For example, data show that CBT leads to greater improvement than no treatment, analytic psychotherapy, pill placebo, nondirective therapy, and placebo therapy (Newman & Borkovec, 1995). CBT is also well liked by clients and is associated with relatively low dropout rates and significant reductions in need for anxiolytic medication. Despite strong empirical support, however, CBT leads to clinically significant change in only about half the clients treated. Therefore, half of the clients may not satisfactorily benefit from the CBT treatment described here.

The low success rate of CBT may be due in part to the high rate of comorbidity found in GAD participants. However, there is also reason to believe that GAD symptomatology often leads to specific secondary effects that may not be addressed with the current empirically supported CBT intervention (Newman *et al.*, 1999a).

One secondary effect of GAD symptomatology not addressed by CBT is the avoidance of experience and expression of emotions. Research suggests that worry (the central feature of GAD) may actually function to help clients avoid processing their emotions, and such avoidance may negatively reinforce the worry process (Newman *et al.*, 1999a,b). Clinical experience also supports this perspective. In fact, many GAD clients report discomfort with their emotions and a desire to avoid them. As a result, our research group has begun to view avoidance of emotions as similar to other types of avoidance and to experientially work with clients to help them process their emotions (Newman *et al.*, 1999b). The mechanism of change is believed to be similar to that of exposure to other feared situations.

Another effect of GAD symptoms not addressed by CBT is problematic interpersonal functioning. As noted above, persons diagnosed with GAD tend to have a high rate of comorbid axis II disorders and interpersonal problems. Clinical experience suggests that many of these interpersonal problems may arise from the tendency of persons with GAD to continually focus on and avoid any and all perceived potential threats (Newman *et al.*, 1999a). Included in the list of potential threats are such things as feeling that others do not like them and feeling emotionally vulnerable in front of others. Attempts to avoid such threats typically lead to withdrawn, self-absorbed, and distracted interpersonal behavior. Moreover, because their attention is focused primarily on subtle avoidance to keep them safe, persons with GAD fail to notice the impact of their behavior on others. Such an impact can include the appearance of being devoid of empathy or caring for others, lacking in spontaneity, and being distant and difficult to read. For example, M. reported that she was very lonely living apart from her husband, but that she had avoided talking to fellow students about these feelings. She reported that whenever anyone asked her what it was like to live apart from her husband, her response would be to make a joke. She believed that people would not like her if she were serious and spoke about her personal pain. Therefore, she continuously avoided being vulnerable and open with other people. The consequence was that people stopped asking her about her life, and M.'s interpretation of this was that they were not interested. In the end, her attempt to avoid being viewed negatively by others had the impact of cutting them off and keeping them distanced from her, which perpetuated her loneliness. As noted above, our research group has begun to actively incorporate therapeutic techniques to work with clients to identify and change avoidant self-defeating interpersonal behavioral patterns (Newman *et al.*, 1999b).

The limitations of CBT have several implications when dealing with a managed care organization. First, it may be helpful to conduct a thorough initial assessment of the client's axis I and II symptomatology as well as their ability to express a range of emotions. If the client appears to have symptoms of additional disorders or is unresponsive to initial CBT interventions, it may be useful for therapists to cite research relevant to the potential necessity of additional intervention strategies or added therapy time. It may also be helpful to cite data showing that symptomatic GAD clients tend to have poorer physical health and to visit the medical doctor much more frequently (Newman, in press). Such data may make the case that spending more money on psychological treatment of GAD may save money in terms of health care costs.

OUTCOME AND FOLLOW-UP

As previously noted, approximately 50% of clients who complete CBT treatment benefit from it in a clinically meaningful way (e.g., are in the range of a normative sample). M. is an example of such a client. Toward the end of therapy, M. was going through a particularly stressful time preparing to defend her Masters thesis. Nonetheless, she reported that it was not nearly as stressful as it would otherwise have been had she not been in therapy. For example, this stress had not kept her from being able to sleep, and she had felt that it was not a big deal.

When M. was asked to describe which therapy techniques were most helpful to her, she first focused on the cognitive restructuring. She indicated that she routinely felt better by thinking about her personal data and the fact that worrying in the past had not helped her. Therefore, telling herself that worrying only caused her grief and wasted her time worked very well to keep her focused on accomplishing the task at hand. By doing this, she indicated that she had been able to make a choice not to worry.

M. also reported that before therapy she had looked at everything as black or white. However, now she was seeing the gray areas and colors and as a result felt that she was able to gain much more from her life and her relationships. Moreover, her day-to-day experiences were so much more fulfilling.

M. further stated that she appreciated the PMR and breathing. For example, at times when she worked herself up cognitively and then breathed slowly, she noticed that it helped her slow down and think more rationally. In addition, doing the physical relaxation was a concrete method that helped her understand that when she let go of tension or slowed her breathing, it made a very big difference in her tension level. In addition, M. reported that she no longer felt concern about interacting with people when they were sick, and she was able even to rub raw chicken juice all over her hands and arms.

After therapy, when M. was reinterviewed with the ADIS-IV, she reported that being asked about particular symptoms highlighted how much more emotionally regulated she felt. In fact, immediately following therapy, M. no longer met criteria for GAD or for specific phobia. Further, her assessor severity rating at that point was a 2 (slightly disturbing, not really disabling) for each of these disorders. At 1-year follow-up, she also did not meet GAD criteria and her severity rating continued to be a 2. However, at this point she again met criteria for a specific phobia with a moderate severity rating.

DEALING WITH RECIDIVISM

There are several potential reasons for recidivism in GAD clients. The first reason, alluded to earlier, is that for some clients the current empirically supported CBT may be insufficient due to axis I and II comorbidity as well as secondary effects of GAD symptomatology not addressed by CBT. For these clients, an attempt to reapply the same interventions targeting the same symptomatology may not be the most helpful solution. Instead, I would recommend a thorough assessment of comorbidity, fear of emotions, and interpersonal functioning before determining the optimal course of treatment. Once the therapist is fully knowledgeable about the extent of the symptomatology, the treatment can be tailored to target whatever symptoms the client may be experiencing.

Another potential reason for recidivism may be that without the watchful eye of the therapist, the client discontinues regular practice and application of CBT techniques or that, over time, the client slowly gets out of the habit of using CBT techniques. In this case, a few booster sessions may be all that is necessary to reacquaint clients with the techniques they had learned. Sometimes, it may be the case that the client is going through a particularly stressful period that contributes to exacerbation of their symptomatology. In this instance, the client may need more than a booster session to help get them through the current stressor.

SUMMARY

In summary, GAD is a disorder that is believed to result from a hypervigilance toward external threat. Such hypervigilance leads to habitual cognitive, behavioral, and physiological responses to internal and external cues. Each response feeds on the response before it to spiral up into intensified anxiety and worry. To reverse this process, CBT for GAD targets cognitive, behavioral, and physiological responses by teaching clients new adaptive strategies to replace maladaptive ones. Such strategies include cognitive restructuring, breathing retraining, progressive muscle relaxation, self-control desensitization, and targeting of any subtle behavioral avoidance.

The CBT targeting of various GAD symptoms has demonstrated a high level of effectiveness. In fact, CBT is considered the gold standard treatment for GAD and is the only therapy that is empirically supported. However, it leads to clinically significant change in only about half of those treated. This suggests that there is room for improvement.

Evidence as to what types of additional interventions may prove most efficacious can be found when one examines areas in which GAD clients appear to be less functional. First, persons with GAD often have negative patterns of interpersonal behavior, something that is not routinely targeted in CBT for GAD. These patterns are due to the inattention of GAD clients toward their impact on others. This inattention occurs because the clients are so focused on keeping themselves safe. The second area of problematic functioning is that worry functions to help GAD clients avoid primary emotions. Such avoidance leads to negative reinforcement of their worry process. Given these two areas of dysfunction, additional interventions that target the impact of GAD clients on others and that expose them to their emotions may increase the effectiveness of the current CBT therapy. As mentioned earlier, a clinical trial is underway to test the addition of interpersonal and emotional processing techniques (Newman *et al.*, 1999b) to standard CBT techniques. It is hoped that integration of these additional techniques will lead to clinically significant improvement in a greater number of participants than CBT alone.

ACKNOWLEDGMENTS

Preparation of this manuscript was supported in part by National Institute of Mental Health Research Grant MH-58593. I would like to thank Louis G. Castonguay for his helpful comments on an earlier version of this manuscript.

REFERENCES

American Psychiatric Association (1994). *Diagnostic and statistical manual of mental disorders* (4th ed.). Washington, DC: Author.

Barlow, D. H., & DiNardo, P. A. (1991). The diagnosis of generalized anxiety disorder: Development, current status, and future direction. In R. M. Rapee & D. H. Barlow (Eds.), *Chronic anxiety: Generalized anxiety disorder and mixed anxiety-depression* (pp. 95–118). New York: Guilford.

Borkovec, T. D., Abel, J. L., & Newman, H. (1995). The effects of therapy on comorbid conditions in generalized anxiety disorder. *Journal of Consulting and Clinical Psychology, 63,* 479–483.

Borkovec, T. D., Newman, M. G., & Pincus, A. (2000). Comparison of applied relaxation/self-control desensitization, cognitive therapy, and their combination on immediate and long-term outcome among GAD clients. Manuscript in preparation.

Brown, T. A., & Barlow, D. H. (1992). Comorbidity among anxiety disorders: Implications for treatment and DSM-IV. *Journal of Consulting and Clinical Psychology, 60,* 835–844.

Brown, T. A., DiNardo, P. A., & Barlow, D. H. (1994a). *Anxiety Disorders Interview Schedule for DSM-IV (ADIS-IV).* Albany, NY: Graywind.

Brown, T. A., Barlow, D. H., & Liebowitz, M. R. (1994b). The empirical basis of generalized anxiety disorder. *American Journal of Psychiatry, 151,* 1272–1280.

Chambless, D. L., Sanderson, W. C., Shoham, V., Johnson, S. B., Pope, K. S., Crits-Christoph, P., Baker, M., Johnson, B., Woody, S. R., Sue, S., Beutler, L., Williams, D. A., & McCurry, S. (1996). An update on empirically validated therapies. *The Clinical Psychologist, 49,* 5–18.

Durham, R. C., Allan, T., & Hackett, C. A. (1997). On predicting improvement and relapse in generalized anxiety disorder following psychotherapy. *British Journal of Clinical Psychology, 36*(Pt. 1), 101–119.

Goldfried, M. R. (1971). Systematic desensitization as training in self-control. *Journal of Consulting and Clinical Psychology, 37,* 228–234.

Mancuso, D. M., Townsend, M. H., & Mercante, D. E. (1993). Long-term follow-up of generalized anxiety disorder. *Comprehensive Psychiatry, 34,* 441–446.

Meyer, T. J., Miller, M. L., Metzger, R. L., & Borkovec, T. D. (1990). Development and validation of the Penn State Worry Questionnaire. *Behaviour Research and Therapy, 28*(6), 487–495.

Newman, M. G. (in press). Recommendations for a cost offset model of psychotherapy allocation using generalized anxiety disorder as an example. *Journal of Consulting and Clinical Psychology.*
cost-effective therapies. Manuscript submitted for publication.

Newman, M. G., & Borkovec, T. D. (1995). Cognitive–behavioral treatment of generalized anxiety disorder. *The Clinical Psychologist, 48,* 5–7.

Newman, M. G., Zuellig, A. R., Kachin, K. E., & Constantino, M. J. (1997, November). *Examination of the reliability and validity of the GADQ-IV: A revised self-report measure of Generalized Anxiety Disorder.* Poster presented at the 31st annual meeting of the Association for Advancement of Behavior Therapy, Miami, FL.

Newman, M. G., Castonguay, L. G., & Borkovec, T. D. (1999a, March). Cognitive behavior therapy for generalized anxiety disorder: Strengths and limitations. In L. Castonguay (Chair), *Improving behavior therapy for generalized anxiety disorder: An integrative approach.* Symposium presented at the annual meeting of the Society for the Exploration of Psychotherapy Integration.

Newman, M. G., Castonguay, L. G., & Borkovec, T. D. (1999b, March). New dimensions in the treatment of generalized anxiety disorder: Interpersonal focus and emotional deepening. In L. Castonguay (Chair), *Improving behavior therapy for generalized anxiety disorder: An integrative approach.* Symposium presented at the annual meeting of the Society for the Exploration of Psychotherapy Integration.

Reich, J., Perry, J. C., Shera, D., Dyck, I., *et al.* (1994). Comparison of personality disorders in different anxiety disorder diagnoses: Panic, agoraphobia, generalized anxiety, and social phobia. *Annals of Clinical Psychiatry, 6*(2), 1994, 125–134.

Rogers, M. P., Weinshenker, N. J., Warshaw, M. G., Goisman, R. M., Rodriguez-Villa, F. J., Fierman, E. J., & Keller, M. B. (1996). Prevalence of somatoform disorders in a large sample of patients with anxiety disorders. *Psychosomatics, 37,* 17–22.

Sanderson, W. C., Beck, A. T., & McGinn, L. K. (1994). Cognitive therapy for generalized anxiety disorder: Significance of comorbid personality disorders. *Journal of Cognitive Psychotherapy, 8,* 13–18.

CHAPTER

Somatization Disorder

Behavioral Medicine and Counseling Center
Danbury, Connecticut

Case Description
Assessment
Treatment Conceptualization
Treatment Implementation
Concurrent Diagnoses and Treatment
Complications and Treatment Implications
Dealing with Managed Care and Accountability
Outcome and Follow-Up
Dealing with Recidivism
Summary
References

179

CHAPTER

Somatization Disorder

Behavioral Medicine and Counseling Center
Danbury, Connecticut

Case Description
Assessment
Treatment Conceptualization
Treatment Implementation
Concurrent Diagnoses and Treatment
Complications and Treatment Implications
Dealing with Managed Care and Accountability
Outcome and Follow-Up
Dealing with Recidivism
Summary
References

179

Effective Brief Therapies: A Clinician's Guide
Copyright © 2000 by Academic Press. All rights of reproduction in any form reserved.

The mind–body connection has puzzled and fascinated clinicians and researchers for centuries. Several theories and hypotheses have been suggested in an attempt to understand this complex relationship without any definitive answers. It is agreed, however, that unconscious conflicts and psychological stressors are at the heart of that relationship. Hormonal and neurochemical factors are believed to be involved in transformation of such psychological states into physical events (Asaad, 1996).

CASE DESCRIPTION

Somatoform Disorders include several conditions in which the presenting physical complaint cannot be explained by any known medical condition. Patients typically visit several physicians and emergency rooms, and undergo numerous tests and procedures in an attempt to uncover the cause of their ailment. Physical examination and diagnostic tests are often normal in these patients, yet all reassurances are not adequate to quell their anxieties and fear of the "real" problem. Such patients tend to avoid exploring any psychological issues, and vigorously resist being referred to mental health professionals.

Somatization Disorder refers to recurrent multiple physical symptoms and complaints in the absence of any physical evidence to substantiate the complaints made by the patient. It is important to note here that the condition can also occur in individuals who suffer from actual medical illnesses. In such instances, the patient will present with an exaggerated clinical picture that far exceeds what is expected based on the nature of the medical illness and objective findings. Somatization disorder occurs in relatively young people, mostly in women under the age of 30. The disorder often assumes a chronic course that can interfere with social and occupational functioning.

Conversion Disorder refers to the presence of certain symptoms or deficits involving motor or sensory functions that cannot be explained based on physical examination or diagnostic procedures. Examples include hysterical paralysis, loss of vision, and psuedoseizures. The disorder occurs more frequently in women than in men and is more common in rural areas and populations of lower socioeconomic status. For most patients, the course is brief; however, in some, the condition could become lengthy and recurrent.

Hypochondriasis is defined as excessive preoccupation with and fear of disease or a strong belief in having a disease based on a false interpretation of trivial physical signs or symptoms. The disorder strikes men and women equally, and tends to assume a chronic course.

Body Dysmorphic Disorder refers to the preoccupation with a defect in appearance based on a false conviction that a certain part of the body is ugly or deformed. The defect is either entirely imagined, or is minor, but exaggerated by the patient (American Psychiatric Association, 1994). The preoccupation can become severe and may cause a great deal of stress and interference with the patient's social life and occupational functioning. Patients can go to extremes trying to "fix" the imagined defect, and may become socially isolated because of being embarrassed about their appearance. The disorder usually begins during adolescence and assumes a chronic course. It affects males and females equally. De Leon *et al.* (1989) reported that Body Dysmorphic Disorder can also be frequent among women at menopause.

Pain Disorder within the context of somatoform disorders refers to severe pain that may be triggered or exacerbated by psychological factors. The degree of the pain cannot be explained on the basis of the physical condition of the patient. The pain may cause significant distress or impairment in social and occupational areas. Pain disorder can occur at any age and can be short-lived or chronic. It is more frequent in females than males.

The etiology of somatoform disorders is not well understood. Kellner (1991) reviewed several theories that attempted to explain the underlying causes of somatization disorder. He cited genetic, psychiatric, physiological, behavioral, and psychodynamic factors. In most patients, a combination of these factors is often present. Most patients seem to present with multiple psychiatric symptoms, including depression, anxiety, and panic attacks. Personality disorders are frequent diagnoses on axis II. Psychosocial stressors are often reported or identified in these patients. Physiological abnormalities in various systems may exist in some, while in others early childhood experiences and learned abnormal perceptions are considered likely contributing factors. The psychodynamic interpretations of somatic symptoms are most fascinating. They include repressed hostility, anger, attention seeking, secondary gain, suppression of emotions, and using bodily metaphors to communicate an unconscious conflict or express emotional distress (Asaad, 1996).

Mersey (1989) outlined several factors that could contribute to the development of conversion disorder. These included the patient's attempt to seek attention, the presence of a borderline or histrionic personality disorder, a history of childhood deprivation or abuse, and severe stress. He added that a large number of patients present with a conversion disorder as a hysterical exacerbation of an actual physical illness. Slater (1965) suggested that damage to the brain or intoxication with certain drugs such as anticonvulsants may predispose some individuals to experience conversion symptoms.

The cause of hypochondriasis is somewhat similar to other somatoform disorders. Several theories have been suggested, including disturbed object relations, repressed hostility, masochism, guilt, conflicted dependency needs, defense against feelings of low self-esteem, perceptual and cognitive abnormalities, and reinforcement for playing the "sick role" (Martin & Yutzy, 1994).

No specific cause has been suggested to explain Body Dysmorphic Disorder. Several authors have considered it to be a subtype of another psychiatric disorder, such as social phobia, obsessive-compulsive disorder, depression, hypochondriasis, or delusional disorder (Martin & Yutzy, 1994).

Pain disorder in the context of somatoform disorders is considered to be induced or exaggerated by psychological or social factors. These include unconscious conflicts, attention seeking, dependency issues, preexisting personality organization, and secondary gain. In addition, there are significant cultural and individual differences with regard to pain perception, tolerance, and expression (Chapman & Turner, 1990). Pain occurs more frequently among patients with psychiatric diagnoses, including depression and panic disorder compared to the general population (King & Strain, 1994).

ASSESSMENT

Patients with somatoform disorders are typically reluctant to undergo psychiatric evaluations or treatments. They concentrate on their physical complaints and visit various medical specialists and hospitals repeatedly. Therefore, these patients are always referred to mental health professionals by their primary care physicians or other health care providers. Occasionally, a family member may insist on bringing the patient to a mental health professional after all medical avenues have been exhausted. It is always necessary to communicate with the treating physician in order to ensure that all medical causes have been ruled out.

Careful and detailed psychiatric evaluation must, in addition to assessing physical complaints, explore various psychiatric disorders that may be associated with somatoform disorders. Such detailed assessment may offer the key to the treatment. It is important to note here that some patients with an actual physical illness may develop a somatoform condition. In such cases, the symptoms of the real illness are greatly exaggerated, or some unrelated and unlikely complications are imagined. In addition, patients who are known to have chronic recurrent somatic complaints in the absence of any physical explanation may be at a special risk. Such patients, at times, may not be taken seriously, and their complaints may be dismissed as "psychosomatic," when indeed they may represent an actual physical disorder, which in some instances could be serious. Therefore, both the primary care physician and the psychotherapist must always communicate and balance risk based on each episode.

In order to make the diagnosis of Somatization Disorder, DSM-IV (APA, 1994) requires the presence of several symptoms in four different categories:

1. Four pain symptoms involving the head, abdomen, pelvis, joints, or other areas of the body.

2. Two gastrointestinal symptoms, for example, nausea and bloating.

3. One sexual symptom, such as impotence or irregular menses.

4. One pseudoneurological symptom, such as paralysis, numbness, loss of voice, seizures, or amnesia.

In Conversion Disorder, there are usually one or two symptoms involving motor or sensory dysfunction similar to those outlined in the fourth category noted above.

Certain serious medical illnesses — including multiple sclerosis, systemic lupus erythematosus, myasthenia gravis, endocrine disorders, and certain occult malignancies — may present with atypical and inconsistent features that may be misdiagnosed as a somatoform disorder. Therefore, it is extremely important for all those who treat patients with vague and multiple symptoms to keep an open mind and consider all possibilities (Asaad, 1996).

TREATMENT CONCEPTUALIZATION

Treatment of patients with somatoform disorders can be very frustrating and challenging at the same time. No patient should be accepted for treatment for a "psychosomatic" disorder unless all possible physical causes have been considered and ruled out. This is obviously the responsibility of primary care physicians and other medical specialists. However, it is very important to communicate with the referring physician and obtain the medical facts in order to develop an appropriate treatment plan.

The goal of therapy is clearly to minimize or eliminate physical complaints and treat the accompanying psychiatric problems. Support and reassurance have a very limited value in such instances. Patients are rarely reassured, even by negative medical tests or physical exams. Therefore, the therapist needs to explore the underlying conflicts that may be contributing to the problem. Careful investigation of psychosocial stressors can be of extreme diagnostic as well as therapeutic value. Kellner (1991) suggested that psychological testing may be helpful in establishing the diagnosis in certain patients with somatoform disorders. Psychiatric disorders — including anxiety, depression, and personality disorders — are often present in patients with somatoform disorders, and they should be treated adequately.

It is important to know in advance that this patient population is very resistant and difficult to manage. In most cases, progress may be slow and limited. Therefore, the therapist must set realistic goals and expectations and plan for a long-term relationship with the patient.

TREATMENT IMPLEMENTATION

As indicated earlier, patients with somatoform disorder are rarely willing to submit to a psychological evaluation. They come reluctantly to the therapist, show poor insight, and are very resistant to ongoing psychotherapy. For this reason, such patients are very difficult to treat and can be very challenging.

The therapist must listen with empathy to the lengthy list of physical complaints and should acknowledge the distress that is endured by the patient. While the therapist should not agree with the patient's convictions, he or she must not oppose them. Such a stand may lead to more resistance and could damage the therapeutic alliance. During the course of therapy, it may be helpful to the patient to maintain regular appointments with his or her primary care physician with limited access to diagnostic procedures (Smith *et al.*, 1986). This strategy will provide the patient with ongoing reassurance, allowing the therapist to probe into the underlying psychological conflicts. Regular communication between the psychotherapist and primary care physician is of vital importance to the success of the treatment.

The role of the therapist in the early stages of treatment should focus on gathering detailed psychosocial history that may be very essential later in the course of treatment. He or she should attempt to identify any particular stressors that may be linked to the onset or exacerbation of any physical symptoms. The therapist will then help the patient see the connection between the psychological problems and the onset of the physical symptoms. As the patient accepts that connection as a contributing factor to his or her physical distress, the therapist may then help the patient develop coping mechanisms to deal with the psychological stressors effectively. Early interpretations should be avoided, and patients should be led carefully to find for themselves the relationship between their physical complaints and psychological conflicts. The process can be tedious and lengthy, but when successful it can be extremely rewarding to both the patient and the therapist.

Psychotherapeutic techniques employed with somatic patients must be eclectic and flexible. Cognitive, behavioral, insight-oriented, and supportive modalities are all useful depending on each individual case. Biofeedback, hypnosis, and relaxation techniques may be helpful in some cases.

Since depression, anxiety, or even panic attacks are frequently present in association with somatoform disorder, psychotropic medications any be needed as well. Antidepressants, anxiolytics, and mood stabilizers are used frequently in such patients with positive results.

The ultimate goal of therapy is to identify the underlying psychosocial factors that are contributing to the physical complaints and help the patient develop coping mechanisms to deal with the underlying problems without resorting to somatic means. With successful psychotherapy, gradual resolution of the physical symptoms often begins to evolve, and psychological symptoms then begin to replace the physical complaints, which can then be dealt with within the ongoing therapeutic process. The emergence of psychological symptoms should be considered a positive sign and a healthier way to express the conflicts. At that point, the treatment plan may need to be revised to address the new clinical presentation.

CONCURRENT DIAGNOSES AND TREATMENT

As noted earlier, other psychiatric problems often accompany somatoform disorders, and may be severe enough to warrant separate diagnoses on axis I or II. Most commonly, these patients suffer from major depression or dysthymia. Generalized anxiety disorder and panic disorder are also common. Insomnia is a common complaint. Some patients may become addicted to pain killers and anxiolytic drugs due to ongoing prescription of such agents. Alcohol abuse is also common. Personality disorders that are encountered among patients with somatoform disorders include histrionic, borderline, and antisocial personality disorders.

Concurrent disorders must be treated adequately, utilizing all available means, including psychotropic medications and various modalities of psychotherapy, including group therapy and family counseling. Patients who become addicted to prescription drugs or alcohol must be identified and treated as deemed appropriate. Detoxification and rehabilitation may be necessary in some cases.

COMPLICATIONS AND TREATMENT IMPLICATIONS

The most common complication of somatoform disorders is development of serious marital or family problems. The spouse and other family members may be supportive to some extent. However, due to the chronicity of the condition and the negative effect it may have on marital and family life, it is inevitable for the relationship between the patient and his or her spouse or others to suffer, leading to ongoing tension and deterioration of the quality of the family life. Similarly, work or school performance may deteriorate due to repeated absences and preoccupation with various heath issues. Serious financial problems may be a natural outcome of unemployment and high medical expenses.

As indicated earlier, patients may develop a chemical dependency on various pain killers and tranquilizers, which will further worsen their overall condition. In some patients, repeated physical complaints and visits to doctors and the emergency room may lead to the performance of unwarranted invasive diagnostic procedures or even surgeries, which may cause actual injuries and further complications.

Finally, it is worth emphasizing again that patients with a known history of multiple and repeated somatic complaints may not be taken seriously every time they present to an emergency room or doctor's office with yet another complaint. Consequently, genuine medical problems may be misdiagnosed as "psychosomatic," and hence go untreated for a longer period of time, missing the opportunity of early diagnosis and treatment, which may lead to grave consequences.

Therefore, it is essential to attend to all problems that could be identified and use all available treatments. Medical interventions should be utilized when appropriate, and ongoing communication among various treating health care providers is essential. Drugs with addictive potential should be used cautiously and should be monitored closely. Early intervention may help avoid social and vocational deterioration.

DEALING WITH MANAGED CARE AND ACCOUNTABILITY

As managed care became a reality, the focus of treatment of various mental disorders shifted from long-term modalities to brief, problem-oriented therapies. This dramatic change in therapeutic approach has led, in some instances, to inadequate treatments with limited success. Since somatoform disorders tend to take a chronic course, they have been most affected by the restrictions imposed by managed care. Most managed care plans offer a very limited number of outpatient visits to treat such disorders. As a result, and since patients are typically ambivalent about psychotherapies, they welcome the termination of psychiatric treatment and return to their medical providers for reassurance and answers. Ironically, managed care organizations may allow further medical visits to various specialists and expensive diagnostic procedures for such patients. The cost of such investigative tests often exceed by several times the cost of providing long-term psychiatric care for these patients.

Most mental health providers are aware that managed care organizations shift the responsibility and liability to the provider, despite the fact that such organizations have full control over access to diagnostic tests and treatments. In order to protect oneself from liability, it is important to continue to document in writing the need for treatment and the risks involved in any shortcuts imposed by managed care organizations. Additionally, providers must know that denial of payment is not a legitimate reason to stop treatment, and patients must be informed of their options.

OUTCOME AND FOLLOW-UP

The prognosis in most cases of somatoform disorders is guarded due to the chronicity of the conditions. Symptoms tend to wax and wane from time to time, and in some instances they can be continuous. Comorbid medical as well as psychiatric conditions are likely to prolong the course and worsen the situation. For this reason, every effort must be made to treat any accompanying condition adequately. In some patients, the disorder may be short-lived and most symptoms may resolve spontaneously.

At the conclusion of the active phase of treatment, patients should be told that the door would always be open for them to return to treatment if the symptoms reappear. Monthly or bimonthly visits may be helpful in order to provide the patient with the support system needed to sustain their improvement. This will also allow the therapist to address any stressful situations that may arise in the future. Patients on psychotropic medications need to be monitored regularly. Visits to the primary care physician should be limited but scheduled as necessary. This will provide the patient with adequate reassurance without abusing the system.

DEALING WITH RECIDIVISM

As indicated above, somatoform disorders are likely to become chronic, and patients are likely to return from time to time with various complaints. It is wise to prepare for such events and keep such patients involved in treatment on an infrequent basis. These patients may also benefit from self-help support groups. Educating the patient and the family about the nature of the disorder is essential in order to minimize recidivism. But when patients suffer from a severe and long-lasting somatoform disorder, several areas may be affected. These include family, social, and vocational aspects. Attention must be paid to all affected areas in order to ensure comprehensive treatment and a more lasting recovery.

SUMMARY

While most people are able to express their emotional conflicts in terms of such psychological symptoms as anger, anxiety, depression, or others, many individuals seem to unconsciously "convert" these symptoms into somatic complaints that present in the form of pain, dysfunction, or loss of function. The choice of the symptom is often determined by the background of the individual and personality organization. Psychological factors that may contribute to the onset of somatoform disorders include repressed hostility, anger, attention seeking, inability to express emotions, and secondary gain. Hormonal and neurochemical factors are most likely involved in the mechanism of somatoform disorders.

These disorders appear more often among women, and seem to affect young adults more often than other age groups. In addition, major psychiatric disorders can accompany somatoform disorders, including major depression, panic disorder, and generalized anxiety disorder. Substance abuse and iatrogenic complications are also common among these patients. Family, social, and vocational disturbances are frequent complications.

It is important to note that some patients with known "psychosomatic" complaints may be misdiagnosed as such, while in fact they may be suffering form a genuine physical disorder. Frequent medical evaluation may be necessary, and ongoing communication between the psychotherapist and the primary care physician is essential.

Patients are usually resistant to treatment, which tends to be difficult and frustrating at times. An eclectic approach is most useful, and the use of psychotropic agents any be needed. Prognosis is guarded with variable outcome.

Prompt and adequate psychiatric attention to patients with somatoform disorders and implementation of appropriate therapies can be of great help to these patients and may prove cost-effective in view of the lengthy and costly diagnostic procedures and medical treatments.

REFERENCES

American Psychiatric Association (1994). *Diagnostic and statistical manual of mental disorders* (4th ed.) Washington, DC: Author.

Asaad, G. (1996). *Psychosomatic disorders: Theoretical and clinical aspects.* New York: Brunner/Mazel.

Chapman, C. R., & Turner, J. A. (1990). Psychologic and psychosocial aspects of acute pain. In J. J. Bonica (Ed.), *The management of pain* (Vol. 1, 2nd ed.). Philadelphia: Lea & Febiger.

De Leon, J., Bott, A., & Simpson, G. M. (1989). Dysmorphophobia: Body dysmorphic disorder or delusional disorder, somatic type? *Comprehensive Psychiatry, 30,* 457–472.

Kellner, R. (1991). *Psychosomatic syndromes and somatic symptoms.* Washington, DC: American Psychiatric Press.

GHAZI ASAAD

King, S. A., & Strain, J. (1994). Pain disorders. In R. E. Hales, S. C. Yudofsky, & J. A. Talbott (Eds.), *The American psychiatric press textbook of psychiatry* (2nd ed.) Washington, DC: American Psychiatric Press.

Martin, R. L., Yutzy, S. H. (1994). Somatoform disorders. In R. E. Hales, S. C. Yudofsky, & J. A. Talbott (Eds.), *The American psychiatric press textbook of psychiatry* (2nd ed.). Washington, DC: American Psychiatric Press.

Merskey, H. (1989). Conversion disorders. In *Treatment of psychiatric disorders* (Vol. 3). Washington, DC: American Psychiatric Association.

Slater, E. (1965). The diagnosis of hysteria. *British Medical Journal, 1,* 1395–1399.

Smith, G. R., Monson, R. A., & Ray, D. C. (1986). Psychiatric consultation in somatization disorder. *New England Journal of Medicine, 314,* 1407–1413.

CHAPTER

Pain Disorder

Robin M. Masheb

Yale University School of Medicine
New Haven, Connecticut

Robert D. Kerns

Yale University School of Medicine
VA Connecticut Healthcare System
New Haven, Connecticut

Case Description
Treatment Conceptualization
Assessment
Treatment Implementation
    Reconceptualization
    Skills Acquisition and Skills Practice
Concurrent Diagnoses and Treatment
Complications and Treatment Implications
Dealing with Managed Care and Accountability
Outcome and Follow-Up
Dealing with Recidivism
Summary and Conclusions
References

Effective Brief Therapies: A Clinician's Guide

A diverse group of theoretically informed psychological treatment approaches for individuals experiencing chronic pain have been described (Gatchel & Turk, 1996). Several of these approaches have received empirical support. Self-management approaches based on the cognitive-behavioral perspective on chronic pain and employing a range of cognitive and behavior therapy techniques have received particularly strong support (Turk *et al.*, 1983). Details of a brief cognitive-behavioral therapy (CBT) approach for promoting management of chronic pain will be highlighted in this chapter.

CASE DESCRIPTION

Dan is a 47-year-old twice-married father of three children who was referred to our interdisciplinary pain management program for comprehensive evaluation and possible help in management of chronic knee pain. Psychosocial evaluation and treatment are generally key components of the program. Dan was born and raised in Connecticut. After receiving a high school diploma, he married, obtained a job as a maintenance worker, and had one daughter, now 23 years old and living on her own. Dan's first marriage ended in divorce after several years. He has since remarried and has two more children, a girl who is 15 years old and a boy who is 11 years old. Dan was employed in his last position for 12 years prior to a work-related injury 15 months ago. Currently, he is not working and is collecting disability benefits.

Dan's previous psychotherapy experience was approximately 20 years ago, when he attended weekly outpatient couples sessions with his first wife. This treatment lasted approximately 5 months. Following his divorce, Dan was prescribed a low-dose tricyclic antidepressant by his primary care physician for symptoms of depression. Dan discontinued the medication after 3 months, stating that his depression had remitted. More recently, Dan's primary care physician prescribed Prozac 20 mg because of symptoms of depression and feelings of worthlessness that he attributed to not being able to work.

Dan's current health status is notable for hypertension and obesity in addition to his chronic knee pain and apparent mood disorder. His hypertension is currently well-controlled with medication. Dan is 5' 10" and weighs 296 pounds. He smokes one pack of cigarettes per day. His obesity and tobacco use are both presumed to contribute to the elevated blood pressure. His medical history also includes a fall from a ladder at work that resulted in injury to his left knee 5 years ago. Dan was initially able to return to work within 6 months of the injury, during which time he was treated with a regimen of physical therapy and nonsteroidal antiinflammatory medications. He reinjured the knee 15 months prior to his referral to our pain program in a second job-related incident. Results from physical examination and imaging studies were suggestive of soft tissue and cartilage damage. Knee replacement surgery was indicated; however, Dan's orthopedic surgeon determined that Dan was not a good surgical candidate, given his level of depression and obesity.

Dan presented at his initial intake for the pain program wearing a knee brace and using a cane. Mental status examination was notable for speech that was impeded by a stutter. He made good eye contact. Signs of anxiety included fidgeting and knee bouncing. Dan displayed a number of "pain behaviors," in particular grimacing when standing or sitting, and rubbing his knee at times. He reported depressed mood and decreased interest in his usual activities. He acknowledged psychomotor symptoms of depression that included sleep disturbance, increased appetite and weight, and decreased energy and libido, as well as cognitive symptoms such as worthlessness, hopelessness, and thoughts of death. He denied suicidal ideation. He denied excessive use of alcohol and use of illicit substances.

In addition to his primary complaint of left knee pain, Dan complained of pain in his left shoulder and right knee. Both Dan and his doctor attributed the shoulder pain to use of the cane, and pain in his right knee from exerting extra weight on that knee. In addition to the underlying pathology in his knee and associated pain, Dan presented with several associated problems and complications. Dan experienced a high level of interference in functioning and increasingly elevated experiences of affective distress. Dan reported that he could not return to his job because pain limited his ability to sit or stand for long periods of time, and because his doctor had restricted him from lifting more than 5 pounds. He had refused vocational retraining for alternative careers because he believed that knee replacement surgery would help him get back to his old job as a maintenance worker. In addition to the interference in his occupational functioning, Dan reported that his knee pain limited his overall mobility. This included interference with his ability to perform household chores, such as shopping and cooking, and to engage in activities with his children and wife. Dan reported that his roles as father and husband had been disrupted. Dan also complained that the pain was associated with growing feelings of frustration and irritability.

TREATMENT CONCEPTUALIZATION

Contemporary models of chronic pain emphasize the multidimensional nature of the experience. One leading model, the biopsychosocial model, also elaborated as a diathesis-stress model of chronic pain (Kerns & Jacob, 1995), emphasizes the multidimensional nature of the chronic pain experience, as well as the importance of identifying multiple contributing factors or concurrent problems (e.g., obesity, marital dysfunction). Four primary domains of the chronic pain experience are emphasized, including the underlying disorder or structural problem, the experience of pain itself, and associated experiences of functional impairment and disability, and affective distress. According to the model, potential contributors cut across biological, psychological, and social or interpersonal domains. Furthermore, individuals may vary greatly in the degree to which impairment or dysfunction is present in a specific domain, the relevance of specific contributors, and the degree to which there is an interrelationship among the domains. This model was applied in Dan's case to aid in the development of an integrative conceptualization of his experience of chronic pain and associated problems. This conceptualization was subsequently applied in the development of an individually tailored and prescriptive treatment plan (Kerns, 1994). As is commonly the case, this treatment plan was multidisciplinary and multimodal in nature.

A first step in the application of the biopsychosocial model to an individual case is articulation of each of the four primary problem domains and their hypothesized interrelationships. This is done in order to develop a comprehensive description of the individual's experience of chronic pain. In Dan's case, this included a thorough medical, particularly orthopedic, evaluation of the pathology of his left knee, with additional evaluation of his shoulder and right knee complaints. Evaluations conducted by his referring physician were viewed as adequate at the time of his referral, and more extensive medical evaluation was determined not to be indicated. Importantly, in Dan's case, there was a clear consensus among his providers and apparent acceptance by Dan and his family about the specific diagnosis and proposed medical intervention. More commonly, uncertainty or ambiguity is present at the time of referral to a tertiary care pain program, and efforts that focus on clarification and acceptance of the medical diagnosis and implications are important first steps in the evaluation process.

The second key domain, and almost always the primary concern of the referred patient, is the experience of pain itself. Careful attention to both the qualitative and quantitative aspects of the experience of pain is critical. Dan described his left knee pain as constant, but fluctuating in intensity, and was able to articulate several variables that he had identified that were relatively reliably associated with either increases (e.g., ambulation, stair-climbing, or sitting for prolonged periods of time) or decreases (e.g., elevating the leg, application of heat) in pain intensity. Dan directly attributed pain to his injured knee, and held beliefs that even transient increases in pain were signs of impending additional trauma or escalating pathology.

The third key domain in the model emphasizes level of functional limitations. Dan's functioning had become increasingly problematic. Not only had he stopped working, but his frequency of pleasurable and constructive activities had greatly decreased. Dan's daily activities had become limited to sleeping, eating, and watching TV. Dan no longer cooked, food shopped, cleaned, or did laundry. He had also stopped activities with his children, such as helping with homework or attending sporting events. He was opposed to seeking alternative careers or job retraining, and preferred to rely on disability benefits for income. Importantly, Dan believed that his functional limitations were a direct and uncontrollable result of his damaged knee and associated pain. Additionally, he felt compelled by his pain to limit activities because of concerns about additional trauma, and ultimately, greater pain and disability.

The final domain relates to commonly associated feelings of emotional distress, including fear and anxiety, depressed mood, and irritability, frustration, and anger. Development of associated symptoms of mood and anxiety disorders are also common. With minimal prompting, Dan readily acknowledged escalating, pervasive, and diffuse feelings of distress, and emphasized feelings of hopelessness and helplessness. He described pervasive negative automatic thoughts of being a failure as a father and husband because of his inability to work and bring in an income. Dan also reported thoughts that his family would be better off without him; however, he denied suicidal intentions or plans. Physiological arousal and muscle tension associated with pain and anxiety were additional problem areas identified. In particular, any event related to money triggered significant anxiety, worry, and distorted thinking. For example, the patient's interactions with his lawyer often triggered catastrophic thinking that he would lose his disability benefits.

Concurrent problems such as obesity, smoking, abuse of prescription medications, and high utilization of health-care services were also identified. Dan had gained 45 pounds during his 15 months of disability leave, which his primary care physician attributed to a combination of high caloric intake and inactivity. Dan had a 17-year history of unsuccessful dieting that was precipitated by weight gain following his second marriage. Dan found it increasingly difficult to control his food intake without a structured workday, and was binge-eating approximately twice daily. In addition, he had ceased his usual exercise routine for fear of exacerbating his knee problem. He also reported smoking more frequently because of boredom. Finally, Dan had poor strategies for managing his medical care. He would take up to twice the prescribed dose of medication and schedule frequent emergency doctor visits.

Dan's marriage and family had also been negatively affected by his pain condition. Susan, his current wife, had taken on many of Dan's old responsibilities, including attending the children's sports activities, taking out the garbage, and cooking. She was employed full-time as a payroll administrator for a large company and had also increased her part-time handmade jewelry business to make extra money for the family while Dan was out of work. These changes had more broadly resulted in a significant decrease in time spent in pleasurable activities involving the children. Sexual interaction and satisfaction between Dan and Susan had similarly diminished. Conversely, frequency of negative interaction between Dan and Susan and among the family members was increasing. An escalating experience of marital and family distress was apparent.

Several hypotheses about potentially relevant contributors to the development of additional sites of pain and apparent pathology and to Dan's escalating experiences of pain, disability, and distress were generated. Possible biological contributors included Dan's general deconditioning secondary to decreases in activity and exercise, specific effects of his increased weight and poor health behaviors, and additional effects of poor body mechanics related to distorted ambulation and the use of a cane. It was also hypothesized that dysregulation of brain neurotransmitter systems secondary to persistent pain was further contributing to escalating symptoms of a major depressive disorder, including a significant sleep disorder, amotivation, chronic fatigue, appetite changes, and depressed mood and irritability. Heightened sympathetic nervous system arousal and stress reactivity were further hypothesized to be contributing to elevated muscle tension and pain, as well as generalized feelings of fear and anxiety.

Multiple interrelated behavioral and cognitive contributors were also apparent. Limited vocational skills certainly undermined his ability to pursue alternative jobs in the face of his injury. More broadly, lack of well-developed avocational interests contributed to his overall declining level of pleasurable and constructive activity. As already mentioned, his increasingly sedentary lifestyle was further hypothesized to contribute to his deconditioning, as well as to his apparent mood disorder. Dan's generally passive style of coping and poor problem-solving skills were viewed as particularly important. Dan's avoidance and withdrawal from his usual roles as husband and father contributed to his decreased ability to assert himself, in particular with his children. For example, his 15-year-old daughter often complained that it was not fair that the family did not have money to buy certain things, and blamed him. Her angry outbursts served as triggers for Dan's negative thoughts of being a failure as a provider, and feelings of inadequacy. He reported thinking that he had lost his authority over her since he was no longer the breadwinner of the family. Instead of setting limits with his daughter, Dan developed a passive style of coping and allowed her to speak to him in a disrespectful manner.

The broader family and social context was also emphasized in the developing conceptualization of Dan's experience of chronic pain (Kerns, 1996). Susan's style of responding to her husband's complaints of pain has been studied in the empirical literature and has become known as a "solicitous" style of responding. For example, when Dan complains, she may bring him food or a drink, take over a household task (e.g., cooking dinner), or suggest that he take a nap. This type of interaction between Dan and his wife was hypothesized to be maintaining Dan in the "sick role" and Susan in the "caregiver role." The availability of disability compensation was additionally highlighted as a potentially important, and unfortunately common, contributor.

Identification of these numerous interrelated problem domains, as well as articulation of several factors hypothesized to be contributing and/or maintaining these problems, served as the basis for the development of a comprehensive plan for additional evaluation and the initial stages of a multimodal treatment plan. It was determined that more extensive evaluation by the program psychologist and rehabilitation specialists was indicated. The goals of the evaluation were specification of a finite number of specific goals for treatment and a development of a time-limited goal-oriented plan, and integrated treatment plan.

ASSESSMENT

Recognition of the range of psychosocial factors that contribute to chronic pain has led to the increasing importance of a comprehensive psychological assessment for the chronic pain patient (Turk & Melzack, 1992). The biopsychosocial perspective has been particularly influential in the development of assessment approaches that are specific to the evaluation of chronic pain conditions. Consistent with this perspective, assessment should be multidimensional in nature and incorporate methods designed to assess the key domains of the chronic pain experience, including structural pathology, pain intensity, disability, and distress, as well as a number of factors often hypothesized to contribute to the development and perpetuation of problems in these domains.

The most frequently used method for assessment of chronic pain is a psychosocial interview. The interview typically begins with the gathering of demographic information and details of the pain condition. The patient's functioning in a range of areas is assessed (e.g., occupational functioning, family functioning, social and recreational functioning, and ability to perform activities of daily living). Psychological well-being is also evaluated, including comorbid psychiatric illnesses and psychological functioning, with particular attention to major depression, affective distress, sleep disturbance, and alcohol and drug abuse and dependence. If the patient is prescribed pain medication, inquiry about medication adherence or abuse is necessary. Finally, attributions about the origins of pain, factors that contribute to fluctuations in symptoms, and beliefs about self-management are assessed.

In the past 20 years, there has been a dramatic increase in the number and breadth of measures of aspects of the chronic pain experience. Instruments range from those designed to assess single constructs, such as coping with pain or pain-related anxiety, to instruments that serve as screening measures, or measures of treatment gains. A number of multidimensional pain inventories, designed to assess the multiple facets of the experience of pain, have also been developed and validated with chronic pain patients. Self-report questionnaires, diaries, behavioral observation, and reports from others (e.g., spouses), as well as additional structured and semistructured interviews, are important adjuncts to the basic pain interview to collect more specific information regarding problem areas. Turk and Melzack (1992) provide a detailed examination of a wide range of commonly used instruments in the assessment of the chronic pain patient.

Following completion of a semistructured pain interview from which the information described above was derived, Dan was administered a comprehensive set of questionnaires and inventories designed to further specify, and quantify, key problem areas and likely contributors. Central to the psychological evaluation was the administration of the West Haven–Yale Multidimensional Pain Inventory (WHYMPI; Kerns et al., 1985). This inventory has several advantages over other available instruments in that it is informed by cognitive-behavioral theory, is psychometrically sound, is comprehensive in its content, and is brief and easy to administer and score. It has become one of the most widely used measures in pain treatment settings.

Dan was also asked to complete additional self-report measures designed to assess pain intensity and pain behaviors (i.e., frequency of distorted ambulation, facial/audible expressions of pain and distress, and help-seeking); disability and functioning, depression, anxiety, and anger; marital and family functioning, and communication; pain-related coping and problem-solving competence; diet, exercise, and tobacco use; and overall physical and psychological well-being. Scores on each of these measures were examined with specific regard to the hypotheses generated in the initial interview and with an eye to specification of targets and goals for treatment.

Not surprisingly, Dan reported particularly high levels of pain and pain behaviors, extremely low levels of activity and perceptions of severe functional limitations and disability attributed to pain, and moderately high levels of generalized emotional distress. Specific measures of depression and anxiety corroborated interview data and suggested the concurrent diagnosis of major depressive disorder. Marital and family dysfunction were also noted, but the level of dysfunction or dissatisfaction was noted to be only in the mild range. A general style of passive and avoidant pain-relevant coping was noted, as were pervasive perceptions of low self-control and poor problem-solving confidence. Several disturbing patterns of health-damaging behaviors were quantified. A moderately severe binge-eating disorder was confirmed in addition to his tobacco dependence and lack of exercise. Not surprisingly, he scored particularly low on the measure of global physical and psychological well-being.

Concurrent evaluation by a physical therapist, occupational therapist, and vocational rehabilitation specialist was also completed. The physical therapy evaluation further documented generalized deconditioning in addition to specific muscle weakness in his lower extremities bilaterally. Physical therapy and occupational therapy evaluations identified developing problems in his shoulders and hands, attributed to poor body mechanics and the use of the cane. Poor understanding of these problems that likely contributed to poor judgments about activity, exercise capacity, and principles of energy conservation were also noted. The vocational evaluation identified several potential areas of vocational interest and established a framework for future discussions about vocational retraining.

TREATMENT IMPLEMENTATION

Based on the results of the comprehensive evaluation, the multidisciplinary pain treatment team met with Dan and his wife to develop a specific, integrated plan for treatment. This process led to agreement on an intensive rehabilitation and treatment plan to be delivered over a 3-month period, involving several outpatient visits each week to the pain center. Responsibility for each prescribed treatment component was delegated. Dan's orthopedist was consulted and met with the client to discuss activity and exercise guidelines. A nutritionist was consulted for dietary guidelines and reasonable weight loss goals. Dan's primary care provider was engaged and reinforced a plan for participation in a three-session smoking cessation program and concurrent use of a nicotine patch. A progressive and structured home exercise program was prescribed and monitored by the team physical therapist. The goals of this program were to increase functional capacity and conditioning, to improve body mechanics, and to strengthen muscles in the legs. An educational session was scheduled with this therapist to more specifically target improved body mechanics and energy conservation. Vocational counseling was also scheduled. Cognitive-behavior therapy that targeted improved self-management of pain, increased activity, and reduced depression was also prescribed. The team psychologist was assigned the role of case manager and coordinator of care, in addition to the role as cognitive-behavior therapist. Monthly team meetings involving the core group of providers were scheduled to discuss Dan's progress and to identify refinements in the initial treatment plan.

Cognitive-behavior therapy (CBT) for pain has been well-described in the existing clinical and empirical literatures, and is now routinely available in many specialized pain treatment centers (Turk *et al.*, 1983). The approach is informed by cognitive-social learning theory and the principles of behavior modification and cognitive therapy. CBT for pain has many similarities to application of this therapeutic approach for many other psychological and behavioral disorders. CBT pain treatment is time-limited, structured, and goal-oriented. The therapeutic process emphasizes the collaborative relationship between patient and therapist. This collaborative process is particularly exemplified at the point of a transition between the assessment phase and the initial treatment sessions, when specific, quantifiable goals for treatment are negotiated. This process helps establish clear expectations and parameters for treatment. Expectations as to active participation in the treatment process are also established, including expectations for skill practice and other homework assignments to be completed outside the formal treatment setting.

Treatment is individually tailored and prescriptive in nature and is based directly on the results of the comprehensive evaluation. However, there are several common treatment targets. These include, but are not limited to: (1) negative cognition, primarily perceptions of helplessness and hopelessness regarding the experience of pain and its management; (2) inactivity and frank disability; (3) physiological arousal, particularly heightened muscle tension, and stress reactivity; and (4) heightened pain intensity. Other common problems that are often targeted include sleep disturbances, marital and family dysfunction, and symptoms of mood and anxiety disorders. Similarly, specifically identified contributors to the experience of pain, disability, and distress are also targeted. These can include training in alternative patterns of pain-relevant communication, assertiveness training that targets restrictions in the expression of negative emotions, and general problem-solving skills training.

Turk *et al.* (1983) have provided a detailed model for CBT for chronic pain that incorporates three interrelated phases of treatment. Central to effective treatment is the patient's developing *reconceptualization* of the experience of pain as chronic, as opposed to acute, and manageable, but not curable. Development of a perspective of self-control that emphasizes development of an active problem-solving approach to pain management is reinforced by a process of *skills acquisition* and *skills practice*. This framework will be employed below to provide an overview of Dan's treatment.

Reconceptualization

The aim of the reconceptualization phase was to help Dan understand the multidimensional nature of his knee pain, and to provide a rationale and model for CBT in the treatment of chronic pain. Building on the evaluation feedback session, he was encouraged to broaden his perspective of the pain problem to include the several concurrent problems previously identified. In Dan's situation, his pain encompassed inflammation, stiffness, fatigue, and soft tissue and cartilage damage, as well as pain in other sites (e.g., shoulder) as a consequence of using a cane and poor body mechanics. He was asked to identify other areas of his life that had been affected by this condition. In collaboration with the psychologist, Dan acknowledged a low frequency of pleasurable and constructive activities, inactivity and lack of exercise, and occupational disability. He also reported distress that included depressed mood, anxiety about money, negative beliefs about his ability to take a self-management approach, passive coping strategies, and marital dissatisfaction. Concurrent problems — such as obesity, smoking, abuse of prescription medications, and high utilization of health-care services — were also identified.

The CBT model was explained to Dan. He was informed about the relationship among thoughts, feelings, and behaviors, and how these three areas can exacerbate pain, disability and distress. The assumption in CBT is that the way in which people think, feel, and behave in response to their pain condition is learned, and that they are reciprocally related. Dan was asked to describe his symptoms in the context of the CBT model. For example, Dan was able to describe that when he awakens with knee pain his thoughts start racing. He thinks that his pain is never going to go away, that it is only going to get worse, and that he is never going to be able to work again. Dan readily understood that these thoughts led to a depressed mood, increased anxiety, and behavioral consequences. He calls his doctor for more medication, and he calls his lawyer to find out the status of his disability. When his doctor refuses to prescribe more medication without a visit, and his lawyer says there is no news, Dan feels helpless. His thoughts turn to "nobody cares" and "nobody is helping me." His increased sense of despair leads to increased physiological arousal. Thus, Dan is stuck in a vicious cycle in which his thoughts, feelings, and behaviors interact and worsen each other. The cycle also does not have to start with the symptoms. Dan may have first gotten the bad news from the lawyer that his disability hearing was delayed. This may have led to catastrophic thoughts, which then may lead to increased pain.

Skills Acquisition and Skills Practice

The purpose of CBT is to break the cycle. Intervention commonly targets the experience of pain, disability, and distress simultaneously with the expectation that a reduction in symptoms in any one domain may have positive benefits in the other domains as well. Skills training that targets deficits in each of the domains is used to promote effective self-management of the pain condition. For the physiological symptoms, self-regulation techniques such as diaphragmatic breathing and relaxation exercises are commonly taught. Cognitive restructuring, coping skills training, and problem-solving techniques target patterns of negative and distorted thinking, restrictions in the use of cognitive coping skills and a pervasive style of avoidant and passive coping, and perceptions of low self-control and self-efficacy. Behavioral methods — such as training in appropriate goal-setting, contingency management to encourage and reinforce increased productive and pleasurable activities, and stimulus control tech-

niques that target poor sleep hygiene and other health risk behaviors —
are also commonly employed.

The primary aim of the skills acquisition phase is to expose the
patient to a range of new skills and gain some initial success in effecting
the desired cognitive and behavioral changes. Success in this phase of
treatment is viewed as critical in order to encourage continued practice
and, ultimately, to develop an active problem-solving and self-management approach to chronic pain and its associated problems. In the skills
acquisition phase, introduction of each new skill is broken down into small
subgoals that are identified through collaborative problem-solving discussions with the patient. The patient is encouraged to try the new skill not
once, but for a period of time, to see if it has been effective, and to keep
records, in the form of self-monitoring, to determine progress. The patient
is reinforced with verbal praise for completion or partial completion of the
assignments. The therapist and patient work to identify and remove obstacles to progress toward each goal. Based on self-monitoring, and response
to each intervention, assignments are made increasingly more difficult, but
easily attainable to shape the appropriate behavior.

In this treatment phase, Dan was taught several self-regulatory skills
that directly targeted his elevated pain intensity as well as his symptoms
of stress, anxiety, and generalized and site-specific physiological arousal.
These included training in diaphragmatic breathing, progressive muscle
relaxation, and visual imagery. At first Dan was instructed to schedule two
10-minute practice sessions per day in situations with few, if any, distractions. After several weeks, Dan reported being able to induce a relaxed
state in a matter of moments during periods of high stress or pain regardless of distraction. Susan was taught diaphragmatic breathing in a couples
session. Noticing the benefits herself, she served to remind Dan of practicing the self-regulatory skills. Cues placed in Dan's home (e.g., stickers)
were used as signals to scan the body for tension areas and induce a relaxed
state with the skills.

Dan and the therapist worked together to identify behavioral goals
that would target previously identified problems. Problems related to his
functional disabilities (e.g., low frequency of pleasurable and constructive
activities, inactivity and lack of exercise, and occupational disability) and
passive coping style (e.g., prolonged periods of bedrest and overuse of
prescription medications) were most appropriate for behavioral intervention. The therapist worked with Dan to establish behavioral goals to increase activities and exercise, and to decrease bedrest and medication use.
A written contract was made each week (e.g., cooking dinner twice this
week, and limiting bedrest to two 15-minute sessions per day). Verbal

reinforcement and rewards chosen by the patient were used for reinforcement of attaining goals.

It is important to ensure that the client has successes with goal-setting, and that the rewards are meaningful. For example, cooking was meaningful for Dan because it was an activity he previously enjoyed. Goals that were easy enough for Dan to achieve, but hard enough so that they were perceived as challenges, were particularly successful in encouraging general behavioral activation and more specific goal accomplishment. If Dan did not meet the goal, that was an indication that the goal was too difficult. Problem-solving discussions attempted to break these larger goals into smaller components. For example, making dinner was initially too difficult, so the goal was changed to making a salad for dinner twice a week. The behavioral goal-setting procedure was highly individualized to encourage small but meaningful changes in Dan's life.

Cognitive restructuring skills were also used in Dan's treatment. He learned to identify trigger situations that provoked negative feelings, cognitive distortions, and maladaptive behaviors. For example, Dan's wife had become accustomed to preparing dinner every night. When he attempted to fulfill his goal and offer to make dinner, Susan said, "I'll do it, I can do it faster." This situation caused Dan to feel useless and depressed, to think, "I'm not a good father, husband and provider; I'm a failure," and to utilize maladaptive coping strategies like sitting on the couch in front of the TV and letting his wife cook dinner. Dan was taught to identify types of cognitive distortions (e.g., dichotomous thinking and negative self-statements). Dan also learned to challenge his negative thoughts with a variety of strategies (e.g., evaluating evidence for and against being a good father, husband, and provider).

Following a period of initial success with new skills, Dan was encouraged to continue his practice of these skills and increasingly apply them in his daily life. Potential problem areas were identified and became a focus for problem-solving discussions in the sessions with the psychologist. Several strategies were employed to encourage maintenance of gains and to prevent relapse. These strategies are described in some detail in the following sections.

CONCURRENT DIAGNOSES AND TREATMENT

Three concurrent diagnoses were specifically targeted in conjunction with the primary focus on improved self-management of pain. These included Dan's obesity, his use of tobacco, and the major depressive disorder and associated anxiety symptoms. These problems were each specified and elaborated as important targets for intervention during the comprehensive evaluation and feedback sessions with Dan and Susan. As such, they were conceptualized from this initial phase as critical components of an overall treatment plan.

Dan and Susan readily acknowledged that an evolving pattern of overeating and inactivity were direct contributors to his weight gain. It was equally clear that surgical intervention and successful rehabilitation following surgery were contingent on successful weight loss. These perceptions translated into Dan's acceptance of treatment components that directly targeted dietary changes and exercise and activity. Three treatment components were specifically identified. These included consultation with a dietician/nutritionist, engagement in an aquatic exercise program, and psychoeducational group treatment sessions delivered by a psychologist in conjunction with a structured weight management program. The psychologist responsible for delivering the group therapy program was also assigned responsibility for coordinating and monitoring Dan's participation in the dietary counseling and swim programs.

Depression and anxiety, as well as Dan's tobacco use, were specifically addressed in the context of the CBT for pain management. It is important to recognize that major depressive disorder has particularly been noted to have a high coprevalence rate among individuals experiencing chronic pain (Banks & Kerns, 1996). Many studies suggest that the rates of depression may be as high as 50% for individuals seeking specialized treatment for chronic pain, a rate considered higher than for virtually any other acute or chronic illness population. Similarly, rates of anxiety disorders among individuals experiencing chronic pain are also noted to be particularly high. Important interrelationships between the experience of heightened pain, inactivity, and depression and anxiety symptoms have also been extensively studied in the empirical literature on chronic pain. These observations have contributed to a relatively routine effort to address symptoms of depression and anxiety disorders in delivery of psychological treatments, particularly CBT, for chronic pain.

In Dan's case, strategies focusing on promoting behavioral activation, generally, and increases in productive and pleasurable activity, more specifically, were primary tools, designed to promote improved mood in addition to the more obvious and direct goal of decreasing disability. In addition, cognitive therapy techniques designed to identify and reduce the frequency of negative and distorted thinking were also important, both to promote self-management of pain and to reduce depressive thinking. Dan's sleep disorder was targeted via education about the importance of good sleep hygiene, and stimulus control techniques to alter poor sleep habits.

Symptoms of cognitive and physiological anxiety and arousal were targeted via training in the range of self-regulatory techniques already described. As with the strategies for targeting depressive symptoms, this aspect of the therapeutic approach was framed as important in reducing pain, but also was described as important for reducing the experience of stress and indirect effects on pain and disability. The specific importance of learning more adaptive and active approaches to coping with stressful life events, including pain and its associated problems, was emphasized in this context. A model of stress management that emphasized the role of personal responsibility and the possibility of self-control of stress responses was presented. The validity of this model was reinforced by way of collaborative problem-solving discussions in the treatment sessions, by training in specific stress management skills, and by assignment of specific homework targeting improved problem-solving and stress reduction. The aquatic exercise program was also framed as an important component of an overall effort to reduce experiences of anxiety and stress reactivity.

Tobacco use was targeted in the context of a consideration of the importance of adopting a more generally healthy lifestyle. Rationale discourse emphasized the pros and cons of quitting smoking and included specific consideration of factors associated with tobacco use that likely increase the experience of pain and negative thinking (e.g., feelings of guilt and poor self-control). Brand-fading, establishment of a quit date, and gradual reduction of tobacco use were incorporated as specific goals during the treatment process.

COMPLICATIONS AND TREATMENT IMPLICATIONS

CBT for chronic pain has been demonstrated to be effective for a substantial proportion of individuals referred for such treatment, yet problems with engaging a significant minority of referred patients, and problems with nonadherence to treatment recommendations, drop-out, and relapse continue to be concerns. In Dan's case, a major factor thought to be important in determining his successful engagement in treatment was his belief that he had no personal control over his pain, and that he depended on physicians and medications, and ultimately surgery, to relieve his pain. Consistent with this belief, he also perceived that his obesity, overall disability, and level of affective distress were direct consequences of his pain and that these problems were unlikely to be resolved in the absence of surgery and complete pain relief. Conversely, he strongly believed that self-management of his pain was impossible and, therefore, that the likelihood of improvement in his overall situation was low.

The transtheoretical model of behavior change and its recent application in the chronic pain treatment literature proved helpful in informing the evaluation and treatment process (Kerns *et al.*, 1997). Dan's beliefs about lack of value of a treatment program emphasizing self-management and lifestyle change were viewed as being consistent with a *precontemplation* stage of readiness to adopt a self-management approach to chronic pain. That is, he held beliefs that were inconsistent with the self-management approach, and he evidenced little interest in pursuing this treatment perspective during the initial evaluation phase.

On recognizing Dan's lack of readiness for the treatment program that was being developed, his beliefs became a specific target for intervention. Efforts were made to demonstrate an understanding of his reluctance. A discussion involving Dan, Susan, and the internist was held that drew attention to the limitations of the medical perspective and the opportunities associated with a self-management approach. A specific obstacle in Dan's case was that, while he felt the medical approach was limited in its effectiveness, he believed that engaging in psychological treatment or adopting a self-management approach meant that his pain was purely psychological in nature. The internist carefully worked with Dan to discuss the multidimensional nature of pain, and to challenge Dan's all-or-nothing beliefs that his pain had to be either purely physical or purely psychological. Other examples of his experiences were elicited that reinforced a perspective of personal responsibility and the possibility of behavior change and subsequent improvements. These discussions were further reinforced in the evaluation feedback session, and Dan began to consider the potential value of the team's recommendations. His statements began to reflect his willingness to *contemplate* participation in the prescribed treatment program. A decisional balance technique was used at the beginning of treatment to further assist Dan in articulating the pros and cons for a psychosocial treatment approach. Initial successes in the treatment program began to reinforce his developing self-efficacy beliefs and his apparent readiness to become an active participant in his treatment program.

A second major obstacle in Dan's treatment was that he had adopted an identity from his disability. In particular, efforts made to assist him in becoming employed were met with resistance because of his compensation from disability benefits (i.e., secondary gain). In this case, the therapist focused on decreasing Dan's perceptions of disability by helping him to become a more productive member of the household, rather than focusing on outside employment. Targets such as increased exercise, participation in pleasurable family-related activities, and consideration of alternative hobbies and avocational activities were emphasized. Goals more directly related to work were set aside initially, with the expectation that they would be reconsidered pending improvement in other areas of functioning and ultimately in the context of additional vocational counseling and/or retraining.

There are a number of other obstacles that make adopting and maintaining pain management techniques difficult. Treatment regimens involve time and planning that the client may not feel provide sufficient improvement to justify the effort required. Clients may not see a direct correlation between techniques such as relaxation exercises and self-monitoring because of the complex nature of pain that creates fluctuating symptoms. Thus, when a patient experiences symptoms, he or she may be frustrated that the relaxation exercises do not bring immediate relief or interpret exercise as a factor that exacerbates the pain. The client may also neglect doing exercises in the absence of symptoms. Finally, cognitive-behavioral techniques are often not intrinsically motivating. Relapse prevention strategies and interventions targeted at self-reinforcement of pain techniques, even in the absence of pain, are critical to increase adherence, avoid premature termination, and ensure maintenance of treatment gains. Each of these several concerns were relevant in Dan's case, but none posed an overwhelming or unusual obstacle to treatment participation or adherence to treatment recommendations.

A final factor influencing treatment is the response by the spouse to reports of pain from the patient. Susan's "solicitous" style of responding (e.g., taking over a household task such as cooking dinner) to Dan's verbal and nonverbal expressions of pain served to reinforce his role as the patient. Incorporating Susan in the treatment was important in promoting reinforcement of effective coping behaviors (e.g., preparing a salad) and decreasing ineffective coping behaviors (e.g., watching TV while Susan makes dinner).

DEALING WITH MANAGED CARE AND ACCOUNTABILITY

Multidisciplinary treatment, as well as CBT, for chronic pain have been demonstrated to be cost-effective treatment alternatives compared to more expensive and often unsuccessful medical and surgical treatment options

(Flor *et al.*, 1992). These approaches meet managed care expectations in several important ways. Perhaps most important to many third-party payers is the fact that treatment is structured, prescriptive, goal-oriented, and time-limited. For example, CBT has been demonstrated to be effective in as few as eight outpatient sessions. These treatments are thus associated with minimal direct costs that can be clearly specified prior to entering treatment. Prior approval for specific treatment plans and associated costs is particularly consistent with managed care concerns.

CBT also meets managed care goals because it is a treatment that has demonstrated efficacy. Studies have demonstrated clinically significant results compared to no treatment or minimal treatment conditions, and equivalent results to other empirically supported treatment approaches. In a review of empirically supported psychological treatments, CBT has been shown to be efficacious as a specific treatment for pain associated with rheumatic diseases, low back pain, irritable bowel syndrome, and heterogeneous samples of chronic nonmalignant pain conditions. Importantly, among the multivariate outcomes demonstrated, successful return to work has been demonstrated in several efficacy and effectiveness studies of multidisciplinary treatment such as that prescribed for Dan.

Finally, multidisciplinary treatments and CBT have been demonstrated to be associated with significant cost-offset effects, that is, reduction in expenditures for relevant health-care services during the period subsequent to effective pain treatment. For example, one problem area identified during Dan's assessment was a large number of unnecessary health-care visits. When Dan experienced an increase in pain, he would contact his doctor to make an appointment and/or increase his medication. One goal for Dan was to establish doctor visits at regular intervals and to eliminate appointments made for increases in pain symptoms. Consolidation of care by eliminating unnecessary specialist involvement and reinforcement of Dan's relationship with his primary care provider as the sole coordinator of his care was particularly useful in reducing subsequent medical costs.

One concern that has been raised is related to the managed care practice of mental health "carve outs," that is, separately contracting for the management of mental health service delivery systems. In such situations, medical cost-offset benefits of mental health treatment for chronic pain may not be realized directly by the mental health managed care system, but rather may be accrued by the medical managed care system. Mental health managed care systems may, therefore, absorb only the costs associated with interventions such as CBT and may be reluctant to authorize them.

OUTCOME AND FOLLOW-UP

Effectively measuring outcome of chronic pain treatment is critical from numerous perspectives. From the patient perspective, specific, quantifiable feedback may serve to reinforce treatment gains and adherence to a plan of continued self-management. From the perspective of the third-party payer, demonstration of effective treatment is critical in order to justify such treatment approaches. Finally, clear demonstration of positive results can be helpful in creating an incentive for staff in dealing with very complicated and challenging clinical problems.

Treatment that offers pain relief without improvement in disability and distress is insufficient. For example, from the perspective of some third-party payers, especially workers' compensation systems, return to work is a primary concern. As such, a multidimensional approach to evaluating changes in the chronic pain experience is indicated. Evaluation of specifically identified goals or targets for treatment is an important component of outcome evaluation. Readministration of psychometrically sound tests and measures that were administered prior to treatment is also a sound strategy and avoids biases inherent in relying solely on retrospective self-reports of the patient.

At the end of the prescribed active treatment phase, Dan and Susan were interviewed about the accomplishment of specific activity-related goals that had been negotiated prior to treatment and his adherence to the prescribed medication regimen. A diagnostic interview was conducted to evaluate the presence and severity of symptoms of major depression. In addition, Dan completed a packet of questionnaires identical to the one he had completed prior to treatment. Similar evaluations were conducted by the other members of the interdisciplinary team. The data from the evaluation were exchanged in a team meeting, and a formal feedback session was scheduled involving the team and Dan and Susan.

The couple agreed that Dan had made a moderate degree of progress toward meeting each of his activity goals. Specifically, they reported that he was spending substantially less time reclining during the day. He routinely contributed to a variety of household chores, spent considerably more time on a weekly basis with the children, was continuing to participate in the aquatic program, and had begun to develop an daily exercise regimen at home. The couple also agreed that he had reduced his use of prescribed pain medication by 50%. Dan had quit smoking midway through the treatment program. He had exceeded his goal for weight loss, and weighed 266 pounds at the end of treatment. On the several questionnaires, Dan reported a 25% reduction in his average level of pain, a 50%

reduction in his reports of perceived interference and disability, and a 75% reduction in depressive symptom severity. In fact, at the end of treatment Dan no longer met criteria for current major depressive disorder. Level of anxiety symptoms remained virtually unchanged. Other measures suggested a substantial change in Dan's thinking, with specific reference to his experience of pain. He now endorsed a substantial increase in his reliance on active, as opposed to passive, pain-coping strategies, a dramatic increase in perceptions of self-control related to pain, and a strong commitment to maintaining a self-management approach to his chronic pain condition. Dan reported a significant change in Susan's characteristic manner of responding to his expressions of pain. Specifically, he reported, and Susan agreed, that she was much more likely to cue and praise activity, particularly household chores and involvement in family-related activities, and less likely to acknowledge his expressions of pain and disability. Overall, the couple reported an extremely positive view of the treatment program and the outcomes achieved.

At 3 months following treatment, the couple again participated in a formal, albeit less intensive, evaluation. Dan continued to report a reduction in pain, ongoing increases in activity, and a positive mood. He reported that he was continuing to exercise on a daily basis and to participate in the swim program. He continued to abstain from tobacco. He reported few symptoms of depression, and especially acknowledged improvement in his sleep. Importantly, he had lost an additional 12 pounds. The orthopedic surgeon agreed to schedule surgery on his knee.

DEALING WITH RECIDIVISM

The final treatment sessions and three scheduled booster sessions at monthly intervals following completion of the active treatment program were dedicated to anticipating and planning for relapse by identifying future problems. Behavioral coping strategies were developed and practiced to handle these problems. Predicting setbacks was an important part of treatment, so that Dan was not surprised when they occurred. Relapse prevention strategies included: (1) identifying high-risk situations that may increase pain or disability, or decrease mood; (2) identifying early signs of relapse such as increases in pain or disability, or decreases in mood; (3) rehearsing cognitive and behavioral skills for responding to high-risk situations or early signs of relapse; and (4) practicing self-reinforcement for effective coping behaviors. The goal of these strategies was to help Dan take on the role of the therapist for himself after the active treatment ended.

In fact, as already noted, Dan had little difficulty maintaining and expanding on initial treatment gains. He only experienced one significant "pain flare" during the 3 months subsequent to the active treatment phase. In this context, Dan successfully avoided relying on increased doses of pain medication, but rather contacted the team psychologist for some additional emotional support and constructive problem-solving that encouraged his planned use of several active coping strategies, especially activity–rest cycling, mental relaxation skills, and goal-directed activity. Fears of relapse and escalating feelings of helplessness diminished quickly as Dan perceived a sense of mastery and competence in coping with even more severe pain levels.

SUMMARY

This chapter has described application of cognitive-behavioral therapy in the context of an interdisciplinary approach to chronic pain management. A specific case was utilized to provide an example of the common components of this approach. The case exemplified several key aspects of the multidimensional experience of chronic pain and the importance of developing a comprehensive and multimodal plan for treatment that targets the complexity of problems experienced by many individuals.

Several future directions for continued development and refinement of this approach have been cited in the existing clinical and empirical literatures. It has already been noted that several published studies support the efficacy of CBT for chronic pain. However, replication of these studies with larger sample sizes and additional specific pain disorder populations continues to be indicated. Effectiveness studies that are designed to assess the utility of the approach in clinical, as opposed to academic/research, settings are also needed. Importantly, future outcome studies should incorporate methods for assessing cost-effectiveness and cost-offset effects.

Refinements in CBT designed to improve the level of successful engagement of otherwise appropriate patients in this treatment approach, to improve adherence to the treatment recommendations, and to reduce drop-out and relapse rates are also important. Integration of strategies that have been developed and applied in other areas of behavior change — for example, motivational interviewing techniques, patient centered counseling approaches, and relapse prevention strategies — may hold particular promise in this regard. Increased adoption of a prescriptive approach to matching patients with particular problems or characteristics to more specific and individually tailored treatment components may also prove useful in improving outcomes.

REFERENCES

Banks, S. M., & Kerns, R. D. (1996). Explaining high rates of depression in chronic pain: A diathesis–stress framework. *Psychological Bulletin, 119,* 95–110.

Flor, H., Fydrich, T., & Turk, D. C. (1992). Efficacy of multidisciplinary pain treatment centers: A meta-analytic review. *Pain, 49,* 221–230.

Gatchel, R. J., & Turk, D. C. (1996). *Psychological approaches to pain management: A practitioner's handbook.* New York: Guilford.

Kerns, R. D. (1994). Pain management. In M. Hersen & R. T. Ammerman (Eds.), *Handbook of prescriptive treatments for adults.* New York Plenum.

Kerns, R. D. (1996). Family therapy for adults with chronic pain. In R. J. Gatchel & D. C. Turk (Eds.), *Psychological approaches to pain management: A practitioner's handbook.* New York: Guilford.

Kerns, R. D., & Jacob, M.C. (1995). Toward an integrative diathesis–stress model of chronic pain. In A. J. Goreczny (Ed.), *Handbook of health and rehabilitation psychology.* New York: Plenum.

Kerns, R. D., Turk, D. C., & Rudy, T. E. (1985). The West Haven–Yale Multidimensional Pain Inventory. *Pain, 23,* 345–356.

Kerns, R. D., Rosenberg, R., Jamison, R. N., Caudill, M. A., & Haythornthwaite, J. (1997). Readiness to adopt a self-management approach to chronic pain: The Pain Stages of Change Questionnaire (PSOCQ). *Pain, 72,* 227–234.

Turk, D. C., & Melzack, R. (1992). *Handbook of pain assessment.* New York: Guilford.

Turk, D. C., Meichenbaum, D., & Genest, M. (1983). *Pain and behavioral medicine: A cognitive–behavioral perspective.* New York: Guilford.

Sexual Dysfunction

N. McConaghy and M. Lowy

Department of Psychiatry
Prince of Wales Hospital
University of New South Wales
Sydney, Australia

CASE DESCRIPTION

In the initial interview Mr. W. D., aged 37, reported that following an accident 5 years previously his sexual desire had diminished, though he could still get an erection if he saw an attractive woman in the street. A chair had collapsed under him, resulting in his receiving spinal injuries for which he was still receiving regular physiotherapy and pain-killing medication. He constantly needed to change his posture to reduce pain, which he did through this and subsequent interviews, often standing for part of the time. He said that subsequent to the accident he had become lethargic about seeking opportunities to have sexual activity, though he felt he had always been intimidated in sexual situations. His initial sexual experience was at the age of 17, when he ejaculated rapidly. This caused him to avoid further attempts until his early 20s, when he again ejaculated rapidly and his female partner abused him concerning this. Since then he rarely attempted intercourse, mainly when he had been drinking, and then he had difficulty in obtaining or maintaining an erection. This led to him rejecting the advances of women so that he did not establish any noncasual relationships. He added that he had missed out on two terrific women, both of whom were married to other men now. Both were willing to have intercourse with him, and he used every technique to reject this, such as telling them he felt guilt due to his good Catholic background.

At the age of 27, he had a further negative experience following rapid ejaculation when again the woman involved reacted negatively. A few months later he went to a prostitute but was unable to obtain an erection. This increased his tendency to avoid sexual relations with women with whom it was likely he could have had long-term relationships. He considered that he was drinking too heavily at this time and 6 months before the accident attended a residential drug and alcohol rehabilitation program, following which he ceased to take alcohol and has continued to attend Alcoholics Anonymous meetings regularly. At the time of the injury, he was sharing a flat with a woman who made sexual advances to him that he rejected, adding that eventually when he did not have sex "she kicked him out." His comments concerning her indicated that he expected his female partners to be very physically attractive, but he showed no evidence of empathy with her possible feelings of being rejected. He said he continued to masturbate in private using appropriate sexual fantasies but indicated that his erection took longer to develop and was not as full following the injury. Later that year he met a woman he did find attractive, but when she slipped into a negligee he felt too anxious to respond and said his back was causing him too much pain, adding, "I felt terrible, I had to leave. Since then I've been punishing myself." His only subsequent attempt at intercourse was with a prostitute 2 months previously, and he said with her he was shaking and could not get an erection.

In regard to his background, he said that all his siblings had university degrees, and he had always felt inadequate because his father was such an achiever and was critical of him when he was drinking heavily. However, he did reasonably well scholastically in his education as a boarder in a Catholic college, which due to the fees would be available only to middle- to upper-class families. He became a chartered accountant and prior to the accident had a well-paid job from which he resigned to commence drug and alcohol rehabilitation. Following the accident, he was unable to work full-time, so that his income had been markedly reduced. He was unable to play rugby, squash, golf, or tennis, all of which he had played regularly prior to the accident. He said that he was now living alone in a one-bedroom "dive," adding that he could not ask women of his own social or psychological level to visit him there. However, he did maintain friendships with women whom he considered met these standards. He would entertain them at considerable expense, taking them to the theater or opera and to restaurants popular with the socially elite, giving them flowers and other gifts. Currently, he was involved in legal action for compensation that the parties involved were continuing to delay.

TREATMENT CONCEPTUALIZATION

In the initial interview, Mr. W. D. showed evidence of longstanding feelings of inadequacy in relation to both his ability to perform sexually and what he saw as a failure to meet the academic standard expected by his family. At the same time, he clearly saw himself as belonging to an elite group socially and psychologically and expected any woman with whom he formed a relationship to be similarly qualified and to be well above average in physical attractiveness. Though at one level he was aware that his reduced income and physical limitations reduced his ability to attract such a woman, he did not show any evidence of a need to reduce his expectations in this respect.

The initial aims of therapy were to increase his self-esteem and reduce his anxiety about his sexual performance. Investigation to determine if neurological and possibly vascular factors were influencing his ability to obtain an erection was also indicated, particularly in view of the issue of compensation. In our experience, patients' self-esteem is often improved sufficiently by the process of seeing them regularly in the context of a supportive relationship in which positive aspects of their behavior are emphasized while specific treatment is directed at improving their performance in relation to their presenting problem. For such patients, it would seem that over time the fact that a person whom they like and respect is prepared to see them regularly and to express approval of them in itself increases their self-esteem.

In Mr. D.'s case, the series of negative experiences in individual sexual encounters would have continued to reinforce his sexual performance anxiety. It was considered that this could best be reduced by a modified Masters and Johnson approach (McConaghy, 1993), in which he would be encouraged to establish a relationship in which initially he would attempt sexual activity only gradually. Initially this should be restricted to kissing and cuddling while he and his partner remained fully clothed. Only when he felt relaxed in this situation and became aware of becoming sexually aroused and experiencing at least partial erection should he proceed to cuddling and mutual sexual stimulation with himself and his partner naked, having agreed with her in advance that sexual intercourse would not be attempted. However, if either of them desired it they could reach orgasm by masturbation or oral sex. This would require that at an early stage in the relationship he would discuss with his partner the fact that he was having problems and was receiving treatment in relation to his sexual performance. His reservations about his ability to do this were explored and he accepted he would do so. Only when he was regularly obtaining an erection sufficient for intercourse were he and his partner to attempt this.

As his anxiety about possible premature ejaculation could be a factor reducing his motivation to attempt to form a relationship in which he and his partner would ultimately have intercourse, he would be reassured that if this occurred specific treatment for this would be initiated. The specific treatment that would be recommended was the "stop–start" procedure initially recommended by Semans (McConaghy, 1993). His partner would be asked to sit between his legs facing him, and masturbate him. He would monitor his arousal and when he felt he was about to ejaculate tell his partner, who would then cease stimulation until told the sensation had disappeared. She would then recommence masturbation. Subsidence of erection could occur temporarily. As he became aware he could prolong erection prior to ejaculation, his anxiety that he will ejaculate prematurely would diminish. Semans believed that ejaculation occurred more rapidly when the penis was wet, and as the subject became able to prolong erection with the technique, he advised use of a lubricant with masturbation. When the subject could prolong erection indefinitely when masturbated with his penis lubricated, Semans considered the moist surface of the vagina would no longer produce premature ejaculation. Only when the patient maintained erections for a sufficient time was he to attempt intercourse, initially with him adopting a supine position and his partner sitting above him to initiate penetration. If the stop–start technique were not effective, the alternative described by Masters and Johnson (McConaghy, 1993) could be used. When during masturbation ejaculation was imminent, they recommended not temporary cessation, but use of the "penile squeeze." The partner was told to place her first finger on the patient's glans penis, the second finger just below it, and her thumb under it, so she could firmly but not painfully squeeze the glans. This inhibited ejaculation and usually resulted in some loss of erection. Masturbation was then recommenced as with the stop–start procedure.

Another source of anxiety that could reduce his motivation to form a relationship was that he would not obtain or maintain an erection adequate for intercourse. The fact that he considered his erection less adequate following his injury naturally would exacerbate this concern. This was dealt with by informing him that he would be investigated for any organic factors that could contribute to his erectile dysfunction. It was also considered that, even if no such factor were found (and, as will be discussed, negative findings do not totally exclude the possibility that such factors are present), he would be trained to use intracavernosal injection to produce an adequate erection. This procedure would then be available to him as a source of reassurance concerning any anxiety that his erection would remain inadequate as he and his partner continued to cuddle together and sexually stimulate each other while nude. Sildenafil citrate (Viagra) was unavailable at the time, but would seem preferable initially if the patient were able to afford this more expensive alternative.

ASSESSMENT

The range and complexity and, therefore, the cost of techniques for assessing sexual dysfunctions, in particular erectile dysfunction, has increased markedly in the last decade, so that avoidance of unnecessary assessment has become salient. Only assessments should be employed that provide information that will increase the therapist's ability to ensure the best

outcome for the client at the least cost, except when medicolegal considerations require assessments for such additional purposes as providing
objective evidence of a client's disability.

For clinical as opposed to research needs, the unstructured interview
remains the major form of assessment of sexual dysfunctions, as its flexibility as compared to the structured interview allows it to serve a number
of functions. An appropriate relationship with the client can be established
more easily, and if the client finds particular issues difficult to discuss
due to guilt or embarrassment they can be supportively encouraged
to do so. In addition, it enables the clinician to determine whether underlying the client's presenting problem are generalized emotional and relationship problems requiring attention, and it allows investigation of the
possible presence of personality disorders. Such disorder may be of major
importance in determining the outcome of therapy for sexual disorders
(McConaghy, 1993).

Assessment is initiated by asking clients the nature of their problem
or why they have sought help, and responding only as much as necessary
to maintain the flow of information within reasonable limits of relevance.
The reasons given for seeking treatment provide the initial information for
assessing the client's motivations, both conscious and unconscious. Assessors with a more traditional behavioral orientation will seek detailed information concerning the nature of the client's problematic behaviors and the
specific stimulus situations in which they occur. Assessors with a psychiatric orientation will inquire concerning a past history of similar problems,
other illnesses, previous treatment, childhood and adolescent relationships
with parents and siblings, social and sexual relationships and practices,
including coercive sexual acts carried out or experienced, sexual fantasies,
educational and work history, and current domestic, social, sexual, and
occupational situations, including the nature and extent of recreational
interests and activities, and use of recreational drugs, including alcohol
and tobacco, and medications. The possibility of memory or intellectual
impairment may require specific investigation. Severity of depression requires assessment if there is evidence of reduced enjoyment of life events
or of appetite or sleep disturbance. The mode of termination of the clinical
interview is of major importance, and adequate time must be left for this,
so that the client leaves with a clear awareness of the next stage of management and is satisfied with its appropriateness.

In Mr. D.'s case, as indicated above, the clinical interview revealed,
in addition to sexual dysfunction, problems with self-esteem and possibly
unrealistic expectations concerning a partner.

Physical assessments for sexual dysfunction can include, in addition to physical examination and consideration of the effects of any medications, hormonal screening for diabetes, impaired thyroid function, and hypogonadism. Nocturnal penile tumescence assessment may be used to discriminate erectile dysfunction of psychogenic versus organic etiology. More sophisticated investigations include duplex Doppler color ultrasonography usually with intracavernosal injection. Further invasive testing with penile cavernosography is restricted to men whose erectile function is severely compromised (Rosen & Leiblum, 1992). Physical examination enables exclusion of such conditions as Peyronie's disease and hypogonadism.

Erectile disorder, hypoactive sexual desire, and sexual pain disorders are sexual dysfunctions for which investigations are indicated. They are essential in all men with hypoactive sexual desire and in those whose erectile disorder is not situational. Situational erectile disorder is that occurring with some but not other partners, or with all partners but not in private masturbation, where no pressure to produce an erection is experienced. While controversy persists concerning what endocrine screening should be routine to be cost-effective, it would seem that in men under the age of 50 testosterone needs to be measured only in those with low sexual desire and abnormal physical examination and prolactin only in those with low sexual desire, gynecomastia, and/or testosterone less than 4 ng/ml (Buvat & Lemaire, 1997).

With Rigiscan nocturnal penile tumescence testing, Mr. D. showed several episodes of erection on each of the three nights tested, most of the episodes showing a rigidity and expansion within the normal range. It is usually accepted that this normal response indicates that the erectile dysfunction is psychogenic rather than due to vascular or neurogenic factors. However, when Rigiscan assessed base and tip rigidity exceeding 60% of the maximum, direct assessment of buckling force has found that this may be lower than the 550 g considered adequate for vaginal penetration (Allen *et al.*, 1993).

Intracavernosal injection of prostaglandin E1 10 μg produced full rigid erection in Mr. D., indicating that there was no significant vascular impairment. It was not possible to totally exclude neurological damage as in part responsible for the diminution in erectile ability noted by Mr. D. following the accident. Current procedures, including biothesiometry, bulbocavernosus reflex latency, and somatosensory-evoked potential measurements are limited to assessment of the afferent somatic pathway of the pudendal nerve and do not evaluate the autonomic control of penile tumescence (Schaivi, 1992).

TREATMENT IMPLEMENTATION

As Mr. D. reported good erections when he self-injected Prostaglandin E1 10 μg intracavernosally, it was considered that use of the injection would increase his confidence in attempting sexual intercourse. He did so when he visited a prostitute but was aware of a high level of concern that he would not be able to maintain the erection and failed to do so when he attempted penetration. He accepted reassurance that this was due to his high level of performance anxiety and that when this was reduced by a gradual approach to sexual activity in the context of a long-term relationship he would maintain the erection just as he did when he used the injection when alone.

He agreed to attempt to form such a long-term relationship with one of the women with whom he had remained friendly, but it appeared that she would need to meet his high standards, referred to earlier. As it seemed likely that he would not be able to find a partner that would meet these standards, it was considered that strategies should be employed in a attempt to reduce his expectations in a nonconfrontational manner. It was pointed out that some women, though prepared to see him from time to time to be taken to entertainments, might not be willing to form such a long-term relationship with him, as they would be aware of his reduced circumstances and physical limitations. At the same time, his continuing to see himself as attractive physically and in personality was not unrealistic, as he was tall and well-built and had a good social background and interests.

The woman with whom he initially began a more regular relationship, Margaret, was described as attractive and a "high flier," meaning that she had a well-paid position. He continued his pattern of inviting her to expensive entertainments, while telling her that he would like to gradually establish a more intimate relationship. She responded by saying that their relationship would be platonic, and he was uncertain whether in time they could become sexually involved or whether she was merely "using him." Concurrently he had met Pat, whom he had known some years previously when he was drinking heavily. He described her as raring to go, but he did not find her attractive, as she was overweight. I suggested that he attend social events run by an organization called "Parents without Partners," which other patients had found a useful venue for meeting partners. It was also attended by a number of people seeking partners who were not parents. Mainly they were of a lower social class than Mr. D., and it was thought it might make him somewhat more realistic in the standards he set for his partners. He followed this suggestion, indicating that he was motivated to adopt behavioral changes that could help him, but decided that all the woman he met there were unmarried mothers who only talked about their kids.

He discussed possible involvements with other women he had met socially — one a fitness trainer whom he considered might be lesbian, and a stockbroker whom he invited to the ballet. She cooled towards him after he took her to a charity ball mainly attended by the upwardly socially mobile. He had to ask her to leave early, as his back had become very painful. He decided he could not relax with her, as she cut him off when he referred to his emotional sensitivity. He then added that Pat, though plump, was gentle in nature and was very pleased with his response to Alcoholics Anonymous. His interest in Pat was reinforced by the suggestion that personality was important as well as appearance and that in view of his physical problems it would be much easier to establish a relationship with a woman with nurturing qualities. It was suggested that, just as with Alcoholics Anonymous, he could continue to see Pat "a day at a time." He accepted this suggestion, and in the context of their continuing relationship they commenced sexual activity, initially not attempting intercourse as instructed.

He missed attending a few interviews, and when I saw him again a few months later he said this was because he was recovering from an influenza attack. Just subsequent to our last interview, his father had received the Order of Australia, and he felt that this had increased the pressure on him to succeed. In the interval, he had commenced intercourse with Pat using intracavernosal injection, but not telling her he was doing so. He recounted with relish her statements of how impressed she was with the size and strength of his erection. He had not experienced premature ejaculation.

I did not consider it useful to make speculative interpretations concerning possible reasons for his failure to attend interviews but emphasized that he was obviously responding well and that he should be gratified at his ability to overcome his anxiety. I then questioned him about the quality of his erection during the period when he and Pat were cuddling without attempting intercourse. He said that at times it may have been sufficient for intercourse, though it was not as full or rigid as the erection produced by injection. I suggested that their relationship appeared sufficiently established that he could tell Pat he had been using the injections. Indeed, he had already told her that due to the accident his back pain had reduced his confidence about his sexual performance. Once he informed her of this, they could attempt intercourse on the occasions when his erection seemed adequate during foreplay. He could then use the injection if it was not maintained. He agreed to do this and at the next interview reported that on some occasions they were able to have enjoyable intercourse without his using the injection, and he felt comfortable using it when this was not the case. I pointed out that at times, when his erection was not maintained in this situation, rather than using the injection, he and Pat might enjoy their sexual activity using the techniques they had used earlier in their lovemaking in the period prior to attempting intercourse.

CONCURRENT DIAGNOSES AND TREATMENT

As indicated above, in addition to the primary diagnosis of erectile dysfunction, Mr. D. showed personality difficulties reflected both in a longstanding negative self-evaluation in regard to his sexual performance and a somewhat excessive self-evaluation in regard to the standard of sexual partners he could attract. Both these issues were dealt with by encouraging him to form a long-term relationship in which it was expected he would become more realistic concerning them. An additional problem was revealed when at his next interview he reported that Pat wanted a break from their relationship as she felt he was too assertive both in giving her advice and becoming angry when she did not follow it. She also complained about his sexual demands. When she discussed problems in her work, he would tell her how to solve them when she was seeking only reassurance and support. Also, she felt he was using their sexual activity to reassure himself about his performance rather than as an expression of affection and a source of mutual pleasure. Their last meeting had concluded with her asking him not to contact her, but she would contact him when she felt ready. He felt he had been excessively angry in their relationship and attributed this both to his being in more pain, as during his illness he had not been able to carry out his usual exercises in the swimming pool, and also to the insurance company delaying his compensation case further when he expected it was about to be concluded. It was suggested that it could be helpful for Pat to attend a joint interview with him, but he said she believed in natural healing and so had an associated aversion to therapists that would prevent this. In addition to counseling concerning means of correcting his inappropriate behaviors, it was decided to make an audiotape of a desensitization procedure in which he would be trained to relax and then visualize scenarios in which he previously behaved inappropriately but in which he now completed appropriately while remaining relaxed (alternative behavior completion: McConaghy, 1993). He was then asked to listen to the tape at home four times a week.

COMPLICATIONS AND TREATMENT IMPLICATIONS

Priapism is the most serious complication of intracavernosal therapy, though it is relatively uncommon with agents other than papaverine. The likelihood of permanent cavernosal damage if erection lasts more than 7–8 hours is extremely high, so that decompression must be carried out prior to this time and a protocol must be in place for the patient to contact the therapist at all times if the erection persists longer than four hours (McMahon, 1999). Penile fibrosis may be a complication of intracavernosal injection therapy, particularly when papaverine is used. Chew *et al.* (1997) reported that its incidence with prostaglandin E1 varied from 0 to 15%. In their own study of 245 men who had been self-injecting an average of 5.2 times a month for 29 months, 23% were found to have penile fibrosis. They considered it mandatory to examine patients for fibrosis prior to commencement of treatment and at regular intervals subsequently. Patients should be warned of the possibility of this complication and be instructed on how to self-examine so they can report any early changes. As papaverine is potentially hepatotoxic to liver function, it should be monitored if it is used for self-injection. Pain and burning is a further possible complication, which is reported to be more common with use of prostaglandin E1 than papaverine.

External vacuum devices are reported to produce adequate erections when intracavernosal injection fails to do so and to have less severe side effects and higher patient acceptance (Althof & Turner, 1992). These investigators considered the common side effects of hematoma, ecchymosis, and petechiae, and the less common one of discomfort with the tension ring, diminished as the patient gained more experience with use. Due to its ability to potentiate the hypotensive effects of nitrates by producing a large sudden drop in blood pressure, use of sildenafil (Viagra) as an alternative to intracavernosal injection or an external vacuum device is contraindicated in men using prescribed nitrates in any form for treatment of angina pectoris or for recreational purposes. Before prescribing it, resting EKGs should be carried out on men with no history of coronary artery disease who are over 50, or younger men with increased cardiovascular risk factors. Abnormal findings or a history of coronary artery disease now asymptomatic following treatment with nonnitrate medication or surgery make advisable obtaining the opinion of a cardiologist as to its safety (McMahon, 1999).

Hypogonadal patients for whom testosterone supplementation is indicated should be informed that the treatment can produce an increased risk of prostate cancer. They should have rectal examination for prostatic changes and blood prostate-specific antigen (PSA) level estimations prior to initiation of the treatment and at regular intervals while it is maintained. Svetec *et al.*, (1997) advised that any significant increase in PSA level should not be attributed to testosterone replacement but be evaluated.

DEALING WITH MANAGED CARE AND ACCOUNTABILITY

Managed care and the related accountability have not yet been introduced into Australia and so were not an issue in Mr. D.'s management. That he was seeking compensation was relevant in that the universal government-funded system of Medicare that pays the bulk of medical practitioners' fees does not do so while there is a possibility that such fees will be paid for by compensation. Many practitioners are prepared to wait for payment until after the issue of compensation is decided.

A further issue in relation to compensation is that some patients consciously or unconsciously are not motivated to improve, as failure to improve can be reinforced by greater compensation. Patients who show this pattern of illness behavior usually report that prior to the incident for which they are seeking compensation they were in perfect health and showed no evidence of the symptoms they attribute to the incident. In contrast, Mr. D. reported sexual difficulties prior to the accident and throughout his treatment appeared highly motivated to improve with treatment.

OUTCOME AND FOLLOW-UP

When I saw Mr. D. again following his listening regularly to the audiotape for the treatment of his inappropriate anger, he said that Pat had "given him the flick." He was understandably depressed, and I pointed out that even if their relationship were not reestablished he had made considerable progress in dealing with his sexual and relationship problems. On his next attendance, he reported that Pat had called and they agreed to see each other again. He had finally been given a definite date for the compensation court case. Pat had agreed to appear in court to give evidence about his emotional instability in their relationship, but their relationship was to be "on hold" until after the case. He was suffering the additional stress in that his long-term Alcoholics Anonymous sponsor was dying of cancer, and D. was visiting him regularly in a nursing home.

When I saw him after the court case, he and Pat had resumed their relationship. They had commenced using the "rhythm method" rather than condoms for contraception after they both agreed that there was no risk of sexually transmitted disease. Her beliefs about natural healing prevented her from using the contraceptive pill. He felt that the lack of need for condoms had improved his sexual confidence, though he still considered there was some lack of feeling persisting since his back injury. At the following interview, he reported that he and Pat had become engaged and they were looking at houses to buy and planning to have a family soon. He and I agreed on infrequent follow-up over the next 12 months.

DEALING WITH RECIDIVISM

The partners of men whose erectile dysfunction has responded to treatment may respond negatively, particularly if the response has occurred by use of intracavernosal injection or an external vacuum device without their views being solicited or their being involved in the treatment process. They may not be willing to have intercourse when the procedure is used, feeling it results in a lack of spontaneity or in their being treated as a sex object rather than a person. Therapists should bear in mind the consistent finding of community surveys that couples' sexual satisfaction is related to their emotional relationship and not to the presence of sexual dysfunctions (McConaghy, 1993). LoPiccolo (1992), in developing a postmodern sex therapy, emphasized that sexual dysfunctions may play an adaptive role in maintaining the couples' equilibrium and that the therapist should remain alert to this possibility. If the partner were not previously involved in the therapy, this involvement should be sought if the nature of any recidivism suggests the partner's response could be a contributing factor.

SUMMARY

A case history is presented of a man with sexual inhibition associated initially with rapid ejaculation and subsequently erectile dysfunction exacerbated following a spinal injury that was somewhat incapacitating. Despite these difficulties, he had somewhat unrealistic expectations concerning potential female partners. The treatment planned was to encourage him to form a long-term relationship in which his anxiety about his sexual performance could be reduced and his expectations become more realistic. He was trained to use intracavernosal injection to produce an erection to increase his confidence to form a relationship. He established a relationship in which he agreed to approach sexual involvement gradually and not to attempt intercourse initially. He subsequently had successful intercourse using intracavernosal injections. A problem with his excessive anger then became apparent for which additional treatment was effective, and his relationship with his partner is currently progressing satisfactorily.

REFERENCES

Allen, R. P., Smolev, J. K., Engel, R. M., & Brendler, C. B. (1993). Comparison of Rigiscan and formal nocturnal penile tumescence testing. *Journal of Urology, 149,* 1265–1268.

Althof, S. E., & Turner, L. A. (1992). Self-injection therapy and external vacuum devices in the treatment of erectile dysfunction: Methods and outcome. In R. C. Rosen & S. R. Leiblum (Eds.), *Erectile disorders assessment and treatment* (pp. 283–312). New York: Guilford.

Buvat, J., & Lemaire, A. (1997). Endocrine screening in 1022 men with erectile dysfunction: Clinical significance and cost-effective strategy. *Journal of Urology, 5,* 1764–1767.

Chew, K. K., Stuckey, B. G., & Earle, C. M. (1997). Penile fibrosis in intracavernosal prostaglandin E1 injection therapy for erectile dysfunction. *International Journal of Impotence Research, 4,* 225–229.

LoPiccolo, J. (1992). Postmodern sex therapy for erectile failure. In R. C. Rosen & S. R. Leiblum (Eds), *Erectile disorder assessment and treatment* (pp. 171–179). New York: Guilford.

McConaghy, N. (1993). *Sexual behavior: Problems and management.* New York: Plenum.

McConaghy, N. (1996). Treatment of sexual dysfunctions. In V. B. Van Hasselt & M. Hersen (Eds.), *Sourcebook of psychological treatment manuals for adult disorders* (pp. 333–373). New York: Plenum.

McMahon, C. G. (1999, April). *GP Newsletter.* Australian Centre for Sexual Health, Sydney.

Rosen, R. C., & Leiblum, S. R. (1992). Erectile disorders: An overview of historical trends and clinical perspectives. In R. C. Rosen & S. R. Leiblum (Eds.), *Erectile disorders assessment and treatment* (pp. 3–26). New York: Guilford.

Schaivi, R. C. (1992). Laboratory methods for evaluating erectile dysfunction. In R. C. Rosen & S. R. Leiblum (Eds.), *Erectile disorders assessment and treatment* (pp. 141–170). New York: Guilford.

Svetec, D. A., Canby, E. D., Thompson, I. M., and Sabanegh, E. S. (1997). The effect of parenteral testosterone replacement on prostate-specific antigen in hyogonadal men with erectile dysfunction. *Journal of Urology, 5,* 1775–1777.

CHAPTER

Exhibitionism

Barry M. Maletzky
Department of Psychiatry
Oregon Health Sciences University
Portland, Oregon

Effective Brief Therapies: A Clinician's Guide

INTRODUCTION

Although clinically significant advances in understanding and treating the paraphilias have been made in the past two decades, many mental health professionals still believe that deviations, such as exhibitionism, cannot be treated. In fact, with present-day techniques, between 60 and 95% of sexual offenders in treatment can be rendered unlikely to reoffend (Maletzky, 1998). While treatment goals may include enhanced social skills, improved partner communication, and more assertive behavior, lack of recidivism remains the gold standard of therapy, and justifiably so considering community safety. As exhibitionism is rarely punished by incarceration, outpatient programs have remained the venue of treatment for most exposers, underscoring the need for effective supervision by corrections officers, and thorough liaison between treatment and supervisory personnel.

Crucial differences exist between treatment for most mental conditions and for sexual offenders. These stem largely from the involuntary nature of treatment in these disorders. Only rarely does an offender present himself[1] for therapy. Most often, such offenders, including most exhibitionists, are referred by their attorney after being charged with a crime or by a probation officer after sentencing. In fact, most exhibitionists are not inalterably opposed to treatment; they simply would not have sought it on their own. Most offenders, however, become aware that they are in control of their treatment and begin to cooperate with it, and benefit, as well.

However, that point may be reached only after a bumpy journey on a road not easily traveled. Moreover, there is no formula to fit each patient. While a standard set of techniques has been defined for exhibitionism, the manner and timing of their use differs among patients. Hence, the following case, while typical in some ways, must be regarded as simply one instance of how an offender is treated in one particular clinic. A pedophile or rapist might be treated altogether differently, based on diagnosis, manner of offending, and level of commitment to treatment. Hopefully, this case will serve as example of, rather than template for, the many methods in use today for treating the paraphilias.

CASE DESCRIPTION

B. is a 33-year-old automobile salesman who, from his late teens, was in the habit of cruising in his car and staring at women. After he married at 25, this habit diminished but returned to a greater degree by 29, such that he took more opportunities to cruise on his way home from work and on

---

[1]The male gender is usually employed when referring to sexual offenders; over 90% of such offenders in the literature and in clinical practice are male.

weekends. This increased when Mrs. B. was away on business trips in her capacity as a sales representative.

As B. stared at women, he became increasingly aroused and would stimulate himself by rubbing his genitals. He began parking on streets where women frequently passed or in mall parking lots to stare at women and masturbate. Occasionally, a woman who was not aware of what he was doing would look back, or even smile in a friendly fashion; this may have stimulated him to become bolder. He began masturbating as women passed by, then progressed to making sounds so women would look, such as opening a window or coughing. Eventually, he began calling women over, pretending to ask for the time or directions, while openly masturbating. B. described intense pleasure, first at being smiled at, and eventually at being seen. Actual reactions were mixed: Most women left abruptly; a few smiled; fewer still expressed disgust.

At first, B. exposed infrequently. With pleasurable experiences, however, and no severely adverse consequences, the frequency gradually increased, so that by 31 he was exposing three times weekly. At that point, he was charged with indecent exposure after he exhibited himself outside his vehicle. He told officers that he simply had to urinate and was heading for nearby bushes. He escaped prosecution when the victim failed to attend a scheduled arraignment; the charges were dropped.

B. was not as lucky with the index offense. Parked in a lot as two women walked by, he began masturbating and called them over, ostensibly to ask directions. One of the victims noted his license number. Officers arrived at B.'s house within 6 hours. Originally, in full denial, B. entered a *no contest* plea, allowing him the edge of maintaining that this was all a mistake. According to B., he was only scratching a genital rash, an ego-sustaining fabrication allowing him to appease his wife, who was at first horrified by the charge against him. At sentencing, B. received 2 years probation with mandated treatment. Although adamant that he did not need treatment, he was surprisingly cooperative after his initial evaluation, perhaps due to the realization that compliance was essential to complete his probation.

B.'s history was not particularly eventful or traumatic. He was raised by strict parents and, perhaps, developed a sense of relief from scrutiny when not observed, such as when he was at camp or college. This may have contributed to the increased exposing activity when his wife was away on business trips. He did well in high school but dropped out after two semesters in college. On his own and away from home, he spent considerably more time on social rather than educational pursuits and recognized he lacked the maturity to benefit from higher education. Skilled technically, he obtained a series of computer technician jobs, until this field became glutted, which forced him to turn to automobile sales. Although his income improved, it was erratic and never matched his wife's in amount or consistency. Perhaps this fueled resentment toward her. They argued more frequently in the 2 years prior to his arrest, often about the frequency of her business trips. They had no children at the time of B.'s entry into treatment.

This description begs the question of whether, in this case, B.'s exposing was secondary to marital problems. Frequency of exposing increased when Mrs. B. was away, and his resentment of her career might have led to anger displaced onto all females by exposing. Countering this facile explanation, however, was the gradual onset of the exhibitionism arising years before the marriage and the lack of a correlation between frequency and satisfaction of sexual activity, as reported by B. and his wife, and the occurrence of exposing. At many points in their relationship, sexual activities were judged intensely satisfying, yet B. repeatedly exposed. At other times, particularly after arguments, B. and his wife abstained for up to 1 month at a time, yet exposing did not automatically increase. This matches many case reports in the literature and clinical experience: exposing cannot automatically be regarded as a compensatory response.

B. entered treatment reluctantly but was not uncooperative. Strangely, Mrs. B. was even more uncertain about treatment. It would take patience and skill to enroll this couple in the therapeutic process.

TREATMENT CONCEPTUALIZATION

Treatment would certainly be more easily accomplished and effective if B.'s denial were broached first. The ideal medium to achieve this was group therapy. In that venue, pressure could be brought to bear by others who had denied, then admitted, their inappropriate behavior. This modeling effect would be important in accomplishing change. This view accepts the premise that he was guilty; we believed this was so based on his history, victims' accounts, his guilty plea, and the results of his assessment, to be discussed below.

Group also is a low-cost entry into treatment for offenders usually hard hit financially by attorneys' fees, court costs, and fines. By getting acquainted with other offenders, stereotypes are often broken. Many offenders are otherwise law-abiding individuals involved in stable relationships, with jobs and families. By appreciating this, offenders lose the defensive edge that many hold on entering treatment; denial is subsequently lessened as well. Group also offers the opportunity to share with new offenders the basics of a treatment program and to review principles of relapse prevention and cognitive restructuring. Finally, group offers a means of support wherein more experienced offenders can share observations, reinforce positive behaviors, and provide validation of emotions to reassure new offenders they are not alone.

Group approaches alone usually cannot provide the attention that most offenders need. Individual therapy must be employed following an orientation group, so that idiosyncratic modes of offending can be understood and controlled. Sexual arousal is unique to each individual. Within the broad category of exhibitionism, each individual might be aroused by different elements of a situation: the type of victim, the setting, or the type of exposure. Each step of the process must be analyzed and appropriate measures instituted on an individual basis.

It would also prove important to enlist the aid of Mrs. B., not only because she could undo elements of treatment if she were opposed to it, but because she could serve as an important vehicle in monitoring, control, and environmental change.

Although a standard repertoire of techniques is available for therapists treating exhibitionists, each must be modified taking into account the patient's individual characteristics. Methods acknowledged as useful and believed to be necessary in this case included:

1. **Aversive conditioning,** including covert sensitization and assisted covert sensitization (Maletzky, 1991): pairing scenes of exposing with negative images and foul odors.

2. **Aversive behavior rehearsal** (Wickramaserka, 1980): staff observing the patient exposing.

3. **Plethysmographic biofeedback** (Maletzky, 1991): providing feedback to the patient about his erectile responses to enhance self-control.

4. **Masturbatory reconditioning** (Abel & Becker, 1984): pairing deviant imagery with aversive self-stimulation or making such imagery boring by repetition.

5. **Vicarious sensitization** (Weinrott & Riggan, 1997): showing videotapes in which an offender suffers severe consequences.

6. **Relapse prevention** (Maletzky, 1997): outlining steps in the exposing process and identifying points of intervention.

7. **Cognitive restructuring** (Murphy, 1990): identifying faulty cognitive processes.

8. **Empathy training** (Murphy, 1990): familiarizing the patient with exposing's short-term and long-term effects on a victim.

Particularly important in this case, we believed, would be trust-building, followed by aversive behavior rehearsal and plethysmographic biofeedback.

Exposing does not parallel other paraphilias, such as pedophilia or rape, in that attraction to a deviant stimulus is either vague or absent. Deconditioning exposing behavior is thus not as direct as we would prefer. Nevertheless, conditioning procedures are used because they have been shown to work. Their elaboration requires careful planning and collaboration with the patient. Moreover, effective therapy requires more than conditioning alone because exposing constitutes a set of behaviors rather than a set of attractions to deviant stimuli. Indeed, exposing may represent an aberration of a primate urge: the first step a male chimpanzee may take in initiating sexual activity is to expose his erect penis to a female. Therefore, additional techniques (chief among these, aversive behavior rehearsal) and additional partners in therapy (chiefly, a spouse and probation officer) are needed to strengthen treatment.

The therapist addressing exhibitionism cannot employ simple slides or videotapes depicting inappropriate stimuli. Most exposers are attracted to normal sexual stimuli. However, in deconditioning we can use stimuli such as videotapes or audiotapes depicting exposing scenarios and slides of attractive women looking at the camera in an interested or amused manner, combined with suggestions of exposing. It is vital to listen to the patient about what is arousing for him.

We envisioned a 12-week course of an orientation group followed by 4 to 6 months of weekly individual therapy employing the techniques mentioned above and involving Mrs. B. from time to time. This active treatment phase was likely to be followed by six monthly boosters. While this would involve an eventual 15-month treatment course, hardly brief compared to other therapies covered in this text, an average course for similar sexual offenders across the nation now is 36 months, some 12 months longer than B.'s probation. Thus, the 15-month treatment course was shorter than average, yet still within his prescribed period of supervision, altogether a reasonable compromise in his case.

ASSESSMENT

The Clinical Interview

Among technological advances in testing instruments, the clinical interview remains the most direct and comprehensive way to obtain information about the patient. While this needs to be buttressed by other assessment techniques, especially in the case of sexual offenders, who may not always tell the entire story, the interview still provides rich data on which to base treatment. For example, from the interview, we learned about B.'s strict upbringing, his desire for freedom from scrutiny, and his marital problems.

While the goals of the clinical interview for sexual offenders are similar to those for other patients, special focus on sexual developmental history is necessary, including sexual abuse (B. was not a victim; only 27% of sexual offenders are), early sexual experiences, and memories of masturbation fantasies. While sexual exploration in preteen years is normal, a singular experience stood out in B.'s memory. He recalled that at the age of 9 a female cousin 2 years older inadvertently barged into the bathroom while he was bathing. His parents told him to simply avert his eyes while she relieved herself. He recalls a mixture of embarrassment, arousal, and curiosity. He began masturbating at 11 to a fantasy of his cousin seeing him naked.

In other areas of sexual development, B. declared, at times vigorously, to have no abnormalities, not uncommon when obtaining a history from a sexual offender. He claimed to have no problems with potency or premature ejaculation, no interest in deviant attractions, such as to young girls or boys, aggressive sexuality, voyeurism, fetishism, or bestiality. While professionals in this field often discount such idealistic sexual histories as laundered, in fact, we have no objective evidence that most offenders are falsifying their histories. However, many cases are known in which exhibitionism coexists with voyeurism, frotteurism, or obscene telephone calling. Moreover, if we had relied on the interview exclusively, we would not have learned about B.'s prior exposing charge or his chosen means of exhibitionism. Offenders have important reasons not to share information, not only to avoid further prosecution, but to protect egos already wounded by social exposure.

Review of Materials

A review of materials relevant to each case should occur, even prior to a first meeting. Such materials consist of police records, the presentence investigation, and prior psychological evaluations. A review of the presentence investigation revealed several police reports about a man of B.'s description exposing in the general neighborhood. These observations did not meet the criteria needed to generate legal charges, but fueled suspicion that B. was involved.

Psychological Testing

Although psychological assessment procedures are often helpful with other types of disorders, they have questionable value with sexual offenders. A number of assessment procedures have been proposed, such as the Multiphasic Sex Inventory and the Clarke Sexual History Questionnaire. However, these provide information more readily obtained through personal interactions. Attempts to correlate sexual offending with responses on a variety of instruments, such as the MMPI, have revealed no personality pattern indicative of offending. We, therefore, administered no psychological tests to B.

The Polygraph

Controversy has surrounded use of the "lie detector" since its inception decades ago. Yet its significance has been enhanced in recent years in evaluation and treatment of the sexual offender. Some studies (Ahlmeyer & Heil, in press) have demonstrated a greater openness just prior to and after a polygraph in offenders when compared to those not required to undergo such testing. While the device cannot prove guilt or innocence, its use has enabled many offenders to benefit from treatment to a greater extent.

Prior to his plea, B. was enjoined by his attorney from taking a polygraph, but the test was mandated at sentencing. B. was shaken to learn that, while he passed all other questions, he showed evidence of deception on questions about exposing, not only related to the present offense but those in the past. At the time, he claimed to be nervous, but this finding, coupled with group pressure and plethysmograph results (described below), prompted his first confession 3 weeks after his test.

The polygraph continued to be important in B.'s treatment. At random intervals, generally at 3 months, he was asked to complete an interval test. Prior to the test, the therapist would urge him to be honest: "We want you to pass this test; so let's review everything that's happened recently to make sure you get it off your chest." We believe this approach is appropriate for patients who pose potential risks to the community.

The Penile Plethysmograph

Originally designed to assess impotence, the plethysmograph has become widely used to measure sexual preferences. Figure 13.1 depicts the instrument and its penile gauge. B. placed this small gauge around his penis and listened to, and viewed, scenes of exposing and of other sexual activities, including normal sex, sex with boys and girls, and aggressive sex. During this time, the plethysmograph was recording his penile circumference

Figure 13.1. The penile plethysmograph and gauge. Courtesy of Behavioral Technology Inc., 24 M Street, Suite 1, Salt Lake City, UT 84103.

changes. It is surprising, given the intrusive nature of this assessment, that deviant arousal patterns *are* often seen.

Offenders are capable of faking suppression of deviant arousal. Moreover, the nature of exhibitionism does not lend itself well to plethysmography. Modern plethysmographs, however, incorporate tests to ensure attention to stimulus presentations and add measurements of GSR and respiration to enhance validity of response. Ratios of deviant to nondeviant arousal can also be employed to compare the presence and severity of offending potential. Many studies (reviewed in Howes, 1995) have demonstrated the reliability and validity of plethysmograph tests for many types of offenders. Indeed, most men without a history of exposing will not become aroused when listening to or watching exposing scenes.

Unfortunately, many offenders show no arousal to any stimuli. Such results should never be used as proof that a problem does not exist or that treatment is not needed. However, false positives are rare. Therefore, when B. showed arousal to consenting heterosexual scenes and to audiotapes describing exposing situations, we were suspicious that he had an exposing problem and hopeful that we could use the plethysmograph in providing treatment and assessing its efficacy. B.'s initial plethysmograph findings are reproduced in Figure 13.2.

These findings, combined with the evidence of deception on the polygraph and the criminal clinical history, indicated a problem of exposing. This underscores the importance of using multiple assessment techniques, especially because initial evaluations, and later treatment reports, may be used as a basis for decisions regarding parole or probation, adequacy for supervision, and need for community safety.

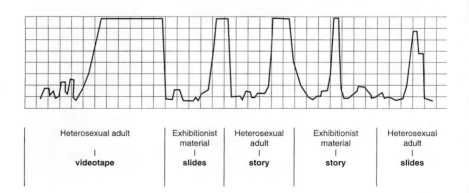

Figure 13.2. Initial plethysmograph tracing.

Assessment of Risk

Professionals are often asked to render opinions of risk to authorities. While a complete literature exists about such assessment (Hanson & Bussiere, 1998) beyond the scope of this chapter, a review of B.'s case reveals factors involved in predicting risk, taken from a variety of studies and presented in Table 13.1, with those applying to B. marked appropriately. However, these models are derived from studies with pedophiles, child molesters, and rapists. While factors such as job and relationship stability and prior criminal history *may* be related to recidivism with exhibitionists, the number of victims and relationships to them, as well as the use of force, may be tangential. No study to date has attempted to predict risk in exhibitionists alone.

TABLE 13.1

Factors Indicating Risk to Sexually Reoffend

1.	Multiple victims*
2.	Victims both male and female
3.	Male victims
4.	Multiple paraphilias
5.	Victims not well-known to offender*
6.	Victims not living with offender*
7.	Extrafamilial victims*
8.	Force used in the sexual offense
9.	Presence of pretreatment deviant arousal*
10.	Denial
11.	Refusal to enter treatment
12.	Past treatment failure
13.	Past supervision violation
14.	History of nonsexual criminal activity
15.	Developmental disability
16.	Unstable employment history
17.	Unstable history of relationships

*Factors that apply to B.

TREATMENT IMPLEMENTATION

Orientation Group

Following the assessment process, B. was assigned to Orientation Group. Table 13.2 lists the components of each group session. These groups were

TABLE 13.2

Components of an Orientation Group

GROUP ONE Why am I here? Common problems of sexual offenders	GROUP SEVEN Relapse prevention Four interventions discussed
GROUP TWO What is treatment? Cognitive and behavioral theory overview Change and choice	GROUP EIGHT Typology of offenders Etiology of offenders
	GROUP NINE Victim empathy Assessment overview
GROUP THREE Polygraph and penile plethysmograph Probation and parole (guest parole officer)	GROUP TEN Cognitive distortions Self-talk Fantasy
GROUP FOUR Behavioral techniques overview (Aversive conditioning, positive conditioning, etc.) Vicarious sensitization tapes viewed	GROUP ELEVEN (guest therapist) The clarification process Family and marital therapy Social skills
GROUP FIVE Power and control Sexual offender deviant cycles	GROUP TWELVE Sexual impulse control training Treatment planning
GROUP SIX Deviant cycles (continued) High risk situations	

Additional group components

Completion of workbook

Completion of polygraph examination

Completion of penile plethysmograph

Weekly homework

Reading handouts and completing worksheets

Group exercises

Treatment progress report sent to referral source every 4 weeks

partly didactic and included a heterogenous array of 8–10 offenders. As part of group, B. underwent polygraph and plethysmograph tests. After listening to offenders describing their experiences and, following the polygraph and plethysmograph results, B. admitted to a problem with exposing during the eighth session, an effort for which he received significant support.

Group provided a didactic and expressive forum in which B. received information and was encouraged to tell his story. He learned about chains of deviant behavior, triggering stimuli, and ways to abort the offending process early on. He had never considered that his behavior created victims; by examining how a victim of exhibitionism might be affected (increased anxiety and fear of venturing out alone) and how his justifications affected self-scrutiny ("I'm not making physical contact; therefore, I'm not hurting anyone"), B. came to a better appreciation of the need to invest effort into change. By discussing concerns about his marriage, he was opening the possibility for change in that area as well.

Group also allowed clinic staff to carry out an ongoing process of evaluation. Therapists and the clinic director met to review the evaluation, the polygraph and plethysmograph results, and the reports of group performance. Following completion of group, the team recommended continuing treatment on an individual basis specifically targeting deviant arousal and exposing behavior.

Individual Therapy

When B. learned of the recommendations for individual therapy, he was reluctant and pointed out the gains made in group. However, he agreed, perhaps with the knowledge that refusing might provoke probation problems. The first three individual sessions were devoted to trust-building. As treatment progressed, the therapist began a series of techniques specific to B.'s offending history. Most sessions included a mixture of techniques, with much overlap and sequence shifting based on individual circumstances. Each weekly session consisted of approximately 1 hour of treatment. After 6 months, sessions were decreased to monthly for 6 additional months to provide boosters strengthening initial change.

Aversive Conditioning

The therapist reviewed scenes of how B. usually exposed, then tape-recorded six scenes, adding endings that were decidedly aversive:

> You are driving to the store when you see several attractive women in a parking lot. As you stare at them, you become very excited, have an erection, and massage your penis through your pants. A brunette walks by, really close. She's about 27 and really well-built. You can see her body and you're getting excited. You

unzip your fly and pull your penis out. You masturbate as she
watches. You want her to see how big and aroused you are. You
call her over to the car and she approaches with a smile. There's
another woman behind her . . . it's your wife! She's coming
over! You're getting sick to your stomach. She might catch you
in the act. Chunks of your lunch catch in your throat. You try to
gulp them down but can't. You vomit into your lap and onto
your penis. It's disgusting to be exposed like this. You quickly
clean yourself and drive away quickly before your wife can
recognize you. As you get away from exposing you feel better.
You can breathe the fresh air coming in through the window as
your stomach settles down and that horrible smell is gone.

While such scenes on their own constitute *covert sensitization*, B.'s
therapist strengthened their aversive nature by presenting a foul odor
(rotting meat and feces) at the point where aversive imagery began, then
removed it on escape from the deviant behavior. The addition of an actual
aversive stimulus changed the technique into *assisted covert sensitization*.

B. was asked to listen to these scenes at home using a bottle of foul
odor four times each week. However, B.'s therapist did not assume he
would follow through and performed the procedure in office sessions as
well, presenting three scenes each session during a total of 15 out of 25
sessions. The therapist also asked B. to view videotapes and slides of
exposing situations while pairing them with foul odors. These types of
pairings were done during 8 of the 25 sessions. This was done even after
the plethysmograph revealed a marked decrease in deviant arousal by the
10th session. Aversive conditioning was not contingent on demonstration
of deviant arousal, because the plethysmograph cannot be relied on to
provide totally accurate information due to false negatives.

Aversive Behavior Rehearsal (ABR)

While this procedure has provoked controversy, it is believed to produce a
marked reduction in urges to expose. As opposed to all other techniques
devised for sexual offenders, its use was originally intended specifically
for exhibitionists.

After building trust, B.'s therapist described the procedure and obtained his written consent. On three occasions thereafter, B. was asked to
expose to his male therapist and one female and one male staff member in
situations comparable to his real-life exposing. The therapist asked B. to
drive to a vacant parking lot, call staff to his vehicle, expose, and attempt
to masturbate for 3 minutes. Under these conditions, B. experienced no

arousal, but, instead, anxiety and embarrassment, turning a previously reinforcing situation into an aversive one. Following each such session, B.'s therapist met with him to review his feelings and provide support. While it might have proven more convenient to have B. expose himself in a laboratory setting and, indeed, most ABR sessions are performed that way, reproducing as closely as possible the actual situation in which B. exposed proved helpful in generalizing treatment effects.

The anxiety caused by this procedure can be severe, and, while it can be expanded to treat other types of offenders (such as having a child molester show with life-size dolls how he abused a victim), it is essential to explain the procedure thoroughly beforehand and provide support immediately thereafter. Some offenders refuse this approach, even under conditions of supervision. It should not be made a requirement of treatment, except in resistant and dangerous cases.

Plethysmographic Biofeedback

During eight sessions, B. was asked to attach the plethysmograph gauge, then listen to or observe scenes of exposing while watching a series of biofeedback lights. These lights were connected to the plethysmograph such that each 5% of arousal illuminated one bulb above the next in a vertical series. If none of the bulbs were lit, there was no arousal. If 10 were lit, there was 50% arousal; if all 20 bulbs were lit, there was 100% arousal. By viewing the lights, B. could gain immediate feedback on his level of arousal.

During early sessions, the therapist asked B. to allow arousal to exhibitionist material, then try to reduce it by 50%. In subsequent sessions, B. was asked to lower his arousal, eventually below 10%. During some of the later sessions, he was instructed to try to increase his arousal to normal stimuli while keeping deviant arousal as close to zero as possible. B. was able to achieve these levels and gain a sense that he was controlling his arousal, as opposed to other techniques in which he was a passive recipient of conditioning.

Masturbatory Reconditioning

During sessions 5 through 15, B. was asked to masturbate four times each week to scenes of exposing until the point of ejaculatory inevitability, at which point he was then asked to switch to scenes associated with normal activity. He was then asked to make that switch earlier and earlier in the course of masturbation until, by the 14th session, he was masturbating entirely to normal fantasies. This had the effect of gradually fading out deviant fantasies and strengthening normal ones.

Also, between sessions 15 and 20, B. was asked to masturbate to normal fantasies three times each week until ejaculation, then to continue masturbating for 30 minutes thereafter to deviant fantasies. This paired exhibitionist fantasies with the point of minimum possible arousal and created a boring and aversive situation connected with those scenes.

For the fantasy change and satiation techniques, B. was instructed to speak his fantasies aloud and tape-record the sessions in his home, then allow his therapist to privately listen to the tape. This partially ensured compliance; trained therapists can often detect faking in these difficult assignments.

Vicarious Sensitization

In this procedure, B. viewed a series of videotapes depicting adverse consequences of offending. Table 13.3 lists some of the themes conveyed in these tapes. While B. had viewed four tapes in the orientation group, individual viewing is thought to help avoid the diluting effect of group therapy, where it was easy for B. to distance himself from other offenders. Unfortunately, the tapes were not extended to include exhibitionism. Nevertheless, they may have had a generalized effect. Many of the scenes elicit a visceral rather than simply a cognitive reaction. In one scene, a victim

TABLE 13.3
Vicarious Sensitization Videotaped Vignettes

1. An experienced inmate describes the brutal rape of a young male sexual offender in prison; the offender is chased across the prison yard.

2. Neighbors, outraged about an offender's sexual abuse of several girls in their community, chase, then corner him, force him to undress, and subject him to cruel ridicule.

3. A victim describes the revenge she would like to extract from her offender while, on-screen, scenes are shown of an actual surgical castration and phallectomy.

4. An adolescent offender is shunned by several groups of high school girls, who whisper about him, point, and make jokes; he complains to friends, who remain unsupportive, that he cannot get a date.

5. Several victims are shown in various states of psychological disarray because of their sexual abuse: a young girl attempts suicide; an older woman mourns her life traumatized by the sequelae of the abuse.

describes what she would like to do to an offender off-screen, while a castration is shown on-screen.

It is difficult to know to what extent each single technique contributes to overall treatment efficacy because research isolating techniques and exposing some offenders to placebo conditions are difficult and ethically uncertain. B. identified vicarious sensitization and relapse prevention as the two most helpful techniques eliminating attraction to exposing.

Relapse Prevention (RP)

A mainstay of most sexual offender treatment programs, RP derives in part from treatment efforts initially directed against alcoholism. B. was asked to describe a chain of deviant behavior, beginning with antecedent conditions (driving or shopping alone, wife going on a trip), attendant emotions (frustration, anger, sense of freedom, sexual arousal), preparatory behavior (driving to a parking lot, general self-stimulation), usual mode of exposing, and emotions thereafter (pleasure mixed with guilt).

This process made B. more aware of predisposing conditions and helped him develop a personalized RP plan:

1. B. agreed to drive the same route to and from work each day. This route was not the most direct, but it avoided the shopping centers where B. had exposed in the past.

2. B. called his wife when he arrived at work and when he left. She knew how long the drive took.

3. B. agreed to never shop alone.

4. B. agreed to never drive alone, except to and from work.

5. B. agreed to allow his wife's sister to be his monitor when Mrs. B. was away. He called her at designated times to report his whereabouts, estimated time of arrival, and so on.

6. B. agreed that certain areas, where he had exposed before, were off limits.

7. Mrs. B. agreed to limit her business trips to a minimum.

8. B.'s probation officer participated in joint meetings to help formulate these plans.

9. B. carried out assignments in a workbook for sexual offenders (Eldridge, 1998) that details steps in the RP process.

Cognitive Restructuring

B. entered treatment with assumptions common to many sexual offenders. He was asked to explore messages he gave himself about exposing. Table 13.4 lists examples among men who expose, with those which B. expressed marked with an asterisk. While behavioral and emotional changes are required for treatment generalization, these messages could have allowed B. to continue exposing without self-scrutiny. B.'s therapist challenged his assumptions that he was hurting no one or that he was different from other offenders. He was then able to grasp more personally the need to monitor his automatic assumptions and challenge them aggressively. B. was also asked to keep a log of the times he caught himself with these preconceptions and the mental steps he took to counter them. Through self-tracking, additional antecedents, such as anger after arguing with his wife, surfaced.

TABLE 13.4
Examples of Assumptions and Justifications among Men Who Expose

Category	Self-statement
Attributing blame	"The way she was dressed, she was just asking for it." "I wouldn't have done it if I hadn't been drinking."
Minimizing, or denying, sexual intent	"I was just looking for a place to pee."*
Debasing the victim	"She was a slut anyway." "She was always a liar."
Minimizing consequences	"I never touched her, so I couldn't have hurt her."* "Exposing is no big deal." "She smiled, so she must have liked it."*
Deflecting censure	"It's not like I raped (or molested) anyone."* "This happened months (years) ago; why can't everyone forget about it?"
Justifying causes	"If I wasn't molested, I wouldn't have exposed." "If my wife weren't away so much, I never would have exposed."*

*Those which B. initially endorsed.

Empathy Training

Although considered separately by most therapists, empathy training is an extension of cognitive restructuring in that it enhances awareness of the suffering that offending can cause. B. was asked to read and listen to victims' experiences in their own words and voices. Most exhibitionists are surprised at the extent of harm exposing may cause. The tone in these sessions was not harsh or accusatory; rather, the therapist allowed B. to reach his own conclusions based on the evidence. He was then encouraged to write letters (that he would not send) to several of his victims describing his patterns of exposing, his motivations, and apologizing for his behavior — an exercise, but a helpful one, nonetheless. Through consistent exposure to the victimization process, B. was better able to put his behavior into perspective and less able to deny its impact on others.

Marital Counseling

Beginning at the 12th session, B. was referred to a specialist in couples' counseling. While this counseling could have been undertaken by his own therapist, the marital issues seemed serious enough to warrant specialist intervention. Through this therapy, Mrs. B. altered her perception of treatment to a more positive image. During several sessions, some of the RP procedures involving Mrs. B. were reviewed. Her observations and suggestions proved helpful in providing information about B. and resolving some of their conflicts. For example, B. agreed to spend 2 hours three times each week with his wife without their children to discuss the week's events. Mrs. B.'s participation appeared to enhance his treatment efforts, perhaps with the message that he was not the only one who needed to change.

Booster Sessions

By the 20th session, B. showed no deviant arousal and had passed all polygraphs at 3-month intervals. He was asked to return for one session each month during the next 6 months to undergo assisted covert sensitization and to discuss ongoing RP efforts. The booster sessions were designed to provide reinforcement and generalization of treatment effects. B. kept his logs over that period and reviewed them with his therapist as well.

CONCURRENT DIAGNOSES AND TREATMENT

In treating exhibitionism, it is important to be aware of comorbid disorders. Particularly prominent are voyeurism, frotteurism, obscene telephone calling, and hypersexuality (Freund & Watson, 1990). B. denied any of these deviant patterns, and no evidence could be found that they existed. Nonetheless, an emphasis in treatment is responsible sexuality, with an eye toward preventing further abuse. Procedures of sexual impulse control, safety in sexual relationships, and the morality of sex are discussed, usually at group level. B. participated well in these discussions, although their eventual impact is not testable at this time.

Depression and alcoholism are believed to be present more often in sexual offenders than in the general public. Fortunately, B. had no evidence of these afflictions.

COMPLICATIONS AND TREATMENT IMPLICATIONS

One of the possible complications of aversive conditioning is generalization to nondeviant stimuli. B. expressed a fear that he might experience diminished arousal to normal sexual stimuli, especially because many of the stimulus configurations approximated normal sexual scenes. However, few, if any, cases have been reported in which a patient loses arousal to normal stimuli, possibly because of the specificity of the deconditioning techniques. B. experienced no reduction in normal arousal throughout treatment.

Most offenders do not enter treatment voluntarily; this can alter expectations and cast a therapist and system *against* the patient, leading to a decrease in trust. This situation has yielded challenges but has proven workable through careful trust-building involving reflective listening techniques and a nonjudgmental demeanor. By respecting B., and allowing him initially to maintain the dignity of denial, the therapist instilled sufficient confidence so that he was eventually able to openly discuss his exposing.

DEALING WITH MANAGED CARE

Most insurance carriers, including Medicare, argue that sexual offending is a choice, not an illness. Lacking any scientific evidence otherwise, providers have been unable to alter this perception. However, as with the drug and alcohol treatment movement of the 1980s, mandated coverage for sexual offender treatment has been considered in several states. Although B. worked steadily and had the means to pay for sessions, he often expressed resentment for having to pay for mandated treatment. B.'s therapist listened to his arguments, expressed concern about his finances, and worked out a schedule of partial payments.

ACCOUNTABILITY

The sexual offender may pose a threat to the community during treatment if another crime occurs. Therefore, B.'s therapist provided monthly reports to his probation officer detailing the progress of treatment and plethysmograph and polygraph results. During two sessions, B.'s probation officer participated in discussing his program and the role the therapist might play in B.'s RP plan. At the end of treatment, B.'s therapist and the clinic director prepared a report to his probation officer detailing what was accomplished and the steps B. should take to prevent lapses.

Because B. was treated as an outpatient, an initial concern was his safety to be at large. Actuarial prediction schemes for risk have been published; however, these relate to child molesters, pedophiles, and men who rape. Risk has not been as extensively studied in exhibitionists. Nonetheless, B. displayed some of the general predictors of risk for sexual offenders outlined in Table 13.1. He also showed signs of safety. We believed he could be safely treated in the community as the risk for reoffending is lowest in the few months following arrest, allowing time to promote treatment change.

OUTCOME AND FOLLOW-UP

The means employed to measure success in treating sexual offenders are under constant scrutiny due to concerns about repeat victimization. While self-report and patient and therapist rating scales are helpful when assessing outcome with a voluntary patient population, we could not rely entirely on subjective impressions to ascertain B.'s safety to be at large. Therefore, a variety of outcome measures were employed to measure progress.

Disclosure

While not measurable, the level and quality of disclosure about sexual offending remain important elements in determining treatment efficacy. Although treatment could have proceeded in the absence of a full admission of complicity, it would have been slow and contentious. Fortunately, through the orientation group, B. talked about his offending. His disclosure was never complete, as he maintained that some of the incidents were mistakes. However, we believed that it was crucial to reinforce disclosures that did occur. Thus, we did not push for admission of every detail, allowing B. latitude in the interest of enhancing the therapy process. However, some clinicians believe that *full* disclosure is necessary.

One of the elements of disclosure is not only admission of the problem to a therapist or group but to people affected by the crime. B. was able to tell his wife about his exposing, perhaps hastened by the realization that she would be called into therapy. Some offenders require help from a therapist in telling a partner or family member. Such sessions are valuable, even when the offender has made in-home disclosures, to be certain the admission is reasonably complete.

Sexual Logs

Although self-reports cannot be relied on exclusively in measuring treatment effects, they are helpful with roughly gauging progress and compliance. B. kept a log of overt (intercourse and masturbation) and covert (fantasies, urges and dreams) sexual acts daily. Overt exhibitionist acts declined from a baseline of 6 each week to 3 at 3 months and a reported 0 at 6 months and at 1- and 2-year follow-ups. Similarly, covert exhibitionist acts declined from 15 each week at baseline to 5 at 3 months and a reported 0 at 6 months and at 1- and 2-year follow-ups.

Reports of a Partner

Another person's observations can be important in assessing outcome, even if the observer is not always objective. Mrs. B. verified that B. maintained the house and community rules jointly established at the beginning of treatment and that he was listening to homework tapes. She could detect no evidence of exposing or deviant fantasies by the end of treatment and at 1 and 2 years. It is possible that B. simply became more skilled at hiding exposing events, although with the accumulation of evidence from many follow-up visits this appeared unlikely.

The Polygraph

B. had failed several questions about exposing on his initial, full-disclosure polygraph. With disclosures in group, repeat polygraphs at 3, 6, 12, and 24 months revealed no further evidence of deception, with B. claiming no further exposing. At the 6-, 12-, and 24-month sessions, he claimed no further deviant fantasies or urges. While a polygraph cannot be used alone to determine if events did or did not occur, in combination with the other measures described it was reassuring to see this evidence of treatment effect.

The Penile Plethysmograph

B.'s abnormal arousal to exhibitionist stimuli provided a baseline that could repeatedly be measured to assess treatment progress. Thereafter, the plethysmograph was utilized in every other treatment session, not only to measure ongoing treatment efficacy, but to monitor reactions during conditioning sessions. Foul odors were effective in reducing arousal, at least within sessions. Generalization, however, could not be guaranteed from B.'s results. A plethysmograph at the end of treatment, and at 1- and 2-year intervals, showed continued absence of deviant arousal, with maintenance of normal arousal. Figure 13.3 depicts B.'s plethysmograph at the end of treatment. These tests were conducted with novel stimuli to guard against accommodation.

An additional technique to protect against faking, aside from requiring attentional responses, is to determine inhibition of response. In testing sessions, B. was first shown normal stimuli, which elicited an erectile response. The time to detumescence was recorded on presentation of an exposing stimulus. Some studies have shown that offenders take longer than normal males to suppress an erection when faced with a deviant

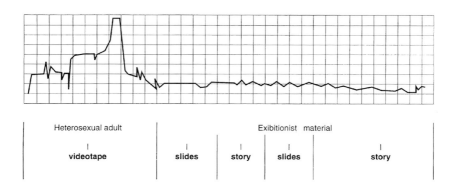

Figure 13.3. Final plethysmograph tracing.

stimulus. Indeed, B. at first could not suppress his erection to exhibitionist scenes, even when instructed to. However, by the third month the time to detumescence was less than 20 seconds, just slightly greater than normal in our clinic. By 6 months, no deviant arousal was noted.

Criminal Records Search

Computerized police records can be searched for any evidence of a sexual crime at any time during or after treatment. Checking official records revealed no additional sexual crimes that B. had not divulged. Further record checks at 3 and 6 months and at 1- and 2-year follow-ups revealed no repeat charges or arrests.

Despite efforts at follow-up, the permanency of treatment has always been in question. With his permission, B.'s data were entered into the records of our ongoing outcome project in which strict criteria are used to define success:

1. Treatment completed with greater than an 80% attendance rate.

2. No overt or covert deviant sexual behavior in the last year.

3. Passing most recent polygraph.

4. No evidence of deviant arousal on latest plethysmograph.

5. No evidence of new charges for a sexual crime.

Table 13.5 presents outcome data from more than 8000 offenders treated in our clinic since 1973, based on primary sexual offending diagnosis and employing the above criteria. These are raw data and should not be interpreted as representing controlled research. Fortunately, a number of smaller and better controlled studies in our literature (reviewed in Maletzky, 1998) have documented equal success rates in similar programs.

DEALING WITH RECIDIVISM

Not all exhibitionists are as successfully treated as B. While we cannot be certain B. will *never* commit another sexual crime, indicators appear posi-

TABLE 13.5

Percentage of Offenders Meeting Criteria for Successful
Treatment Outcome ($N = 8,000$)[a,b]

Type of offender (N)	% (N)
Child molester, female victim (2,416)	93.7 (2,264)
Child molester, male victim (840)	90.6 (761)
Heterosexual pedophile (1,112)	90.3 (1,004)
Homosexual pedophile (1,376)	83.7 (1,152)
Exhibitionist (1,760)	86.5 (1,522)
Rapist (496)	78.8 (391)
Total (8,000)	88.7 (7,094)

[a]Criteria for successful outcome: (1) completed all treatment sessions; (2) no overt or covert deviant sexual behavior; (3) no evidence of deviant arousal on plethysmograph; (4) passed exit polygraph; (5) no record of any sexual crime during or after treatment.

[b]Follow-up periods ranged from 1 to 25 years.

tive. Booster sessions are helpful in this regard, as are group sessions, which are offered free after formal therapy ends.

When an offender lapses (has urges) or relapses (commits incidents), a number of approaches should be considered:

1. **Plethysmographic reassessment**. Has deviant sexual arousal reoccurred? If a different type of offending has occurred, is there other deviant arousal? It is not uncommon for exhibitionists to sexually offend in other ways, such as inappropriate touching (frottage), peeking, voyeurism, and obscene telephone calling. Unfortunately, a plethysmograph cannot be specific here, nor in men with hypersexuality. Nonetheless, a plethysmograph for reassessment can be valuable as a first step in analyzing treatment failure.

2. **Additional techniques**. If exposing has reoccurred, additional and diverse means of employing ABR might be helpful. The therapist should also help the patient identify the earliest steps in a chain leading to new deviant behavior, and implement ways to block these precursors. The offender's partner should be included in some of these discussions as well. If deviant arousal is present, additional aversive conditioning, perhaps using novel unconditioned stimuli, such as foul taste, should be considered.

3. **Referral**. If drug and alcohol abuse are compromising recovery, referral to a specialized program should be considered. If a psychiatric disorder is present, referral to a psychiatrist might be worthwhile. More commonly, a difficult decision must be made about whether the present program is appropriate and flexible enough to serve this particular patient. Referring the patient to a different therapist in the same clinic or to another clinic should be considered before determining that the patient cannot be treated, especially if progress appears to be blocked by lack of trust, personality conflicts, or communication struggles between therapist and patient.

4. **Medication**. In a few dangerous offenders, medication to reduce sexual drive might be helpful, particularly in cases when an offender remains in the community but cannot control impulses to molest or to rape. Even in cases of mandated medication by a court or corrections division, informed consent is necessary. While serotonin-reuptake inhibitors such as Prozac are reported to lower sexual drive, the chief medication employed for reducing drive is depo-Provera. Dangerous offenders receiving bimonthly injections have rarely reoffended (Grubin & Mason, 1997). Unfortunately, medication can never be regarded as the sole treatment for sexual offending because most men will discontinue it once probation ends, yet it produces no permanent change. It must be combined with the cognitive and behavioral methods already described in a comprehensive treatment program so that eventually it can be discontinued, preferably prior to the end of supervision, and at a time when these more long-lasting methods have taken hold.

SUMMARY

Most clinicians can pick out successful cases for presentation. B.'s case, however, is not atypical. The majority of exhibitionists and, indeed, of sexual offenders in general, will not commit further sexual crimes after the type of treatment presented here. Some offenders, however, may be dangerous to be at large and at increased risk for reoffending while engaged in treatment. Among these are true pedophiles, who are preferentially attracted to children or are predatory to them, and men who have repeatedly raped or who have bonded aggression to sexual arousal. While the cognitive and behavioral techniques described for B. might still apply, they might best be used in an institutional setting with such men to guard against community risk.

B.'s case illustrates the need for, and usefulness of, group and individual therapy. Group was particularly helpful with breaking through denial, while individual therapy provided more specific techniques tailored to B.'s particular problems. Therapy was not only technique-driven, as there was time in sessions to discuss marital issues contributing to exposing. However, it was important to recognize that the primary goal was to stop exposing rather than to uncover background factors responsible for exhibitionism. The exact and combined etiologies of sexual offending remain beyond our ken. We are obligated, nonetheless, to use methods that have been demonstrated to be effective in reducing risk.

For B., treatment was not unduly lengthy or at catastrophic cost. Some pedophiles or rapists, however, can require 2 or 3 years for effective treatment. Still, the money saved from repeated prosecution and incarceration, and more importantly, the improved quality of life for victims and offenders, are incalculable. It is fortunate that effective treatment techniques for the sexual offender have been developed in the past two decades, but equally important that we continue to develop new methods, and test existing ones, to prevent victimization in the future.

REFERENCES

Abel, G. G., & Becker, J. V. (1984). *The treatment of child molesters* (NIMH Grant MH36347-01202 and BRSA Grant 903,E5040). New York: New York State Research Foundation for Mental Hygiene.

Ahlmeyer, S., & Heil, P. (in press). The impact of polygraphy on admissions of victims and offenses in adult sexual offenders. *Sexual Abuse: A Journal of Research and Treatment.*

Eldridge, H. (1998). *Maintaining change: A personal relapse prevention manual.* Thousand Oaks, CA: Sage.

Freund, K., & Watson, R. (1990). Mapping the boundaries of courtship disorder. *Journal of Sex Research, 27,* 589–606.

Grubin, D., & Mason, D. (1997). Medical models of sexual deviance. In D. R. Laws & W. O'Donohue (Eds.), *Sexual deviance: Theory, assessment and treatment* (pp. 434–448). New York: Guilford.

Hanson, R. K., & Bussiere, M. T. (1998). Predicting relapse: A meta-analysis of sexual offender recidivism studies. *Journal of Consulting and Clinical Psychology, 66,* 348–362.

Howes, R. J. (1995). A survey of plethysmographic assessment in North America. *Sexual Abuse: A Journal of Research and Treatment, 7,* 9–24.

Maletzky, B. M. (1991). *Treating the sexual offender.* Newbury Park CA: Sage.

Maletzky, B. M. (1997). Exhibitionism: Assessment and treatment. In D. R. Laws & W. O'Donohue (Eds.), *Sexual deviance: Theory, assessment and treatment* (pp. 40–74). New York: Guilford.

Maletzky, B. M. (1998, October). *Treatment outcome, technique efficacy and assessment of risk: A five to twenty-five year follow-up of 7,500 sexual offenders.* Paper presented at the annual conference of the Association for the Treatment of Sexual Abusers, Vancouver, B.C.

Murphy, W. D. (1990). Assessment and modification of cognitive distortions in sex offenders. In W. L. Marshall, D. R. Laws, & H. E. Barbaree (Eds.), *Handbook of sexual assault: Issues, theories and treatment of the offender* (pp. 331-342). New York: Plenum.

Weinrott, M. R., & Riggan, M. (1997). Vicarious sensitization: A new method to reduce deviant arousal in adolescent sex offenders. *Archives of Sexual Behavior, 27,* 211–219.

Wickramaserka, I. (1980). Aversive behavior rehearsal: A cognitive-behavioral procedure. In D. J. Cox & R. J. Daitzman (Eds.), *Exhibitionism: Description, assessment and treatment* (pp. 123–149). New York: Garland.

CHAPTER

Bulimia Nervosa

J. Scott Mizes and Deanne Zotter Bonifazi
Department of Psychology
West Chester University
West Chester, Pennsylvania

Case Description
Treatment Conceptualization
Assessment
Treatment Implementation
  Stage 1
  Stage 2
  Stage 3
Concurrent Diagnoses and Treatment
Complications and Treatment Implications
Dealing with Managed Care and Accountability
Outcome and Follow-Up
Dealing with Recidivism
Summary
References

Bulimia nervosa is a psychological disorder characterized by binge eating, purging through self-induced vomiting (or other means), and intense body dissatisfaction. It afflicts primarily teenage and young to middle-aged women, although men are not immune to the disorder. Bulimia nervosa is a vicious disorder that knows no socioeconomic bounds, afflicting poor inner-city women and persons such as Diana, Princess of Wales, with equal tenacity. Bulimia is a terrible disorder to suffer with, as it consumes your life, destroys your self-esteem, and leaves you physically weakened, depressed, and feeling alone. The fact that bulimia is an eating disorder is somewhat of an ironic play on words, as this is a disorder that literally "eats away" at your body, your relationships, and your soul. In this chapter, using the hypothetical case of Jenni, we will discuss and illustrate the assessment, treatment, and difficulties encountered in treating a person with this most challenging disorder.

CASE DESCRIPTION

Jenni, age 23, has struggled with bulimia nervosa since her teens. Although there have been periods of time when she felt in control of her eating, she currently reports feeling out of control. Her binging and purging behaviors have escalated such that she is binging and vomiting 4 to 6 days a week. She is 5 feet 6 inches tall and weighs 129 pounds.

Jenni is the youngest in a family of five, having two older brothers. Her parents married when both were young, and separated when Jenni was in high school. The separation was prompted by her mother (who Jenni describes as overweight) learning that her father was having an affair with his bookkeeper at work. Although Jenni had always been overly concerned with her appearance, she recalls her weight becoming more of a concern after the separation. She began dieting and exercising to become thinner. Soon she began a romance with the school's basketball star and got into a partying crowd. She got drunk with her friends yet still managed to juggle her "A student" status with her newly found popularity. When her boyfriend left her for another girl, Jenni fell into a depression. She started to stay home more and more, staying in her room and exercising late into the night. She also began dieting more restrictively, thinking that if she were thinner and prettier her boyfriend would again find her desirable.

Over time, Jenni felt unable to continue the restrictive dieting. After a particularly stressful day at school, Jenni recalls coming home and eating a piece of chocolate cake. "Before I knew what had happened, I had eaten the entire cake!" In a panic (fearing weight gain), Jenni immediately went to the bathroom and induced vomiting. After this, Jenni felt relief and excitement — now she could eat anything she wanted and "get rid of it." She recalls the happiness she felt as she began to relax her dietary controls and decrease her exercise. Within a few months, however, Jenni began noticing increases in her weight. This greatly distressed her, and she resumed her restrictive dieting practices, although she was unable to stop the urges to binge. She would binge and purge three or four times a week. Jenni continued these patterns until her high school graduation, when she vowed to put an end to her bulimia and make a fresh start in college.

Jenni attended a major university about 2 hours from her home. She had high hopes for a new life and got off to a good start, joining several campus organizations and making many friends through the sorority she joined. In the sorority, she found friends who were similarly appearance-conscious. They would try "fad diets" and exercise together. Although she would occasionally binge and purge, these episodes were infrequent. A trauma in December of her sophomore year, however, changed everything. She got drunk and was raped by a senior fraternity brother at a sorority party. She was so embarrassed that she told no one. She began to binge and purge more frequently to escape the violent memories and to comfort herself. "Food took over my life again, but this time I was so out of control!" Jenni began avoiding parties and other events where she might see the rapist, and had trouble concentrating on her work. After a year of deteriorating academic performance and increasing social isolation, Jenni found herself binging and vomiting daily. Her sorority sisters called her parents and she was hospitalized. After 2 weeks in an eating disorders unit, Jenni returned to school against the advice of her treatment team. She had gained some control over her binge-eating and was determined to complete the school year.

Jenni was very busy during her senior year, completing an internship at a local business and taking extra classes in an attempt to raise her GPA. Although her eating and social life were restricted, she went for weeks at a time without binging and vomiting. While on her internship, Jenni met Joe, 8 years her senior. She fell in love for the first time. When they had been drinking, Jenni was able to overcome her fear of sexual relations. Jenni graduated in May and landed a sales job in a pharmaceutical company. Joe proposed to Jenni 6 months later. As the wedding approached, Jenni and Joe began to have problems. Joe traveled a great deal for his job and Jenni found it increasingly difficult to tolerate his absences. She began exercising obsessively when she was alone. To alleviate her concerns that Joe was being unfaithful to her when he traveled, Jenni decided to fly to the city where Joe was working. She found Joe with another woman and immediately ended the engagement, feeling humiliated and betrayed. Jenni retreated into her work and her eating disorder. She spent long hours at her office and, in addition to increasingly severe dieting and exercise, she gradually began to binge and purge almost daily. In addition, she began taking laxatives.

Jenni's current eating patterns involve skipping breakfast each morning (only drinking black coffee), eating a salad, soup, or pretzels for lunch, and snacking on hard candy all afternoon. She gets takeout dinners nightly and eats in front of the television. Four to six nights a week she purges her dinner by vomiting, followed by binge-eating on doughnuts, chocolate cookies and cakes, and/or ice cream. This makes her feel miserably full and ashamed. Sometimes she continues the cycle of vomiting and binge–eating, while at other times she exercises late into the night. On the weekends, Jenni sometimes will binge and vomit up to five times a day. At times when she feels the binging has been particularly excessive, she will use laxatives, taking as many as six at a time.

Jenni sought treatment because she believes the bulimia is having a negative impact on her career. Due to her late night binge–purge episodes, she has a hard time getting up in the morning, which has led to increasing lateness at work. Other problems at work (e.g., her short temper with others and her increasing forgetfulness) are creating a crisis situation in which she fears she may lose her job.

TREATMENT CONCEPTUALIZATION

Jenni's current weight represents a body mass index (BMI) of 21, which is well above the criterion for anorexia as specified by ICD-10 (i.e., a BMI of 17.5). The weight cutoff of the ICD-10 criterion, as opposed to the DSM-IV criteria, is preferred because it is more clear cut. This is because the DSM-IV criteria are based on 85% of "expected weight," which is an elusive construct, and number, to define. Specific information about weight will also be important in the psychoeducational part of Jenni's treatment. A BMI of 23, which represents an average healthy weight, is 142 pounds for her height. The cutoff for being overweight is a BMI of 25, and is based on the point at which medical consequences of excess weight begin to occur. For Jenni, this point is 155 pounds. The significance of this is that there is no MEDICAL reason for her to attempt weight loss as long as her weight is 155 or below. This is an extremely important recognition for Jenni to make, as one of the most central parts of her recovery is to give up the ultimately impossible goal of trying to weigh less than her body is genetically designed to weigh. Only when she gives up this quest, and the attendant body dissatisfaction, will she truly overcome her bulimia.

A brief overview of Jenni's history will illustrate several common themes in the development of eating disorders for many patients. Having said this, it is important to keep in mind that there is not just one "pathway" to bulimia; rather, several different etiologic courses are possible. It is also important to note that a strong genetic vulnerability to eating disorders has been recently established, though the exact biologic mechanisms of this risk are not currently known. This is important to keep in mind, as Jenni's case illustrates the triggering role of psychosocial stresses in the expression of eating disorder symptoms. However, the stressors described in Jenni's case are for the most part neither unique nor unusually catastrophic; that is, many other women experience these same stressors and do not develop eating disorders.

Jenni's eating disorder history illustrates a common theme among eating disorder patients; that is, the stressors that are particular threats to self-esteem are the most likely to lead to initiation, intensification, or return of eating disorder symptoms. The first threat to her self-esteem was her parents' separation while she was in high school, due to her father having an affair. Undoubtedly, this threatened her sense of security, and perhaps her sense of lovability in her father's eyes. The fact that her mother was overweight creates the grounds for both mother and daughter to conclude that father left mom because she was fat. Of course, detailed inquiry into the specific meaning Jenni placed on her parents separation, especially as it relates to her own self-esteem and views of what women must accomplish to be attractive, is necessary in order to fully understand the impact this family disruption had on her. Psychodynamic or systems theorists may be inclined to interpret her eating disorder symptoms as an attempt to distract her parents from their problems, or to get them to join again to address her problems. There is little research evidence to support these interpretations as generally applicable to eating-disordered patients and their families, although it is possible for these dynamics to occur in individual cases.

The second stressor was the breakup with her first boyfriend, who left her for another girl. Jenni's response was to intensify her dieting, and to become depressed. Jenni's belief that being thinner and prettier would win her boyfriend back was likely a hypothesis she derived from her mother's experiences, and an idea certainly well-articulated by the media. However, although her boyfriend may have been unusually superficial, odds are that the reasons for the breakup were much more complex than this; for example, stemming from their young age and not being ready to stay in a long-term relationship (a developmentally normal state of affairs), areas of incompatibility between them, or perhaps aspects of her own behavior. This illustrates the role of simplifying assumptions in cognitive schema in eating disorders, as described by Vitousek and Hollon (1990). That is, Jenni conceptualizes her experience of a relationship ending in simple, concrete terms that miss the complexity of the probable reasons for the breakup. Thus, by defining the problem as due to her weight she accomplishes two important things. First, she prevents herself from a more realistic, and likely painful examination of what "really" happened and her potential contribution. Additionally, she provides herself with a seemingly simple, concrete solution; that is, become thinner and her boyfriend problems will be gone. This may seem much more attainable to her than accepting her boyfriend's rejection, or considering how she might change in the future.

Jenni's development of binge eating, and then purging, after she is unable to continue restrictive dieting, is a common course of events. This situation illustrates the effects of dietary restraint on the development of binge eating in susceptible people. Although there has been some argument on just what is the concept of dietary restraint, for our purposes we will define it as a generalized cognitive set to limit food intake, independent of whether one is actually currently limiting food intake, such as by dieting. This cognitive set is characterized by a variety of rigid, often black-and-white, rules about what constitutes acceptable and unacceptable eating. Dietary restraint sets up susceptible people to binge eating in several ways. The first is mainly biological in that calorie deprivation can be sustained for only so long before the body "rebels" and makes up for the calorie deficit by binge eating. Second, dietary restraint makes eating in response to strong emotions more likely. Strong emotion, especially negative emotion, undermines the extreme self-control necessary to maintain calorie deprivation. Third, the rigid black-and-white food rules create an abstinence violation effect when the person is eating a small amount of a forbidden food. Thinking that they have blown it, the person gives up and eats more of the forbidden food than they would have otherwise. Lastly, dietary restraint creates the conditions for "craving" the forbidden foods by increasing their appetitive value because they are "off limits." This can be referred to as the "grass-is-greener-on-the-other-side-of-the-fence" effect.

Development of binge eating also illustrates a characteristic of bulimia patients: the use of avoidance-based coping rather than problem-based coping (Christiano & Mizes, 1997). We can speculate that Jenni has already shown this tendency in the manner in which she coped with her parents' divorce and her own relationship breakup. However, as the binge eating and purging develop, they become a major coping mechanism for regulating negative emotions. As such, they are primarily avoidance-based coping strategies in that they serve to "mask" or avoid her emotional distress. This is in contrast to adaptive problem-focused coping strategies, which would address the problems that create stress in her life directly and attempt to solve them.

The unfortunate rape Jenni suffered again returns us to the theme of threats to self-esteem as triggers of bulimic behavior. Also, the accompanying posttraumatic stress disorder symptoms create a variety of intense and upsetting emotions and probably residual body sensations that only intensify her overreliance on avoidance-based coping. Sadly, this avoidance-based coping will make her PTSD symptoms worse, as seeking a safe emotional environment in which to reexperience the trauma is one of the most helpful things for reducing and resolving her PTSD symptoms so that they do not become chronic. The temptation is to see the rape as a direct causal agent in her eating disorder symptoms. However, the available research would suggest that rape, sexual assault, and physical abuse are not specific risk factors for bulimia, but rather general risk factors for a variety of psychological problems. Having said that, Jenni's body image disturbance is likely to be complicated beyond the typical concerns of shape and weight seen in eating disorder patients. Specific negative "body memories" from the rape, as well as generalized negative views of her body as disgusting, may likely complicate the picture.

ASSESSMENT

Assessment of bulimia should include evaluation of general and eating disorder–specific psychopathology; should include assessment of psychological, nutritional, and medical status; and should use multiple assessment methodologies. These methodologies should include standardized psychological questionnaires, interviews, and behavioral assessments approaches. The focus here will be on psychological assessment.

From a cognitive-behavioral perspective, assessment often starts before the patient begins treatment. Thus, Jenni would be sent a detailed eating disorder–specific questionnaire that gathers information about frequency of binge eating and purging, current eating patterns, foods avoided or most likely to be purged, preferred binge foods, medical symptoms associated with eating disorders, current weight, lowest and highest weights, self-defined ideal weight, family history of obesity, history of or current presence of suicidal ideation and acts, current and previous use of alcohol and drugs and indicators of pathological use, and general psychiatric and medical information. (A few such questionnaires are available; the reader can contact the senior author for the one developed in our program.) In addition to the efficient collection of basic information, this preintake information serves several other functions. First, it frees the clinician to clarify basic issues regarding her eating problems, using the questionnaire information as a starting point for discussion. For example, it can be quickly noted that Jenni indicated on the questionnaire that her eating problems began in her teens, and then the clinician can inquire about the psychosocial circumstances that may have triggered emergence of the eating disorder. Second, completing the questionnaire enlists Jenni in the process of thinking about her eating disorder *systematically*, and in a manner consistent with a cognitive-behavioral therapy (CBT) approach. Third, asking Jenni to complete the questionnaire introduces her from the outset to the basic CBT philosophy of out-of-session homework, and gives the clinician initial information on her willingness to complete such assignments. As a practical matter, our clinical experience is that the vast majority of eating disorder patients complete the questionnaires; thus, it is a clinical "red flag" when this does not occur.

There are several good sources of information to glean during an intake interview for eating disorders. Due to space considerations, we will not comprehensively review the eating disorders intake interview here. Rather, we will focus on some of the more unique aspects of a CBT interview, as well as unique aspects of Jenni's case that require assessment. The first aspect of the CBT interview is that is focuses on specific eating behavior in *detail* and does not assume that it is a mere symptom to be touched on lightly before getting down to the "real" issues. It is very common for patients who have previously received traditional treatment to comment that little was asked by previous therapists about their eating, purging, and other weight control behaviors. Though some patients are embarrassed by their eating habits (usually more likely to occur for a first-time patient), many are relieved that someone is talking with them directly about what is so obviously one of their major concerns. Although not spoken about extensively in even more current CBT guides on the intake interview, one of the changes in our approach in recent years is a very detailed assessment of body dissatisfaction. This includes a global rating of level of body dissatisfaction, as well as a detailed body part-by-body part discussion of body dissatisfaction. Body dissatisfaction is not a static construct, so it is important to assess triggers that increase body dissatisfaction, such as having eating forbidden foods, certain clothes, negative moods, weighing oneself, and so on. It is also useful to assess specific body image avoidance behaviors, such as not looking at oneself in the mirror, avoiding wearing revealing clothes, or wearing excessively baggy clothes. Finally, it is useful to assess cognitions and schema that are part of the body dissatisfaction. The fundamental question to answer is: What about weight gain is so upsetting to the client? In Jenni's case, weight gain may be associated with fears of being unlovable and abandoned, particularly by men.

Assessment of general psychopathology can be accomplished via the MMPI. In Jenni's case, in addition to a clinical interview, her depression and PTSD symptoms can be assessed psychometrically via the MMPI. The MMPI can also help assess her personality disorder features. Different eating disorder centers use different eating disorder questionnaires. We use the following: the Eating Disorders Inventory-II, the Revised-Restraint Scale, and the Mizes Anorectic Cognitions Questionnaire. In a case like Jenni's, these assessments are not needed to make the diagnosis. However, they provide important evidence for Jenni that her eating behavior and related cognitions and schema are NOT normal, even though many of her previous sorority sisters, and perhaps current friends, have some level of body dissatisfaction, fear of weight gain, and eating preoccupation. Also, feedback on her questionnaire scores can be a good way to begin teaching her about basic concepts used in CBT treatment, such as dietary restraint.

More recently, we have added assessment of the patient's readiness to change due to the well-known resistance of eating disorder patients. The model we and others have used is the Stages of Change model by Prochaska et al. (1992), which has been adapted to eating disorders. We use a stages-of-change algorithm to help determine if the patient is a precontemplator, contemplator, or in the action stage. Additionally, we use a decisional balance questionnaire (based on work by Kelly Vitousek, personal communication, November 1992) to assess the relative pluses and minuses of both anorexic and bulimic behavior. The vast majority of eating disorder patients are at the precontemplator or contemplator stage, particularly as related to what we view as the ultimate bottom line of recovery from an eating disorder, that is, giving up all effort to regulate body weight and shape in an effort to be something that one is not. Given that Jenni has left treatment prematurely before, and that the major stimulus for her seeking treatment currently is job problems, she very well may be at the precontemplation stage relative to her eating disorder. As such, her decisional balance questionnaire would likely reveal that she perceives that her bulimia provides her more benefits than it costs her. Accordingly, she would be expected to be hesitant to give up her bulimia.

TREATMENT IMPLEMENTATION

Cognitive-behavioral therapy continues to be supported as the treatment of choice for bulimia nervosa (Whittal *et al.*, 1999). The CBT protocol for bulimia has been well articulated by Fairburn *et al.* in their 1993 manual. While implementation of CBT varies somewhat across treatment facilities, most rely on the basic formulation developed by Fairburn and his colleagues. CBT emphasizes the importance of maladaptive cognitions in the etiology and maintenance of bulimia nervosa. A fundamental belief of many individuals with bulimia, including Jenni, is "I *must* be thin to be worthwhile." Given this belief, their problematic eating patterns become easier to understand. Combined with the emphasis on cognitions is an emphasis on the problematic eating behaviors themselves. Of utmost importance is getting the individual to replace their pattern of dietary restraint, binging, and purging, with more normal eating patterns. In fact, many bulimics in recovery have reported the return to normal eating as one of the key elements in promoting their recovery.

CBT can be viewed as a three-stage process. Stage 1 (lasting approximately 8 weeks) involves building a solid therapeutic relationship, introducing a pattern of regular eating and weekly weighing, and educating the client on various aspects of their disorder and the CBT approach to treatment. Stage 2 (lasting approximately 8 weeks) is more cognitively oriented and involves cognitive restructuring of the thoughts, beliefs, and values that help to maintain the disorder. A key feature in this stage is addressing shape and weight concerns. In addition, identifying triggers to binge–purge episodes and training in problem-solving to deal with these triggers is essential. Finally, Stage 3 (lasting approximately 3 weeks) focuses on relapse prevention techniques.

Stage 1

Establishment of a good working relationship between client and therapist cannot be overemphasized when the client is struggling with bulimia. In many cases, these individuals have been very secretive about their disorder and are filled with shame and embarrassment. In addition, most will be ambivalent about giving up their bulimic symptoms. In order for clients to discuss such ambivalence openly, a sound relationship is necessary. This is true with Jenni, who is in the precontemplation stage. An additional factor with Jenni is the sex of the therapist. Given her history with men, it may be especially difficult for her to trust a male therapist. While there is no evidence that the sex of the therapist influences the outcome of CBT for bulimia, it is important not to overlook this variable with someone like Jenni. Regardless of the client's history, male therapists working with females with bulimia need to have a true understanding of the relentless and pervasive societal pressures placed on females to be thin, beautiful, and successful. Failure to recognize the impact that these societal messages have on girls/women will certainly undermine a male therapist's effectiveness.

Explaining the rationale for CBT and the process that treatment will follow (e.g., collaborative relationship between client and therapist, weekly homework assignments) is an important first step in establishing rapport with the client. Reviewing the completed assessment measures with the client in a warm nonjudgmental manner may also help in establishing the relationship. A supportive discussion of the decisional balance questionnaire is essential, particularly for the majority of patients who record more benefits to their symptoms than costs. With Jenni, emphasizing the costs she already recognized (e.g., threats to her employment) and introducing other disadvantages not previously recognized (e.g., potential physical complications) helped to increase her motivation and move her closer to the action stage of change. Often, reviewing the client's perceived advantages and disadvantages of their disorder helps bring to light various inaccurate beliefs on the part of the client and can set the stage for discussion of psychoeducational principles and later cognitive restructuring. For example, Jenni felt her restrictive eating patterns were advantageous because she believed they helped her to lose weight. As Stage 1 progresses, this belief can be confronted by presenting evidence on the ineffectiveness of dieting and the relationship between dieting and binge eating.

Self-monitoring of intake, binging/purging behaviors, and cognitions is the cornerstone of CBT for bulimia and should be introduced during the first session. Self-monitoring provides the therapist and client with a more precise picture of the eating problem. The importance of self-monitoring should be emphasized to the client. Clients are instructed to carry a monitoring sheet with them at all times and to record all episodes of eating or drinking immediately after each episode. Clients should record the time, the amount they have eaten or drank, the location of the eating episode, whether the client felt the episode was a binge, whether they induced vomiting and/or took laxatives after the episode, and the context in which the eating episode took place. The context could include thoughts, feelings, and/or events that influenced the eating. Exercise should also be monitored to ensure that it is not excessive. As therapy progresses, monitoring sheets are used to assess eating patterns, help identify triggers to binge episodes, record dysfunctional thoughts and beliefs, and ultimately assess progress as the number of binge–purge episodes decrease. (See Figure 14.1 for a sample of Jenni's monitoring sheet.)

Each session should include a review of the monitoring sheets. Early on in therapy, particular attention should be paid to the accuracy of the monitoring (e.g., were episodes recorded immediately, are there any omissions, are amounts eaten recorded). Any difficulty the client had with monitoring should be explored and resolved while all attempts at monitoring should be praised. A client who does not comply with monitoring will sabotage treatment. Initially, Jenni's self-monitoring sheets were filled with vague and incomplete entries. In this circumstance, a return to the discussion of Jenni's decisional balance questionnaire, a review of the importance of monitoring, and directly addressing her avoidance-based coping led to increased compliance.

Given a bulimic client's extreme fear of weight gain and the fact that their eating patterns will change during treatment, establishing a pattern of weekly weighing is necessary in order for clients to be able to monitor their weight in an objective way. Clients should be instructed to weigh themselves *once* each week during a morning of their choice. They should then record their weight and any accompanying thoughts or feelings on their monitoring sheet.

Educating the client on their disorder is essential. Topics to be discussed include the roles of dietary restraint and purging on binge eating, ineffectiveness of purging, adverse physical consequences of binging and purging, and body weight, including the myth that with enough effort we can sculpt our bodies to whatever shape we desire. Providing clients with written materials (e.g., Garner's 1997 chapter on psychoeducational principles) can be an effective means of introducing this information. With Jenni, much time was spent addressing the cyclical nature of her eating disorder. That is, her dietary restraint and the accompanying dichotomous thinking style left her susceptible to binge eating in response to hunger and negative emotion. Binge episodes in turn led to purging behaviors in response to guilt over eating and fear of weight gain. Knowing she could

Day _Friday_   Date _3/20_

Time	Food and Liquid Consumed	Place	B	V/L	Context
6:00	Black coffee (2 cups)	Kitchen & Bedroom			Very tired.
9:00	Black coffee (2 cups)	Work			Feeling very hungry.
1:15	1 bowl of vegetable soup 2 saltine crackers Diet soda	Work			Too busy to think — have lots of work to finish before the weekend!
3:00	4 pieces of hard candy	Work			
7:00	Pasta primavera from the Italian Bistro with garlic bread; Diet soda	TV room		V	I hate my life! I hate my body!
7:30	half a bag of chocolate chip cookies; 1 pint chocolate –chocolate chip ice cream	TV room	B	V	Feeling sorry for myself. . . Another Friday night and I'm home all alone. . . I have no life! I'm a loser!
9:50	entire pan of brownies with vanilla ice cream and chocolate sauce	Kitchen	B	V	Why am I doing this??? I'm a fat pig!
11:45				L	Feeling very fat. I exercised for 15 minutes but I'm just not in the mood to exercise. . . I'm tired and feeling depressed. Took 4 Ex-Lax.

Figure 14.1 A sample monitoring sheet obtained early in Jenni's treatment.

purge her food also contributed to the large amount of food consumed during a binge and the frequency of binge episodes. Shame and self-disgust following purging led to increased efforts to control intake that caused the cycle to continue. Jenni also needed to learn about the ineffectiveness and dangers of using laxatives (as well as the other physical complications of bulimia). Much time was also spent addressing set point theory (e.g., Keesey, 1993) and how Jenni exerts a great deal of effort trying to weigh less than her body is genetically designed to weigh.

As mentioned previously, helping clients to engage in a pattern of regular eating is particularly helpful in recovery. This is referred to as prescribed eating and involves instructing the client to eat three planned meals a day with two or three planned snacks. Meals and snacks should be planned such that there is no more than 3 hours between eating episodes. Clients should be instructed not to eat between the planned meals and snacks, and not to purge or engage in any compensatory behaviors after eating. This prescribed plan of eating should be adhered to regardless of the client's appetite or any other circumstances. As is often the case, Jenni initially selected all low-calorie foods as she began prescribed eating. Early on in treatment, this is acceptable. The goal is to get the client to eat average amounts of food regularly throughout the day, regardless of the caloric content. Clients should be warned about feelings of fullness and the urges to purge following eating. The client should develop a list of pleasurable alternative behaviors and should be instructed to engage in one of these behaviors whenever feeling tempted to purge. Jenni was able to distract herself in her work during the day, and she found that bubblebaths and creative writing (short stories) helped at nights.

As was true with Jenni, many clients will resist the prescribed eating, fearing weight gain. The client should be assured that prescribed eating rarely results in weight gain. Although the client will likely be eating more frequently, they will be less likely to binge, thereby reducing their overall caloric intake. Using completed monitoring sheets to calculate the large number of calories consumed during a binge may help demonstrate this point. Some clients may increase their exercise in reaction to prescribed eating. Although all exercise need not be discouraged, exercise should be monitored to ensure it does not become excessive. With Jenni, it was necessary to introduce prescribed eating gradually, beginning with eating breakfast daily, then adding a mid-morning snack, and so on. Seeing no changes in her weight, she was better able to accept the prescribed eating.

By the end of Stage 1 (8 weeks into treatment), clients should understand many of the factors that contribute to the maintenance of their disorder, including dietary restraint and the use of purging behaviors.

Clients should also be engaging in prescribed eating. In addition, through regular examination of the self-monitoring sheets, clients should begin to recognize specific triggers that lead to binge episodes. Stage 1 took slightly longer than 8 weeks with Jenni due to her initial ambivalence toward giving up her bulimic symptoms and her reluctance about prescribed eating. By the end of Stage 1, however, reduction in the frequency of Jenni's binging and purging (including abstinence from laxatives) was seen, as is the case with most clients. When this is not the case, and/or significant emotional distress persists, the possibility of a comorbid condition (e.g., major depression) must be considered. Antidepressant medication may be beneficial with this subgroup of clients. Furthermore, hospitalization and/or treatment approaches other than CBT should be considered.

Stage 2

While continuing the tasks in Stage 1 (e.g., prescribed eating, self-monitoring), dieting and binging are targeted more specifically in Stage 2. The aim is to cease binging and all efforts at dieting. The therapist should demonstrate how dieting leads to binge eating by using examples from the client's monitoring sheets showing increased binge episodes following periods of restraint. Whereas in Stage 1 the goal of prescribed eating was getting the client to eat regularly throughout the day, Stage 2 focuses more on *what* the client is eating. That is, it is now important to be sure the client is not restricting their caloric intake and not eliminating feared foods from their eating. Individuals with bulimia have a tendency to separate foods into "good" and "bad" categories, allowing themselves only the "good" foods and leaving themselves vulnerable to binge on the "bad" foods. It is essential to help clients break this dichotomy by gradually introducing the feared foods into their diet. For example, Jenni was asked to list foods she likes but does not allow herself to eat. She then ranked these foods from least to most feared. Over a period of several weeks, Jenni was then instructed to progressively incorporate these foods into her planned meals and snacks, beginning with those least feared and working her way to those most feared. Clients should be instructed to only attempt introduction of feared foods at times when they feel relatively in control of their eating. As clients begin to relax their rigid controls over what they eat, they should be encouraged to relax other controls over eating such as practicing eating in a variety of settings (e.g., restaurants, parties).

Once clear triggers to binge episodes have been identified, training in problem-solving skills should take place. Triggers are often interpersonal in nature, as was the case for Jenni. By the beginning of Stage 2, Jenni was aware that feelings of loneliness and painful memories of her fiance's betrayal frequently led to binge eating episodes. She found watching other people enjoying each other's company left her feeling terribly alone. This often happened when she would see a couple on a date at the restaurant where she would pick up dinner or when watching television shows involving relationships. Problem-solving for Jenni involved recognizing the problem when it was occurring and then finding alternative ways of dealing with her painful memories and feelings of loneliness.

During Stage 2, clients should begin increasing their awareness of the thought processes that accompany the onset of a binge as well as thoughts that go through their mind whenever they are tempted to restrict or weigh themselves. These cognitions should be recorded on monitoring sheets and can then be examined and restructured using the methods devised by Beck and colleagues (1979). Quite often, cognitions associated with a binge episode are dichotomous in nature (black-and-white thinking). Cognitions associated with restrictive dieting behaviors and weighing often involve strong beliefs about the importance of being thin. It is critical that concerns about weight and shape be directly targeted in therapy, as body dissatisfaction is highly related to relapse in bulimia nervosa. Standard cognitive restructuring techniques should be used along with an exploration of the origin of the beliefs. For example, Jenni believed she must be thin and attractive to be loved. This idea is commonly portrayed in the media and became salient to Jenni when her father left her overweight mother for another woman. Examining the validity of this belief and the implications of this belief (e.g., people are superficial, love is superficial) enabled Jenni to develop effective counterarguements against dysfunctional thoughts stemming from this faulty belief. A discussion of body misperception is also important in tackling weight and shape concerns. Although typically not overweight, individuals with eating disorders tend to feel fat, particularly during periods characterized by negative affect. Clients should understand this tendency and be instructed not to trust their own perceptions of their body size. Finally, one cannot fully address body and weight concerns without discussing the impact of the media's portrayal of woman. Clients should be encouraged to stop reading fashion magazines, and to look at supermodels and other media images with disdain and skepticism. When necessary, cognitive restructuring should also be used to address dysfunctional thoughts not directly related to eating or body image. For example, Jenni had many cognitive distortions related to men.

These contributed to her inability to trust men, her loneliness, and her overall dissatisfaction with her life.

At the end of Stage 2, significant progress is usually seen. Clients have relaxed many of their controls over their eating, are able to identify and counteract dysfunctional thoughts, and are able to identify and cope with situations and/or feelings that previously would have resulted in a binge episode. While some clients cease binging and purging entirely, most, like Jenni, may binge and purge infrequently. Clients should be made aware that progress typically continues even after treatment has ended.

Stage 3

The final stage of therapy aims at ensuring that the progress made will be maintained. Sessions are usually scheduled at 2-week intervals. Clients should understand that progress is not necessarily linear but instead is likely to follow an irregular pattern of successes and setbacks. Having a predetermined plan for dealing with difficult times, differentiating "slips" from a full-blown relapse, and learning from "slips" in order to help avoid them in the future are all key elements in relapse prevention. Clients should be instructed to consider the aspects of treatment that were most helpful and then, with the therapist's assistance, develop a written plan for dealing with times when they believe their eating is becoming problematic. Finally, clients should again be cautioned against temptations to diet.

CONCURRENT DIAGNOSES AND TREATMENT

Comorbidity in bulimia nervosa has recently received research attention in terms of descriptive psychopathology. There has been little work on the needed modifications in treatment of bulimia in the face of comorbid psychological diagnoses. The most common comorbid conditions are depression, anxiety disorders, posttraumatic stress disorder secondary to sexual/physical abuse and rape, and personality disorders. In terms of specific personality disorders, borderline disorder is frequently seen in bulimic patients, at least among a treatment-seeking population. In general, cluster B personality disorders (anxious, fearful) are the most common seen in this population. Research has shown that patients with personality disorders have a poorer response to treatment, and typically need treatment of a much longer duration to experience clinical benefit.

In most cases, specific treatment of depression is not needed, as the moderate depression that frequently accompanies bulimia improves after basic CBT treatment. This is likely due to the improvements in self-esteem and body image that occur as a function of CBT treatment. Additionally, improvements in nutrition and physical status also likely contribute to improved mood, and decreased fatigue. Of course, in the case of a clear comorbid major depressive episode, more direct treatment of the depression may be necessary. In this case, antidepressants may be considered (particularly the selective serotonin reuptake inhibitors) for their positive effect on both depression and binge eating. In the few studies that have assessed changes in anxiety due to CBT treatment, there is usually a decrease in anxiety. However, little is known about treatment of bulimia when various other anxiety disorders are present.

One specific anxiety disorder that has received much attention in research on bulimia is posttraumatic stress disorder. Jenni's case illustrates the common clinical presentation of bulimia, a history of physical/sexual abuse or rape, and associated PTSD. Jenni presented symptoms of PTSD that require future investigation, as she reports avoidance behavior related to the trauma (i.e., avoiding parties, as she was raped at a party), intrusive memories of the rape, increased social isolation (which may have been due to the social isolation associated with both PTSD and bulimia). She also reports fear of sexual relations. Moreover, she seems to report a basic mistrust of others, and anger and irritability, which often occur with PTSD.

There is much debate on whether sexual/physical abuse and rape are risk factors for bulimia. Some researchers see it as a general risk factor for psychopathology in general, as these events are clearly major psychosocial stressors. Others see abuse and rape as specific risk factors for bulimia nervosa. In Jenni's case, this debate is not relevant, as her eating disorder problems began before the rape. However, after a period of moderation in her binge eating, the rape triggered a relapse in her binge eating and purging. In fact, when she relapsed, her binging and purging were worse than they were previously.

Clinically, we have found it useful to utilize a coping model in these cases. Specifically, bulimia nervosa patients overrely on avoidance-based coping strategies in the face of emotional distress. They tend to not utilize appropriate problem-focused coping (such as specific problem-solving or assertiveness), nor do they use helpful emotion-focused coping (such as seeking an emotionally supportive listener). We have clinically observed a rigid reliance on avoidance-based coping, particularly among patients with PTSD, and among those with borderline personality disorder. Importantly, the binging and purging becomes an important, and sometimes exclusive, strategy for engaging in avoidance-based coping in the face of painful emotions associated with the trauma. This goes well beyond the typically observed pattern of many bulimics to eat in response to stress, and to purge in the face of fears of weight gain after binge eating. Jenni clearly shows this pattern of avoidance coping to escape painful emotions. After the rape, she described binging and purging to avoid the memories of the rape, with the behavior also providing a way to reduce her emotional distress over the short term. Also, she had intense feelings of betrayal, mistrust, and worthlessness after discovering her fiance's affair. These emotions are likely to trigger similar emotional themes still held over from the rape.

In cases such as Jenni's, the overreliance on problem avoidance has to be addressed directly. Often, these patients will not complete self-monitoring, and will avoid talking about the eating disorder as well as other significant problems. They will also interject a variety of topics into treatment, as part of their strategy to avoid dealing with things directly. In addressing the avoidance coping, it is useful to address the patient's fears about more adaptive coping strategies. For example, they may fear that addressing the problems directly will only make them worse, or that they will be overwhelmed by the intense emotions that are associated with the trauma. Also, they may have deep-seated doubts about their ability to cope with problems, and thus conclude that nothing is likely to change. Other patients fear using emotion-based coping, such as social support, or have deficits in emotion-focused coping skills. For example, they fear telling their problems to another (including the therapist!). They fear that the other person will judge them to be defective and worthless because, after all, that is what they already "know" to be true about themselves. The basic interventions of CBT for bulimia are clearly problem-focused coping strategies. Patients locked into rigid avoidance-based coping are unlikely to utilize these coping strategies, and often may resist them. Addressing their avoidance coping style directly will help minimize unproductive "tugs of war" between the patient and therapist, and also assist the patient in gradually shifting to more adaptive coping strategies.

COMPLICATIONS AND TREATMENT IMPLICATIONS

Both physical and psychological complications are common in individuals with bulimia nervosa. These must be carefully evaluated and managed throughout treatment. Although medical complications are more common among individuals with anorexia, they can occur in bulimia nervosa and, on rare occasions, be life-threatening. A careful medical evaluation by a physician who is knowledgeable about eating disorders is necessary early in treatment. Perhaps the most potentially serious medical complications are electrolyte abnormalities. Disturbances in the electrolytes potassium, chloride, and sodium can be found in those who frequently purge by vomiting, laxatives, or diuretics, and can cause weakness, tiredness, constipation, and depression. Furthermore, although rare, some deaths from bulimia have been linked to hypokalemia (potassium depletion) leading to cardiac arrhythmias. Presence of electrolyte disturbances seems to be related to the severity of purging behaviors and the duration of the disorder. However, this relationship is not a perfect one; thus, all purging bulimics should be evaluated. An additional possible complication in those who use ipecac to induce vomiting is the development of cardiomyopathy. Use of ipecac is rare, but should be carefully evaluated due to the potentially fatal consequences.

Additional medical complications include dehydration from vomiting and/or laxative/diuretic abuse and gastrointestinal bleeding resulting from malnutrition and vomiting. Chronic laxative abuse can also result in gastrointestinal bleeding. Although rare, esophageal rupture can occur in patients who induce vomiting. This is another potentially fatal complication.

In the event a medical emergency arises (e.g., cardiac arrhythmias, serious electrolyte disturbances, significant gastrointestinal bleeding), hospitalization is necessary. Hospitalization may also be indicated with patients who have serious comorbid psychiatric conditions, suicidal ideation, severe depression, or who have shown an inadequate response to outpatient treatment.

Other less serious medical complications include irregular menses and swelling of the salivary glands. These tend to normalize following a return to normal eating and cessation of binging and purging. Frequent vomiting over a prolonged period of time can also lead to erosion of tooth enamel. The use of bicarbonate rinses after vomiting and frequent dental examinations are recommended. Frequent self-induced vomiting occasionally results in spontaneous regurgitation of food, which may complicate treatment.

The abuse of laxatives may result in severe constipation when laxatives are ceased. Rebound water retention should be expected following the cessation of laxative or diuretic abuse. This is often problematic for a bulimic as she becomes quite anxious about the water weight gain. The therapist should assure the client that the rebound water retention is a temporary phenomenon. Normalization of eating and discontinuation of purgatives will gradually reduce this water retention.

Infertility may result from untreated bulimia nervosa. Pregnancy may also be problematic for individuals with bulimia, as changes in body shape and weight can lead to increases in binge–purge episodes. In the event the bulimic patient becomes pregnant, communication among patient, obstetrician, and eating disorder specialist is critical.

As mentioned previously, common psychological complications include comorbid conditions such as depression, personality disorders, anxiety disorders, and PTSD following a history of sexual abuse. Substance abuse is also commonly seen in patients with bulimia nervosa. While CBT for bulimia has been shown to be effective for patients with significant psychiatric comorbidity, treatment may need to be lengthened and/or supplemented in important ways. Antidepressant medications (particularly the SSRIs) have been shown to be an effective adjunct to CBT for those with severe depression. Bulimics who abuse substances should be treated for both problems simultaneously. Research has demonstrated that only treating the substance abuse leads to an increase in eating disorder symptoms and vice versa. Using a twelve-step program or CBT targeting the substance abuse as an adjunct to CBT for bulimia may be beneficial.

The majority of patients who do not respond to standard CBT treatment for bulimia are those with personality disorders. Therefore, if an underlying personality disorder is detected, the therapist's approach and the treatment plan must be altered to accommodate the axis II condition. Often, symptoms of the eating disorder can be examined and treated within the larger context of the personality disorder. For example, a patient with borderline personality disorder can examine her binging and purging along with other impulsive and self-destructive behaviors. CBT techniques aimed at reducing impulsive and self-destructive behaviors in general can be utilized as opposed to specifically targeting the binge–purge episodes.

Patients with bulimia, like Jenni, who have been sexually assaulted often have heightened body image disturbance. For these individuals, the relationship between the assault and their body dissatisfaction needs to be directly explored. In addition, core beliefs about themselves and their world are likely to have been shaken if not shattered. Much time in CBT should be spent addressing these altered core beliefs.

Two final complications that are often found with individuals with bulimia are secretiveness and social isolation. Their secretiveness about their bulimic behaviors often means that very few people, if any, know of their eating disorder. This results in little social support for their recovery. Disclosure of bulimia to a few close friends or family members should be included as a goal of treatment. Therapists should also be aware of a bulimic's tendency toward secretiveness and be cautious of the patient who reports a cessation in binging and purging when clinical judgment suggests otherwise. As a rule, bulimic patients do not intend to be deceitful; they simply do not want their therapist to be disappointed in them and think of them as a failure. This relates to the tendency toward avoidance-based coping addressed earlier. Social isolation also stems from secretiveness and avoidance-based coping, and was a large problem for Jenni. Her social isolation increased her dysphoric feelings and played a key role in her binge–purge episodes. Encouraging increased social contacts through behavioral exercises may assist those with this complication.

DEALING WITH MANAGED CARE AND ACCOUNTABILITY

Managed care has had a tremendous impact on the treatment of eating disorders, especially inpatient treatment. This impact has had more implications for the treatment of anorexia nervosa than for bulimia nervosa. Managed care has resulted in dramatically shortened lengths of stay for anorexia nervosa, such that the length of stay provided is frequently too short to allow for even minimally competent treatment. Weight restoration for anorexia is a major goal for inpatient treatment. The rate of weight restoration that is medically needed and safe in the hospital is 1–3 pounds per week. As many anorectics need to achieve 20–30 pounds of weight gain, it is obvious that this cannot be achieved in the 1- to 2-week hospitalization that many managed care companies allow. Even the month allowed by more generous companies is often insufficient. Recent research has strongly suggested that discharge before achieving approximately 95% of expected weight increases the risk of relapse and rehospitalization. Not only have the pressures of managed care resulted in excessively short hospitalizations, but the financial pressures have led many inpatient eating disorders treatment facilities to close. This has resulted in a significant shortage of needed treatment resources.

The changes induced by managed care have had less of a dramatic impact on treatment of bulimia nervosa. This is largely because bulimia can be treated successfully on an outpatient basis in most cases. There has been scant research on the comparative effectiveness of inpatient versus outpatient treatment for bulimia. However, the general consensus is that patients are less likely to relapse after outpatient treatment because they are learning skills regarding their eating in their home setting. The situation becomes more complex when the patient has significant comorbid conditions that merit hospitalization in their own right. The most frequent examples include severe depression and suicidal risk, borderline personality disorder, or a severe anxiety disorder, such as posttraumatic stress disorder. These clinical issues may be severe enough to get a hospitalization authorized from a managed care company. However, this is usually for stabilization of the comorbid condition rather than treatment of the bulimia. Due to the dramatic decrease in the number of inpatient facilities with expertise in eating disorders, the unit the patient is admitted to is often ill-equipped to adequately treat the bulimia. In addition to lack of hospital resources, expertise in treatment of eating disorders is lacking. Treatment of eating disorders is still a very specialized area, and many professionals do not receive training in this area. Severe medical complications, such as dehydration and/or heart palpitations, may also result in a managed care reviewer authorizing inpatient treatment for bulimia. However, the goal here is medical stabilization, and the hospitalization is often only a few days on a medical rather than psychiatric unit. Clearly, this is insufficient for treating the bulimia.

There are no particular barriers, as compared to other disorders, for managed care companies to authorize outpatient treatment of bulimia. The main barrier is that of inadequate length of treatment for many individual patients. Even though the existing clinical research on CBT for bulimia is for treatments lasting 15–20 sessions, for a substantial percentage of patients this length of treatment is inadequate. This is particularly true for persons with bulimia and significant comorbidity. Although CBT has been shown to be effective in treatment outcome studies, often only one-third of patients are free of their disorder at the end of treatment. Thus, very brief treatment, which is within the parameters that managed care allows, is often inadequate for many patients.

Three aspects of CBT for bulimia make it well-suited for the managed care environment. First, since CBT focuses directly on the eating behavior itself, CBT keeps detailed track of the frequency of binging and purging on a weekly basis. This is in contrast to a variety of other therapies for bulimia that not only do not assess binge–purge frequency but do not make eating behavior an explicit part of treatment. Managed care reviewers respond quite favorably to reports of changes in binge–purge frequencies in utilization reviews of treatment progress. Other treatment parameters, most notably changes in body image dissatisfaction, have not been so readily included in the measurement of treatment progress. Second, CBT appears to lead to faster clinical improvement than the main alternative that has received empirical support (i.e., Interpersonal Therapy). Third, CBT for bulimia has been identified by the Division of Clinical Psychology, American Psychological Association, as an empirically well-supported treatment. This is important, as managed care companies, and to a lesser extent consumers, demand that the treatments given be those that have adequate research support.

OUTCOME AND FOLLOW-UP

The goals of CBT for bulimia nervosa include cessation of all binging, purging, and dieting, and the adoption of healthy attitudes toward one's shape and weight. In reality, few patients accomplish all of these goals. Instead, most respond to treatment with varying degrees of improvement. For example, some may cease binging and purging, but may continue to restrict their eating due to their persistent concerns about shape and weight. Others may resume normal eating patterns and have decreased body image concerns, yet continue to engage in occasional binge–purge episodes. Still others may make modest improvement in all areas, yet still be symptomatic. The therapist should not be overly concerned when terminating a client who is not 100% improved. Throughout CBT, the therapist is helping the client develop skills that the client can continue to use on their own once therapy has ended. For this reason, patients often show continued improvement after successful CBT. Patients should be encouraged to act as their own therapist and use the skills they have gained through CBT before seeking additional treatment.

Our experience is that most patients, like Jenni, are successful at reducing the frequency of binge–purge episodes, while body image concerns remain at some level. It is very difficult to completely rid the client of body image dissatisfaction when they are constantly bombarded by media images of the ideal (i.e., thin) woman and social pressures to diet. It is commonly stated that body image concerns and dieting are normative among females in our culture. While these concerns may not be problematic for a female with no history of an eating disorder, body dissatisfaction and dieting can lead to relapse in a recovering bulimic. Clients should be instructed to recontact the therapist whenever dieting, binging, and/or purging are increasing and the client is not able to affect change on their own.

DEALING WITH RECIDIVISM

Patients with bulimia who have been successfully treated with CBT tend to show good maintenance of change at follow-up. Therefore, relapse should not be expected. Unfortunately, relapse is not entirely uncommon. Often relapse occurs after a psychosocial stressor when the patient feels overwhelmed and fails to use the relapse-prevention techniques discussed at the termination of their therapy. Patients who relapse should be encouraged to examine the causes of their relapse and to utilize the CBT techniques that were most useful to them in an effort to once again gain control over their symptoms. Cutting back on eating and skipping meals are often the first steps toward relapse. Therefore, reinstituting self-monitoring and prescribed eating may be important initial steps in getting back on track with recovery. Patients can often regain control with minimal assistance from the therapist. Those that cannot may benefit from an abbreviated form of CBT.

Those clients who fail to respond to CBT may benefit from a different therapeutic approach. Interpersonal Therapy (IPT) may be a sound alternative. Initial research shows, relative to CBT, that IPT produces modest results at the end of treatment, but actually produces more improvement at long-term follow-up. IPT is quite different from CBT. It is nondirective and focuses only on interpersonal relationships. Eating patterns and shape and weight concerns are not specifically addressed. It is possible that those clients who do not respond to CBT may do quite well with IPT. Antidepressant medications may also help those nonresponders. Research is currently investigating whether those who do not respond to CBT improve with antidepressant medication or alternative forms of therapy. It is possible, however, that nonresponders to CBT may prove intractable. There is some systematic research to support this idea as well as case reports of individuals who have struggled with bulimia for years, with numerous attempts at treatment.

SUMMARY

In spite of the relative poor level of funding from federal and private sources as compared to other psychological disorders, it is amazing how much research has been done on bulimia nervosa, and eating disorders in general. When the first author treated his first patient with bulimia while in graduate school at the University of Arkansas in the late 1970s, the term *bulimia nervosa* did not exist in the DSM, and only a handful of articles existed regarding this condition. Now, 20 years later, we have empirically supported treatments and well-validated assessment approaches. Thus, for patients needing treatment there is definite hope. However, this hope must be tempered with the fact that approximately two-thirds of patients have a treatment outcome that is less than what we and they would hope for (i.e., complete remission of the disorder). Thus, astute clinicians and researchers will continue the search for better approaches to treatment.

REFERENCES

Beck, A. T., Rush, A. J., Shaw, B. F., & Emery, G. (1979). *Cognitive therapy of depression*. New York: Guilford.

Christiano, B., & Mizes, J. S. (1997). Appraisal and coping deficits associated with eating disorders: Implications for treatment. *Cognitive and Behavioral Practice, 4,* 263–290.

Fairburn, C. G., Marcus, M. D., & Wilson, G. T. (1993). Cognitive-behavioral therapy for binge eating and bulimia nervosa: A comprehensive treatment manual. In C. G. Fairburn & G. T. Wilson (Eds.), *Binge eating: Nature, assessment, and treatment* (pp. 361–404). New York: Guilford.

Garner, D. M. (1997). Psychoeducational principles in treatment. In D. M. Garner & P. E. Garfinkel (Eds.), *Handbook of treatment for eating disorders* (2nd ed., pp. 145–177). New York: Guilford.

Keesey, R. E. (1993). Physiological regulation of body energy: Implications for obesity. In A. J. Stunkard & T. A. Wadden (Eds.), *Obesity: Theory and therapy* (2nd ed., pp. 77–96). New York: Raven.

Prochaska, J. O., DiClemente, C. C., & Norcross, J. C. (1992). In search of how people change: Applications to addictive behaviors. *American Psychologist, 47,* 1102–1114.

Vitousek, K. B., & Hollon, S. D. (1990). The investigation of schematic content and processing in the eating disorders. *Cognitive Therapy and Research, 14,* 191–214.

Whittal, M. L., Agras, W. S., & Gould, R. A. (1999). Bulimia nervosa: A meta-analysis of psychosocial and pharmacological treatments. *Behavior Therapy, 30,* 117–135.

CHAPTER

Primary Insomnia

David L. Van Brunt
Department of Preventive Medicine
University of Tennessee College of Medicine
Memphis, Tennessee

Kenneth L. Lichstein
Department of Psychology
The University of Memphis
Memphis, Tennessee

Case Description
Treatment Conceptualization
Assessment
Treatment Implementation
Concurrent Diagnoses and Treatment
Complications and Treatment Implications
Dealing with Managed Care and Accountability
Outcome and Follow-Up
Dealing with Recidivism
Summary
References

Effective Brief Therapies: A Clinician's Guide

CASE DESCRIPTION

Peggy is 47 years old, married, and currently not working outside of the home. Her primary complaint is difficulty in initiating sleep for the past 6 to 7 months, and increasing nighttime awakenings over the past 2 months. She was reluctant to come to the outpatient mental health clinic because she did not see her problem as a "mental" one. She has tried several medications provided by her family physician, observing that she now takes them simply out of habit despite their ineffectiveness. She was referred by her family physician and followed through with her appointment at the insistence of her husband.

TREATMENT CONCEPTUALIZATION

Insomnia is a frequent complaint in the primary care setting, affecting as much as a third of the adult population in the United States (Kroenke *et al.*, 1990). Surveys suggest that about 10 to 20% of adults suffer from insomnia that is severe or chronic. Older insomniacs predominantly suffer from sleep maintenance problems, whereas younger insomniacs more frequently complain of difficulty falling asleep. Insomnia is reported more commonly among females than males, and the incidence of insomnia symptoms increases with age (Ford & Kamerow, 1989).

A clinician's approach to any sleep complaint should include distinguishing an acute sleep complaint or a symptomatic sleep complaint from a primary sleep disorder. The focus of this chapter is on Primary Insomnia, which is distinct from other sleep complaints in both quality and duration. Although other sleep disturbances will be covered briefly for their value in differential diagnosis, the treatment approaches discussed here are directed toward Primary Insomnia specifically. The reader is referred to Thorpy (1990) for detailed coverage of a wide variety of sleep disorders.

Insomnia can be broadly classified as either difficulty initiating sleep (sleep-onset or initial insomnia) or difficulty maintaining sleep (sleep-maintenance insomnia). The latter can be further subdivided into either frequent or lengthy nocturnal awakenings, or early morning awakenings with an inability to return to sleep (terminal insomnia). Sufferers may present with one or any combination of the aforementioned difficulties.

Behavioral intervention for Primary Insomnia begins with understanding a conceptual model of sleep behavior by which to formulate and evaluate treatment. This chapter addresses important theoretical and practical considerations through case conceptualization and treatment progression.

Environmental factors may play a significant role in the initiation or maintenance of sleep problems, and examining these is an important first step. However, it is unlikely that a chronic sleep complaint will be explained solely by environmental disturbances. A more complete conceptualization views primary insomnia from the perspective of conditioning, whereby repeated pairings of the bedtime stimuli with arousal and frustration serve to exacerbate the complaint. In this model, the best-intended efforts by the patient to make sleep better (such as spending more time in bed) paradoxically make the problem worse through more exposure to bedtime arousal and frustration. The anxiety associated with the impending poor night's sleep creates an arousal that is incompatible with sleep. Thus, the bedroom, the bed itself, and rituals associated with going to bed may become conditioned stimuli that continue to elicit insomnia long after any originating stressors are removed.

In addition to the conditioning that can occur during insomnia's development, cognitions unrelated to sleep concerns might play a formative role. Intrusive cognitions may include problem solving, planning future activities, brooding over the day's events, or other thoughts that tend to arouse rather than relax the insomniac.

ASSESSMENT

When assessing a client with sleep complaints, a thorough history is critical. Insomnia can exist as a self-standing clinical issue as with Primary Insomnia, or it can be a symptom of other pathology. Depression, anxiety, bipolar disorder, panic disorder, substance abuse, or a host of other psychological and/or medical maladies may be present. Both comorbid and causative factors should be addressed immediately. Failure to do so may result in treatment failure as the factors perpetuating the insomnia persist or worsen. Frustration stemming from initial difficulties may work against treatment adherence and further interfere with treatment. Medical concerns should be addressed through physician referral. Clinicians should be careful to consider whether the insomnia complaint is of difficulty falling asleep, difficulty staying asleep, or early morning awakenings. Early morning awakenings may be indicative of depression, while awakenings during the night may indicate environmental disturbances, medical problems (such as apnea, pain, or nocturia), or panic disorder.

Because insomnia complaints can sometimes be symptomatic of other axis I syndromes (American Psychiatric Association, 1994), careful psychological examination is required. An initial interview should investigate the following areas of interest:

- The **nature and severity** of the problem (i.e., "6 months of sleep-onset insomnia").

- **Frequency of occurrence**. Although the client's initial report may be global and diffuse (i.e., "all the time"), it is important to follow up for specifics.

- **Date of onset and life circumstances surrounding that time**. This includes any emotional, social, or economic factors or stresses at the time of onset. If the problem is sporadic rather than chronic, determine what circumstances are likely to exacerbate the condition.

- **Detailed sleep history**. Assess what "normal" sleep is for the patient by getting a description of sleep habits preceding the current symptoms (e.g., number of hours slept, number of awakenings).

- **Daytime sequelae**. This includes an evaluation of sleepiness, fatigue, performance, and mood. Do these factors fluctuate with the quality of the previous night's sleep?

- The **patient's emotional and behavioral reactions** during a bad night of sleep. What fears (possibly irrational) are associated with not being able to sleep? What does the patient do when unable to sleep?

- **Sleep hygiene**. The regularity of sleep schedule, exercise, dietary habits (caffeine, nicotine, alcohol), environmental conditions, and napping can all affect sleep.

- **Psychiatric factors**. Is the patient experiencing depressive symptomatology or feeling anxious? If psychiatric factors are uncovered during the initial interview, a more detailed psychiatric diagnostic interview is recommended.

- **Medical factors**. Check for the existence of breathing irregularities, limb twitches, and pain. Refer to physician if appropriate.

- **Medication and other drugs** What medication is being taken, and does the patient smoke, drink alcohol, or use other drugs of abuse? Frequency and quantity of usage should be investigated.

- **Treatment history**. This should include a history of treatment types, treatment response, and compliance with treatment procedures.

- **Patient perspectives**. Ask the patient to theorize about the etiology of his or her complaint. Also, what goal (possibly unrealistic) is the patient hoping to attain through treatment?

If medical causes are suspected, a physician should be consulted as soon as possible. If there is any suspicion of medical concern, or if the history indicates sleep disturbance beyond primary insomnia, consultation with a physician to recommend an overnight sleep study (polysomnography) is appropriate. Because other sleep disorders may produce symptoms similar to those associated with primary insomnia, the process of differential diagnosis can prove to be challenging. Referral of a patient for polysomnography (PSG) may be imperative. PSG involves all-night monitoring of brain activity (EEG), eye movement (EOG), muscle tension (EMG), respiration, and other physiological variables, and is necessary for definitive diagnosis of certain sleep disorders. Some of these disorders are described here, along with the features that the cautious clinician can use to differentiate them from insomnia.

One opportunity for misdiagnosis is present in the case of narcolepsy. Narcolepsy is characterized by excessive daytime sleepiness (EDS), which often results in an inability to stay awake during tasks requiring substantial vigilance (e.g., driving a car). In addition to sudden sleep attacks, narcoleptics may also report cataplexy (loss of muscle tone induced by strong emotions), hypnagogic hallucinations (vivid dreamlike images seen while failing asleep), and sleep paralysis (an inability to move while falling asleep or immediately after awakening). Insomnia and narcolepsy can be confused by the lay observer because of the nighttime sleep difficulties and EDS that may be associated with both disorders. However, many insomniacs do not experience EDS (especially not to the degree found among narcoleptics), and some narcoleptics will not complain of nocturnal sleep disturbance. Other symptoms of narcolepsy (i.e., cataplexy and sleep paralysis) are not reported by insomniacs. The critical tests in diagnosing narcolepsy are PSG and multiple sleep latency tests (MSLTs). MSLTs consist of PSG monitoring during four 20-minute daytime nap opportunities, a requirement for identifying the two narcoleptic earmarks of excessive daytime sleepiness and sleep-onset rapid eye movements (REMs).

Another area of potential confusion lies with circadian rhythm disorders. Many biological functions, including body temperature and the sleep–wake system, follow a rhythmic cycle that lasts about 25 hours (circadian rhythm). Circadian rhythm disorders result when a person's circadian rhythm does not match the demands of his or her environment.

The circadian disorders often confused with insomnia are delayed sleep-phase syndrome (DSPS) and advanced sleep-phase syndrome (ASPS). DSPS involves an inability to fall asleep until much later than conventional times (as governed by the person's environment and social expectations). People suffering from DSPS often cannot fall asleep until sometime early in the morning (2:00–6:00 a.m.) yet will be forced to awaken only a few hours later in order to fulfill daytime responsibilities. Students and night-shift workers are likely to develop this pattern. Patients with ASPS show the opposite pattern, falling asleep and awakening earlier than desired. One sharp distinction, however, is that for ASPS patients total sleep duration is not shortened. For example, an individual with ASPS may be unable to stay awake past 6:00 p.m., despite a desire to do so, and will awaken for the last time the next morning at 1:00 a.m. Thus, DSPS mimics sleep-onset insomnia, while ASPS may imitate terminal insomnia if total sleep duration is not considered.

Despite their similarities, some features of DSPS enable discrimination from insomnia without the use of PSG. A sleep-history assessment with DSPS patients will often reveal a pattern of sleeping unusually late on weekends and holidays, when early morning arising is not required. Sleep length is also an important indicator, because many DSPS patients are able to sleep for a normal length of time when social–environmental constraints are removed. A consistent sleep-onset time favors a diagnosis of DSPS, as it suggests a problem with the time that one is trying to fall asleep rather than a general inability to initiate sleep.

When speaking of obtaining a "proper amount" of sleep, it is important to remember that this amount varies greatly between individuals. Someone sleeping less than 8 hours per night is defined as an insomniac only if he or she is consistently unable to get adequate rest from those hours of sleep. Short sleepers are individuals who sleep for only a short period each night but exhibit no consequent impairment of functioning during the day. They may complain of insomnia because they view their sleep pattern as abnormal, have unsuccessfully attempted to increase sleep length, or fear that dire consequences may result from limited sleep. Some short sleepers attempt to solve their perceived problem by spending more time in bed. Unfortunately, this strategy may result in adverse conditioning to the bedroom environment.

An assessment of sleep history will often distinguish a short sleeper from a sleep-maintenance insomniac. Short sleepers usually report a long history of obtaining a small amount of high-quality sleep (even on weekends and holidays when allowed to "sleep in") while experiencing no impairment in daytime functioning. Insomniacs, by comparison, describe significantly lengthier sleep time prior to their insomnia complaint. The short sleeper who complains of insomnia should be assured that acquiring a limited amount of sleep is not necessarily dangerous or "abnormal," and treatment should involve establishment of more realistic sleep goals. Further, because the nature of sleep changes through the life-span, the focus of treatment should be obtaining satisfactory sleep rather than reaching a fixed number of hours.

A significant health problem that may lead to a complaint of insomnia is sleep apnea. Although apneics do not typically have difficulty initiating sleep, they may complain of sleep maintenance problems. Clues that suggest a diagnosis of apnea rather than primary insomnia include heavy snoring, breathing irregularities, obesity, morning headaches, and sleeping better when sitting upright. Although the prototypical sufferer of obstructive sleep-apnea syndrome is a middle-aged obese male, anyone can develop the problem. Polysomnography is required for a definitive diagnosis of this disorder. Periodic limb movements during sleep (PLMS) may also be mistaken for primary insomnia. Patients with PLMS who complain of sleep maintenance difficulties are often unaware of the cause of their problem. Because of this lack of awareness, the observation of a bed partner can provide valuable information to the clinician during the process differential diagnosis.

Another indicator of PLMS is the presence of restless legs syndrome (RLS). RLS consists of uncomfortable "crawling" sensations in one's legs that interfere with sleep onset, and nearly every person suffering from RLS also suffers from PLMS, although the converse is not true. As with sleep apnea, PSG is required to investigate the role of PLMS in a patient's sleep concerns.

By looking at how the patient sleeps in alternate contexts, as well as how he or she behaves and reacts in various sleep-related situations, the clinician can assess what environmental and behavioral factors may be operating to maintain the problem. While taking Peggy's history, it became apparent that she had inadvertently conditioned herself against sleeping in the desired fashion. She described her current status as only falling asleep when completely exhausted, usually after a couple of consecutive nights of poor sleep. When traveling, however, she would have no difficulty falling asleep at all. She reported anticipatory anxiety surrounding bedtime, and made nightly predictions about how "awful" her sleep would be and how "wasted" she would feel the next day. Not surprisingly, her predictions were often confirmed.

The genesis of Peggy's sleep problems came upon first moving to the local area, a time she described as turbulent and stressful. At that time (about 9 months prior), she was also suffering from the flu. Because of her illness, she made no alarming attributions about her inability to fall asleep easily. After she recovered, however, she began to notice and worry that her sleep was not improving. She immediately began using over-the-counter (OTC) sleep aids. After a couple of months, the OTC medications became less effective, so she brought her insomnia complaint to her family doctor. After trying various medications, she began to doubt she would ever sleep normally again. She was now taking the medications as a matter of habit, fearing that if she stopped her sleep would get even worse. Any attempts to go without medication resulted in frustration and exhaustion.

Peggy showed some indications of anxiety as well. She described herself as generally "high strung," and she had frequent problems with stiff neck muscles and tension headaches developing through the course of the day. In addition to her interviews, Peggy completed a Personality Assessment Inventory (Morey, 1991) and a Brief Symptom Inventory (BSI; Derogatis, 1992) to see if other psychological factors warranted concern. Her testing indicated high levels of anxiety characterized by a worrisome thinking style. However, there was not sufficient distress nor interference with daily functioning to support diagnosis of a comorbid anxiety disorder, and her history did not support the idea that her insomnia was a symptom of other medical or psychiatric factors. Factors mitigating for a diagnosis of primary insomnia in Peggy's case are shown in Table 15.1. In light of these circumstances, a diagnosis of primary insomnia was made.

TREATMENT IMPLEMENTATION

Treatment for primary insomnia can take several directions. Table 15.2 summarizes common empirically supported treatment interventions. In each case, insomnia sufferers must alter their own waking behavior in order to impact their sleep. In most cases, the benefit is obtained only after persistent change on the part of the patient, often after an initial period in which the problem might seem to worsen. A large part of the clinician's job is dealing with adherence to treatment principles, and encouraging the patient to follow through with the components of the treatment plan for long enough to see benefit.

In reviewing the treatment options with Peggy, it became clear that most of the principles of sleep hygiene were already being applied. However, she was responding to the insomnia in fairly common ways, includ-

TABLE 15.1

Diagnostic Criteria for Primary Insomnia (APA, 1994, p. 557)
and Corresponding Patient History

DSM-IV criteria requirement: *Primary Insomnia* (307.42)	Patient's history
Criterion A: "The predominant complaint is difficulty initiating or maintaining sleep, or nonrestorative sleep, for at least 1 month."	Presenting complaint was difficulty initiating and maintaining sleep three of five weeknights (though usually not weekends), lasting over 6 months.
Criterion B: "The sleep disturbance (or associated daytime fatigue) causes clinically significant distress or impairment in social, occupational, or other important areas of functioning."	Significant distress over the sleep loss and its possible implications; curtailing of daytime activities (pt. never sought employment locally) in response to a feared inability to perform; began to turn down social events so she could spend more time in bed.
Criterion C: "The sleep disturbance does not occur exclusively during the course of Narcolepsy, Breathing-Related Sleep Disorder, Circadian Rhythm Sleep Disorder, or Parasomnia."	No other circadian problems, parasomnias, or major medical concerns were noted in medical records, from exams, or by patient report of history.
Criterion D: "The disturbance does not occur exclusively during the course of another mental disorder (e.g., Major Depressive Disorder, Generalized Anxiety Disorder, a delirium)."	Pt. reported intermittent episodes of mild depression and anxiety, but the sleep problem continued unchanged through these periods and between these periods. Patient Did not currently meet criteria for any other mental disorder.
Criterion E: "The disturbance is not due to the direct physiological effects of a substance (e.g., drug of abuse, medication) or a general medical condition."	No evidence of drug abuse. There did appear to be some tolerance to the sleep medications, but the sleep disturbance existed for over a month before these medications were tried. There were no other medications being used (prescribed or OTC) that were associated with changes in sleep.

TABLE 15.2

Empirically Supported Treatment Approaches for Primary Insomnia

Treatment	Description
Sleep hygiene	Instructions given to patient about specific habits and behaviors to increase the probability of good sleep (see Table 15.3).
Stimulus control	Altering the stimuli or exposure to stimuli surrounding bedtime or sleep behavior, and changing the person's own response to the sleep disturbance. Reconditioning the bedroom and sleep environment to produce sleep instead of arousal. The key feature is limiting exposure to the bedroom environment to times when sleep onset is imminent, so that the environment becomes a cue for somnolence rather than arousal. Stimulus control usually involves strict rules about when to enter and leave the bedroom (see Figure 15.2), and establishing new patterns of behavior that can serve as cues for sleep onset (i.e., bedtime routine).
Sleep restriction	Decreasing the amount of time spent in bed to include only hours actually spent sleeping. Once sleep is less fragmented and sleep onset is rapid, the "sleep window" can be expanded. Sleep-restriction therapy consists of the following steps:

1. The amount of time patients are allowed to spend in bed is initially restricted to their 2-week average (though no patient is asked to limit time in bed to less than 4½ hours). Napping or lying down during periods outside of the prescribed time limits is prohibited throughout treatment.

2. Patients choose fixed times to enter and leave bed. As with stimulus control, the importance of a consistent awakening time is stressed.

3. Mean sleep efficiency is calculated as the percentage of time spent sleeping with respect to total time in bed. If sleep efficiency is >90% for a 5-day period, a patient's time in bed is increased by allowing the patient to enter bed 15 minutes earlier. Five days of unaltered sleep schedule always follows an increase of time in bed.

4. If sleep efficiency drops below an average of 85% for a period of 5 days, time in bed is reduced to the mean total sleep time for those 5 days. No curtailment of time in bed occurs during the first 10 days of treatment or for 10 days following a sleep-schedule change.

5. If mean sleep efficiency falls between 85 and 90% during a 5-day period, a patient's sleep schedule remains constant.

Sleep compression	Similar to sleep restriction, except that sleep compression does not immediately reduce time in bed to the baseline sleep-time average. Instead, the patient's time in bed is reduced by gradually delaying the time entering bed and advancing morning arising time.
Relaxation	Systematically lowering autonomic arousal to facilitate sleep onset. Training/practice methods may vary.

TABLE 15.3

Sleep Hygiene Guidelines

Sleep Promoting (habits to increase)	➤ Making a comfortable bedroom environment: ❖ Moderate-cool temperature (1) ❖ Quiet (2) ❖ Dark ➤ Spending 20 minutes in a tub of hot water an hour or two prior to bedtime ➤ Eating a light snack at bedtime ➤ *Regular* exercise in the afternoon ➤ Establishing a regular pattern for getting out of bed
Sleep Disrupting (habits to lose)	➤ Using caffeine 4–6 hours before bedtime (3) ➤ Using nicotine before bedtime (3) ➤ Using alcohol after dinner, or as a "sleep aid" (4) ➤ Doing vigorous exercise within 2 hours of bedtime ➤ Taking daytime naps ➤ Eating snacks in the middle of the nights (5) ➤ Eating heavy or high-fat foods, chocolate, raw fruits, or vegetables right before bedtime.

Comments:
1. A cool temperature is consistent with the body temperature dropping during sleep onset.
2. Consider earplugs or a masking noise (i.e., a fan or white noise generator) if needed.
3. If possible, eliminate using it altogether.
4. Although it may seem to facilitate sleep onset, alcohol fragments sleep and makes it less restful.
5. Awakening may become associated with hunger.

ing staying in bed longer to try to "make up" for lost sleep. This behavior resulted in almost a quarter of each night being spent in bed awake and frustrated. Session time was spent discussing how this pairing of aggravation with her bedroom might actually be a perpetuating factor in her insomnia. She observed that, when on a recent trip out of town, she "slept like a baby" the entire time. She reported feeling more rested and at ease than she had felt in months, and she was surprised to find that on her very first night back home she was unable to fall asleep. She laid in bed awake all night, getting more and more angry at her relapse.

In fact, Peggy had not "relapsed" at all, but rather showed the prototypical pattern of a conditioned insomniac. The bedroom environment itself had become a cue for arousal. With this hypothesis, the most logical approach seemed to be stimulus-control therapy. This treatment approach tries to break the associations between bedroom and arousal, and build an association between bedroom and sleep. The primary method is to restrict exposure to the bedroom to times when sleep is imminent. Of course, this is more easily accomplished when the person has become sleepy enough that sleep onset is likely to be rapid. With her anxious cognitive style and excessive physical tension, adding cognitive therapy (CT) and relaxation training also seemed prudent. We agreed that one aspect to becoming sleepy would be do decrease her overall arousal levels, and she was eager to test this by combining the CT with the relaxation skills.

The first part of her treatment involved establishing her current sleep needs. For insomnia, it is generally good practice to collect nightly information about sleep in the form of a sleep diary (see Figure 15.1). Daily recording eliminates "mental averages" that may obscure otherwise useful information, and allow for more accurate baseline sleep levels by which to set goals and evaluate progress. Peggy agreed to complete such a diary during the week following her first visit, and to bring the completed record back for her second visit. Aside from some basic sleep hygiene instructions (see Table 15.3), no changes were made in her schedule during this first week.

At the beginning of the second session, we reviewed her diary. As expected from her history, her sleep onset latency (the amount of time taken to fall asleep) was in excess of 2 hours. She would typically get into bed with her husband at around 10:30 p.m., where she would find herself angry at how long it was taking to fall asleep. She observed that, although she felt tired at the time she entered the bedroom, she seemed to wake up as soon as she got to bed. Seeing her husband fall asleep almost immediately only served to magnify how long it seemed for her own sleep to begin. Discussing her diary led us toward several things to try during the ensuing week.

First, we calculated a "sleep window" based on the amount of sleep she was actually getting. Subtracting her time awake in bed from her total time in bed yielded an average of 5½ hours per night spent sleeping. She agreed that a wake-up time of 6:30 was reasonable for a daily routine, and we counted back the 5½ hours to arrive at a 1:00 a.m. bedtime. Although initially alarmed at the thought of such a late bedtime, she observed when reviewing her diary that 1:00 a.m. wasn't much later than when she would normally fall asleep anyway. The only thing she was sacrificing was a lot of time tossing and turning in frustration.

Another important component was to ensure consistency in her awakening time and to follow the stimulus-control guidelines (Figure 15.2) strictly. Diaries were kept throughout the treatment process to verify that she was following the protocol, and to obtain estimates of change in

SLEEP QUESTIONNAIRE

Please answer the following questionnaire **WHEN YOU AWAKE IN THE MORNING.** Enter yesterday's day and date and provide the information to describe your sleep the night before. Definitions explaining each line of the questionnaire are given below.

EXAMPLE

yesterday's day ⇒ yesterday's date ⇒	TUES 10/14/97	Day 1	day 2	day 3	day 4	day 5	day 6	day 7
1. NAP (yesterday)	70							
2. BEDTIME (last night)	10:55							
3. TIME TO FALL ASLEEP	65							
4. # AWAKENINGS	4							
5. WAKE TIME (middle of night)	110							
6. FINAL WAKE-UP	6:05							
7. OUT OF BED	7:10							
8. QUALITY RATING	2							
9. MEDICATION (include amount & time)	Halcion 0.25 mg 10:40 pm							

ITEM DEFINITIONS

1. If you napped yesterday, enter total time napping in minutes.
2. What time did you enter bed for the purpose of going to sleep (not for reading or other activities)?
3. Counting from the time you wished to fall asleep, how many minutes did it take you to fall asleep?
4. How many times did you awaken during the night?
5. What is the total minutes you were awake during the middle of the night? This does <u>not include</u> time to fall asleep at the beginning of the night or awake time in bed before the final morning arising.
6. What time did you wake up for the last time this morning?
7. What time did you actually get out of bed this morning?
8. Pick <u>one</u> number below to indicate your overall QUALITY RATING or satisfaction with your sleep.
      1. very poor, **2.** poor, **3.** fair, **4.** good, **5.** excellent
9. List any sleep medication or alcohol taken at or near bedtime, and give the amount and time taken.

Figure 15.1 Sleep diary.

daytime functioning. Oftentimes when patients get discouraged, it is useful to have diary information to show when they are doing well, or to identify specific behaviors that need improvement.

During the third session, Peggy reported some aggravation with the sleep schedule. On one night she felt especially sleepy and opted to go to bed early, but was surprised to find herself awake "as soon as my head hit the pillow." Fortunately, rather than lying in bed frustrated by this turn of events, she got out of bed and began to read in the living room. It is a good

Set a reasonable arising time and <u>stick to it</u>!

Surprisingly, it is *very important* that you cut down your time in bed in order to improve sleep! Set the alarm clock and get out of bed at the same time each morning, <u>weekdays and weekends,</u> regardless of your bedtime or the amount of sleep you obtained on the previous night. You may be tempted to stay in bed later ("Sleep In") if you did not sleep well, but it is important that you get out of bed anyway. This guideline is designed to regulate your internal biological clock and reset your sleep-wake rhythm. *The most important step in setting the biological clock is a regular and consistent arising time.*

Go to bed only when you are sleepy.

Spending too much time awake in bed has two unfortunate consequences: you may begin to associate your bedroom with arousal and frustration, and consequently, your sleep actually becomes shallower. There is no reason to go to bed if you are not sleepy. When you go to bed too early, it only gives you more time to become frustrated. Individuals often reflect on the events of the day, think about the next day's schedule, or worry about their sleep difficulty. These behaviors are incompatible with sleep, and tend to perpetuate insomnia. You should therefore delay your bedtime until you are sleepy, even if it means that you go to bed later than your scheduled bedtime. Remember to stick to your scheduled arising time regardless of the time you go to bed.

Get out of bed when you can't fall asleep or go back to sleep in about 15 minutes. Return to bed only when you are sleepy. <u>Repeat this step as often as necessary</u>.

Although we don't want you to be a clock-watcher, get out of bed if you don't fall asleep fairly soon. How long is long enough without watching a clock? By the time you are asking yourself how long it has been, the answer is "long enough." Remember that the goal is for you to learn to fall asleep quickly. Return to bed only when you are sleepy. The object is to reconnect your bed with sleeping rather than frustration. It will be demanding to follow this instruction, but many people from all walks of life have found ways to adhere to this guideline.

Use the bed or bedroom for sleep and sex only; do not watch TV, eat, or read in your bedroom.

The purpose of this guideline is to associate your bedroom with sleep and comfort rather than wakefulness. Just as you may associate the kitchen with hunger, this guideline will help you associate your bedroom with sleep. Follow this rule both during the day and at night. You may have to move the TV or radio from your bedroom to help you during treatment.

Figure 15.2. Stimulus-control guidelines handout.

practice to predict such difficulties for patients early on, so that when problems occur they are equipped to deal with them in adaptive ways. When Peggy had difficulty, the event only served to reinforce the validity of the case conceptualization and encourage tenacity with the treatment protocol.

Subsequent sessions were spent reviewing adherence to the stimulus-control procedures, learning relaxation techniques (Peggy found biofeedback assisted progressive muscle relaxation most helpful), and learning cognitive restructuring techniques to use when she found herself brooding about daily events. When Peggy found that she was able to fall asleep on the first attempt, we began to broaden the sleep window by advancing the bedtime. She recalled that she used to feel very satisfied after about 7 hours of sleep, and this appeared to be the case when she would travel as well. Although she had some anxiety over "not getting all eight," we discussed how people's sleep needs differ, and she came to realize that she simply didn't need as much sleep as she originally thought.

CONCURRENT DIAGNOSES AND TREATMENT

Insomnia is often associated with affective disorders, although the causal relationship between them can be ambiguous. In addition, insomniacs tend to produce high scores on scales associated with anxiety such as the MMPI Psychasthenia Scale (Levin *et al.*, 1984). Whereas this may indicate some form of psychopathology, it also may reflect a general ruminative style that correlates with the complaints of intrusive cognitions mentioned earlier. Bedtime worry may indicate that failure to adequately dispose of daytime concerns is either causing or perpetuating a sleep difficulty. In such cases, the clinician may find that simply applying sleep hygiene or stimulus-control procedures is insufficient. Clinicians should be prepared to address other concerns with the insomnia patient. Because stress can in itself be a precursor to sleep difficulties, it is wise to assess both the degree of psychosocial stresses and the patient's reaction to these stresses to determine if intervention is necessary. In addition, the persistent lack of consistent and good-quality sleep can become a stress of its own.

Interventions for stress control or comorbid disorders should be considered for inclusion in the treatment plan. Many aspects of stress management training, such as neuromuscular relaxation training, can also be useful tools for patients to help them become more relaxed as bedtime approaches. In Peggy's case, although the severity was not sufficient to warrant diagnosis of an anxiety disorder, she did have some elevated anxiety. Cognitive and behavioral interventions for anxiety are covered in detail elsewhere in this volume and should be implemented with the insomnia patient when indicated.

Complaints of insomnia can also cooccur with some medical disorders, and insomnia may even be a presenting problem that ends in a diagnosis of another medical condition. Medical problems commonly associated with insomnia include neurological disorders (e.g., dementia, parkinsonism), chronic obstructive pulmonary disease, asthma, gastroesophageal reflux, peptic ulcer disease, sleep apnea, and pain syndromes such as fibrositis. See American Sleep Disorders Association (1990) for a more thorough discussion.

COMPLICATIONS AND TREATMENT IMPLICATIONS

When a patient with significant insomnia does not respond to standard interventions, the clinician should first reassess the diagnosis with particular emphasis on other psychological and potential medical factors. The patient's use of medication should be examined closely in consultation with a physician. Possible explanations for nonresponse to treatment are wide ranging and include affective disorder, sleep state misperception, "sick role" behavior, and treatment noncompliance. If the patient has had difficulty adhering to one treatment approach, others should be tried either alone or in combination.

Clients may complain that keeping a restricted sleep window is interfering with daytime functioning. Obviously, it is prudent to advise patients to exercise due caution in operating machinery, driving, or doing any activity that requires vigilance if sleepiness is likely to pose a safety risk. The specific interventions chosen (sleep restriction, sleep hygiene, relaxation training) must balance practicality and likelihood of patient adherence. For example, although in the case presented Peggy was willing and able to incorporate a sleep restriction component, it may be impractical to do so with an individual who works rotating shifts.

DEALING WITH MANAGED CARE AND ACCOUNTABILITY

A primary aim of managed care is to limit costs in both the short and long terms while maintaining acceptable quality standards. This can put clinicians in the awkward role of gatekeeper, with the pressure to balance what is most effective with what appears less expensive. Managed care organizations (MCOs) will hasten to say that they do not deny services, but simply set limits on services for which they will pay. For many clients, however, that is the same thing.

For assessment, it is highly unlikely that the expense of an overnight sleep study will be approved in most cases, unless there is a compelling reason to suspect a severe condition that cannot be otherwise detected. The diagnosis of Primary Insomnia is therefore a clinical one that is based on clinical interviews and, when possible, sleep diaries. Subjective complaints of severity and impact are not trivial, and are sometimes based on unrealistic expectations for sleep or ignorance of changing sleep needs throughout the life-span. In such cases, treatment goals can be accomplished with little change in actual sleep time.

For treatment, nonpharmacological interventions for insomnia have been shown to be cost-effective (Morin & Wooten, 1996), and many health plans covering mental health services will cover behavioral treatments for primary insomnia. As with obtaining reimbursement for any service, it is wise to have relevant and recent data to support one's claims of efficacy. Thorough recordkeeping and outcomes measurement are indispensable to this end. Fortunately, satisfactory treatment results can often be obtained in fewer than eight sessions with motivated clients, with better long-term gains than are usually seen with pharmacotherapy. Some studies suggest that behavior therapy alone has better long-term outcomes than pharmacotherapy combined with behavior therapy or pharmacotherapy alone (Morin & Wooten, 1996; Riedel *et al.*, 1998), though there is still debate over which behavioral approach, if any, is most efficacious.

For Peggy, the referral to our clinic came from the primary care provider (PCP) coinciding with his recommendation that she discontinue the use of sedative hypnotics. This combination made justification for behavioral treatment to Peggy's MCO almost effortless. Establishing relationships with PCPs and providing them with feedback about their clients' progress is not only a good way to minimize administrative reimbursement hassles, but makes for a good referral base as well.

OUTCOME AND FOLLOW-UP

After 6 weeks of stimulus control, relaxation training, and some cognitive restructuring training to decrease worry, Peggy had shortened her sleep latency to about 20 minutes. She had expanded her sleep window back to midnight, so she was getting about 6½ hours of sleep each night with only an occasional interruption. Although this was short of her original goal of 8 hours, Peggy was now getting this sleep without the use of sleep aids, and with much higher ratings of daytime alertness. Since much time in sessions was spent reinforcing the adherence to the stimulus-control and sleep hygiene guidelines, she was confident that she knew how to continue the regimen on her own. She agreed, however, that therapy itself was ongoing and that she was in charge of future gains and maintenance. Peggy also reflected the understanding that some nights may not be satisfactory, but that an occasional "lapse" was normal for anybody. Follow-up telephone calls later confirmed that her bedtime and sleep-onset pattern was becoming more stable, and that she continued to be satisfied with the sleep she was receiving. The relaxation training had become a routine that she practiced twice a day on most days.

Outcome measurement consisted of her sleep diary and a readministration of the BSI she had taken initially. While the sleep diary showed marked improvement, her improvements on the BSI were more modest. However, she did show some reduction in anxiety. Whether this was the cause of sleep improvement or the result of it is unknown, but she clearly showed an overall improved clinical picture. She remained free of medication use as of both the 6-month and 1-year telephone follow-ups.

DEALING WITH RECIDIVISM

Frustration and anxiety are natural consequences of persistent sleep loss, and sleep deprivation may cause significant impairment in some important areas of functioning. The clinician should monitor progress carefully using sleep diaries, patient reports, and other instruments as warranted to determine the client's reaction to the treatment process. Uncompleted diaries can signal nonadherence to the treatment protocols, and time should be spent in the session addressing this. Predicting the difficulties ahead of time and troubleshooting how the client might face these can go a long way toward reducing treatment rejection and relapse.

It is not at all unusual for insomnia problems to get worse before they get better. Although in many cases the hours spent sleeping may not actually decline, from the patient's perspective things may seem much worse. One reason for this is that, even though a patient may have previously only gotten a few hours of sleep during the night, he/she may have spent several hours in bed to get them. When treatment begins, all waking time is spent outside of the bedroom, making awake time much more prominent. Further, there may be some misperception of the sleep state itself; patients may state they were "up all night" when in reality they may have been drifting in and out of a shallow sleep. It is important to reassure patients through examination of their own sleep data that the changes are required, and to use the diary and session time to reinforce adherence to sleep protocols.

Unreasonable expectations can be especially problematic. If patients expect perfect sleep every night once improvements begin, one difficult night can easily set the cycle of worry, frustration, and sleep-countering behaviors in motion. An occasional difficult night is normal with any person, and patients should be aware of how to face this when (not if) that night comes. Even after patients feel the insomnia problem has been solved, they should be aware that adherence to good sleep hygiene principles and stimulus-control guidelines are important preventive methods as well. Once learned, the insomnia cycle can be easily reinstated if they respond to a difficult night with old, maladaptive responses. By predicting the problem and helping patients identify the adaptive response, acute sleep difficulties can be kept from becoming chronic ones again.

SUMMARY

Primary Insomnia is a prevalent sleep disorder that can occur in conjunction with other health problems or exist in isolation. The diversity of symptoms and overlap with other disorders makes careful assessment and differential diagnosis essential for treatment planning. Assessments should include objective measures when possible, but they should not ignore the patient's subjective perceptions of the disorder. Self-report measures are an effective tool in the assessment process. Although such reports may appear to sacrifice precision, the person's subjective experience prompted the visit and therefore should not be dismissed lightly. Sleep-quality variables may be as important in assessment and treatment planning as sleep-quantity variables, and increased sleep length does not necessarily imply increased satisfaction.

Many patients either have already explored pharmacological interventions or may wish to do so in the future. Although pharmacotherapy has demonstrated some short-term gains, it is contraindicated for the treatment of chronic insomnia. Several behavioral treatments are effective at reducing symptoms, but their success is dependent on patient compliance.

REFERENCES

American Psychiatric Association (1994). *Diagnostic and statistical manual of mental disorders* (4th ed.). Washington, DC: Author.

American Sleep Disorders Association (1990). *International classification of sleep disorders: diagnostic and coding manual.* Rochester, MN: Author.

Derogatis, L. R. (1992). *Brief Symptom Inventory (BSI).* Minneapolis, MN: National Computer Systems.

Ford, D., & Kamerow, D. (1989). Epidemiologic study of sleep disturbances and psychiatric disorders — an opportunity for prevention? *JAMA, 262,* 1479–1484.

Kroenke, K., Arrington, M., & Mangelsdorff, A. (1990). The prevalence of symptoms in medical outpatients and the adequacy of therapy. *Archives of Internal Medicine, 150,* 1685–1689.

Levin, D., Bertelson, A. D., & Lacks, P. (1984). MMPI differences among mild and severe insomniacs and good sleepers. *Journal of Personality Assessment, 48,* 126–129.

Morey, L. (1991). *Personality Assessment Inventory.* Odessa, FL: Psychological Assessment Resources.

Morin, C. M., & Wooten, V. (1996). Psychological and pharmacological approaches to treating insomnia: Critical issues in assessing their separate and combined effects. *Clinical Psychology Review, 16,* 521–542.

Riedel, B., Lichstein, K., Peterson, B. A., Epperson, M. T., Means, M. K., & Aguillard, R. N. (1998). A comparison of the efficacy of stimulus control for medicated and nonmedicated insomniacs. *Behavior Modification, 22,* 3–28.

Thorpy, M. J. (Ed.) (1990). *Handbook of sleep disorders.* New York: Dekker.

CHAPTER

Pathological Gambling

Robert Ladouceur, Caroline Sylvain,
and Claude Boutin

Department of Psychology
Laval University
Quebec, Canada

Effective Brief Therapies: A Clinician's Guide

CASE DESCRIPTION

Joan is a 58-year-old proud, passionate, and sociable woman. Divorced 20 years ago, she is the mother of two children and works part-time in a bar. Her annual income is low. She began playing video-lottery machines 3 years ago, following a breakup. From that moment on, her quality of life gradually deteriorated.

From the time gambling began to dominate her life, Joan had experienced severe financial insufficiency. She no longer visited the dentist or hairdresser, and had abandoned all skin-care products, which formerly meant a great deal to her. In order to survive, her activities had become limited to shuttling back and forth between her home, the pawnshop, and various bars.

Two years ago, Joan left the apartment that she had lived in for almost 15 years due to financial constraints. She rented a one-room apartment and preferred to isolate herself from her two children and her friends, for fear of disappointing them. The only friend that she had left was a gambling partner. Ironically, without their common gambling problem, they would probably not have spent time together.

Joan met eight of the DSM-IV (APA, 1994) diagnostic criteria for pathological gambling. She felt obsessed by gambling and fearful of her uncontrollable need to increase the amount of her bets. She unsuccessfully attempted to cease gambling using various methods. Her desires to recuperate her losses and beat the machine were strongly anchored. She lied about her gambling habits, and this saddened her more than anything else since it endangered her relationship with her children. She believed that, in the end, her children would abandon her because she was isolating herself. During the diagnostic evaluation, she reported not yet having committed illegal acts and stated she was too proud to count on others to obtain money to relieve her of a desperate financial situation. She was slowly paying off a credit card whose limit had been surpassed to finance her gambling habit.

Joan did not have any drug or alcohol problems. Moreover, she did not report having any other types of compulsions (e.g., eating, sexual, shopping). Although thoughts of suicide had surfaced, she reported never having seriously considered acting on them. Although Joan appeared somewhat despondent, she was not clinically depressed.

Gambling was never part of Joan's life prior to her recent interest in video lotteries. Her first bet was the result of a friend urging her to do so. She remembers having won $550. From that point on, she became a video-lottery addict and began gambling frequently. On a weekly basis, she engaged in three gambling sessions, each lasting approximately 3 hours. When asked by her therapist to recount the current total amount of her gambling losses, she replied that she preferred not to know and did not wish to respond to that question.

Near the end of the evaluation session, her therapist began to identify the occasions when Joan had successfully restrained herself from gambling despite a strong impulse to engage in the activity. At that moment, he introduced the cognitive-behavioral therapy framework, which emphasizes the inner discourse of the gambler.

TREATMENT CONCEPTUALIZATION

In 1980, the American Psychiatric Association officially recognized pathological gambling as a disorder of impulse control (DSM-III). Since then, prevalence studies have shown that 0.5 to 2.0% of adults met the criteria for pathological gambling over the past 6 to 12 months. The percentage of adults who met criteria over the course of their lifetime ranged from 1.0 to 2.5%. The prevalence of pathological gambling is related to accessibility of gambling activities (Abbott & Volberg, 1996; Eadington, 1997; Jacques et al., 1999). Research also indicates that pathological gamblers become emotionally dependent on gambling, lose control of personal, family, and vocational aspects of their lives, and display several signs of poor psychosocial functioning. These consequences have important social costs for society.

Few controlled treatment studies have been carried out (Blaszczynski et al., 1991; McConaghy et al., 1983, 1998). Most interventions have been reported in case histories that suffer from serious methodological flaws and do not adequately assess therapeutic efficacy. Russo et al. (1984) and Taber et al. (1987), who conducted studies that included a relatively large sample, found that 91.4% of participants gambled less following therapeutic intervention. Lesieur and Blume (1991) reported similar results. Their research revealed that 94% of participants showed an improvement on gambling measures following a therapeutic intervention and that 64% were abstinent from gambling 6 to 14 months after the intervention. Recently, Echeburua et al. (1996) tested the efficacy of different treatment programs. Again, methodological difficulties (e.g., different conditions among comparison groups and absence of validated measures to evaluate pathological gambling) limit the interpretation of findings. In addition to the aforementioned flaws, few treatment programs have been based on theories relevant and specific to the psychology of gambling behaviors.

Using a single-case experimental design, Bujold *et al.* (1994) evaluated a treatment program consisting of four components. The combination of these four components — namely, cognitive correction, problem-solving training, social skills training and relapse prevention — provided positive outcomes. After treatment, subjects did not meet the DSM criteria for pathological gambling, and the results were maintained at 9-month follow-up. More recently, Sylvain *et al.* (1997) evaluated the efficacy of this cognitive and behavioral treatment in a controlled group study. Participants were randomly assigned to a treatment or control group. Posttest results indicate highly significant changes in the treatment group on all outcome measures, and analysis of data from 6- and 12-month follow-ups reveals maintenance of therapeutic gains in 85% of treated subjects. In a subsequent study, Ladouceur *et al.* (1998) evaluated the efficacy of modifying the erroneous perception of the notion of randomness. Results obtained in a single-case experimental design confirm the efficacy of this procedure.

In understanding the motivation to gamble, the acquisition of wealth is assumed to be a primary factor. Ironically, all legalized forms of gambling are designed so that the expected return is less than the wagered sum. Thus, if acquisition of wealth is the individual's goal, the rational consideration would be to avoid gambling. The principal paradox of gambling is therefore that people, in attempting to gain wealth, engage in an activity that is by nature impoverishing. Cognitive theories of gambling resolve this paradox by assuming that gamblers believe and expect to win regardless of the adverse odds.

Studies show that cognitive factors play a key role in the development and maintenance of gambling problems. More specifically, erroneous perceptions about the usefulness of making links between random events appears to be the core misconception held by gamblers (Ladouceur & Walker, 1996, 1998; Walker, 1992). Gamblers employ various game strategies and believe that their abilities will help them win (Ladouceur & Walker, 1996). Many studies have shown the importance of erroneous perceptions held by individuals while gambling. In one such study, participants were asked to think aloud while playing roulette, slot machines, blackjack, and video poker. Results revealed that over 75% of their perceptions were erroneous and that most of them deviated from the notion of randomness. This cognitive misconception plays an important role in the development and maintenance of gambling.

If cognitive factors play a key role in the development and maintenance of this pathology, confronting and correcting these erroneous perceptions would be expected to reduce or eliminate gambling problems. The core cognitive errors lie within the illusion of control and the belief that events are predictable, both of which stem from a misconception of randomness. The main objective of the present cognitive treatment for pathological gambling is to correct gambling misconceptions. This objective is accomplished by increasing the patient's awareness of the fundamental misconception of making erroneous links between independent events, identifying risk situations leading to gambling, and, finally, correcting this fundamental cognitive error. The case history described below will illustrate this treatment procedure.

ASSESSMENT

The next step in understanding problem gambling involves analyzing the consequences of extreme persistence despite substantial loss. The central consequence, and possibly the core factor in causing gambling problems, is the financial loss resulting from this activity. While it may seem obvious that financial loss is a fundamental aspect of gambling problems, this perspective is sometimes not given appropriate emphasis. For instance, only 4 of the 10 criteria used to diagnose pathological gambling in the DSM-IV explicitly refer to loss of money and problems engendered by it. If the financial cost of gambling were emphasized, many of the criteria for identifying pathological gambling could be understood as consequences of this common cause. Walker's (1992) sociocognitive theory of gambling states that false beliefs held by gamblers can lead to chasing losses, changes in mood, withdrawal, irritation, anger, and foolish financial transactions. These changes, combined with a substantial decrease in income, are expected to have a negative impact on the gambler's employment, family, and social life. In addition to financial impoverishment, persistent gambling consumes large amounts of a gambler's time. This time consumption is expected to heavily impact the gambler's family life and employment.

In addition to loss of time and money, there is an additional area of loss that is more difficult to quantify. As previously mentioned, gamblers hold a set of erroneous beliefs about the nature of gambling and their role in relation to the activity. Forcing gamblers to realize that their beliefs are erroneous produces a great deal of stress for them, and can be expected to lower self-esteem and ultimately induce depression.

In addition to the DSM-IV, the South Oaks Gambling Screen (SOGS) is an important evaluative tool. The SOGS was first designed to identify pathological gambling among hospitalized patients (Lesieur & Blume, 1987). This gambling screen is a 20-item scale derived from DSM-III criteria for pathological gambling. Respondents scoring 3 and 4 points are classified as "problem gamblers" and those scoring 5 points or more are classified as "pathological gamblers." This research tool has been translated into more than 20 languages and is the most widely used instrument to measure pathological gambling throughout the world. Although recent studies have shown that the SOGS overestimates prevalence rates when used in the general population, its use as a clinical tool remains adequate.

We have adopted a multistep evaluation procedure. When a gambler calls for help, we return the call within 24 hours. During this first call, we ask the gambler to describe his or her main complaints and subsequently administer the SOGS. If preliminary data collected during the telephone interview suggest that the individual is a pathological gambler, a formal semistructured interview is immediately scheduled in order to identify the nature and history of the problem. Before beginning the scheduled interview, the individual is asked to complete a set of questionnaires designed to evaluate the following areas: depression, anxiety, beliefs about gambling, superstitious behavior (see Ladouceur *et al.*, 1997), and problem-solving abilities. The interview is divided into two sections and covers the following aspects: history of gambling activities; motivation for the consultation; first contact with gambling; first problems with gambling; familial, professional, and marital problems; money lost; and criteria of pathological gambling.

TREATMENT IMPLEMENTATION

In this section, the cognitive approach is applied to Joan's case in order to facilitate understanding of the different steps comprising the therapeutic intervention.

The intervention was based on correcting misconceptions about the basic notion of randomness. The cognitive correction included four components:

1. **Understanding the concept of randomness.** The therapist explained the concept of randomness, that each turn is independent, that no strategies exist to control the outcome, that there is a negative return rate, and that it is impossible to control the game.

2. **Understanding the erroneous beliefs held by gamblers.** This component mainly addressed the difficulty of applying the principle of independence among random events. The therapist explained how the illusion of control contributes to the maintenance of gambling habits and corrected the erroneous beliefs held by Joan.

3. **Awareness of inaccurate perceptions**. Joan was informed that erroneous perceptions predominate during gambling, and the distinction between adequate and inadequate verbalizations was explained.

4. **Cognitive correction of erroneous perceptions**. The therapist corrected inadequate verbalizations and faulty beliefs using a recording of the patient's verbalizations made during a session of pretend gambling.

The therapist first began to increase Joan's awareness of situations that triggered her desire to gamble, and evaluated at-risk situations leading her to gamble. He pointed out that she had previously said that feelings of rejection increased her desire to gamble. When asked to provide examples, Joan replied that she had once returned to gamble when her friend declined an invitation to go for coffee. Risk situations were then discussed. The therapist explained that the refusal situation just described is called an at-risk situation and asked Joan to find other situations that increased her desire to gamble. The therapist identified risk situations that were present before, during, and after a gambling session. These were: refusal/rejection, boredom, free time, a favorable horoscope, feelings of premonition, imagining herself winning, dreaming of a large win, having won the previous evening, having lost the previous evening, having negative emotions (anger, sadness, etc.), and receiving an invitation to gamble.

The therapist then introduced Joan to the basic concepts of cognitive therapy and the idea that at-risk situations are triggers for gambling behavior. The therapist explained that there is a thought preceding every behavior. Joan was asked to write down the refusal situation as being an at-risk situation, along with what she said to herself at that moment. Using the downward arrow, the therapist tried to identify Joan's erroneous ideas regarding gambling. Even though Joan sometimes confounded at-risk situations and thoughts, the therapist encouraged her to continue identifying them. At this stage, the goal was to make Joan aware of the link between at-risk situations, thoughts, and behavior. That week Joan had abstained from gambling three times. The thoughts that provided her with this control were identified and reinforced by the therapist. The downward arrow technique was used to explore Joan's gambling habits (games, bets, numbers, lines, observations, her rules of behavior, etc.) and to identify several erroneous perceptions associated with gambling. Joan's erroneous perceptions regarding gambling were as follows:

- □ Spontaneous attraction to a machine always pays off.
- □ Playing poker helps her to know if she has a good or bad machine.
- □ Wearing a religious medallion or making the sign of the cross is lucky.
- □ Drawing cards helps her predict whether the video-lottery machine will pay or not.
- □ Betting $5.00 at the beginning is lucky because the number 5 is lucky.
- □ The beginning of a gambling session often pays.
- □ The machine often pays out $20.00 and $80.00 if it did not pay at the beginning.
- □ Running out of credits fools the machine into believing there is a new player and a new game.
- □ A small rapid kick to stop the machine helps produce better wins.
- □ Playing using a regular rhythm of 3 seconds pays more.

The search for erroneous thoughts was carried out in detail. Each element of Joan's responses was questioned, but never confronted. During the interview, the therapist never took anything for granted and subquestioned everything. Subsequently, the therapist started establishing the link between thoughts and behavior.

Joan was then asked to provide a correct definition of chance and to differentiate between a game of skill and a game of chance. The therapist explained that we are not used to listening or being aware of what we say to ourselves; thinking is often an automatic process. However, in many cases, our thoughts determine our behavior, and we must act upon these to modify our behavior. We must learn to be more aware of our thoughts.

Next, the therapist asked Joan to define chance in order to verify whether she had a correct conception of it. Premonitions and the notion of destiny entered into Joan's definition of chance. The therapist discussed this conception of chance with her until Joan arrived at an appropriate definition. She finally stated, "Chance means that it is impossible to 'feel' a win or a loss beforehand, or to have any control over the outcome."

Joan and the therapist discussed cognitive errors associated with excessive gambling. The goal was to identify the cognitive errors that provoke and maintain excessive gambling. That week, Joan had gambled almost every day. This behavior was triggered when her gambling partner refused to lend her a dress that she wanted to borrow. Joan took this as a rejection and said that this led her directly to a machine. The therapist observed that this was a refusal scenario and that such a refusal is an at-risk situation. Joan said that she was so upset that she didn't even know what she was doing. When she woke up the next day, she hated herself for being so emotional and went directly to a bar. Gambling calmed her.

The therapist kept looking for erroneous thoughts. Since the thoughts Joan had before gambling were inaccessible, the therapist explored her thoughts during the gambling session. He asked her why she always started gambling by playing poker. She replied that she always tested the machine regardless of how she felt, and that when poker paid well at the beginning she assumed that it was her lucky day.

At this point, Joan provided the therapist with an occasion to question her hypothesis related to poker. He asked if she had ever had a game of poker that had paid well and that afterwards the other games had not paid well. Since she was unsure, he suggested the possibility that telling herself that future games would pay, after having won at poker, encouraged her to continue gambling. She stated that she believed it to be a possibility, but that she still thought that testing the machine worked. The therapist instructed her to systematically monitor what happened after her game of poker in order to provide answers to these types of questions.

The therapist then took the time to identify and challenge additional erroneous ideas. Often, it is erroneously believed that gambling is engaged in for pleasure. More often than not, however, the pleasure quickly transforms itself into a nightmare. The therapist then inquired about other sources of pleasure that had contributed to Joan's happiness prior to her gambling addiction and encouraged her to reengage in these or to find new sources of pleasure.

At this stage of therapy, Joan had gambled twice that week and each time was able to stop before having spent all of her money. According to her, this was a 50% improvement. She told the therapist that she started to understand that the control came from within herself and that she was stronger than the machines. The therapist addressed the fundamental erroneous perception in gambling, the concept of independence between events. This concept is the central point in therapy. Essentially, the patient needs to understand that each turn is new and independent and that it is useless to keep track of the machine's previous payoffs in order to find strategies to increase one's chances of winning. He pointed out that gamblers have a natural tendency to remember wins and forget losses. Observing the poker machines is useless for trying to "feel" beforehand if the machine will pay well or not. This kind of error leads one to consider games of chance as games of skill and to spend more money than desired.

He asked her if she believed that playing on the same machine leads it to fill up and makes it more likely that it will pay. Joan stated that she did. When asked if she had lost even after having "filled" up the machine, she recalled an experience whereby she and three other people spent $2000 on a machine that never did pay the jackpot. This intervention created dissonance in Joan's beliefs.

The concept of illusion of control was introduced by discussing certain strategies Joan used when gambling. The therapist targeted her habit of occasionally emptying the machine of its credits and beginning to gamble again. He discovered that she believed that the machine often pays at the beginning of a session, and that she thought she could fool it into believing that she was a new player. The therapist emphasized the fact that video-lottery machines are nothing more than programmed computers.

Finally, among the different erroneous perceptions, superstitions were the most revealing and most difficult to grasp. The therapist noticed that Joan maintained erroneous beliefs related to positive energy. The therapist's efforts were aimed at training Joan to identify her beliefs regarding energy, which fed her gambling problem. For example, she had gambled once that week and did not know why. She claimed that she was knitting and feeling relaxed when a thought crossed her mind. The thought was related to the fact that she had felt happy all day long. Joan reported that her positive energy encouraged her to gamble since it was often a sign of luck. She interpreted this positive energy as a sign that she couldn't lose and saw it as a way of reimbursing part of her credit card.

Once these erroneous thoughts were identified and written down, the therapist asked her to question their validity. He reminded her that a link exists between what she thinks and what she does. Each erroneous thought was addressed and questioned until Joan was able to reformulate them in a way that was adapted to her reality and the reality of games of chance. Once again, the therapist paid special attention to superstitions and the concept of energy, and pointed out the fact that, with games of chance, nothing can help to predict or feel what will happen. Since her superstitions were strongly anchored, the therapist suggested that she systematically observe her feelings and the results that she obtained. This would ultimately increase her awareness that her thoughts were erroneous.

The goal of the last four interviews was to consolidate these changes. The therapist continually emphasized the fact that Joan's thoughts caused her decision to gamble. He also pointed out that the fact that she was financially disadvantaged increased her desire to make quick wins and led her to maintain superstitions. At the end of the 15th interview, Joan said that she felt less fragile and more in control of herself. What helped Joan a lot was to realize that the power originated within her and that her debts would be reimbursed slowly but surely. Throughout the period involving the last three interviews, she had not gambled and her desire to gamble was almost nonexistent. She claimed that the exercises helped her immensely. At follow-up, Joan had abstained from gambling for the past 6 months.

CONCURRENT DIAGNOSES AND TREATMENT

The two frequent additional diagnoses found in pathological gamblers are substance abuse and depression. With the former disorder, research has shown that 20 to 30% of pathological gamblers seeking treatment also suffer from an alcohol or drug problem. It is of paramount importance for the clinician to determine the relationship between the two problems. The way to proceed when alcohol is to be treated as the primary pathology is as follows. The clinician's focus should be to determine whether the majority of gambling activities take place while the patient is intoxicated. It is typical in such cases that gambling is not the primary pathology and that alcohol abuse needs to be treated first. But in many cases, if not in the majority of cases, an individual will begin gambling without having consumed alcohol, but will undertake drinking as he or she continues to gamble. The person will then become intoxicated and lose control over his or her wagers.

Pathological gambling is often associated with important depressive symptoms as well. In the majority of cases we have seen at our clinic (more than 300 pathological gamblers), depression is the result of important financial, familial, and professional losses. When gambling is halted and the individual remains abstinent, the depression usually wanes. Studies have shown that more than half of pathological gamblers have considered suicide because of important losses in many areas of their lives. Clinicians should pay attention to gambling and depression history. Often, depression is triggered when gambling becomes out of control or when the main purpose of gambling is to chase one's financial losses.

COMPLICATIONS AND THERAPEUTIC IMPLICATIONS

The major complication in the treatment of gambling is adherence and treatment compliance. Dropout rates are very high. As reported in most treatment outcome studies (controlled or cases histories), for every person who completes the treatment there is at least one person who does not. This alarming dropout phenomenon can be explained by the cognitive model of gambling. In an effort to shed some light on this issue, a recent examination of patients who had failed to complete the treatment or who did not show up after the evaluation phase was conducted (Ladouceur *et al.*, 1999). Findings revealed that when patients ask for help, their goal is to stop gambling. This goal, however, is in direct opposition to a secretly held desire to recuperate the losses incurred by gambling. By putting an end to their gambling behavior, gamblers must accept that they will never recuperate their losses and will not be able to reimburse their debts with future wins. It is hypothesized that the gamblers who do not show up for treatment or drop out in the early phases of therapy do so because they are unable to renounce the prospect of gambling as a short-term solution.

This is consistent with Custer and Milt's (1985) description of the three stages of gambling — namely, the winning phase, the losing phase, and the desperation phase. It is during the desperation phase that gamblers resort to borrowing money, and more than half of them will commit illegal acts such as stealing, embezzlement, and fraud. In this phase, they need to recuperate the money they have lost, and, most importantly, they remain convinced that they will. This conviction is sufficient to keep them from giving up hope of a future win and thus leads them to refuse or drop out of therapy.

One method of increasing treatment compliance is to discuss this issue at the end of the first evaluation session. The therapist should explicitly ask patients how they plan to manage their financial problems, how they will reimburse their debts, and how they plan to do so without a final big win!

DEALING WITH MANAGED CARE

The central consequence, and possibly the core factor in causing gambling problems, is the financial loss. Walker (1992), in his description of a sociocognitive theory of gambling, shows how the false beliefs of gamblers can lead to chasing losses, changes in mood, withdrawal and secretiveness, deceitfulness, irritation and anger, and foolish financial transactions. These changes at the individual level, coupled with the large loss in income, would be expected to impact on the family life, employment, and social life of the gambler. Persistence with gambling causes not only financial loss, but also absorbs large amounts of the gambler's time. The time away can be expected to impact heavily on the family and on employment. The impact on the family of excessive involvement in leisure activities or employment is common across activities and may be a cause of family argument and distress. However, it is likely that time away is for most gamblers and their families a minor factor compared to the financial losses suffered by the persistent gambler. Many pathological gamblers will commit illegal and criminal acts. They need new money to chase their losses. Brief and effective treatments exist. Over a period of 12 weeks, treated gamblers who completed the treatment will obtain significant gains. Therefore, treatment should be undertaken as soon as possible, and insurance companies will reimburse the cost since it is now included in the DSM and should be recognized as any other mental disorder.

OUTCOME AND FOLLOW-UP

Single-case experimental studies have been conducted over several years to evaluate this cognitive–behavioral approach to treatment for adults and adolescents suffering from pathological gambling. The results were quite encouraging. A control group comparison study was conducted to further assess the treatment's efficacy (Sylvain *et al.*, 1997). Twenty-nine pathological gamblers participated in the study. The majority of gamblers were video poker players, while others gambled on horse races or casino games. Subjects were randomly assigned to a treatment or a waiting list control group. Results showed that treated subjects improved significantly compared to the control group. Treated individuals met fewer diagnostic criteria, reported less desire to gamble, and had a lower SOGS score. In order to provide clinically relevant results, the percentage of change and end-state functioning (comparing posttest scores to a criterion score) were calculated. Among the treatment group, 12 of the 14 participants improved by 50% or more on three dependent variables and on the end-state functioning criteria, in comparison to 1 of the 15 participants in the control group (85% success rate). Finally, 6- and 12-month follow-up measures indicated that the therapeutic gains were still present, confirming the long-term effects of this therapeutic program. More recently, Ladouceur *et al.* (1999) confirmed the efficacy of using cognitive intervention to stop making erroneous links between independent events.

Research on the fundamental aspects of the psychology of gambling suggests that the core cognitive error lies within the gambler's notion of randomness (see Ladouceur & Walker, 1996; Walker 1992). Gamblers try to control and predict game outcomes that are objectively uncontrollable and unpredictable. It follows that, if the gambler's erroneous perceptions and understanding of randomness can be corrected, then the motivation to gamble should decrease dramatically. The present treatment program has focused on erroneous cognitions concerning randomness as the most important target for change. This central component of the treatment is highly specific and based on a theoretical understanding of cognitions and behaviors related to gambling. That may explain the magnitude of therapeutic gains. Correcting the erroneous belief that links exist between random events plays an important role in the treatment of pathological gambling. Its effectiveness was illustrated in the case history described above. Although it cannot be argued that correcting this basic notion is a sufficient therapeutic objective, research has established that it merits inclusion as a treatment component in all interventions, regardless of the theoretical perspective.

ACKNOWLEDGMENTS

This chapter was written while the first author was receiving research grants from the National Council on Responsible Gaming and Loto-Québec. The authors wish to thank Sandra Hopps and Patrizia Montecalvo for their helpful comments on earlier drafts of this chapter.

REFERENCES

Abbott, M., & Volberg, R. (1996). Gambling and pathological gambling: Growth industry and growth pathology of the 1990s. *Community Mental Health in New Zealand, 9*, 22–31.

American Psychiatric Association (1980). *Diagnostic and statistical manual of mental disorders* (3rd ed.). Washington, DC: Author.

American Psychiatric Association (1994). *Diagnostic and statistical manual of mental disorders* (4th ed.). Washington, DC: Author.

Blaszczynski, A., McConaghy, N., & Frankova, A. (1991). Control versus abstinence in the treatment of pathological gambling: A two- to nine-year follow-up. *British Journal of Addiction, 86,* 299–306.

Bujold, A., Ladouceur, R., Sylvain, C., & Boisvert, J. M. (1994). Treatment of pathological gamblers: An experimental study. *Journal of Behavior Therapy and Experimental Psychiatry, 25,* 275–282.

Custer, R. L., & Milt, H. (1985). *When luck runs out.* New York: Acts on File Publications.

Eadington, W. R. (1997). Understanding gambling. In W. R. Eadington and J. A. Cornelius (Eds.) *Gambling: Public policies and the social sciences* (pp. 3–9). Reno, NV: Institute for the Study of Gambling and Commercial Gaming.

Echeburua, E., Baez, C., & Fernandez-Montalvo, J. (1996). Comparative effectiveness of three therapeutic modalities in the psychological treatment of pathological gambling: Long-term outcomes. *Behavioral and Cognitive Psychotherapy, 24,* 51–72.

Jacques, C., Ladouceur, R., & Ferland, F. (1999). *Impact of availability on gambling: A longitudinal study.* Manuscript submitted for publication.

Ladouceur, R., & Walker, M. (1996). A cognitive perspective on gambling. In P. M. Salkovskis (Ed.), *Trends in cognitive therapy* (pp. 89–120). Oxford: Wiley.

Ladouceur, R., & Walker, M. (1998) The cognitive approach to understanding and treating pathological gambling. In A. S. Bellack and M. Hersen (Eds.) *Comprehensive clinical psychology* (pp. 588–601). New York: Pergamon.

Ladouceur, R., Arsenault, C., Dubé, D., Jacques, C., & Freeston, M. H. (1997). Psychological characteristics of volunteers in studies on gambling. *Journal of Gambling Studies, 13,* 69–84.

Ladouceur, R., Sylvain, C., Letarte, H., Giroux, I., & Jacques, C. (1998). Cognitive treatment of pathological gamblers. *Behavior Research and Therapy, 36,* 1111–1120.

Ladouceur, R., Gosselin, P., & Laberger, M. (1999). *Where have gone all the follow-ups?* Manuscript submitted for publication.

Lesieur, H. R., & Blume, S. B. (1987). The South Oaks Gambling Screen (The SOGS): A new instrument for the identification of pathological gamblers. *American Journal of Psychiatry, 144,* 1184–1188.

Lesieur, H. R., & Blume, S. B. (1991). Evaluation of patients treated for pathological gambling in a combined alcohol, substance abuse and pathological gambling treatment unit using the Addiction Severity Index. *British Journal of Addiction, 86,* 1017–1028.

McConaghy, N., Amstrong, M., Blaszczynski, A., & Allock, C. (1983). Control comparison of aversion therapy and imaginal desensitization in compulsive gambling. *British Journal of Psychiatry, 142,* 366-372.

McConaghy, N., Amstrong, M., Blaszczynski, A., & Allock, C. (1988). Behavior completion versus stimulus control in compulsive gambling. *Behavior Therapy, 12,* 371–384.

Russo, A. M., Taber, J. I., McCormick, R. A., & Ramirez, L. F. (1984). An outcome study of an inpatient treatment program for pathological gamblers. *Hospital and Community Psychiatry, 35,* 823–827.

Sylvain, C., Ladouceur, R., & Boisvert, J.-M. (1997). Cognitive and behavioral treatment of pathological gambling: A controlled study. *Journal of Consulting and Clinical Psychology, 65,* 727–732.

Taber, J. I., McCormick, R. A., Russo, A. M., Adkins, B. J., & Ramirez, L. F. (1987). Follow-up of pathological gamblers after treatment. *American Journal of Psychiatry, 144,* 757–761.

Walker, M. (1992). *The psychology of gambling.* Oxford: Pergamon.

CHAPTER

Cognitive Behavioral Treatment of Trichotillomania

Ruth M. T. Stemberger, Amanda McCombs Thomas,
and Sherry G. MacGlashan
Department of Psychology
Loyola College in Maryland
Baltimore, Maryland

Charles S. Mansueto
Behavior Therapy Center of Greater Washington
Bowie State University
Bowie, Maryland

Case Description
Treatment Conceptualization
Assessment
Case Information Regarding Assessment and Conceptualization
Treatment
Teri's Case
Complications and Treatment Implications
Dealing with Managed Care
Outcome and Follow–Up
Summary
References

Effective Brief Therapies: A Clinician's Guide

CASE DESCRIPTION

Teri, a 20-year-old college student, presented with chronic hair pulling dating from her preschool years. She sought treatment at this time because her pulling had gotten worse, although she could not identify any particular reasons for the exacerbation. Teri's history of trichotillomania began with pulling "itchy" eyelashes in preschool, and pulling "rough" eyebrows in first grade. She moved on to leg hair in fifth grade, pubic and underarm hair in ninth grade, and scalp hair above her forehead in the later school years. Teri had been treated in the past with Luvox, but she could not tolerate the side effects and did not find that it decreased the urges to pull.

TREATMENT CONCEPTUALIZATION

Our approach to treating chronic hairpulling is based on a cognitive behavioral conceptualization that is consistent with, but broader than, the original behavioral conceptualization of hairpulling as a habit (Azrin *et al.*, 1980). As such, hairpulling is viewed as a complex set of behaviors that are maintained by antecedents and consequences. A functional analysis in which the antecedents, behaviors, and consequences are fully understood forms the basis for this behavioral conceptualization. In other words, it is assumed that hairpulling is a function of factors that immediately precede and follow it. It is the clinician's job to work with the client in a collaborative effort to isolate and change the relationships among the antecedents, consequences, and behaviors.

Prior to a discussion of the conceptualization of hairpulling or trichotillomania, two important issues must be addressed. First, this conceptualization will apply to those cases in which the clinician determines that hairpulling is an appropriate target for treatment; in other words, pulling must be creating significant distress in an individual for whom no more prominent conditions overshadow the pulling. Second, this conceptualization assumes that the origins of the pulling are unlikely to be the same as the current maintaining factors. Furthermore, it is assumed that the latter are the most crucial in understanding and treating this condition. Therefore, the purpose of this conceptualization is to identify the factors that have an impact on the current pulling rather than to understand what might have initially caused it.

The first set of factors to consider in hairpulling is the antecedents. Antecedents are comprised of the cues that trigger the urge to pull and the discriminant stimuli that facilitate pulling. For example, if an individual looks in the mirror and sees a hair that is out of place, this may serve as a cue. If she is driving a car and leans her head against her hand, this posture may serve as a discriminant stimulus, which makes her more likely to pull. We have categorized cues as either internal or external to the individual (Mansueto *et al.*, 1997). External cues include settings in which pulling is triggered (e.g., bathroom, car, bedroom) and implements (e.g., tweezers, mirrors), affective states (e.g., boredom, anxiety, irritability), sensations at the site (e.g., tingling, itching, burning), and cognitions (e.g., "I can't stand gray hair," "Eyebrows must be perfectly symmetrical"). Discriminative stimuli also can be categorized as external and internal to the individual. For some people, external factors such as the absence of others or the presence of certain implements (e.g., tweezers and mirrors) facilitate pulling. Internal urges, postures, and thoughts also can make pulling more likely. Examples of these would include thoughts of "I will only pull one" and postures in which the hand is close to the pulling site.

The second set of factors is the behaviors involved in the pulling. Contrary to what the term "hairpulling" implies, this condition actually involves more than the simple pulling of hair. In fact, there are unique patterns of preparation, pulling, and utilization of hair following a pull. Preparatory activities include purposefully going to a setting in which pulling can occur, securing implements, choosing a body site, and conducting visual or tactile searches for a specific type of hair. The pulling itself can occur in various ways. Important variables to consider include handedness, the type of hair selected, how the hair is manipulated (e.g., twisted, twirled, knotted), and the traction with which it is pulled (e.g., gentle, quick). Finally, individuals vary in how they dispose of the hair. They may quickly discard the hair, retain the hair for long or short periods of time, examine the hair, and/or use the hair for tactile stimulation or for oral activities that may include ingestion of the hair or hair root. Because individuals may vary in each of these factors, no one pattern of pulling applies to all clients.

Following the pulling, a variety of factors may impact the likelihood that pulling occurs again, either immediately or at some later time. Possible consequences include positive emotional states (feeling of satisfaction or tension-reduction), negative emotional states (guilt, disgust), changes in the physical sensations at the site (reduction of itching or burning), or a sense that one has/has not achieved a goal. Social consequences can include attention, criticism, and disapproval. For any individual, the relationship between pulling and these consequences may vary, but it is assumed that the consequence of the pulling impacts whether further pulling will occur.

An additional element associated with hairpulling is its cyclical nature. Many people are unlikely to pull just one hair because the consequence of the pull acts as a cue for another pull. One pull can thus lead to a pulling binge. Therefore, damage can result from pulling over short (i.e., during binges) or long periods of time (i.e., multiple incidences of pulling).

ASSESSMENT

The primary goals of the assessment of hairpulling are: (1) to assess for other significant axis I conditions and to determine the relationship between these conditions and the pulling, (2) to complete the functional analysis so that clinically relevant and powerful determinants of pulling can be isolated for intervention, and (3) to determine the probability that the client will engage in the behaviors that are necessary and sufficient for change.

Persons suffering from trichotillomania commonly experience co-morbid conditions. Christenson *et al.* (1991), in their study of 60 adult chronic hairpullers, found that over 80% met criteria for current or past axis I disorders. The most common were mood and anxiety disorders, and 20% qualified for substance abuse or dependence. Part of the clinician's job is to determine whether treatment of any other conditions should supersede treatment for trichotillomania. In most cases of moderate to severe depression, anxiety, or any level of substance dependence, these issues are probably paramount. On the other hand, chronic hairpulling may be the cause of milder forms of anxiety or depression, in which case treatment of hairpulling may alleviate the need for other treatments.

The next stage of assessment is completion of the functional analysis. The best assessment methods for gathering data are semistructured interviews and individually tailored self-monitoring sheets. Semistructured interviews should include detailed information regarding antecedents and consequences as well as specifics concerning the pulling behavior itself. For example, individuals should be questioned about all possible sites from which they might pull, affective states that might be associated with their pulling, their strategies for pulling and disposing of hair or hair roots, and problematic cognitions associated with pulling. Figure 17.1 provides a template for developing a self-monitoring form. Any of the variables included in the template can be employed when individually tailoring a specific client's self-monitoring form.

Once the antecedents, behaviors, and consequences are identified, the next step in the assessment process is to determine the modalities

Template for developing a self-monitoring form

Date	Time Began	Time Ended	Location (Where were you?)	Activity (What were you doing?)	Strength Of Urges (0-10)	Degree of Awareness (0-10) Full	Notable Feelings	Notable Thoughts	Notable Sensations	Site S=Scalp B=Brows L=Lashes P=Pubic O=Other	Strength Of Effort To Resist (0-10)	No. Pulled	Tactics and Results	Comments And Observations

Figure 17.1. Template for developing a self-monitoring form.

through which these function. Possible modalities are cognitive, affective, motoric, sensory, and environmental. The cognitive modality functions when the pulling is maintained by thought patterns before, during, or after the behavior: for example, "eyebrows must be symmetrical" or "I must remove all of the gray hairs." Many clinicians assume that the affective modality is paramount for all cases of trichotillomania, when in fact this appears to be true only in some cases. Affect includes negative feelings such as tension, anxiety, and sadness, but also positive ones such as excitement and satisfaction, and even neutral ones such as boredom. When pulling seems to be primarily a habit, with pulling-related behaviors executed without full awareness, the motoric modality is operative. The sensory modality functions for those whose pulling seems driven by tactile sensations such as itching or by a desire for pleasurable sensations derived from hairpulling. Finally, the environmental modality appears to operate primarily through the principles of classical and operant conditioning. Often, certain settings or the presence of objects that are used as implements for pulling serve as cues for pulling or facilitators (discriminative stimuli) for pulling.

One, or more likely a combination of modalities may be functional for a specific client. Once modalities are identified as important, individually tailored self-monitoring sheets may be designed to further understand the role that these components play in the hairpulling. Standardized assessment instruments may be employed if desired. One example is the Massachusetts General Hospital (MGH) Hairpulling Scale (Keuthen *et al.*, 1995). This self-report measure is brief and easy to administer, and it has been shown to be reliable and valid.

The third major area for assessment is judging whether the client is likely to participate in and benefit from behavioral treatment for chronic hairpulling. Treatment may require clients to tolerate the discomfort of resisting strong urges, engage in potentially embarrassing behaviors (e.g., carrying a "Koosh" ball around, wearing bandages on the fingertips), and engaging in tedious recordkeeping. Consideration must be given to the extent of distress the client feels regarding the hairpulling and its sequelae. Highlighting the emotional distress, physical damage, restriction of activities, and interpersonal conflict suffered due to hairpulling increase the client's motivation for treatment. Clearly, axis II symptomatology can impact a client's willingness or ability to participate in treatment. Compliance with self-monitoring assignments can also give an indication of how likely a client will be to engage in more demanding elements of the prescribed treatment.

CASE INFORMATION REGARDING ASSESSMENT
AND CONCEPTUALIZATION

Through self-report in interviews and individually designed monitoring sheets, it became apparent that Teri pulled an average of 115 hairs daily. She reported that sharp, "bristly," and dark hairs were abhorrent, and she used tweezers to pull them, sometimes digging below the skin and causing damage. She was more likely to pull when she was tired or overworked. She pulled most often in the bathroom using a mirror but would also pull in the car or while working a desk. She was careful to be alone when she pulled.

Using our behavioral model as an aid in conceptualization (Mansueto *et al.*, 1997), Teri's problem was described as involving mainly the cognitive and sensory realms, with external environmental variables playing a significant role.

TREATMENT

Clients often have a goal of eliminating pulling for the rest of their lives. This goal sets them up for failure when inevitable setbacks or relapses occur. In fact, the stress of a relapse can be so great as to increase pulling that much more. Therefore, an important initial step in treatment is to reframe this goal as probably unrealistic and possibly unattainable. A more realistic goal is to minimize pulling so that the client feels a greater sense of control and acquires skills to use when hair pulling urges increase (e.g., during times of stress).

The next step in treatment is to use the information from the self-monitoring to determine which treatment modalities (e.g., cognitive, affective) are likely to benefit the client. Possible treatment strategies are organized by modality in Table 17.1. Many of these interventions are commonly used by cognitive behavioral therapists, while others have been uniquely developed for use with this population. The therapist and client work together to review the possible strategies in the relevant modalities or to develop a new strategy within a modality, and then choose an initial strategy. It is important to take into account the fact that clients will find certain treatments more appealing than others. It can be especially beneficial to choose an environmental manipulation as an initial treatment strategy if the environmental modality plays any role in the pulling. As stated previously, these interventions are often quick and effective and require

TABLE 17.1

Treatment Inventions that Operate Through Identified Modalities

Modality	Cognitive-behavioral strategy	Examples of specific interventions
Cognitive	Cognitive coping	Cognitive correction Coping self-statements
	Cognitive conditioning	Thought stopping Covert sensitization
Affective	Relaxation	Progressive muscle relaxation Controlled breathing
	Emotive	Assertion Journal writing Exercise
	Imagery	Positive visualization Self-hypnosis
	Exposure	Imaginal/*in vivo* exposure
	Medication	Serotonin reuptake inhibitors Antidepressants Anxiolytics
Motor	Awareness training	Self-monitoring Finger bandages Biofeedback
	Response prevention	Gloves Scarves Wet hair rubber fingers
	Competing response training	Fist clenching Holding Koosh Ball Knitting
Sensory	Distraction	Baths Massages Facial masks
	Substitution	Brush hair Nibble food
	Extinction	Prolonged sensory exposure
	Medication	Cortisone cream Lacrilube
	Stimulus control	Dye hair Pull back hair
Environmental	Stimulus control	Remove/cover mirrors Eliminate tweezer Stay out of certain rooms
	Contingency management	Rewards Penalties Covert contingencies Snap rubber-band against wrist Show hair to therapist

little skill acquisition. Once this initial strategy has been implemented, careful recordkeeping will allow the therapist and client to evaluate its usefulness. If it is helpful, but does not eliminate the pulling, another strategy can be added. If the strategy is not helpful or is too difficult for the client to use, an alternative strategy can be chosen. It is also possible to modify the strategy to make it more effective. For example, adding environmental cues to remind the client to use the strategy can be helpful. The process of recordkeeping and evaluation continues throughout treatment. Interventions that apply to each of the modalilties will be described below.

When *environmental stimuli* trigger or facilitate pulling, stimulus control strategies such as removing or covering mirrors, removing implements such as tweezers, purposefully avoiding being alone, and staying out of certain rooms can be powerful interventions. Developing a contingency management plan with rewards for engaging in strategies to prevent pulling and penalties for not using strategies also can be very helpful. (This is often more helpful than rewarding "not pulling" or punishing "pulling.")

Cognitive strategies have been shown to be effective in the treatment of hairpulling when used as part of a larger treatment package (Rothbaum, 1992). Interventions used include cognitive coping (i.e., coping self-statements and cognitive correction) and cognitive conditioning (i.e., thought stopping and covert sensitization). All of these strategies can be easily adapted to hairpulling. For example, a client whose pulling is facilitated by the thought of "I will only pull just one" may benefit from cognitive correction (e.g., "If I pull one, I will pull many more"). In a client whose pulling is cued by a thought such as "I must have a perfectly even bikini line," thought stopping might prove useful. For instance, in this case the client could be instructed to interrupt the thought (snapping a rubber band on her wrist may facilitate this) and substitute an adaptive statement such as "It is okay to have an uneven bikini line." For the therapist, use of cognitive strategies requires significant training in cognitive therapy. In addition, clients must learn the skill of recognizing their own cognitive patterns as well as how to apply these skills. Cognitive interventions can be very effective but work best with a highly motivated and perceptive client.

In clients for whom the *affective modality* is primary, there are numerous commonly used behavioral strategies available. If tension appears related to the pulling, progressive muscle relaxation, with or without imagery, and controlled breathing can be helpful to remove affective cues for pulling. If other strong negative emotions (e.g., anger, frustration) play a role, exercise, journal writing, and assertiveness training might be useful to reduce those feelings. If strong urges to pull are difficult to endure, then exposure to both the stimuli that trigger the urge and to the urge itself can address this problem. For example, some clients experience overwhelming urges to pull while looking in the mirror. For these clients, structured exposure sessions of looking in the mirror while resisting the urge to pull can eventually reduce these urges. Medications are a final possibility for helping to manage emotions related to pulling. Most often, SSRIs, benzodiazipines, and tricylics are used; however, the meager available data suggest that medications are helpful only to hairpullers in the short run (Pollard *et al.*, 1991). It is not clear, however, that medications prescribed to improve affect will reliably reduce urges to pull, though it is certainly worth trying with patients who experience irresistibly strong urges to pull.

Some of the first treatments for hairpulling were developed by Azrin and colleagues (1980) and have come to be known as habit reversal training or competing response training. In this formulation, these strategies seem most appropriate in clients for whom pulling appears to be primarily a *motoric habit*. These individuals can be trained to use a variety of competing responses such as clenching their fists, holding "Koosh" balls, or engaging in any activity that otherwise occupies their hands. Barriers to pulling such as wearing gloves, rubber fingers, bandages on the fingertips, scarves, and hats can be effective aids in response prevention, particularly during the early stages of treatment. Many clients are unaware of their pulling or are unaware of the initial pulls in a hairpulling episode. In these cases, increasing their awareness through self-monitoring or through other awareness-enhancing devices (e.g., wearing a movement-restricting elbow brace, wearing perfume on the wrists) can be very helpful.

The least investigated treatment modality is the *sensory modality*. If negative sensations drive the pulling, prolonged sensory exposure can be helpful in extinguishing the pulling response. Medications such as cortisone cream and Lacrilube can reduce the sensations at the site. When clients seem to use pulling as a means of gaining sensory stimulation, substitutions for pulling can be used. Substitutions that may be helpful include: (1) brushing the hair; (2) handling dental floss, nylon fishing line, koosh balls, or anything that feels like hair to the client; and (3) eating sunflower seeds or other "nibble" snacks that can substitute for hair roots to quell oral cravings. When pulling is cued by visual or tactile sensing of the hair, stimulus control measures such as dying the hair (or eyebrows, etc.) or wearing it pulled back from the face can reduce the likelihood that pulling will be initiated. Activities like baths and massage can provide sensual alternatives to hairpulling at critical times.

At some point in treatment, it may be helpful to elicit support from significant others. Although some clients completely hide their pulling from everyone, in most cases family members and other significant persons are aware of the pulling. Unfortunately, if uninformed and confused about the disorder, significant others can add to the client's stress. This is especially true when the hairpuller experiences the comments and attention of others as punitive. Educating significant others about trichotillomania can reduce possible detrimental influences and opens up possibilities for them to make positive contributions to the treatment process.

In the absence of complicating factors, treatment for trichotillomania can be relatively brief, but treatment that lasts for several months is not unusual. At first, treatment sessions should be conducted weekly, but sessions can become spaced out for longer intervals in later stages of treatment. Phone contacts between treatment sessions can be helpful. After significant improvement in the pulling has been achieved, contact with the therapist can be maintained until the client's self-management skills ensure self-sufficiency.

As mentioned previously, whenever there are concurrent diagnoses, it is important to be certain that hairpulling is the appropriate first target for treatment. Several other conditions have been associated with hairpulling. For example, Christenson et al. (1991) found that 15% of hairpullers also met criteria for OCD. In such cases, it should be determined whether to treat the OCD or the hairpulling first. Because confusion remains, it is worthwhile mentioning here that hairpulling is often viewed as a subvariety of OCD. In fact, overlap and dissimilarities between trichotillomania and OCD have been found, but clear criteria for considering trichotillomania as an OCD variant have not been established (Stanley & Cohen, 1999). In actuality, treatment for OCD disorders and chronic hairpulling is very different; unlike treatment for hairpulling, OCD interventions typically involve exposure and response prevention as core treatments derived from an extinction model of anxiety reduction (Stanley & Cohen, 1999). On the other hand, chronic skin/nail/cuticle picking seems behaviorally and phenomenologically similar to hairpulling as it has been described here (Wilhelm et al., in press). Therefore, treatment approaches derived from this model, with only minor modification, can be applied to these conditions.

With mild cases of anxiety or depression, treatment for these conditions and for hairpulling can often be concurrent. In fact, some of the techniques will overlap when affect appears to be strongly related to the pulling. When depression or anxiety are moderate to severe, or when substance abuse or dependence is present, it is unlikely that clients will be able to manage the requirements of therapy for trichotillomania. This is also true in cases where clients have severe external stressors such as an impending divorce or significant problems with children, finances, or personal health. In these cases, hairpulling is probably best viewed as a secondary treatment issue until the time that such significant life issues are adequately addressed.

TERI'S CASE

Treatment techniques targeting environmental change are often chosen as initial options because clients tend to find them helpful immediately, and they are relatively easy to implement. For the first treatment sessions, the therapist and Teri worked together to come up with a physical barrier to pulling that could aid in response prevention. "Rubber fingers," devices commonly worn by office workers, were chosen. These worked well initially, but Teri reported that they "bugged" her, so bandaids on the fingers were substituted further into treatment. Teri eventually kept bandaids in her purse or pockets at all times in case they were needed. The initial treatment session also involved a discussion about tweezers and whether Teri was willing to give them up. She did agree to do so, but soon found that she pulled nearly as many hairs without them. It became clear after two sessions that Teri needed to keep her hands busy or, without realizing it, she would begin a manual search for sharp hairs to pull. It was hypothesized that Teri would benefit from manipulating objects to provide her with alternative sources of sensations. Teri experimented with various toy-like (e.g., koosh balls, silly putty) objects, and finally, after several sessions, reported that use of a "buff-puff" was most helpful. Two environmental changes that were made at this point involved covering the mirror in her bathroom and putting magazines in the bathroom to keep her busy while she was toileting.

In the second session, the therapist began the process of working on problematic cognitions. Teri reported several variations on the theme of "sharp hairs are intolerable and need to be weeded out." The therapist pointed out that such thought patterns increased the likelihood of pulling and recommended that Teri begin to replace such thoughts with more adaptive ones such as "Sharp hairs are baby hairs," " To have hair, I must let sharp, baby hairs grow," "If I let the baby hairs grow, they won't be sharp anymore." Teri reported that it took almost 8 weeks of constant work before her old thinking patterns were dislodged. As time went on, more replacement cognitions were added, such as "If I pull one hair, I won't be able to stop," and "I will be sorry later if I even pull one."

COMPLICATIONS AND TREATMENT IMPLICATIONS

If treatment is not proceeding well and no reasons are obvious, an un-known complication is probably present. Most likely, it will involve unrec-ognized axis I or II symptomatology or the onset of a new, severe stressor. In these cases, it is best to suspend treatment for trichotillomania until the other problems have been managed effectively. A second complication can be the failure to accurately assess a client's willingness and ability to change. Often, this requires a supportive and frank discussion about the commitment the client needs to make in order for treatment to be success-ful. It is possible that pulling serves some adaptive function for the client (e.g., distraction from life stressors, or providing a reason to form a thera-peutic relationship). In these cases, the pros and cons for change need to be examined in detail. Finally, it is possible that the therapist has made a mistake in identifying the appropriate modality. Clients are at times very unaware of their own behavior and may not give a complete picture of their problem in the initial sessions. Sometimes revisiting the functional analysis or developing new self-monitoring sheets can be very helpful. Finally, it should be noted that trichotillomania is a notoriously difficult disorder to treat, and even the competent, experienced, and motivated therapist will fail to reduce hairpulling in some clients.

Fortunately, Teri's case did not involve any serious complications. She did not have any comorbid disorders, she was in an appropriate stage of change, and no major life stressors occurred during the course of treat-ment. Some minor life stressors — namely, academic stress and the death of an extended family member — did occur. The therapist and client took a brief break from focusing on the hairpulling in order to provide her with support and training in stress management techniques (e.g., progressive muscle relaxation).

DEALING WITH MANAGED CARE

Therapists known to be experienced and competent in treatment of tricho-tillomania are a relative rarity. Once identified as such, substantial num-bers of referrals from the community can be forthcoming. When these therapists are known to the managed care company, they are likely to be targeted for this caseload. If they work outside the managed care system, they may be viewed as an "out-of-network-specialist" and an appropriate referral. It is not unusual for patients to have received treatment for tricho-tillomania from a variety of clinicians with no noticeable improvement. In contrast, the clear treatment plans derived from the model presented here can be very helpful for obtaining managed care approval. Managed care organizations tend to respond well to treatment plans that specify long-term goals, operationally define objectives, and specify the treatment techniques to be employed. In addition, treatment plans required by most managed care programs can provide the therapist and client with useful feedback.

The therapist was not a participating provider in Teri's mental health insurance plan; however, Teri chose to remain in treatment because of the specialized knowledge and skill of the therapist. The treatment plan was submitted and approved. As specified in her insurance plan, Teri was responsible for 50% of out-of-network fees and was willing and able to pay these fees.

OUTCOME AND FOLLOW-UP

As mentioned earlier, expecting the total elimination of pulling may not be a reasonable goal for many hairpulling clients. Instead, clients need to feel that they have learned successful strategies to minimize pulling that they can employ in high-risk situations. Before termination, it is important to have clients expose themselves to such high-stress/high-risk conditions. For example, if removing or covering mirrors is a successful strategy for pulling, prior to termination the client should be able to look at him or herself in a mirror without pulling. Clients also need to have a repertoire of strategies readily available for unexpected high-risk situations. For instance, a client may learn that she needs to carry bandaids in her purse or keep cognitive coping statements on an index card in her wallet for emergency use.

Once the therapist determines that the client has the necessary skills to manage pulling behavior, a mutual agreement to terminate can be reached. At this time, the client must be able to recognize indicators that warrant follow-up treatment. If, for example, the client is able to apply previously learned strategies to a single hairpulling episode, contact with the therapist is probably not necessary. On the other hand, if the client experiences more than one episode, a significant increase in pulling, or extreme worry regarding resurgence, she must be prepared to schedule additional sessions. If a full-blown relapse occurs, it is important for the therapist to revisit the functional analysis and determine whether new patterns of pulling are present. If new patterns have developed, new treatment strategies are warranted.

Teri was seen weekly and biweekly for 6 months; this period included the hairpulling treatment and stress management training and support. Treatment was judged to be very successful; she pulled rarely and felt as though she could manage the pulling. Several meetings were held over the next months to maintain her gains. At one point she experienced a relapse during a out-of-town trip. She called the therapist on her return. An analysis of the situation revealed that she needed to carry barriers, such as band-aids, and sensory toys, such as buff-puffs. Following this relapse and the intervention, she felt more confident in her ability to manage her hairpulling. After an additional session, she and the therapist decided to terminate treatment with the agreement that Teri would call again if she experienced any additional difficulties.

SUMMARY

Chronic hair pulling can be a devastating condition. While at first glance it may appear to be a relatively simple problem, careful assessment of all relevant modalities is likely to lead to a conceptualization of the problem that is detailed and complex. However, when a systematic plan, constant monitoring, and appropriate adjustments are implemented as needed, treatment can be brief and effective. More treatment outcome research is certainly needed, particularly as it pertains to identifying effective treatment options for each individual client.

REFERENCES

Azrin, N. H., Nunn, R. G., & Franz, S. E. (1980). Treatment of hair pulling (trichotillomania): A comparative study of habit reversal and negative practice training. *Journal of Behavior Therapy and Experimental Psychiatry, 1*, 13–20.

Christenson, G. A., MacKenzie, T. B., & Mitchell, J. E. (1991). Characteristics of 60 adult chronic hair pullers. *American Journal of Psychiatry, 148*, 365–370.

Keuthen, N. J., O'Sullivan, R. L., Ricciardi, J. N., Shera, D., Savage, C. R., Borgman, A. S., Jenike, M. A., & Baer, L. (1995). The Massachusetts General Hospital (MGH) Hairpulling Scale: 1. Development and factor analysis. *Psychotherapy and Psychosomatics, 64*, 141–145.

Mansueto, C. S., Stemberger, R. M. T., Thomas, A. M., & Golomb, R. G. (1997). Trichotillomania: A comprehensive behavioral model. *Clinical Psychology Review, 17,* 567–577.

Pollard, C. A., Ibe, I. O., Krojanker, D. N., Kitchen, A. D., Bronson, S. S., & Flynn, T. M. (1991). Clomipramine treatment of trichotillomania: Follow-up report on four. *Journal of Clinical Psychiatry, 52,* 128–130.

Rothbaum, B. O. (1992). The behavioral treatment of trichotillomania. *Behavioral Psychotherapy, 20,* 85–90.

Stanley, M. A., & Cohen, L. J. (1999). Trichotillomania and obsessive-compulsive disorder. In D. J. Stein, G. A. Christenson, & E. Hollander (Eds.), *Trichotillomania* (pp. 225–261). Washington, DC: American Psychiatric Press.

Wilhelm, S. I., Keuthen, N. J., Deckersbach, T., Nelissen, I., Forker, A. I., Baer, L., O'Sullivan, R. L., Jenike, I. M. A. (in press). *Journal of Clinical Psychiatry.*

CHAPTER

Borderline Personality Disorder

Soonie A. Kim and Brian C. Goff
Dialectical Behavior Therapy Program
Portland, Oregon

Case Description
Treatment Conceptualization
Assessment
Treatment Implementation
    Treatment Stages
    Treatment Components
Concurrent Diagnoses and Treatment
Complications and Treatment Implications
Dealing with Managed Care and Accountability
Outcome and Follow-Up
Dealing with Recidivism
Summary
References

Effective Brief Therapies: A Clinician's Guide

CASE DESCRIPTION

Mary Jones[1] is a 41-year-old woman referred to this treatment program by her therapist of the last 5 years. Mary presents at the intake interview following a 1-week hospital stay for a suicide attempt by overdosing on her antidepressant medication. On the day of the attempt, she had become upset with her therapist when he requested she bring her husband to their next appointment. She saw this as an indication the therapist did not believe she was telling the truth about her husband's poor treatment of her. On the way home from the session, she called the therapist from her cell phone, angrily complaining of being misunderstood and speaking vaguely of ending it all. Hanging up abruptly, she went home and proceeded to overdose. When the therapist was unable to contact her at home, he called her husband, who came home from work to find her conscious but drowsy and took her to the emergency room.

Mary reports a long history of recurring bouts of depressed mood and anxiety, beginning when she was an adolescent. She is unaware of what precipitates these episodes, although she states, "I don't handle stress well, especially conflict with other people." At age 17, following a breakup with a boyfriend, she made her first suicide attempt by overdosing on over-the-counter medication. She met and married her husband shortly after this episode, and became pregnant with her son the second year of their marriage. Throughout her 20-year marriage, Mary states she experienced several more periods of feeling hopeless and depressed, during which she contemplated (and made threats of) taking her own life. However, she reports that taking care of her son and going to work helped her to "keep it together." Four years ago, around the time her son was to leave for college, Mary made a second suicide attempt, again with nonprescription medication. Subsequently, she quit her job as a medical office receptionist and began to report feeling depressed and suicidal "all the time," resulting in two to three hospitalizations each year. Mary also has an extensive background of self-mutilating behavior that involves cutting or burning herself. She says this behavior began when she was about 16 and has occurred throughout the years with varying frequency. She reports it often occurs after she has "done something stupid" and is feeling anxious or ashamed. After getting angry at her husband for working late, for example, she states, "I felt so selfish and demanding . . . after all, he works so hard for us." She experienced a strong urge to hurt herself for the rest for the evening, and after her husband had gone to bed, she went into the bathroom and cut. When she feels especially distressed, Mary becomes

---

[1]The following case example is a composite with details added or omitted to protect the confidentiality of Portland DBT Program clients.

numb and "spaces out," a sensation she describes as "being there, but also being removed from myself."

Additional problems include chronic dissatisfaction with her appearance and problems keeping friends. Although not markedly overweight, she reports years of "yo-yo dieting" that usually ended in binge eating and purging. "Shopping sprees" also help Mary feel better about how she looks, although she acknowledges that buying new things provides only temporary relief from feeling "fat and ugly, like a nobody." With regard to friendships, Mary has little difficulty in the early stages of a relationship, but over time she feels "misunderstood" and "taken advantage of," eventually leading to a confrontation and breakup of the relationship. At the time of the intake, however, Mary's primary concern was feeling that her husband was "fed up" with her emotional problems and the resulting burden on family finances. She was also quite fearful that her therapist had "reached his limit with her" and was considering discontinuing treatment.

Mary demonstrates several features indicative of borderline personality disorder (DSM-IV, American Psychiatric Association, 1994): a pervasive pattern of instability in affect (depressed mood and anxiety since adolescence, frequent anger outbursts), difficulty in interpersonal relationships (chronic marital problems, difficulty keeping friends), and poor impulse control (binge eating, purging, and shopping). Fears of abandonment are suggested in her concern over losing her husband and therapist, as are dissociative episodes in her description of "spacing out" when under extreme duress. Finally, Mary demonstrates what some consider the hallmark feature of the disorder: recurring suicidal and self-mutilating behaviors.

TREATMENT CONCEPTUALIZATION

Dialectical Behavior Therapy (DBT) was developed by Dr. Marsha Linehan and her colleagues at the University of Washington as an empirically validated cognitive-behavioral treatment for borderline personality disorder (BPD) (Linehan, 1993a,b).[2] Based on a biosocial theory of BPD, DBT is designed to treat both individual and environmental variables that create and maintain the disorder. According to the biosocial theory, BPD develops in an emotionally dysregulated individual who grows up in an invalidat-

---

[2]The information presented in this chapter is primarily a synopsis of Marsh M. Linehan's extensive writing on DBT. This is a complex treatment that requires serious study and training to conduct effectively. Readers are advised to consult her text on the subject and the companion skills training manual for a more thorough understanding of the model. For more information on training in DBT, contact the Behavioral Technology Transfer Group (B-TECH) (206) 675-8588.

ing environment. These components (emotional dsyregulation and an invalidating environment) transact and evolve over time in response to each other.

DBT formulates emotion dysregulation as the central feature of BPD. Emotion dysregulation, described as a tendency to be emotionally sensitive and reactive, that is, easily triggered, with an intense emotional response and slow return to baseline mood. Emotion dysregulation is hypothesized to be biologically based and may be due to one, or a combination of, factors, including genetics, intrauterine abnormalities, or early childhood events that are traumatic and permanently affect the brain in some way (Linehan, 1997).

An invalidating environment, postulated to be the contributing environmental factor, is described as one that trivializes, disregards, blames, or punishes the person for their emotional condition. Invalidation occurs on a continuum from attempts to help that are experienced as invalidating (e.g., "Why are you so upset?" "There is nothing to be upset about.") to more severe types of invalidation (e.g., verbal, physical, and sexual abuse). Environments can also be invalidating because they are limited in their ability to respond. This may be due to a caregiver's lack of knowledge or skill, or whose lifestyle or personal problems impede appropriate reactions (Linehan, 1993a).

Biological and environmental factors interact and culminate in the individual's inability to modulate emotional experience. This includes problems with identifying and making sense of emotional experience, blunted or escalated emotional responses, and difficulty redirecting attention and behavior to other matters and goals when emotional. According to this model, the severely maladaptive behaviors demonstrated by individuals with BPD are seen as ineffective attempts to resolve problems and regulate emotional experience. This result is not stagnant. Individual and environmental conditions are hypothesized to continually influence and transform one another, resulting in the individual becoming more emotionally reactive and behaviorally dysregulated and the environment more invalidating (Linehan, 1997).

At its core, DBT is a behavioral treatment that draws from an area of applied behavior analysis called self-management. Simply put, self-management of behavior is a process by which clients learn how to define problems behaviorally, monitor these behaviors in context, analyze this information according to models of learning, and develop solutions to change behavior based on their analyses. Solutions usually fall into one of four categories — skills training, cognitive restructuring, exposure techniques, and contingency management. Everything in DBT is a problem to be defined, analyzed, and solved in a collaborative fashion. Cause is not assumed based on personality traits, drives states, or self-object structures, but is hypothesized, according to respondent, operant, and observational learning models. Providing new learning experiences is the central corrective feature of the treatment (Linehan, 1993a).

However, DBT is more than teaching clients how to be their own behavior therapists. Indeed, therapy with individuals with BPD that focuses solely on change often recapitulates their earlier invalidating environment and results in escalated and extreme responding on the part of client and therapist alike (Linehan, 1993a). Thus, in DBT, theory and methods of behavior therapy are balanced with acceptance strategies and skills, all of which are housed in a treatment framework that is "dialectical" in nature.

Dialectics, an area of classical philosophy, within a treatment context promotes searching for synthesis and balance between opposing perspectives or positions. The emphasis in dialectics shifts from an "all-or-nothing" "either/or" perspective to a "both/and" position. Dialectical synthesis in thought is having a particular perspective and maintaining what is true in that position, while at the same time searching for "what's being left out?" or the truth in the opposing perspective. In behavior, dialectical balance is achieved by continually balancing treatment strategies — for example, focusing on change while focusing on acceptance and treating both the client and his or her environment. In emotions, synthesis is sought by integration of pure emotion with reason or logic and intuition, as well as achieving balance between trying to regulate (or change) emotions and accepting (or tolerating) them (Linehan, 1993a).

The core acceptance strategy in DBT is validation. Linehan (1993a) describes various levels of validation, but the essence of the strategy is this: to communicate to the client that his or her responses are real, that they make sense and are understandable within his or her life context or current situation. Validation is not used simply to make clients feel better, but is applied strategically: to provide a balance to the push for change, as feedback to reinforce clinical progress, and to strengthen the therapeutic relationship. It is also used in an attempt to teach clients how to self-validate and is a strategy taught to significant others as part of treating the environment (Linehan, 1993a).

Mindfulness is the core acceptance skill taught in DBT. Drawn from certain Eastern meditation practices, mindfulness is defined as observing one's internal experience (thoughts, feelings, images, physical sensations) and external behaviors (overt actions) in context (the situation those are occurring in) in the present moment. The quality of this experience is nonjudgmental, that is, attempts to judge the experience as good or bad, or to try to explain, control, or change it are suspended. In short, mindfulness is about focusing on one thing in the moment and accepting that moment without reservation. It is important to note that acceptance does not equal agreement, liking, or approval of the experience or situation at hand. Rather, it means to acknowledge what is, as opposed to what should be, and a willingness to do what is needed in order to respond effectively (Linehan, 1993a).

Thus, DBT is an amalgamation of behavior therapy and "acceptance therapy," housed in a dialectical treatment framework that emphasizes synthesis through balance. Based on a biosocial model of BPD, the therapy provides for treating the client and the surrounding environment. Treatment entails devising and implementing new learning experiences, both in the context of the therapeutic relationship and in the client's natural environment.

Very early in her childhood, Mary recalls being labeled as an overly sensitive child, easily upset at the slightest provocation. Combined with this, she describes a highly invalidating home environment. For example, her father had little tolerance for expression of emotion in the home, was rigid in beliefs about what was right and wrong, and had high expectations for his children. She states that living with him was like "walking on eggshells" due to his frequent temper outbursts if things did not go smoothly and according to plan. She describes her mother as fairly nonassertive and complacent, usually agreeing with her father even when she might have disapproved of his actions. In her current home environment, although Mary's husband attends to the family's physical needs, he is frequently gone due to his work, and emotionally "not there" when he is home. Mary indicates feeling very frustrated in her marriage; however, complaints to her husband are often dismissed or trivialized. She is quite confused about "what is really going on" and often feels "wrong and bad," like there is something inherently wrong with her.

ASSESSMENT

DBT, as a behavioral treatment, is assessment driven. Pretreatment assessment begins with a thorough diagnostic evaluation, including unstructured and semistructured diagnostic interviews (e.g., SCID-II, First et al., 1996). Information germane to diagnostic clarity is gathered from a number of sources, including prior psychiatric records and consultation with concurrent providers and significant others. High rates of comorbidity between BPD and other axis I and II disorders underscore the importance of drawing a complete diagnostic picture.

Data regarding concomitant problems, such as disruptive affective states, maladaptive cognitive patterns, and interpersonal problems, can be gathered through the use of a variety of instruments. The degree of detail one would seek in academic research settings is difficult if not impossible to obtain in other settings; however, deciding that no quantifiable data should be sought is equally ineffective. A balance must be struck between gathering exhaustive data on what often is an array of problems and the practicalities of clinical practice. Use of a brief instrument with good psychometric properties that measures affective states (e.g., Brief Symptom Inventory, Derogatis & Spencer, 1982) can provide an objective measure of client status and clinical progress in this area. Additional measures of cognitive patterns (e.g., dissociation) and interpersonal variables (e.g., interpersonal sensitivity) round out a self-report contribution to the assessment.

Early in treatment, a thorough history of prior suicidal and parasuicidal (self-harm behavior without the intent to die) behaviors is also obtained for the purpose of estimating future risk and better management of crises. This information includes detailed data regarding precipitants of past episodes, method and lethality rating, and outcomes.

Diary cards (i.e., self-monitoring inventories) are completed by clients every week and record daily intensity ratings of sadness, anger, fear, agitation, and guilt/shame. Information pertaining to suicidal and parasuicidal thoughts, urges, and actions, and other earlier identified target behaviors are also gathered through these cards. Diary cards are examined in each session, and when a target behavior (e.g., self-harm) occurs, a thorough behavioral analysis is conducted. In this process, detailed information about the target behavior is gathered, along with information pertaining to physical states, emotional and cognitive processes, and environmental factors. The purpose of such data gathering is to elucidate the problem and generate causal hypotheses. In DBT, knowledge regarding the most effective intervention can only be had through assessment, hypothesis development, and testing.

Mary was assessed during pretreatment to meet criteria for borderline personality disorder and major depressive disorder. Although she also engaged in binging–purging and impulsive spending, she was not given additional diagnoses, as these problems are subsumed under a diagnosis of BPD. Many of the BSI clinical scales (Derogatis & Spencer, 1982) were elevated, with the most pronounced being interpersonal sensitivity, hostility, depression, and anxiety. In addition to monitoring intensity of emotions and frequency of suicidal and parasuicidal behaviors on her diary card, Mary recorded instances of binge–purge behavior and episodes of impulsive spending.

TREATMENT IMPLEMENTATION

Clients with BPD often present with a host of problems that can be overwhelming (to client and therapist alike) and may disorganize attempts to deal with any one of them effectively. To prevent this from happening, DBT is structured into stages of therapy and organized along a hierarchy of targets.

Treatment Stages

There are four stages of treatment in DBT: pretreatment, followed by the first, second, and third stages. The goals of pretreatment are to assess and orient the client, and to build commitment. Orientation involves communicating to the client what they can expect from the treatment and the therapist, and clarifying what will be expected of them. This typically entails explaining how DBT may be different from other treatments, providing information about BPD and the biosocial model, and commiserating with the client about the amount of work involved. Building commitment involves getting the client to agree with certain conditions of treatment (e.g., therapy duration, individual and skills group attendance) and mutually arriving at the goals of therapy. The importance of establishing commitment cannot be overemphasized, as failures in commitment (on the part of the client or therapist) are often the cause of treatment impasses and premature termination (Linehan, 1993a). DBT outlines specific strategies for establishing commitment and bolstering it when it inevitably requires revisiting.

The first treatment stage in DBT focuses on decreasing certain "behavioral targets." Behaviors to decrease are addressed in a hierarchical manner and include life-threatening behaviors (i.e., suicidal and parasuicidal behavior), therapy-interfering behavior (i.e., therapist and client behaviors that interfere with the client receiving and benefiting from treatment, and behaviors that burn out the therapist), and quality-of-life–interfering behaviors (i.e., impulsive behaviors that are not life-threatening, severely dysfunctional interpersonal behaviors, other behaviors related to physical or mental health that compromise quality of life). It is in this stage that DBT is especially unique, equipped with a variety of strategies focused on resolution of first-stage targets.

The second stage of DBT is designed to address posttraumatic stress response patterns related to childhood physical or sexual abuse, a common experience among BPD clients. It should be noted, however, that if these response patterns present in the context of life-threatening behavior, or are determined to be therapy-interfering or quality-of-life–interfering, they are appropriately dealt with in Stage 1 of the treatment. The final stage of therapy focuses on making personal and lifestyle changes that enhance self-respect and general quality of life, for example, making career changes or increasing marital satisfaction.

Treatment Components

DBT is a multimodal therapy that utilizes individual therapy, group therapy, telephone consultation, and a therapist consultation group. Treatment components discussed here are as implemented in an outpatient setting (such as in our program and in the DBT efficacy research, e.g., Linehan *et al.*, 1991). Other settings (e.g., inpatient) may utilize a different set of modalities. Implementation of treatment components is guided by the requisite functions of DBT: (1) to enhance client capabilities, (2) to enhance client motivation, (3) to enhance generalization of capabilities, (4) to enhance therapist capabilities and motivation, and (5) to structure the client's environment to support new capabilities (Linehan, 1993a).

Skills training groups are designed to enhance client capabilities (Linehan, 1993b). Skills taught are divided into four modules parallel to four areas of dysregulation for the borderline individual: core mindfulness (for cognitive dysregulation), distress tolerance (for behavioral dysregulation), emotion regulation (for emotional dysregulation), and interpersonal effectiveness (for interpersonal dysregulation). As a psychoeducational group, the physical setting and structure of skills training groups should ideally prompt classroom behavior (i.e., behavior conducive to learning). The standard format of the group is as follows: mindfulness exercise, homework review (e.g., skills practice check-in), presentation of new material, in-group practice (if applicable to topic), homework assignment, and check-out. Skills training groups in our setting last 6 months and are conducted in weekly 2-hour sessions with six to eight clients per group.

The main work of motivating clients to implement skills in DBT is carried out in individual therapy. More than anywhere else, it is in individual sessions that "the therapist blocks or extinguishes bad behaviors, drags good behaviors out of the patient, and figures out a way to make the good behaviors so reinforcing that the patient continues the good ones and stops the bad ones" (Linehan, 1993a, p. 97). Skills training provides clients with information about skills, but emotional, cognitive, or environmental factors frequently prove to be obstacles to using skills. It is in the individual therapy session that these factors are identified and addressed. The focus of any session depends on what has occurred in the hierarchy of targets since the previous session. Solutions to problems are developed out of a detailed behavioral analysis and may take the form of skills training, cognitive modification, exposure, or contingency management.

It is critical that individual treatment be delivered within the context of a strong therapeutic relationship. To this end, the therapist is reminded to weave validation strategies into interventions focused on change, and to balance a reciprocal communication style with one that is irreverent. Reciprocal communication is responsive, warmly engaging, and genuine. "Radical genuineness" is "realness" — being oneself and having a real relationship with the client. In contrast, irreverent communication is unorthodox, paradoxical, and offbeat, but not mean-spirited. Within the context of a good relationship, irreverent communication can get the client and therapist "unstuck" by pushing the interaction "off balance," allowing for a new balance to emerge (Linehan, 1993a). Individual therapy sessions are typically held weekly, and the individual therapist is considered the coordinating therapist among other providers involved in the client's care (e.g., skills trainer, prescriber, PCP, case manager).

Telephone consultation with the individual therapist is the treatment mode that addresses generalization of capabilities to the environment. The purposes of telephone consultation include skills coaching, relationship repair, and crisis intervention. Crisis calls involve conducting a risk assessment, exploring the problem at hand, validating the client's problem and associated pain, developing a solution, and obtaining commitment to a plan. To avoid reinforcing self-injury, telephone calls from a client are not accepted for 24 hours following self-injury (beyond ensuring safety).

Weekly therapist consultation groups enhance therapist capabilities and motivation. Because this treatment component does not include the client, it may be erroneously considered optional. On the contrary, therapist consultation is an essential aspect of DBT. A number of important functions are fulfilled in this treatment component. Therapy-interfering behaviors on the part of the therapist are identified and ameliorated. Therapists are cheered on and supported, and thus reinforced for doing DBT. Team members provide a dialectical balance to the therapist by validating feelings or their current position and simultaneously challenging them to grow and change. The consultation team members explicitly commit to a set of consultation agreements: (1) remain dialectical in interaction with each other, (2) do not act as an intermediary for clients with other treatment team members, (3) understand that intertherapist consistency is not expected, (4) accept that therapist limits may be different from each other and observe those limits, (5) search for nonpejorative interpretations of client's behaviors, and (6) accept that all therapists are fallible (Linehan, 1993a).

It is important that the team reinforce doing effective therapy because clients often unintentionally reinforce the therapist for doing ineffective therapy. What clients sometimes enjoy (and what therapists enjoy doing) is what can be termed "compassion," while "doing what works" may not be enjoyable to either the client or the therapist but can be termed "effective compassion." To illustrate, a client may wish to talk in depth about her feelings related to a recent parasuicidal event (and feel warmly understood and accepted by her therapist for doing so) but may not wish to do a behavioral analysis of the event. The former is compassion, while the latter is effective compassion. Metaphorically, pouring water on the feet of a person in a fiery pit is compassion; giving them a ladder to climb out of hell is effective compassion (Linehan, 1993).

DBT concerns itself with structuring the client's environment to be less reinforcing of maladaptive behaviors and more reinforcing of new behaviors. This is sometimes accomplished through family therapy or couples therapy. In our program, we conduct a group for family members (typically spouses and parents) and friends of program clients. Attendees are taught about BPD and the biosocial model, validation and invalidation, basic principles of learning, and various DBT skills.

Mary responded well to commitment strategies during pretreatment, particularly "devil's advocate" and "weighing the pros and cons" (see Linehan, 1993a). Some time was spent on letting Mary know that DBT was not going to be easy and on educating her about BPD and the biosocial model. Mary's participation in DBT was limited to Stage 1 of treatment: decreasing life-threatening behaviors (i.e., suicidal behavior, self-injurious behavior), decreasing therapy-interfering behavior (i.e., missing individual therapy appointments, not using a phone consult before instances of going to the hospital or self-harm), and decreasing quality-of-life–interfering behavior (i.e., binging–purging, impulsive spending). She was involved in each of the therapy components, and her husband attended the education/support group for family members of clients.

CONCURRENT DIAGNOSES AND TREATMENT

Common axis I disorders concurrent with BPD include mood disorders, anxiety disorders, eating disorders, impulse-control disorders, and substance-related disorders. The interrelatedness of these disorders with BPD can be complex and take a variety of forms. For instance, the chaos and crisis of the borderline individual's life is such that depression seems a natural byproduct. Other disorders may serve to regulate affect (albeit with considerable negative consequences) for the BPD client. Examples include bulimia, substance abuse, and spending, to name a few. The implication for treatment depends on where these disorders occur in the hierarchy of therapy targets. For example, substance abuse could constitute a quality-of-life–interfering behavior (e.g., financially burdensome or interfering with relationships), a therapy-interfering behavior (e.g., coming to therapy intoxicated), or a life-threatening behavior (e.g., driving while highly intoxicated).

When concurrent disorders constitute life-threatening behavior, they are bumped up the hierarchy of targets and DBT strategies are aimed at reducing such behavior. Alternatively, ancillary treatment may be utilized to treat the comorbid disorder when resources within the program are insufficient (e.g., hospitalization for medical stabilization of an anorectic client). When a comorbid disorder involves therapy-interfering behavior, the treatment of that disorder (either within DBT or through a collateral treatment) becomes a priority. Examples include intoxication during therapy sessions, social phobia that interferes with group therapy, or dissociating during therapy (which may be a feature of BPD or may be a comorbid dissociative disorder). Finally, concurrent disorders that interfere with the quality of an individual's life (e.g., bulimia or a chronic pain condition) may become the focus of therapy when life-threatening behaviors and therapy-interfering behaviors are extinguished.

Whatever the concurrent disorder and wherever it falls on the hierarchy of treatment targets, it should be clear that the DBT therapist must also be facile in providing treatments for a host of other disorders. Treatments for depression, PTSD, social phobia, panic disorder, substance abuse, and bulimia that are typically employed within DBT are behavioral or cognitive-behavioral in nature, both because DBT is a behavioral treatment and because efficacy research on these disorders indicates such an approach. DBT functions as an umbrella for these other treatments by providing a theoretical base, as well as a set of guiding principles, assumptions, and treatment strategies.

Mary met the criteria for major depression and, although she did not meet the criteria for an eating disorder or impulse control disorder, she did have problems with binging–purging and impulsive spending. All of these problems were targeted for treatment under quality-of-life–interfering behavior. Mary's depression was most influenced by the emotion regulation skills taught in the skills training group. In addition, some time was spent focused on behavioral activation and in testing of dysfunctional thoughts and beliefs. Mary's binge–purge behavior and impulsive spending were treated using contingency management, exposure with response prevention, and skills training (i.e., mindfulness, distress tolerance and emotion regulation skills) since these behaviors were determined to function primarily as emotion regulators.

COMPLICATIONS AND TREATMENT IMPLICATIONS

Anyone who has conducted therapy with individuals diagnosed with BPD knows how difficult the work is. However, because DBT was developed specifically for this population, there are many aspects of the treatment designed explicitly to address the common problems that arise. One of these problems and a major area of concern in effectively conducting DBT is therapist burnout. In our program, we have found that burnout is often related to: (1) heightened therapist stress in dealing with life-threatening behavior and high frequency help-seeking behavior, and (2) therapist frustration and anger in response to certain client behaviors, for example, help-rejecting complaining behavior or harshly critical and attacking behavior.

Increased stress is an inevitable element of work with high-risk clients. To manage it, the DBT therapist is advised first to synthesize for themselves the dialectic of acceptance and change: to accept their own level of stress, fallibility, and ultimate lack of control, while working to monitor and manage (change) stress in order to avoid counterproductive responses to client behavior. The team consultation group provides help through general support, assistance in problem-solving, and continuous training in DBT interventions. In addition, therapists are encouraged to apply DBT to themselves by using distress tolerance and emotion regulation skills, exercising general self-care strategies (e.g., health maintenance, seeking balance in personal life), limiting the number of high-risk clients on their caseloads (if possible), and observing their own limits with clients (i.e., being aware of and communicating to the client behaviors the therapist is able to tolerate and those that are unacceptable) (Linehan, 1993a).

High-frequency help-seeking by clients is another source of therapist stress. As a preventive measure, clients are oriented at treatment onset (and then numerous times throughout treatment) about the general goals, method, and rationale of DBT. "Selling" the rationale — that behavior is learned through a process of person–environment interactions and that in order to change behavior one must create new learning experiences — is critical. Emphasis on the self-versus-other management of behavior in DBT is highlighted, as are the benefits of this approach over the long run.

Excessive help-seeking is sometimes manifested in clients' use of telephone consultation. First and foremost it should be stated that phone consult is not supportive therapy over the phone; it has specific purposes to which the client is clearly oriented at treatment onset. If a client is overusing phone consult, or not using it for the purposes intended, the therapist addresses the problem quickly and in an open and direct fashion. Solutions might involve teaching the client how and when to ask for help, developing support systems in the client's natural environment, encouraging the client to use distress tolerance skills if help is not immediately available, or some form of contingency manipulation. The success of the intervention depends on the strength and nature of the therapeutic relationship and the therapist's ability to thread the conversation with validation.

Whenever therapists experience negative emotional reactions in response to client behaviors, they are advised to: (1) practice mindfulness to their reactions, noticing their reactions and letting them come and go at will, (2) try changing their perspective, from one of "should" to one conducive to a biosocial and phenomenological outlook, (3) observe their own limits and communicate these to the client in a nonjudgmental manner, and (4) educate the client using self-involving self-disclosure (communicate the effect of the client's behavior on the therapist, the relationship, and the possibility of progress given this effect, while teaching more effective ways of interacting). Seeking consultation is recommended if negative reactions persist, particularly if they may be related to institutional or personal problems (Linehan, 1993a).

In Mary's case, her individual therapist struggled with frustration around Mary's constant help-rejecting, complaining behavior. The typical pattern involved Mary tearfully presenting problems to her therapist, who listened and validated. But as soon as the therapist tried to problem-solve, Mary would respond with statements like "I tried it and it doesn't work," or "You just don't understand, it's not that easy." Mary's therapist brought the problem to her consultation group. The team helped to validate the therapist's view of the problem and associated feelings and reinforced her hard work, but at the same time they provided a dialectical balance by asking the question "What's being left out?" Through this process the therapist was "re-moralized", and with the help of the team began analyzing the problem and developing a variety of interventions to try. These included presenting the problem to the client nonjudgmentally, in terms of the biosocial model, and collaboratively exploring obstacles to change, having a heart-to-heart discussion with the client using self-involving self-disclosure and observing limits, and using irreverent communication with the client to help get her "unstuck."

DEALING WITH MANAGED CARE AND ACCOUNTABILITY

The primary goals of managed mental health care are to oversee cost containment and quality of care. Many aspects of DBT are conducive to this goal. Examples include outcome data demonstrating efficacy (Linehan *et al.*, 1991, 1993; Koons *et al.*, in press), cost savings over the long run for clients who are high utilizers of service ("Integrating dialectical behavior therapy," 1998), emphasis on accountability through continuous monitoring of specific behavioral targets, attention to generalization of treatment gains to natural contexts, phone consult service offering after-hours availability by the primary treatment provider, and a team approach to monitoring adherence to the model and quality assurance.

However, while DBT may further the goals of managed care, the commitment required, in time and money, to effectively conduct the treatment exceeds the limits set by most managed care plans. Typical benefit plans do not cover the basics of even the first phase of a DBT program: 24 individual and 24 group therapy appointments in a 6-month period. Individual sessions for purposes of assessment and orientation prior to entering the 6-month group and services provided during the second half of the treatment are further beyond the scope of treatment generally envisioned by managed care operators.

In Massachusetts, however, a large insurance provider ("New outpatient benefit," 1998), has developed a new outpatient benefit specifically to accommodate the treatment. The benefit covers a 6-month period and provides for all components of the treatment. In our state, Oregon, insurers have not yet devised formal benefit plans to support DBT. As a result, we often have to work with clients on an individual basis to devise unusual and sometimes complicated and cumbersome reimbursement strategies. For some, we have been able to negotiate the transfer of inpatient to outpatient benefits. For others, we bill the insurer for individual therapy only and the client for the group component. For those individuals whose benefits have been exhausted in the first half of the program and are under financial hardship, we sometimes reduce our fees and modify program expectations to permit them to participate in the group component alone during the second half of treatment. Although measures such as these have expanded our ability to provide DBT services, many eligible clients are excluded from treatment due to lack of resources. It is clear that continued advocacy and education are necessary to convince managed care companies to increase short-term costs in order to realize long-term benefits.

At the time Mary started treatment, she had approximately 15 visits left of her outpatient mental health benefit. Her insurance provider was willing to transfer some of her inpatient benefit for outpatient use, which, combined with her remaining 15 visits, covered pretreatment stage sessions and the time period she was in the 6-month skills training group. She used her insurance benefit for individual therapy only (the more costly of the two treatments) and paid out of pocket for the group at a reduced fee. At the end of the skills training group, Mary's insurance benefit was exhausted. She chose to continue in the program and began paying out of pocket for individual therapy. Individual sessions were cut back to twice a month for the next 3 months, then once a month for a period of 3 months, and were eliminated during the last 3 months she was in the program. Throughout this time, Mary attended a weekly Phase 2 group, which she paid for out of pocket at a reduced fee.

OUTCOME AND FOLLOW-UP

Outcome variables for a client in DBT obviously depend on the specific target problems of the client. In measuring outcome with our clients, we look at frequency and intensity of suicidal and parasuicidal behavior, use of crisis services (e.g., visits to ER and/or crisis center), and psychiatric hospital or respite center stays. In addition, we assess improvements in reported intensity of various emotions and outcomes related to earlier identified quality-of-life–interfering behaviors. The majority of the outcome data we collect in our private practice setting is derived from the BSI (Derogatis & Spencer, 1982), client diary cards, and a behavioral outcome interview. Data are collected throughout the 6-month skills training group for all clients, and may be continued beyond the skills group for clients with persisting Stage 1 targets. We also solicit consumer satisfaction data through a program evaluation questionnaire completed by clients at the end of the skills training group.

In Linehan's (1991) initial efficacy trial, she compared the efficacy of DBT to treatment as usual (TAU) over a 1-year time period. As attrition is typically high in this population (approximately 50%), it is significant to note that DBT attrition was less than 17%. Compared to the control group, the DBT clients had fewer parasuicidal acts and lower levels of medical risk of parasuicidal acts. The DBT clients had fewer inpatient psychiatric days than the control group as well (8.46 days per year for DBT as compared to 38.6 days per year for TAU). During the follow-up year, DBT clients had higher Global Assessment scores, better work performance, fewer suicidal acts, lower anger scores, better self-reported social adjustment, and fewer inpatient psychiatric days (Linehan *et al.*, 1993). A recent study (Koons *et al.*, in press) replicated Linehan's findings and also found DBT clients to show significant reductions in suicidal ideation, hopelessness, depression, and anger expression. Other studies have shown the long-term cost savings of DBT, particularly for clients who are high utilizers of inpatient psychiatric services ("Integrating dialectical behavior therapy," 1998).

Outcome for Mary was assessed primarily from her BSI scores, target cards, and a behavioral outcome interview. By the end of the 6-month skills training group, Mary's BSI clinical scores uniformly showed improvement. The most prominent improvement was noted in the hostility and interpersonal sensitivity scales. Target cards reflected a decrease in suicidal ideation, with no attempts past the second month of treatment. Self-harm behavior decreased in frequency overall and occurred only three times between the third and sixth months of treatment. Purging was extinguished by the end of the 6-month skills training group; however, little improvement was made in binge eating and impulsive spending. Mary went to the ER twice during the first month of treatment and was hospitalized one of these times. Intensive work with her individual therapist around these episodes resulted in Mary staying out of the hospital during the remainder of the program.

DEALING WITH RECIDIVISM

Despite good outcome data, we are not suggesting that 1 year of DBT (much less 6 months) is a panacea for clients with BPD. Although in theory clients move smoothly through a series of treatment stages over a circumscribed period of time, in reality they frequently move forward and backward over an undeterminable period. While this process is understandable given the chronic and pervasive nature of the disorder, it highlights the need to develop strategies for maintaining clinical change.

Although attention to maintenance of treatment gains can be found throughout DBT, we have formalized the teaching of maintenance strategies within a self-management skills unit. Didactic presentations and homework in this unit address basic self-management principles and techniques, as well as information drawn from Marlatt & Gordon's (1985) work in the area of substance abuse relapse prevention. For instance, one assignment involves clients developing a "personalized" relapse prevention plan where they identify relapse triggers and warning signs that signal initiation of skills use.

To further solidify the acquisition of treatment gains after our 6-month skills training group, clients are offered the opportunity to enter a "Phase 2" group. The purpose of this group is to refine skill knowledge and reinforce the use of skills in day-to-day living. A primary task in this group is conducting group problem analyses of client target behaviors, with skill review and refinement occurring in the process, as well as teaching about the self-management model. Phase 2 groups meet once a week and are an hour in length. Clients make a commitment to Phase 2 groups in 3-month intervals. Some of our clients remain in these groups for several months beyond the initial 6-month skills training group.

Mary reduced her individual therapy and joined a Phase 2 group after the 6-month skills training group. During the 9 months she was in the group, Mary focused on managing emotional reactivity, reducing binge eating and impulsive spending, and exploring and changing dysfunctional interpersonal patterns. She engaged in self-harm behavior twice during this time period. The contextual factors of each of these lapses were emphasized (e.g., an argument with her husband), and self-management principles were presented to prevent future lapses. At the end of treatment, Mary had not had a suicide attempt or psychiatric hospitalization for a period of 14 months. She and her husband were referred to a marital therapist outside the program. She had obtained a volunteer position at a local hospital 3 days a week and was looking forward to, at some point, going back to work full-time.

SUMMARY

DBT is an innovative approach to treating BPD, combining the theory and methods of cognitive-behavioral therapy with acceptance strategies and skills. Both are housed within a dialectical treatment framework that emphasizes synthesis through balance, and are delivered by way of a therapeutic relationship that stresses "effective compassion" and "radical genuineness." Although DBT is not designed to be a brief treatment, its time-limited approach is intended to foster improvements in behavior more quickly than traditional treatments, where clients may be in (or more typically, in and out of) therapy for several years, if not a lifetime.

DBT is multimodal, composed of individual therapy, skills training group, telephone consultation to the client, and team consultation group. It is also multifunctional in that each treatment modality is designed to address specific therapeutic functions, particularly enhancing client capability and motivation, and generalizing capability to natural contexts. In addition, DBT provides for "treating the environment" through both the team consultation group and the ancillary family and friends group component. A team-based approach also serves to monitor adherence to the model and promote quality assurance, and can be useful in preventing therapist burnout, a major area of concern in working with difficult-to-treat borderline clients.

DBT places a strong emphasis on accountability. Treatment goals are well-defined, interventions are systematically applied, and client progress is closely monitored. Indeed, at this time, DBT is the only treatment for borderline personality disorder with empirical validation, and research continues to be conducted to refine the model and increase our knowledge of what does and does not work with this population. Although we still have a long way to go in this process, it is our belief that DBT is a first step in the right direction.

REFERENCES

American Psychiatric Association (1994). *Diagnostic and statistical manual of mental disorders* (4th ed.). Washington, DC: Author.

Derogatis, L. R., & Spencer, P. M. (1982). *Brief Symptom Inventory: Administration, scoring, and procedures manual, I.* Baltimore: Clinical Psychometric Research.

First, M. B., Spitzer, R. L., Gibbons, M., Williams, J. B. W., & Benjamin, L. (1996). *User's guide for the Structured Clinical Interview for DSM-IV Axis II Personality Disorders (SCID-II).* New York: Biometrics Research Department, New York State Psychiatric Institute.

Integrating dialectical behavior therapy into a community mental health program (1998, October). *Psychiatric Services, 49,* 1338–1340.

Koons, C. R., Robins, C. J., Tweed, J. L., Lynch, T. R., Gonzalez, A. M., Morse, J. Q., Bishop, G. K., Butterfield, M. I., & Bastian, L. A. (in press). Efficacy of dialectical behavior therapy in women veterans with borderline personality disorder. *Journal of Consulting and Clinical Psychology*.

Linehan, M. M. (1993a). *Cognitive-behavioral treatment of borderline personality disorder*. New York: Guilford.

Linehan, M. M. (1993b). *Skills training manual for treating borderline personality disorder*. New York: Guilford.

Linehan, M. M. (1997). Dialectical behavior therapy (DBT) for borderline personality disorder. *The Journal of the California Alliance for the Mentally Ill, 8,* 44–46.

Linehan, M. M., Armstrong, H. E., Suarez, A., Allmon, D., & Heard, H. L. (1991). Cognitive-behavioral treatment of chronically parasuicidal borderline patients. *Archives of General Psychiatry, 48,* 1060–1064.

Linehan, M. M., Heard, H. L., & Armstrong, H. E. (1993). Naturalistic follow-up of a behavioral treatment for chronically parasuicidal borderline patients. *Archives of General Psychiatry, 50,* 157–158.

Marlatt, G. A., & Gordon, J. R. (Eds.) (1985). *Relapse prevention: Maintenance strategies in the treatment of addictive behaviors*. New York: Guilford.

New outpatient benefit: Dialectical behavior therapy (1998, July 16). *Clinical Alert, 2,* 1–3.

CHAPTER

Histrionic Personality Disorder

William I. Dorfman
Center for Psychological Studies
Nova Southeastern University
Fort Lauderdale, Florida

Case Description
Treatment Conceptualization
Assessment
Treatment Implementation
Concurrent Diagnoses and Treatment
Complications and Treatment Implications
Dealing with Managed Care and Accountability
Outcome and Follow-Up
Dealing with Recidivism
Summary
References

Effective Brief Therapies: A Clinician's Guide

CASE DESCRIPTION

Alexandra was a tall, thin, rather attractive woman of 49 years with deep lines marking her tanned skin. She was dressed in a tight-fitting black dress and had heavy makeup and long hair, all of which seemed somewhat inappropriate for her age. She glided into the examiner's office and draped herself very dramatically on the couch, letting out a deep sigh. "I hate this . . . I've been crying for 6 years." Before the clinician could inquire further, she went on: "I met an old patient of yours at the supermarket and was telling her about my problems. She recommended you and told me you were 'wonderful.' "

As the interview continued, the patient related her history and complaints in vague, disjointed, highly emotional, and self-dramatizing terms. Her manner initially made it difficult for the examiner to create a coherent and detailed chronology of her past or present difficulties. Sorting through this emotionally charged and highly impressionistic account of her past history, however, the examiner began to construct a picture of a woman who, for her entire life, had felt victimized emotionally, physically, and financially by every important figure in her life. Alexandra stated that she had "escaped" from a cold and discounting home environment, quit college, and at age 18 married a man 15 years her senior. She described him as physically abusive, controlling, and insistent on cutting her off from her friends and family. After 3 years of marriage and two children, she divorced him and went to work for a large advertising agency, where she felt she enjoyed much success. She quickly found herself in a new and intense relationship, which ended when the man reportedly assaulted her and "left her for dead." The patient claimed that she tried to cope with this trauma by suing this man in what turned out to be a protracted and ultimately unsuccessful court battle. She stated that as a result of the assault she was diagnosed with mild head injury, severe depression, and posttraumatic stress, as well as panic disorder, for which she required extensive psychotherapy and medical treatment throughout the next 15 years.

Alexandra went on to explain that she had been fired from her successful position in advertising after she lodged a sexual harassment compliant against her boss, who had allegedly made a "pass" at her. Without a job or income to support her, Alexandra endured mounting stress, loneliness, and chronic feelings of emptiness, all of which left her feeling totally "incapacitated" and reportedly unable to leave her apartment for long periods of time.

The patient reported that she married again a year later to a successful businessman with whom she "shared" a thriving advertising firm for

5 years. Once again, however, she became a "victim." She reported that he too abused her physically, "stole" her money, and left her "destitute" and demoralized, which had lasted up to the present time.

At the time of the initial interview, Alexandra stated that she was living alone, separated from her second husband for 6 years, and estranged from her two grown children, who were "unsympathetic" to her situation. She had not worked for 7 years, had applied for disability, and was totally dependent on her mother for financial support. She was engaged in a constant legal battle with her estranged husband for back alimony and had been unable to pay her attorney for representing her. She felt that the attorney had also "victimized" her with poor legal representation. She complained of chronic anxiety and depression, anhedonia, exhaustion, sleep disturbance, and pervasive feelings of emptiness and inadequacy. Since she had suffered from these problems for the better part of her life and had sought no therapy during the previous 4 years, the psychologist inquired as to why she was seeking assistance at that time. Without further elaboration, and with tears streaming down her face, she answered, "I realized that I was going to hurt myself if I didn't get help." When pressed for further details, she added that she had recently had an altercation with her boyfriend of 4 years, whom she felt was "cheating" on her.

TREATMENT CONCEPTUALIZATION

The Diagnostic and Statistical Manual of Mental Disorders, Fourth Edition (DSM-IV) (American Psychiatric Association, 1994) defines a personality disorder as an enduring pattern of inner experience and behavior, both inflexible and pervasive, which is "stable and of long duration and its onset can be traced back at least to adolescence or early adulthood" (p. 633). From this perspective, the clinician must realize that "treating" histrionic personality disorder in a brief therapeutic framework is a challenging endeavor. The self-defeating pattern of cognitive, emotional, and interpersonal functioning characteristic of this disorder is a result of multiple determinants of biology, psychological experience, and social learning and, consequently, is unlikely to be modified significantly in very brief interventions. It is rare, however, for patients to seek treatment for their histrionic personality disorder. Rather, they are likely to complain of the consequences of their self-defeating style. They often complain of feeling "overwhelmed" with life and unable to manage their affairs, of being engulfed intermittently by waves of anxiety and depression, of being disillusioned or abandoned by an intimate relationship, and, not infrequently, of being plagued by somatic symptoms for which no physical basis has been found. Such was the case with Alexandra. As in all effective brief therapy, it is imperative that the clinician carefully define a "focus" for treatment that is guided by the patient's most pressing concerns, assess the feasibility of changing the targeted issues, and, of course, determine the pragmatics of time and availability of visits (Budman & Gurman, 1988). In brief therapeutic approaches, the histrionic personality disorder will rarely be defined as the primary focus of treatment. More typically, the therapist will "address" the personality disorder during the treatment process in order to minimize rather than permanently alter the individual's cognitive, interpersonal, and affective behaviors. It is these behaviors that frequently have given rise to the patient's psychological difficulties, which have helped him or her to defend against awareness of repressed conflicts, and / or have helped to maintain and perpetuate a self-defeating lifestyle. The psychologist's insight into the development and dynamics of this histrionic style will enable him or her to diagnose the disorder and to empathize with the patient's self-perception and perception of the world. Ultimately, this psychological "leverage" will enable the clinician to successfully treat the identified problems.

Histrionic personality disorder may be most comprehensively conceptualized using an integrative theoretical model. In the treatment of Alexandra, this integration combined an interpersonal, short-term dynamic perspective that emphasized the developmental influences of her childhood experiences and parental interaction with a cognitive approach focusing on her resulting belief system and cognitive schemata (Beck & Freeman, 1990; Horowitz, 1997; Levenson, 1995; Millon, 1999; Strupp & Binder, 1984). With each patient, however, the therapist must draw out from his/her therapeutic armamentarium those theoretical formulations that seem to best explain the origins and maintenance of the patient's difficulties. Most importantly, these formulations must inform effective and time-sensitive treatment interventions.

For many female histrionics, childhood and adolescent experiences are characterized by parental conflict and marital schism, which lead her to turn away from an often cold, competitive, and rejecting mother and turn to a more indulgent father. Typically, the father is superficially supportive and affectionate, but only in response to his daughter's "cuteness," flirtatiousness, and dramatic flair. Alexandra felt that in order to meet her needs for warmth and affection she had to "perform" for her father, since expressions of genuine feelings or moderate displays of emotion were ignored. Eventually, in the development of the histrionic personality, these performances do not result in fulfillment of the individual's needs, and he or she later often resorts to emotional outbursts, demanding behavior, self-dramatization, seductiveness, and even physical illness to gain control of his/her parents. Such was the case with Alexandra. She felt that even these displays would elicit no response or, at best, an inconsistent one from her father.

Adolescence brings a shift from a focus on parental relationships to those involving peers. Alexandra remembers her teenage years as a time when she began to emphasize her physical appearance. She learned that this attracted the attention that she desperately craved. In spite of this superficially seductive self-presentation, the person developing a histrionic style may be quite guilty about his/her attractiveness and anxious about any real sexual involvement. He/she nevertheless turns to others who respond positively to seductive manipulations while turning away from those who arouse feelings of jealousy and competition. As Alexandra turned toward boys and later men, however, she became highly dependent on them for her sense of identity, overvalued them, and chose men who were controlling, unavailable, or hurtful. The painful history of such relationships had left her with the feelings of disappointment, inadequacy, depression, and anxiety for which she sought treatment.

Partly as a result of these developmental experiences, the person with histrionic personality disorder (HPD) often develops a set of beliefs, cognitive distortions, and underlying assumptions about the world that help to determine their behavior (Beck & Freeman, 1990). Such persons believe that they are inadequate and incapable of managing their lives, and crave constant love and nurturance from everyone. Fearing rejection and desperate for attention, Alexandra had "performed," manipulated, and demanded her way through life. Whether playing the role of the seductress or injured victim, she continually sought protection, rewards, and affection from others. The histrionic cognitive style, described by Shapiro (1965) as impressionistic, diffuse, global, and lacking in detail, further distorts the individual's views of their problems, undermines a well-differentiated sense of self, and leads to a profound lack of identity. From the perspective of cognitive theory, such diffuse, illogical, and vague thinking leads to the intense, overblown emotional "storms" and poor problem-solving skills that had become characteristic of Alexandra.

Finding a specific treatment focus in Alexandra's treatment was crucial. In light of the time-limited nature of the treatment, it was decided that psychotherapy would address three areas of concern. First, the therapist would deal with the acute emotional distress that seemed to overwhelm Alexandra and prevent her from effectively managing her other difficulties. The development of a supportive and empathic relationship would strengthen a working alliance and allow the patient to begin to contain and modulate her emotions. Next, using a combination of cognitive challenges, communication skills training, and insight-oriented interpretive links to both her early family experience and her "in therapy" or transferential behavior, the therapist addressed the patient's distorted self-concept and maladaptive interpersonal style. Specifically, he focused on how her feelings of inadequacy and fear of rejection resulted in her assuming the "victim" role in order to receive caring and support from others, including the therapist. Finally, the focus of therapy was turned to helping Alexandra develop the confidence to return to work and attain some degree of independence. The therapist's expectation was that she would leave the relatively brief therapeutic experience functioning at a higher level than when she arrived, but certainly not "cured" of a very well-ingrained approach to life.

ASSESSMENT

Accurate diagnosis and treatment planning require multiple sources of information, but none is more useful than a careful clinical interview. Here the clinician can call upon his or her own emotional reactions to the presentation of the person with HPD. The patient's dramatic displays of emotion, vague and "broad-brush" description of problems, seductiveness, or even warmth and charm may strike the examiner as superficial or insincere. Therapists often feel as if they are watching a theatrical performance. However, while subjective reactions to patients serve as important cues to HPD, diagnosis and assessment must ultimately rely on more empirically and clinically supported criteria established through clinical interviews and testing.

As we saw with Alexandra, the histrionic patient will typically present for treatment with complaints of generalized anxiety, dysphoria, physical problems with no organic basis, or general feelings of malaise or "existential angst." The patient will frequently have difficulties with intimate relationships, feel disillusioned or out of control, and portray his/her experience in vivid, colorful language full of exaggeration and hyperbole. The examiner will often notice in the patient a strong interest in fashion and great attention to physical appearance and attractiveness. The patient may initially relate to the examiner with ease, charm, and warmth designed to elicit approval and sympathy. When the clinician fails to provide the reassurance and concern that the patient craves, frustration and anger typically emerge.

The clinician must also watch for the expressions of helplessness and dependency that are characteristic of persons with HPD. Often such patients will think of the psychologist as "omnipotent" and will expect magical cures or instant solutions to problems that do not require their active participation. They will deny responsibility for their problems and blame life circumstances or uncaring people in their lives. They feel their problems will be solved if they can attract enough attention from others through their entertaining or demanding behavior.

In response to the examiner's questions, the patient will often respond impulsively, relying on immediate impressions and "hunches" rather than careful recollections. When the interview has concluded, the clinician may realize that he/she has little real information and no chronological view of the patient's history. Only careful questioning and delicate probing over time will reveal the patient's underlying despair and fears.

The DSM-IV (APA, 1994) has established criteria for Histrionic Personality Disorder and reports a prevalence rate of up to 15% in clinical populations, where it is diagnosed more frequently in women than men. The gender differential, however, may be influenced more by sex-role stereotypes in our society than by actual occurrence. The DSM-IV defines the disorder as "a pervasive pattern of excessive emotionality and attention seeking, beginning by early adulthood and present in a variety of contexts" (p. 657).

The DSM-IV lists eight criteria for diagnosis, including the following: the need to be the center of attention; interpersonal behavior characterized by sexually seductive or provocative gestures; shallow and labile expressions of emotions; use of physical appearance to gain attention; impressionistic and vague speech; self-dramatization and exaggerated emotion; high suggestibility; and a perception of more intimacy in relationships than actually exists.

In addition to clinical observation, the psychologist can employ a variety of objective and projective assessment tools to assess for the disorder. The Minnesota Multiphasic Personality Inventory-2 (MMPI-2) was very useful in evaluation of Alexandra and revealed a profile of elevations (T scores > 65) including Scales 3 (Hysteria), 2 (Depression), and 1 (Hypochondria). The Millon Clinical Multiaxial Inventory-III (MCMI-III) also provides the diagnostician a useful objective measure with a specific "Histrionic" scale. Projective devices like the Rorschach and the Thematic Apperception Test (TAT) also have unique patterns of scores and themes that further clarify the conflicts and perceptual styles of persons with HPD. Often, patients will respond impulsively to the stimuli in these projective measures, expressing their immediate affective reaction with statements like "Ugh, get this away from me" or "What a sad picture; I feel like crying."

Treatment Implementation

In early therapy sessions, Alexandra communicated about her loneliness, lack of meaning in life, and the hurt she had experienced at the hands of the many men in her life. She mentioned nothing of her own responsibility. After the second session the therapist was able to determine that Alexandra's current distress was precipitated by the recent infidelity of her current boyfriend and her fear of being abandoned by him. This rejection had seemed to remind her of the old losses she had suffered and left her feeling angry and depressed. Her previous boyfriend had reportedly left her 3 years earlier after she had become pregnant with his baby. She aborted the child and claimed feelings of guilt and shame over her decision since that time. She admitted that she was so unhappy being alone, however, that she took him back soon after the abortion. During the early sessions, she also related more experiences of being victimized by various men in her life, including her divorce lawyers, the mental health professionals who never seemed to "understand" her, and physicians who were unable to find causes for her chronic headaches, feelings of weakness, and gynecological pain. She leaped from one complaint to another, never focusing very long on any single issue, frequently manifesting a lability of affect in which she would laugh and sob within the same session.

During these initial sessions, empathy and the communication of respect and caring were central to engaging Alexandra and developing a working alliance. The therapist patiently listened to Alexandra's dramatic expressions of pain, reflected her feelings, and clarified her vague feeling states with specific words. He would ask questions and clarify her dramatic emotional experience, trying to establish cause-and-effect links around the events that were overwhelming her. Rather than intervening prematurely in Alexandra's specific interpersonal problems or internal conflicts, the focus of treatment was on helping her contain her emotional "storms" and experience her feelings in more manageable doses. The therapist discussed specific triggers that the patient might face between sessions and explored how she might respond to them. She planned with the therapist how she might react if her boyfriend called, or how she would respond to the suicidal thoughts that had been frightening her. Alexandra responded positively to the therapist's interventions; her acute feelings of distress diminished and she felt encouraged that her emotional experience was being validated. The development of a safe atmosphere where her concerns could be expressed and contained in manageable doses had the effect of reducing Alexandra's acute depression and anxiety. Over the course of therapy, however, she did occasionally regress when faced with disappointments or perceived rejections, or when she was confronted by the therapist about manipulative and attention-seeking behavior.

The middle phase of therapy addressed some of the interpersonal conflicts, cognitive schemata, and other self-defeating behaviors that had brought Alexandra to treatment. After neutralizing some of the emotionality that helps the person with HPD avoid awareness of underlying despair and fear, the therapist could begin to touch on Alexandra's issues as they manifested themselves both within and outside of therapy. In essence, the psychologist could begin to help her identify and modify what Strupp and Binder (1984) as well as Levenson (1995) refer to as a "cyclical maladaptive pattern." This pattern, developed early in her relationship with parents, defined her interpersonal style and fostered thought and belief patterns that helped create much of her unhappiness.

Psychotherapy next began to focus on helping Alexandra understand how her dependency and fears of abandonment allowed her to stay in the destructive relationship with her current boyfriend. The therapist helped the patient to verbally label her feelings and to identify the beliefs and self-statements that helped create them. Dealing with her emotions through cognitive therapeutic approaches was quite foreign to Alexandra. Accustomed to impressionistic, "gut" feelings and "hunches," she was frustrated by having to "think through" problems and by being asked to take responsibility for creating her upsetness. She was motivated early in therapy, however, to avoid further abuse from her boyfriend and was willing at least to question her long-held beliefs that she was "inadequate," "helpless," and "in need of his undying love." At times the psychologist would suggest that she write down the thoughts that accompanied her feelings or list the pros and cons of a specific decision she was about to make. This helped reduce impulsivity and heightened her awareness of the causes for her difficulties. The therapist also introduced assertiveness training to help Alexandra confront her friend calmly and confidently without the temper tantrums and dramatic emotionality she had usually employed. On one occasion, for instance, when she felt he was cheating on her once again, she drove to his apartment and broke several of his windows! Even though she continued to feel lonely and quite needy, the patient was able to stop calling him, to refuse to accept his controlling behavior, and to end the relationship prior to termination of treatment.

One of the most challenging goals in therapy was helping Alexandra to learn more effective interpersonal skills and to alter her global and impressionistic style of thinking and reacting to situations. As the turmoil that motivated her to seek therapy began to subside, the clinician began to address the more pervasive issues that fostered her identity as a "victim." As Alexandra "told her story," the psychotherapist helped her understand the value of this script in gaining attention, sympathy, and concern from others. While these dramatic manipulations worked on a short-term basis, the long-term effects on her relationships and the false sense of "identity" that these manipulations fostered were devastating. The therapist encouraged her to consider using verbal expression as a way to seek attention rather than seductive gestures or emotional outbursts. He helped the patient to identify some of the frustrations she had experienced as a child when she attempted to gain attention from her parents and to understand how some of her dramatic emotional displays as an adult paralleled these early experiences. When confronted with this insight, Alexandra often became genuinely sad and tearful. At other times when confronted with her manipulations in interpersonal situations she would become enraged, sometimes threatening to walk out on such an "unfeeling" therapist.

The patient was asked to generate alternative ways of getting what she wanted that would be more "honest" and satisfying. The clinician would respond and identify her genuine expressions of feeling and ignore the unauthentic emotions. He would always respond calmly and in a respectful manner, always conscious of his own emotional reactions to her provocations. He would redirect her attempts to avoid upsetting issues and memories, help her focus on upsetting experience, and ask her to logically evaluate her understanding about how these problems came about. In essence, he would continually reinforce her responsibility for and control over her life and redirect her from an external to an internal view of herself and the world.

As the therapy progressed, the clinician began focusing on Alexandra's need for emotional and financial independence. Returning to the workforce, ending her dependency on her mother, and risking failure in a job were frightening for the patient.

The therapist challenged her belief that becoming independent would lead to abandonment by others. Her irrational beliefs included notions that she was incapable of managing life on her own and that she was worthless and could be safe only if she were taken care of by someone stronger. The therapist responded to her strengths and helped her acknowledge them. He began to create a new and more healthy interpersonal experience for her, one in which she could see herself as a competent adult rather than a victimized child.

Alexandra decided to take a part-time job working as an assistant night manager in a hotel. She could dress up, be charming with the guests, and earn a little money. Unfortunately, she made some mistakes during her training period and was criticized by her supervisor. When he challenged her judgment in solving a guest's problem, she later reported that she began feeling "weak" and had a "seizure" in which she lost consciousness temporarily. A thorough neurological exam revealed no problem, but Alexandra was unwilling to return to the hotel. This pattern of physical complaints threaded through her therapy in the form of feelings of fatigue and malaise, back pain, and reported autoimmune disorders for which no physical basis could be found. These symptoms would often emerge when Alexandra was under stress, had a court date to deal with her divorce, or when a therapy session uncovered painful material. Like her emotional outbursts, somatization would elicit attention from her mother and her physicians, strengthening her position as a "victim." The therapist treated these physical displays like the behavioral ones. He showed respect, inquired about actual medical findings and, in their absence, explored with the patient how her somatic complaints might be stress related and serve to distract her from more painful emotional issues that she was avoiding.

CONCURRENT DIAGNOSES AND TREATMENT

Histrionic Personality Disorder rarely serves as a patient's presenting "complaint." More typically, as we have seen in the case of Alexandra, patients will present with symptoms of depression, anxiety, physical dysfunction, and pain for which they have found no medical explanation. The DSM-IV (APA, 1994) notes that HPD is associated with higher rates of Major Depressive Disorder, anxiety disorders, somatoform disorders, including Pain and Conversion Disorders, and comorbid diagnoses of other personality disorders, particularly those in the "dramatic cluster" (Borderline, Narcissistic, Anti-Social Personality Disorders). Marital problems will frequently be the focus of attention as couples address the relationship conflicts exacerbated by the histrionic style. The treatment of these comorbid disorders is beyond the scope of this chapter. The reader is referred to the discussions of these psychological impairments in the appropriate chapters of this volume.

Alexandra received the diagnoses of Major Depressive Disorder and Posttraumatic Stress Disorder in addition to HPD. Additionally, she displayed features of several other syndromes but did not consistently meet the full criteria for formal diagnosis. She complained of intermittent panic attacks, agoraphobic avoidance, and frequent conversion-like symptoms, including seizures. In such complex cases, the clinician must first conceptualize how each of these symptoms contribute to the patient's overall clinical picture and then develop an integrated approach to their treatment. Without a clear treatment plan, the patient's shifting clinical presentations from session to session could result in a disjointed "treatment-of-the-week" approach.

Alexandra initially presented with a significant degree of subjective distress that clearly impaired her ability to attend to and profit from psychotherapy. She experienced not only depression-related feelings of hopelessness and despair, but concentration problems, distractibility, and neurovegetative symptoms, including sleep and appetite disturbance. In order to address these problems as quickly and effectively as possible, the clinician decided to refer her to a psychiatrist who treated her with antidepressant medication and a mild sedative for sleep. While the possibility exists that such medical "solutions" will reinforce the dependent cravings in the patient with HPD and appear to offer "magical" cures, the immediate relief of the medication helped Alexandra focus on therapy more quickly and allowed for a more successful time-limited intervention.

COMPLICATIONS AND TREATMENT IMPLICATIONS

Treating the patient with HPD is a challenge for both the novice and seasoned clinician. Various treatment complications can arise in managing the therapeutic relationship with the patient with HPD, including transference and countertransference reactions, suicidal threats, and premature termination.

The patient's initial response to the therapist is often to view him/her as a "savior" who will be altogether attentive and nurturing. The patient is likely to be complimentary, sometimes seductive, and always dependent on the therapist to "make everything all right." The therapist must be alert to these interpersonal maneuvers and avoid responding to them inappropriately. It is difficult at times to avoid feeling flattered by the patient's compliments or the emotional "high" of being needed by the patient. Unwary clinicians can find themselves being seduced into meeting the patient's unrealistic demands and trying to "rescue" the patient from uncomfortable life circumstances. This only reinforces the "cyclical maladaptive pattern" that the therapy is designed to alter.

Alexandra made frequent demands for "answers" as well as for special considerations from the psychologist. She asked for letters requesting release from jury duty and refunds for unused plane tickets because her psychological problems made it "impossible" to concentrate or travel. The clinician evaluated the appropriateness of each request and explored her possible motivation for avoiding situations. Firm limits must be set and followed, and emotional reactions to the patient's frustration must be carefully processed. The therapist must be careful not to allow the frustration or anger engendered by the patient's manipulations to color his/her judgment about what may be very appropriate requests for assistance. The clinician can become overly cautious and defensive, and this can result in punitive rather than therapeutic reactions towards the patient.

Suicidal ideation, gestures, or bona fide suicide attempts are always serious concerns in the management of any patient. The dramatic behavior of the patient with HPD increases the probability that manipulative suicidal threats or gestures will become part of the clinical picture. The clinician must take every threat seriously and carefully evaluate its lethality. Obviously, serious risks will require the therapist to protect the patient from self-destructive impulses. Clearly, manipulative behavior must be contained, confronted, and explored in the context of its plea for attention. As therapy progresses, the patient must learn more effective ways to meet emotional needs and to express anger.

Finally, premature termination is always a major concern in the treatment of the patient with HPD. Patients often lose interest in therapy, experience an immediate reduction in emotional distress as a result of support from the therapist, or leave therapy when their manipulations are ignored or confronted. In order to minimize premature dropout, clinicians must take care to develop a nonjudgmental, trusting environment in which the patient can confront difficulties. Goals for treatment must be practical, aimed at providing immediate as well as long-term gains, and reflective of the patient's "real" as opposed to "false" self.

DEALING WITH MANAGED CARE AND ACCOUNTABILITY

The managed care industry has revolutionized health care in our country, and nowhere has the impact of this revolution been more significant than in the treatment of psychiatric disorders. In this new environment, practitioners have been challenged to modify their historically long-term treatment approaches to allow for more time-limited interventions. Managed care organizations are no longer willing to pay for interminable therapy or treatment that is not "medically necessary." Such a policy represents a significant challenge for the treatment of personality disorders. Most managed care companies allow for solution-focused, brief interventions directed at ameliorating acute distress within a relatively limited number of sessions. It will be obvious to the reader at this point that for the patient with HPD substantial changes in behavior are unlikely if the intervention is too brief.

Managed care organizations require that clinicians be accountable for the treatment they deliver and justify all visits by regularly submitting treatment plans that are consistent with the patient's diagnosis and degree of impairment. The goals must be measurable and treatment interventions clearly defined. In treating patients with HPD, the practitioner must establish a focus for treatment that is directed toward symptoms and behaviors that are impairing functioning and that are likely to be impacted by brief treatment. Alexandra's depressive and anxiety symptoms were a primary focus of treatment and were addressed within the context of her personality disorder. From the perspective of managed care, however, it is generally unwise for a clinician to establish a personality disorder as the sole focus of clinical attention.

All patients, and certainly those who are prone to developing strong dependent attachments, need clear limits and boundaries in therapy. When there is a strong likelihood that therapy visits will be limited, the psychologist must be clear with the patient about these limitations at the outset of treatment. If at a later time the insurance company terminates visits, with or without the practitioner's agreement, patients are less likely to feel abandoned or angry about being misled.

Managed care will continue to call for brief and effective treatments for psychological disorders. Psychologists and other mental health practitioners who want to be reimbursed for their services will be challenged to design time-sensitive and empirically validated treatment approaches that are uniquely effective in treating personality disorders.

OUTCOME AND FOLLOW-UP

Alexandra was treated in psychotherapy on a biweekly basis over the course of 5 months. She then agreed to reduce the frequency of treatment to monthly visits for the next 3 months, after which she was terminated. She was seen for a total of 13 sessions. The patient was given the option of returning for additional "booster" sessions when she felt they were necessary.

At the point of termination, the patient was not experiencing any acute symptoms of depression or anxiety. She reported occasional dysphoria, especially when she was reminded of a past relationship or felt particularly lonely. She was able to end the relationship with her controlling boyfriend and reported no contact with him up to the time of termination. Her dramatic and manipulative behavior had reduced in frequency during therapy sessions, and she was even able to develop some insight about her exaggerated needs for attention. When under stress she continued to be quite emotionally reactive and to complain of headaches, dizziness, and other somatic derivatives. She never stopped focusing on her appearance and often expressed concerns that she was unattractive and aging too quickly. The therapist received a telephone call from Alexandra about 3 months after termination soliciting his advice on whether she should undergo a facelift. She felt that this surgery might boost her self-confidence.

Alexandra clearly benefitted from her psychotherapy but is likely to continue to manifest histrionic personality traits, especially when under stress. At the time of her last phone call, she told the therapist she was planning to go job hunting after she had undergone facial surgery.

DEALING WITH RECIDIVISM

Recidivism is very likely in the treatment of personality disorders, since patients will continue to be affected by stressful situations that elicit or are created by their maladaptive coping and interpersonal styles. Brief therapy can reduce these acute episodes and, over time, help patients manage their psychological weaknesses more effectively. It cannot, as has been noted, "cure" the disorder. Rather than consider a patient's return for treatment of their personality disorder as "recidivism," the clinician can adopt a view of treating such patients at different points in their lives as difficulties arise. This is not unlike the role of the physician who treats a patient with a chronic physical disorder whenever the need arises. Cummings and Sayama (1995) have described this approach as "intermittent psychotherapy throughout the life-cycle."

Alexandra's personality style is unlikely to be altered substantially through a brief therapy intervention. Psychotherapy did impact her functioning, however, and provided her with a perspective and some coping skills that will undoubtedly serve her in the future.

SUMMARY

This chapter reviewed the assessment and treatment of Histrionic Personality Disorder from a theoretically integrative perspective. Combining elements of psychodynamic and cognitive-behavioral psychotherapies, the treatment of a 49-year-old female patient was presented, along with information regarding comorbid diagnoses, treatment outcome, and recidivism. Discussion of the management of this disorder within the current health-care environment was also presented.

Patients with HPD can at one moment be charming and entertaining, and at another, demanding, infantile, and impulsive. They are challenging not only for the novice but also for the seasoned therapist. To experience any success with patients with HPD, therapists must understand their insatiable need for attention and admiration; appreciate their strategy of trying to fulfill all their needs by focusing their attention totally outside themselves; and commit themselves to helping their patients feel safe and trusted as they examine their "inner world" of thoughts, conflicts, and identity. Perhaps most importantly, the therapist must instill the hope that the patient can experience emotional fulfillment by drawing upon his/her own inner resources rather than depending solely on other people.

REFERENCES

American Psychiatric Association (1994). *Diagnostic and statistical manual of mental disorders* (4th ed.). Washington, DC: Author.

Beck, A. T., & Freeman, A. (1990). *Cognitive therapy of personality disorders.* New York: Basic Books.

Budman, S. H., & Gurman, A. S. (1988). *Theory and practice of brief therapy.* New York: Guilford.

Cummings, N., & Sayama, M. (1995). *Focused psychotherapy: A casebook of brief, intermittent psychotherapy throughout the life cycle.* New York: Brunner/Mazel.

Horowitz, M. J. (1997). Psychotherapy for histrionic personality disorder. *Journal of Psychotherapy Practice and Research, 6,* 93–107.

Levenson, H. (1995). *Time-limited dynamic psychotherapy.* New York: Basic Books.

Millon, T. (1999). *Personality-guided psychotherapy.* New York: John Wiley & Sons.

Shapiro, D. (1965). *Neurotic styles.* New York: Basic Books.

Strupp, H. H., & Binder, J. L. (1984). *Psychotherapy in a new key: A guide to time-limited dynamic psychotherapy.* New York: Basic Books.

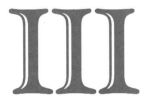

PART

SPECIAL ISSUES

CHAPTER

Considerations for Gay and Lesbian Clients

Sandra J. Coffman and G. Dorsey Green

Independent Practice
and
University of Washington
Seattle, Washington

Effective Brief Therapies: A Clinician's Guide

CASE DESCRIPTION

Sheryl is a 25-year-old white woman living in Seattle, Washington. She has a good job as a paralegal and lives in a nice apartment in a pretty area of the city. Sheryl has come to therapy because she thinks she is depressed. Sheryl says that while she has had ups and downs for years, she really "hit bottom" 2 or 3 months ago. She reports that she is feeling "blue" and is tearful quite often. She says she is waking most mornings at about 3:30 a.m. and cannot return to sleep, resulting in chronic fatigue. While Sheryl has not spent much time with her friends recently, she had enjoyed outings with them when they occurred. She says that even though she is still participating in some of her favorite activities, she takes little pleasure in them. Sheryl reports that she cannot read as easily as before, as she is having difficulty concentrating. She is worried that her work is suffering because of these concentration problems and reports that decisions are hard to make. Sheryl admitted during intake that she has occasionally wished she were dead, although she denies any active suicidal ideation. Sheryl is not initially sure why she would be feeling so depressed right now.

Sheryl grew up in a small city with her brother, sister, and parents. Her father is a dentist, her mother a school librarian. Sheryl graduated from a large university and then trained as a paralegal. When she got a job in a Seattle law firm, she moved to the West Coast. When asked about changes in libido during the first session, Sheryl reluctantly told the therapist that she has been in a sexual relationship with her best friend for the last 7 months. Sheryl also reported that while she enjoys sex with her friend, her interest in sexual activity had dropped markedly in the last 2 months. As she and the therapist explored Sheryl's thinking about her relationship, Sheryl revealed she had told no one about this relationship and that she had no positive images of lesbian or bisexual women. To the contrary, she held many negative beliefs about women who have romantic or sexual relationships with other women. These attitudes were reinforced by Sheryl's family and her religious training. She and her family are Southern Baptists, and even though Sheryl had not attended church in Seattle, she reports agreeing with most of the Church's teachings.

TREATMENT CONCEPTUALIZATION

The authors chose a diagnosis of depression with underlying internalized homophobia to demonstrate the use of brief therapy with lesbians, gays, or bisexual (l/g/b) clients. It is the rare l/g/b person who grows up with no damage to her or his self-concept given the prevalence of the antihomosexual beliefs and prejudice in North American culture.

Most major institutions in our society maintain a strong bias or laws against homosexuality. Several of the most obvious examples of this cultural bias include the sodomy laws that include consensual same-gender sexual behaviors, the national Defense of Marriage Act, which prohibits same-gender couples from marrying legally, and the widespread belief that homosexuals are sick or sinful.

Internalized homophobia "is the gay person's direction of negative social attitudes toward the self, leading to a devaluation of the self and resultant internal conflicts and poor self-regard" (Meyer & Dean, 1998, p. 161). Internalized homophobia does not take root until a person self-identifies as gay, lesbian, or bisexual. Then these negative cultural beliefs and attitudes suddenly develop a more personal salience.

Research has shown that gay men and lesbians who have high levels of internalized homophobia are more likely to suffer psychological distress than are more self-affirming lesbians and gay men (Meyer & Dean, 1998; Shidlo, 1994). As men and women develop a positive lesbian/gay or bisexual identity, their internalized homophobia lessens and their overall mental health improves (Shidlo, 1994). Based on his research into the connection between internalized homophobia and psychopathology, Shidlo recommends that lesbians and gay clients routinely be assessed and treated for internalized homophobia. It is crucial that therapists working with this population are knowledgeable about the lesbian/gay/bisexual affirming resources available to their clients.

Internalized homophobia is based on maladaptive beliefs and attitudes that the l/g/b person will need to change in order to feel positive about her or himself. The following composite case illustrates how a therapist may expose and address these self-critical beliefs using Cognitive-Behavioral Therapy (CBT). While this case is fairly straightforward and obvious once the underlying beliefs are exposed, internalized homophobia frequently appears in more subtle ways. Examples include the gay man who never seems to be able to fall in love and partner, or the woman who drinks excessively whenever she desires a sexual encounter with another woman. Clinicians need to learn about their own beliefs concerning l/g/b people to ensure that they do not unintentionally collude with either the subtle or obvious signs of internalized homophobia.

The many current varieties of CBT all share two fundamental assumptions about cognitive activity: (1) that it affects mood and behavior, and (2) that it may be monitored and altered. It is also assumed that behavior change can be effected through cognitive change (Dobson, 1988). This chapter will focus on the cognitive-behavioral therapy described by Beck and his colleagues (Beck *et al.*, 1979) as brief and time-limited, and based on a sound therapeutic relationship between the therapist and client. This therapy provides an educational, structured, directive, problem-oriented approach to mood and behavior change. CBT initially includes behavioral activation to energize and motivate clients and to increase feelings of competence and pleasure in life. CBT then utilizes the Socratic method of inductive questioning to illuminate and challenge the client's maladaptive thoughts and assumptions.

Cognitive-behavioral therapy is a focused form of psychotherapy based on the connection between psychological disorders and dysfunctional thinking. Feeling and thinking are also influenced by and connected to behavior and the social and interpersonal environment of an individual (Fallon & Coffman, 1991). Problems, interpersonal relationships, and mood disorders can be modified by changing the environment and/or by changing the way a person views his/her situation. If one's thinking is found to be dysfunctional, modifying this thinking would provide improvement in mood or behavioral symptoms. Theorists assume that modifying underlying core beliefs about the self, the world, the future, or others leads to a durable improvement in one's mood (Beck, 1995).

Cognitive therapy is centered on a cognitive conceptualization of the disorder (in this case depression) and of the particular client, and may be charted using the Core Conceptual Diagram (Beck, 1995). Although this conceptualization may change over time with increasing information, therapists are encouraged to guess at core assumptions even from the first session. They can then tie treatment decisions to this unique conceptualization and choose from a variety of techniques (e.g., cognitive, behavioral, and experiential) to modify underlying maladaptive ideas. Clients are also taught to watch for certain typical forms of thinking errors and to become more accurate reporters to themselves about the world and themselves.

Core ideas about the world and the self, and personal styles of organizing and interpreting information and experience are commonly acquired in early childhood. Although originally useful for the individual, these core ideas and the compensatory behaviors that flow from and reinforce them are often both restrictive and taken for granted. Clients may not realize that their core beliefs may blind them to alternative, more accurate viewpoints and thereby keep them stuck in repetitive behavior patterns. Alternative possibilities may not appear on the horizon until the client learns to question his/her thinking and behavior.

Keeping a daily record of automatic thoughts helps clients to track cognitions and to eventually correct dysfunctional thinking and identify typical thinking errors. Patterns may emerge from this cognitive data that may highlight patterns in automatic thinking as well as underlying assumptions. Tracing the meaning of terms and symbolic meaning via a "downward-arrow" technique (Beck *et al.*, 1979) helps unearth underlying beliefs. Imagery and role-playing techniques are also included to expose and change beliefs and assumptions (Young, 1989).

For example, someone dissatisfied with his/her work environment could either work to change the environment (e.g., by becoming more assertive, participating in a union, or restructuring work responsibilities), to change his/her view of him/herself and the job, or both. Using both an activity schedule and a thought record, he/she could gather evidence to indicate whether or not he/she had a complete and accurate view of work responsibilities. He/she could seek feedback about work performance or examine his/her own expectations for work, including watching for a tendency to personalize negative information or to think in a global way. If he/she suspected homophobia was harming advancement at work, he/she could try any or all of these approaches. A core conceptualization diagram (Beck, 1995) could also search for internalized homophobia, which might take the form of self-statements such as "All lesbians are defective" or "If I were straight, I would be a better person."

ASSESSMENT

Since the client described herself as being depressed, she was given a Beck Depression Inventory (BDI) (Beck *et al.*, 1979) at her first session, and scored 25. Both dysthymia and bipolar disorders were ruled out using the DSM-IV: the client did meet criteria for major depressive episode, single occurrence. Sheryl was also isolating herself, though this may have resulted from being in the early stages of a romantic relationship. She also found previously enjoyable experiences, such as hiking and singing in a choir, to be less pleasurable. Her BDI score on item 9, which measures suicidality, was 1 and was further explored with the client. She admitted infrequent suicidal thoughts but had neither a plan nor intent. She was deterred by her relationship, her strong ties to her family of origin, and her religious beliefs. She also seemed undefensive in discussion of her suicidal feelings and readily agreed to discuss any future ideation or thoughts with the therapist.

Cognitive Conceptualization. Cognitive therapy includes a cognitive conceptualization of each case (Persons, 1989). Therapists are encouraged to guess at a client's core beliefs early in therapy and to refine this idea as additional evidence is revealed, sometimes via the downward-arrow technique. Early in therapy it appeared that this client felt herself to be lovable, but only if she was heterosexual. She felt lovable because she saw herself as a child of God and felt that "God loves me." However, she assumed that "God doesn't accept or like homosexuals." She therefore concluded, "If I'm homosexual, God doesn't love me." This assumption flowed from some fundamental religious beliefs, including "all homosexuals are sinful."

Her current love relationship required her to face her long-suspected attraction to women, which she felt isolated her from God's love. She also feared that being attracted to women would mean she hated men (and that men would hate her). These painful ideas were explored in later sessions when evidence for and against these ideas was collected. Alternative ways of viewing God's love and her attraction to women were also explored. Various options were pursued to develop a new core belief that would allow Sheryl to love women and also experience God's love, thus maintaining her core belief of lovability.

TREATMENT IMPLEMENTATION

Treatment followed the standard protocol for using CBT with depressed clients (Beck *et al.*, 1979), while also paying special attention to thoughts and beliefs about sexual attraction and orientation and to thoughts about what it might mean to the client to define herself as bisexual or lesbian. An outline of the sessions follows.

Session 1 (BDI = 25)

The plan/agenda for this session was: introduce self and therapeutic orientation; address bureaucracy, including insurance (referred by primary care physician, managed care referral for five sessions, can apply for extension); solicit her description of problem and what brought her to therapy (depression); assess suicidal ideation and hopelessness; obtain brief history of depressive episode and current symptoms (first sexual relationship with a woman, ongoing for 7 months); introduce CBT model, and explain and administer BDI.

The client came to therapy to decrease depression and feelings of hopelessness and self-criticism. She was confused by the happiness she was experiencing in her first sexual relationship with a woman, since she felt homosexuality to be wrong. She was also confused about the impact of this relationship on her mood and how this relationship affected her sexual orientation. The therapist confirmed her diagnosis of depression and expressed hope about helping her learn skills to increase happiness and to help her clarify the meaning of her current relationship. The client did not want to include her girlfriend in therapy at this time, seeing individual issues as her priority.

Homework that was assigned: Develop and prioritize goals for therapy; read and react to *Coping With Depression* (Beck & Greenberg, 1995); complete an Activity Schedule (Beck *et al.*, 1979).

Session 2 (BDI = 28)

The agenda was to review the Activity Schedule; obtain a history of relationships (with men and women); review client's goals (be less depressed, explore conflicted feelings about relationship with girlfriend, decide whether to spend more time with other friends).

The client prioritized her goals for therapy and discussed the Activity Schedule, which highlighted the absence of social contact outside her relationship. She agreed to begin planning more social activity with other friends. Since she and her partner were also in a rut, she wanted to try going hiking together, an activity she had previously enjoyed.

She revealed past pleasurable experience, platonic and sexual, with men in high school and college but was surprised to find herself enjoying her current relationship even more. This stirred deeply held religious values about homosexuality being wrong. She was fearful that her parents and siblings would not accept her. She also recognized the contradictory possibility that they might still love her given their strong family ties and love. Discussing this seemed to decrease her feelings of hopelessness and gloom.

Homework that was assigned: continue Activity Schedule; plan social activity with friends; increase exercise; plan hike with partner.

Session 3 (BDI = 19)

The agenda was: review homework (Activity Schedule, looking for patterns of depression and also of pleasure and competency); plan additional pleasure and social contact (hikes with friends, reading, time with girlfriend including movies, dinner, or music); explain Dysfunctional Thought Record (Beck *et al.*, 1979) and begin one in session about feelings about her girlfriend; assign Activity Schedule and first three columns of thought log.

The client reported surprise and pleasure that she could positively influence her mood with social contact and pleasurable activities. However, her fun with her girlfriend continued to bring on depression and self-loathing as she believed homosexuality to be wrong in the eyes of God. She feared losing God's love and her sense of being lovable. These religious and social ideas were explored further and used as the beginning of a thought record. It was clear that her mood was changed by these thoughts. This and other examples clarified the model of cognitive therapy, which made sense to her.

Homework that was assigned: complete first three columns of thought record; increase exercise; increase social contact with friends and fun with girlfriend.

Session 4 (BDI = 20)

The agenda was: review homework (thought record, exercise, social contact, and pleasure with girlfriend); complete fourth and fifth columns on thought record in session.

Since the client was still experiencing significant depression and was still confused about her sexual orientation, the therapist introduced the option of requesting additional sessions from the managed care company. Together the client and therapist reviewed the extension request form and discussed the ramifications of including the sexual orientation issues. The client felt strongly that she did not want any mention of sexual orientation concerns, so the therapist respected this request after explaining that its exclusion might decrease chances of the organization offering more sessions.

The client was agreeable with mentioning her continuing depression and with the phrase that "her Seattle lifestyle conflicted with her religious upbringing." The thought record was reviewed and extended to include examples in session of the fourth and fifth columns, providing alternative explanations for depressive automatic thinking. Since the client felt sure she, and others, could identify lesbians, gays, and bisexuals by appearance, homework was assigned to test this idea.

Homework that was assigned: watch for thoughts on Broadway (a street frequented by many l/g/b as well as other people of alternative and traditional lifestyles); see if she could identify gays vs. "punks" vs.

"straights" vs. "granolas" and "alternatives"; continue thought record, at least first three columns.

Session 5 (BDI = 19)

The agenda was: review mood and homework; review thought record (logs) (did five columns); explore her feelings about homosexuals not being loved by God.

The client used the thought log to explore the connection between her depressed mood and her critical thoughts about bi/homosexual people. She was able to see this connection but was unable to produce any alternative ideas. She was intrigued with the therapist's suggestion that some religious people might hold different views of bi/homosexuality than the church in her hometown. Sheryl was open to exploring beliefs of other congregations in Seattle.

Homework that was assigned: read Saturday newspaper church guide and gay news and look for affirming congregations (churches that have publicly welcomed and declared their support of l/g/b people) and decide if she wants to visit; skip a week of therapy to see how she does and if further sessions are granted; explore contact with family (phone, Email); diminish avoidance and test negative predictions.

Session 6 (BDI = 15)

The agenda was: probe perception of why her depression was dropping; introduce idea of relapse and relapse prevention; review thought records and other homework; discuss possibility that God might love homosexuals; discuss possibility that church doctrine can be fallible and can change over time; discuss bisexuality.

The client reported that her depression had lifted considerably as a result of increased social contact with friends. She was also heartened and curious over her observation that the lawyer she liked best in her law firm was likely a lesbian. She was also hopeful and curious about the existence of affirming churches, and was willing to explore them further. If she felt spiritually at home in such an environment, she was hopeful that she might experience God's love for gays and lesbians. This might open up the possibility that God might love her, no matter what her sexual orientation.

She also reported that she had found her homework assignment both confusing and liberating. She realized that she couldn't always guess a person's sexual orientation; many overlapping categories confounded this issue (such as politics, style, cultural, and ethnic orientation). So she found the Broadway street experience confusing, which meant that other rigid ideas about herself and others might be misleading or incomplete.

Homework that was assigned: read *Is the Homosexual My Neighbor?* (Scanzoni & Mollenkott, 1994); visit an affirming church.

Session 7 (BDI = 12)

The agenda was: discuss her visit to affirming church; discuss asking lawyer to lunch; practice downward-arrow technique about religious beliefs; contrast those beliefs with core belief "I'm lovable."

The client was quite moved by her visit to an affirming church. As hoped, this provided an opportunity to examine her ideas about homosexuals being unloved by God. Her basic idea, "I'm lovable," had always rested on the foundation assumption "Since I'm a child of God, God loves me." Her sense of lovability was therefore dependent on feeling loved by God. Since she had been taught that God does not accept or like homosexuals, she had concluded "If I'm bisexual or homosexual, God won't love me."

Growing up in the rural United States, she was not aware of having met any homosexuals. By contrast, the gay scene in Seattle jolted her with culture shock. When she acted on her attraction to her friend, she developed a new idea: "If I'm attracted to women I must hate men (and probably men will hate me)." These assumptions were elucidated via the downward-arrow technique, by asking what an idea might mean to the client, and going for deeper and deeper meaning, rather than simply disputing or asking for evidence.

The most global idea that emerged was that "homosexuals are sinful and sick," which she thought she had learned in church. Her recent visit to the affirming church had brought these old ideas to the fore. It also provided a more flexible model for acceptance of homosexuals by the clergy and, perhaps, God. The client was hopeful that she might be able to find a way to both be loved by God and act on her attraction to women.

Homework that was assigned: talk with partner about going to church together; continue reading; consider idea of terminating or requesting further sessions after the 10th.

Session 8 (BDI = 14)

The agenda was: debrief partner's reaction to shifting self-definition and the possibility of coming out; solicit reactions to reading; discuss therapy ending and whether she desires extension of referral.

The client was pleased to be feeling less depressed and more like a lovable person again. She had found her partner supportive of her quest for self-understanding. They were able to discuss various ways in which they might define their relationship, both to themselves and to others. Neither was ready to discuss this relationship with their parents, but they could imagine this discussion occurring in the future.

The connection between core beliefs and assumptions and behavior was explored in the session. The client was able to develop alternative beliefs about being both bi/homosexual and a child of God: "God loves you if you struggle to lead a good and righteous life, regardless of your sexual orientation."

The client wanted to act as if she is bisexual and see if that fit for her. She was exploring new religious beliefs about homosexuals. Although this remained complicated for her, she felt confident that her depression would remain low if she continued to stay active and examine and challenge critical self-talk and beliefs. She also decided she could stop therapy after the 10 sessions allotted, knowing that she might also desire future booster sessions.

Homework that was assigned: go to Gay Bingo or to a lesbian bar alone or preferably with partner; return to church; continue thought records to be less self-critical.

Session 9 (BDI = 9)

The agenda was: debrief social activity (bingo or bar visit); discuss self-identification and terminology; review evidence for new belief; put on cue card; discuss relapse prevention; introduce idea of self-sessions.

The client reported she felt she has new "breathing room in her body," a better sense of self, and faith in her spiritual connection to God. She was happy to be enjoying her relationship with her girlfriend and wanted to further explore new ways of looking at her life.

Sheryl developed a list of situations and thoughts that might make her vulnerable to a relapse of depression and countered them with new ways of viewing herself and situations. These views flowed from and were consistent with her new core belief about God's love extending to people who struggle to lead a righteous life, regardless of sexual orientation. The therapist role-played her old beliefs and Sheryl countered with the new ones, and found them convincing.

Her feelings and thoughts about termination were explored. She saw herself as now extending her therapy on her own and agreed to practice holding therapy sessions alone, role-playing both therapist and client voices (self-sessions).

Homework that was assigned: consider what was most helpful in therapy and anything that was not helpful; review therapy goals and progress; consider patterns in ending relationships and if the ending of therapy is similar, different or same as other relationship endings; explore feelings about termination and continuing to use skills on own; try self-session.

Session 10 (BDI = 7)

The agenda was: discuss feelings about termination; discuss possibility of booster sessions (needs referral) if depression returns; review patterns in ending relationships; review relapse prevention; review therapy goals; discuss what she liked or disliked about therapy.

The client was feeling somewhat sad about termination but felt confident about her ability to try her new skills. She understood the possibility of asking for another referral if she needed a booster session or if she could not interrupt a slide into depression. She predicted that coming out to her family might require some support. Reviewing her goals increased her confidence and optimism, since she had made a good start on all of her goals.

Sheryl said it felt good to be ending therapy after 10 sessions; she had been fearful that she would get dependent on therapy. She had found the structure and skill-building focus helpful. Although exploring her feelings about her sexual orientation had been painful, she felt these discussions had been very important. Finding that some religious people accept homosexual and bisexual people allowed her to begin to imagine that God might still love her, which contributed greatly to the lifting of her depression and the creation of hope about the future. The one part of therapy she found uncomfortable without being sure it would help was the role-play in the previous session. The session ended with the therapist offering future assistance if desired, but also expressing optimism about the client's skills and future.

CONCURRENT DIAGNOSES AND TREATMENT

While it appears that Sheryl was depressed, there are two other probable diagnoses to evaluate and treat. It is quite likely that Sheryl was experiencing anxiety due to her romantic relationship with her best friend. There was a strong possibility that Sheryl's family would not approve of this relationship if they knew about it. It is not unheard of for parents and siblings to break off relationships with a lesbian/gay or bisexual family member. Sheryl may have had information about her family's feelings and beliefs about homosexuality that increased or warranted her anxiety.

Sheryl was also conflicted about the teachings of the Southern Baptist Church. She valued her connection with the church, even though she was not an active attender. Sheryl also had no conception of a healthy lesbian/bisexual woman. She may have become anxious if she decided to continue this relationship without having any idea of what her life could be like as either an undisclosed (closeted) or disclosed (out) lesbian/bisexual. It is probable that as Sheryl's depression lifted the anxiety would become more apparent.

The second diagnosis was internalized homophobia. While this is not an official DSM-IV diagnosis, internalized homophobia can psychologically cripple someone, and if present, must be treated to reduce the risk of recurring depression and anxiety. Sheryl appeared to suffer from high levels of internalized homophobia. Her lack of positive exposure to and information about lesbian and bisexual women left her particularly vulnerable to the anti-lesbian/gay teachings of her church and of mainstream society. Newly self-identified lesbian, gay, or bisexual people are inundated with an entirely new, usually negative self-image and do not usually have family support for learning to survive in the face of society's hostility.

COMPLICATIONS AND TREATMENT IMPLICATIONS

The direction of Sheryl's therapy raises a number of implications for treatment. As she continues to explore her sexual orientation and relationship with God, Sheryl is likely to feel more positive about being a lesbian or bisexual woman, resulting in her becoming more comfortable and perhaps active in some aspects of the l/g/b communities in Seattle. This activity could include singing in a lesbian or l/g chorus, joining an l/g/b support group in an affirming congregation, participating in an l/g/b outdoors club, or any number of other activities.

These experiences would probably further boost her self-esteem as a lesbian or bisexual woman. As a result, Sheryl might choose to come out to her parents. Parents' responses are unpredictable and range from imme- diate support of their child to completely breaking contact with their l/g/b daughter or son. The personal and clinical experience of one of the authors suggests that parents take an average of 3 years to adjust to a child's announcement of being lesbian, gay, or bisexual. Most parents seem even- tually to accept their child and may even become true advocates of l/g/b legal and social rights. However, Sheryl has no guarantee that she will be able to continue relationships with her family as before. Sheryl might eventually decide to move in with her girlfriend. Some same-gender cou- ples have commitment ceremonies or marriages in affirming churches and synagogues. More commonly, moving in together is equated with the intention to have a long-term committed relationship.

Alternatively, Sheryl might decide that she really is bisexual and choose to be partnered with a man. This decision usually happens after the initial same-gender couple breaks up. If Sheryl were to choose a male partner, she could either retain her sense of being loved by God as a bisexual woman, regardless of the gender of her partner, or alternatively deny the lesbian relationship as a mistake.

One less likely treatment complication might result if Sheryl quit therapy after two or three sessions. She could, as some people have done, decide that being a lesbian/bisexual woman was too difficult for her or too conflictual given her religious beliefs. At this point, she might go to a therapist or clergy member to help her "get over her attraction to women" so that she could find and marry a male partner. She might choose celibacy so as to retain God's love. There is a slight possibility that she could kill herself early in the term of such therapy. Suicidality might result if she sees herself as broken and unfixable and therefore unlovable. However, the indications early in this therapy case were that Sheryl meant to continue therapy until she felt better.

DEALING WITH MANAGED CARE AND ACCOUNTABILITY

The client had been referred by her primary care physician, as mandated by her managed care health insurance, for treatment of depression. Her physician had offered her antidepressants, but she preferred to try psycho- therapy first. The physician knew that CBT had been shown to treat depression successfully in numerous clinical trials, and so made the ther- apy referral.

The managed care company only allotted the client five sessions of therapy, even though the client's insurance policy covered 20 sessions of psychotherapy annually. Since her BDI was still quite high at the fourth session, the clinician initiated a discussion of whether the client felt she was improving with CBT and whether or not she wanted to come for additional sessions if the managed care company would comply with the request for additional sessions. The client was encouraged by the CBT and felt she was learning useful skills to decrease depression, so five additional sessions were requested. The therapist discussed the ways the managed care company's questions could be answered and raised issues of confidentiality with the client. The client did not want the matter of sexual orientation reported, even though she understood that including this complicating factor might facilitate the request for additional sessions. So only depression, the initial presenting complaint, was discussed in the request for more sessions.

The managed care company granted an extension for five sessions, and further progress was made in therapy. Both client and therapist felt she could stop after 10 sessions, although they concurred that additional booster sessions might be useful in the future should the client not be able to spot and/or interrupt any relapse in depression. Should the client decide to come out to her parents, additional sessions might be requested at that time for planning, support, or debriefing.

OUTCOME AND FOLLOW-UP

Over the course of 10 sessions of CBT, Sheryl became less depressed. She successfully identified and challenged the core belief that she was lovable only if she were heterosexual. She explored affirming religious congregations and developed more tolerance for l/g/b sexual orientations, her own and others'.

Research has shown that l/g/b men and women who are active in l/g/b-affirming activities and friendships have higher self-esteem and less psychological distress than those who are more isolated (Herek *et al.*, 1998). Sheryl's experience is consistent with this prediction. It is probable that she will continue to strengthen her lesbian or bisexual self-identity and involvement in l/g/b-related activities. She is quite likely to begin attending church again, when she finds one that matches her spiritual needs, thus further decreasing depression and making relapse less likely.

There is no formal follow-up in this case. Sheryl has said that she would contact the therapist for a booster session or support if she needed it. Given her positive experience in 10 sessions of CBT, there is a very good chance Sheryl will follow through on her statement.

DEALING WITH RECIDIVISM

Early in therapy, the idea of relapse was presented as a natural part of healing and growth. It was argued that any relapse that might occur during the course of therapy would provide an opportunity to practice new skills. Relapse during therapy can also provide practice for any future relapse of depression.

However, the client did not relapse during treatment, possibly because of having only 10 sessions and possibly due to the gradual reduction in her depression. The idea of relapse was discussed again in Session 6, at which time her depression had diminished somewhat. The client was coached to view any future relapse as an opportunity to examine her thoughts and images for depressive self-talk, including internalized homophobia. She could also examine her environment for stresses or negative situations, which she could try to change.

Relapse was again discussed in Sessions 9 and 10, and included discussion of what kinds of situations or self-talk might precipitate relapse into depression. The client made a list of the skills she might use to head off any further slide in mood. For example, she would check to see that she was getting enough sleep, was eating regularly and well, and was getting sufficient exercise and pleasurable social contact. She stated that she might return to doing thought records and would particularly watch for thoughts associated with her old core assumption that "God doesn't love homosexuals." She visualized herself substituting her new assumption, "God loves you if you struggle to lead a good and righteous life, regardless of your sexual orientation," for her old belief.

The client felt excited about trying her new skills on her own and could imagine herself handling any future relapse. She understood the danger in viewing relapse as catastrophe and the advantage of viewing it as useful information. She also knew she could return for booster sessions should she need assistance with future relapse. Additional resources were also presented for help with relapse, such as support groups or reading.

SUMMARY

Sheryl's case is a good example of the effectiveness of CBT for depression exacerbated by internalized homophobia. She was a particularly good candidate for brief therapy because her initial core belief about her lovability was positive and only recently had been modified to include the limitation "*if* I am heterosexual." CBT works well to counteract internalized homophobia, which is dependent on irrational beliefs for its power over people. It is very difficult to live in the United States and not absorb the negativity and bias against lesbian/gay/bisexual people. As a result, we argue that it is essential to include an assessment of internalized homophobia in any client who is l/g/b, who is considering one of those sexual orientations, or who is or has been involved in a same-gender sexual relationship.

The structure of CBT is helpful for these populations because it leaves the data gathering about beliefs and personal conclusions to the client, not the therapist. The collaborative client-centered focus of CBT facilitates the client's development of more helpful core beliefs and allows him/her to trust these new beliefs as his/her own, not just as the creations of a liberal therapist. Finally, after clients have challenged the old beliefs and developed new ones that better fit their current knowledge and environment, they may choose to act in a way that best meets their needs, not the therapist's. And empowering individuals is, after all, what therapy does at its best.

ACKNOWLEDGMENTS

The authors are grateful to Keith Dobson, PhD, Steve Holland, PhD, Christopher Martell, PhD, and Ann Stever for their helpful critique of this manuscript.

REFERENCES

Beck, J. (1995). *Cognitive therapy: Basics and beyond*. New York: Guilford.
Beck, A. T., & Greenberg, R. L. (1995). *Coping with depression*. Bala Cynwyd, PA: The Beck Institute.
Beck, A. T., Rush, A. J., Shaw, B. F., & Emery, G. (1979). *Cognitive therapy of depression*. New York: Guilford.

Fallon, P., & Coffman, S. (1991). Cognitive behavioral treatment of survivors of victimization. *Psychotherapy in Private Practice, 9*, 53–66.

Dobson, K. S. (1988). *Handbook of cognitive-behavioral therapies.* New York: Guilford.

Herek, G. M., Cogan, J. C., Gillis, J. R., and Glunt, E. K. (1998). Correlates of internalized homophobia in a community sample of lesbians and gay men. *Journal of the Gay and Lesbian Medical Association, 2*, 17–25.

Meyer, I. H., & Dean, L. (1998). Internalized homophobia, intimacy and sexual behavior among gay and bisexual men. In G. Herek (Ed.), *Stigma and sexual orientation: Understanding prejudice against lesbians, gay men, and bisexuals* (pp. 160–186). Thousand Oaks, CA: Sage.

Persons, J. (1989). *Cognitive therapy in practice: A case formulation approach.* New York: Norton.

Scanzoni, L. D., & Mollenkott, V. R. (1994). *Is the homosexual my neighbor?: A positive Christian response.* San Francisco: Harper.

Shidlo, A. (1994). Internalized homophobia: Conceptual and empirical issues in measurement. In B. Greene and G. Herek (Eds.), *Lesbian and gay psychology: theory, research, and clinical applications.* Thousand Oaks, CA: Sage.

Young, J. (1989). Schema-focused cognitive therapy for personality disorders: Part II. *International Cognitive Therapy Newsletter, 4*, 4–6.

Considerations for Clients with Marital Dysfunction

Gary R. Birchler

Department of Psychiatry
University of California, San Diego

William Fals-Stewart

Department of Psychology
Old Dominion University
Norfolk, Virginia

Correspondence should be sent to Gary R. Birchler, PhD, VA Outpatient Clinic (116A4Z), 8810 Rio San Diego Drive, San Diego, CA 92108. Tel: (619) 400-5181, Fax: (619) 400-5171.

CASE DESCRIPTION

Jeffrey, a 32-year-old construction worker, met Linda, a 29-year-old nurse, when he was hospitalized briefly following surgery for a broken arm. Jeffrey was a big, good-looking, soft-spoken man. He had a high school education, but earned a good income. He loved to party with friends and be physically active. Linda was an attractive brunette who loved to party with Jeffrey and their friends. When they met she also made a good living. In addition to being very physically and sexually attracted to one another, Jeffrey liked Linda's independence and assertiveness; she liked his easy-going, fun-loving nature and kind-hearted manliness. They dated for 6 months, lived together for 3 months and decided to get married. Linda became pregnant within 2 months of marriage and gave birth to a son. Minor problems between the partners emerged as they encountered the stresses of maintaining dual careers, buying a home, caring for an infant, and attempting to maintain their active drinking and social lives. Unfortunately, coming home alone from a party one night, Linda was intoxicated and had an automobile accident. She was paralyzed from the waist down. She lost her job, was confined to a wheelchair, and her body image and social functions were altered drastically. The family's entire role structure and living routines had to be modified. Within a year of the accident, the couple sought marital therapy when Linda threatened separation because Jeffrey was continuing to "go out and drink" with his buddies, while she was confined to working a job she did not like and taking care of her son. Their communication had deteriorated, their sex life was nonexistent, and they were fighting almost daily over domestic responsibilities.

TREATMENT CONCEPTUALIZATION

Since the advent of the social learning approach to marital dysfunction in the late 1960s and early 1970s, behavioral marital therapy (now more appropriately referred to as behavioral couple therapy) has always been conceptualized as a short-term approach. While no standard number of sessions has been prescribed, the typical number of sessions described in the literature has ranged from 10 to 25, each lasting 60–90 minutes. The present chapter presents a brief approach that is best described as an integrated behavioral-systems approach. For practical purposes, when the terms "marriage" and "marital" are used, they are generally meant to be interchangeable and to include unmarried couples attempting to maintain a long-term intimate relationship. Therefore, discussions in this chapter would be relevant to cohabiting unmarried couples of the same or opposite sex.

As a further introduction to considerations for clients with marital dysfunction, it should be noted that marital distress, discord, and breakup remain pervasive in our culture. Though the following trends and findings are sobering if not demoralizing regarding the institution of marriage, let us consider a number of important and generally substantiated phenomena: (1) more than 90% of the population of the United States participate in marriage; (2) the divorce rate remains about 50% for first-time marriages; (3) while the remarriage rate is approximately 75% for men and 67% for women, the redivorce rates for these groups are about 61 and 54%, respectively; (4) the majority family unit in the United States today is the single-parent family, and the single parent often is en route to becoming remarried, attempting to blend two or more families; (5) 40% of the presenting complaints of adults seeking outpatient mental health services involve adult intimate-relationship dysfunction; (6) in general, married adult females, particularly married adult males, are physically and emotionally healthier than their single, especially formerly married, counterparts; (7) the rate of comorbidity for clinical depression and marital distress in one or more partners is about 50%; (8) the rates for domestic violence in the United States are high, and the (reported) incidence is increasing; (9) in general, children exposed to persistent marital conflict and family violence do poorly emotionally and physically relative to their counterparts raised in maritally stable and satisfied families; and, finally, (10) for many people divorce is the most stressful life event that one may encounter in life, second only to the death of a close family member. There tends to be major emotional and physical illness complications during and after the 1- to 2-year acute phase of the divorce process. Needless to say, given the serious and compounding implications of these marriage and divorce trends, we must continue to develop societal-level and family-based root-cause prevention programs and more effective remedial treatments for marital dysfunction.

To date, the most frequently cited scientifically validated treatment approach for marital dysfunction is behavioral couple therapy (BCT). In fact, while other approaches have some relatively new and impressive scientific support, BCT is the only form of couple therapy that the Clinical Psychology Division of the American Psychological Association lists as meeting the criteria for "empirically validated treatment" (Crits-Christoph et al., 1995).

The authors have developed an approach that potentially employs all of the major components of BCT, plus a conceptual base that also includes features of family systems theory and cognitive-behavioral couple therapy (Birchler *et al.*, 1999). Used as a framework for assessment and treatment, the heuristic tool is called the "7Cs" of long-term intimate relationships. The 7Cs are comprised of **Character** features, **Cultural and ethnic factors, Contract, Commitment, Caring, Communication**, and **Conflict resolution**. Obviously, the authors did not originate these domains of consideration; however, packaging them as the 7Cs and using them as a specific framework to evaluate and treat couples who present with marital dysfunction has been quite helpful in the development of our brief treatment program.

We will define the 7Cs and note some concepts underlying these domains of personal and interpersonal function as they relate to being in a couple relationship. First and foremost, we are concerned with the (inter)personal abilities and emotional qualities of the two individuals attempting to create the relationship. In our framework, *Character features* refer to the aggregate of features and traits that form the individual nature of a person. At one end of the continuum of the potential for interpersonal intimacy is an individual who, by virtue of often complicated biopsychosocial misfortunes, has certain handicaps, personality traits, emotional vulnerabilities, and perhaps limited personal resources or pathological characteristics such that s/he is not a good candidate for maintaining an adult intimate relationship. At the other end of this continuum is the individual who is capable of loving and being loved in the broadest sense of emotional and physical health. S/he is responsible, resourceful, can adapt to varying and stressful circumstances, is able to consistently give and get positive responses, and can achieve a healthy and functional balance of independence and interdependence in the relationship. In the domain of Character features, theoretical factors relating to individual development, the course of mental illnesses, mate selection, and attachment theory are important considerations for clients with marital dysfunction.

Cultural and ethnic factors refer to the cultural, ethnic, racial, religious, family-of-origin, socioeconomic, and other societal variables that collectively form the past and present contexts in which individuals and couples exist. Certainly, given these important and diverse developmental and contextual parameters, many adjustments by the couple are required and the potential exists for many types of conflicts to occur, both between the partners and between the couple and their extended families or the community. In this domain, cultural diversity, the presence of family of origin issues and values (i.e., family systems theory), sex-role preferences, and role strain are relevant considerations.

As applied in our framework, the notion of *Contract* comes from mate selection theory, family systems theory, and social exchange theory. The contract between the partners may refer to *explicit* agreements between the two for the doing or not doing of something specified and expected. However, in close relationships Contract features are more often a complicated set of *implicit* expectations about definition, certain benefits, and the types of interactions within the relationship. In or out of awareness, contract problems suggest that individual partners' expectations do not match their experiences and significant dissatisfaction and intrapersonal and interpersonal conflicts result.

Commitment is thought of as the state of having pledged, devoted, or obligated oneself to another — to be involved, remain loyal, and to maintain the relationship over time. Commitment is a complicated interpersonal variable and can cause much insecurity and distress for a couple. We attempt to simplify the notion by focusing on at least two aspects. First, are partners committed to stability (e.g., no threats or behavioral steps toward separation or divorce; no intention of leaving one another)? Second, are both partners committed to quality, that is, are they willing to invest in an ongoing process to maintain high quality and to improve the relationship through emotional involvement and collaborative work? In the absence of these types of commitment, prognosis is poor regarding remediation of marital dysfunction.

Caring, obviously an important element of an intimate relationship, is considered from the perspective of social learning theory. We refer to the partners' abilities to express relational behaviors that promote emotional and physical intimacy, including mutual affirmation, support and understanding, demonstrations of affection, and pleasurable sexual activities. Also, partners need to establish an effective balance between partner-care and self-care regarding the activities of daily living, the experience of pleasant events, and sources of personal and couple satisfaction.

For the past 30 years, *Communication* effectiveness has been a basic conceptual component of BCT. We define effective communication as the open and honest sharing of information between two people — when the messages intended and sent by the speaker are exactly the same as the messages heard or received by the listener. In our approach, the analysis of couple communication and subsequent communication training are usually fundamental to remediation of marital dysfunction.

Finally, *Conflict resolution*, the last of the 7Cs, refers to the personal skills and interpersonal patterns of interaction that facilitate effective decision-making, individual and joint problem-solving, management of anger, and resolution of marital conflict. Social learning theory and empirical research suggest that people are often deficient in the skills of problem-solving, anger management, and conflict resolution, and that, given the proper motivation to improve the relationship, couples usually can be trained to make significant improvements in this important domain of dyadic function. Having described the 7Cs and briefly noted some conceptual and theoretical links, let us now describe our general treatment format, the elements of assessment, and how they relate to 7C formulation.

ASSESSMENT

Consistent with the traditional practice of BCT, multimethod assessment is considered an important and distinct phase of therapy. BCT typically employs three assessment methods: semistructured interviews, paper-and-pencil questionnaires, and a sample of marital conflict communication. The evaluation period takes from three to four sessions, the objective being completion of a comprehensive evaluation of the marriage. Typically, during the first session, introductions occur and a discussion takes place concerning such administrative items as the therapist's policies on fees, confidentiality, length of sessions, office hours, and so forth. The first meeting is devoted to hearing partners' presenting complaints (i.e., what brings them each to therapy), exploring their respective goals and expectations for treatment (i.e., who and what do they want changed), and taking a brief history concerning when and why they got married, their courting and newlywed experiences, and the development of their current problems. Given sufficient rapport-building and validation of partners' respective experiences, the first session typically ends with an agreement to complete the evaluation process, distribution of the marital assessment questionnaires, and a brief description of the upcoming assessment procedures.

The subsequent one to three evaluation sessions begin with collection of the questionnaires, which are designed to assess various areas of satisfaction and dysfunction related to the 7Cs (e.g., the *Marital Relationship Assessment Battery*, Birchler, 1983; the *Marital Satisfaction Inventory*, Snyder, 1979; the *Dyadic Adjustment Scale*, Spanier, 1976). During the second session, the couple also provides a sample of their problem-solving communication so that their basic communication skills can be analyzed. These interactions usually are videotaped and are available for playback to the couple. In almost all cases, we employ a combination of conjoint and individual interviews. During the latter we learn about Character features, family-of-origin cultural issues, personal histories, and certain information most effectively obtained in an individual session (e.g., domestic violence issues, plans to separate and divorce, commitment to therapy). To conclude the assessment phase, our program features a carefully planned feedback session. The therapist, in dialogue with the couple, integrates the multimodal assessment information, formulates the problems according to the 7Cs, and then co-constructs the treatment plan. This meeting is strategically designed to influence and motivate the couple to enter therapy, or possibly not, depending on the couple's prognosis, motivation, and current appropriateness for conjoint therapy. Occasionally, the nature of the problems or existing levels of motivation are such that engaging in marital therapy is not indicated. In such cases, one or both partners may be referred for individual or group therapy.

Case Description: 7C Analysis

Regarding Jeffrey and Linda, the conjoint and individual interviews, combined with information from the paper-and-pencil measures and the observed conflict communication sample, resulted in the following 7C analysis. Jeffrey's Character features included a history and tendency to abuse alcohol. He had a variable work history and typically had poor work satisfaction. In Linda's current view, he was a hopeless procrastinator who was dissatisfied with his life. Based on paper-and-pencil measures and interview, he was found to be moderately depressed because of his marital problems and work situation. Linda also had a history of alcohol abuse; however, since the accident, she had stopped drinking and became very sensitive and critical when her husband and their friends drank. Jeffrey complained that she was dominating and controlling about the "right way" for him to do things. He claimed she was often argumentative and moody. Interviews and questionnaires indicated that Linda also was depressed about her physical disability, her life situation, and her deteriorating marriage.

Jeffrey and Linda did not present with significant cultural and ethnic problems. Both partners came from working-class upbringings, observed traditional family values, and shared the same ethnicity and religion. Both were interested in working to support the family lifestyle. Jeffrey's male-bonding activities did cause some conflict, especially after Linda's accident. During his upbringing, women made virtually no demands on him. The females in Linda's family typically were independent and had a moderate antimale bias. Against this background, Linda's disability interfered significantly with her need for independence, and Jeffrey resented some of the domestic roles and responsibilities thrust on him. Both parents loved and were involved in their son's emotional and physical development.

The initial marital contract was clear, and the couple functioned fairly well until Linda's accident forever changed the nature of their relationship. She lost a satisfactory job, and the family's financial needs require her to retain a much less satisfying one. This was a detrimental change. She could no longer engage in the work and play activities that brought her satisfaction. Moreover, additional domestic burdens fell to Jeffrey. Both partners frequently were exhausted. The changes in Linda's bodily functions affected not only her activities of daily living, but also the couple's previously special sexual relationship. Presently, neither partner was getting what they wanted from the marriage. What had been complementary personality styles became very annoying, and conflict prevailed.

The contract for Jeffrey and Linda had changed so drastically that marital satisfaction was low and commitment moderately shaken. On the one hand, both partners had a history of ending previous relationships when things did not go well. On the other hand, they were very committed to coparenting their son and they came from families where divorces did not occur. It seemed as though Jeffrey was more committed to stability and less committed to change and therapy, whereas Linda was less committed to stability without change via therapy.

The expression of caring in their current relationship was moderately impaired. Before the accident, the couple described a relationship with high-quality caring, from emotional support to an active and enjoyable sex life. However, during the past year, poor adjustments following Linda's injury had taken their toll. The couple was beginning to display occasional disrespect for one another during increasingly frequent and intense arguments. Moreover, consistent with this process, they had failed to recover their sexual relationship.

For Jeffrey and Linda, communication was functioning much like caring, in that, before Linda's accident, the couple reported a smooth-functioning communication system that resulted in relatively few misunderstandings and arguments. Currently, when interacting about their son and when they were not angry with one another or stressed about their work situations, they still reported effective communication and problem-solving abilities. However, they reported that their conflict-resolution and anger-management skills also had worsened since the accident. As Linda attempted to get Jeffrey to do things in a timely and proper manner, increasing arguments ended in angry yelling matches or took the form of a demand/withdrawal pattern. Typically, the more Linda became frustrated and made demands, the more Jeffrey withdrew, stayed out drinking with his friends, and came home to an even more resentful wife.

On a 7-point scale, ranging from 1 (very vulnerable) to 4 (mixed) to 7 (strength), the therapists and couple evaluated the marital relationship as follows: Character features = 4, Cultural and ethnic factors = 6, Contract = 2, Commitment = 4, Caring = 4, Communication = 5, and Conflict resolution = 2. The primary problem was the current contract between the partners, which had changed abruptly and resulted in increasing domestic- and work-related stressors. Despite previously strong communication skills and expressions of caring, these areas of couple function were deteriorating and they were not managing conflict well at all.

TREATMENT IMPLEMENTATION

Following the assessment phase, the length and course of marital therapy are quite variable. The limits of managed care notwithstanding, our couples typically meet for 55–60 minutes weekly for 2 to 5 months. Of course, some couples terminate prematurely and a few others can make slow but steady progress for over a year. The length of treatment also depends on the number and severity of the problems, on whether improvement/modification is needed in one or more of the 7Cs, and on the basic motivation and functional capacities of the partners and the therapist. Occasionally, partners have incompatible or hidden agendas as they enter marital therapy. In such cases, helping couples to work effectively as a team toward open, agreeable, and attainable goals can be challenging, especially if spouses have spent many years entrenching themselves in polarized and unrewarding patterns of interaction.

Based on the vast empirical research associated with BCT, there are certain core behaviorally oriented skill-acquisition interventions that can be offered to many couples either at the outset or during the course of therapy. These classic treatment components include communication and problem-solving training and/or behavioral exchange activities that are designed to enhance intimacy and reduce conflict (Jacobson & Margolin, 1979). Psychoeducational behavior-change interventions are believed to work best with couples who are younger and not severely distressed, more emotionally engaged, less polarized in their disagreements, and willing to practice collaboration, accommodation, and compromise to reach compatible goals. Regarding the 7Cs, BCT interventions also are much more likely to be successful in brief therapy to the extent that the couples' problems are mild to moderate and occur in the domains of Cultural and ethnic factors, Caring, Communication, and Conflict resolution. Major compatibility problems in areas of Character features, Contract, and Commitment present significant challenges and suggest a poor prognosis for brief conjoint treatment. In practice, the specific interventions and techniques employed to help a particular couple reach their treatment goals can vary significantly from case to case. As an overview of broad-based BCT-related interventions, let us indicate the relationship between the 7C domains emphasized in our model and typical BCT treatment components. Behavioral couple therapists typically feature: (1) interventions and homework exercises designed to strengthen mutual commitment and the expression of caring behaviors; (2) psychoeducational experiential training in communication and problem-solving (i.e., conflict-resolution) skills; (3) a review of partners' expectations and beliefs about the relationship (i.e., Contract) and modification of any negative or otherwise dysfunctional thoughts that may impede the processes of acceptance or change; and (4) specific directed behavior change strategies designed to help people modify maladaptive personal behaviors and dysfunctional relationship interactions.

Specific intervention procedures are employed to build on the couple's strengths and optimal modes of learning and to address the problems highlighted by the 7C evaluation process. These directive procedures include videotape feedback of both spontaneous and planned communication and conflict interactions, role-playing both ineffective and effective verbal exchanges, therapist coaching and modeling, in-session communication exercises, weekly homework assignments to strengthen aspects of the 7Cs, monitoring self-observed cognitive and self- and spouse-observed behavioral variables, and reading assignments from communication training manuals (e.g., Notarius & Markman, 1993).

Based on clinical experience, we have some ideas of how to sequence the emphasis on 7C domains. This discussion also may serve to help practitioners anticipate certain criteria by which to accept couples for brief marital therapy. Concerning Character features, individualized therapy (and not conjoint therapy) usually is indicated when either partner is actively psychotic, actively abusing alcohol or drugs, battering his or her partner, suffering from an acute exacerbation of a severely disabling mental illness (e.g., major depression, bipolar affective disorder, posttraumatic stress syndrome, or other anxiety disorder), or manifests certain severe and treatment-resistant forms of personality disorders. The existence of these problems suggests poor prognosis for brief marital therapy, and, considering the treatment options presented throughout this guidebook, a referral for individual therapy would be most appropriate.

Cultural and ethnic factors by themselves, independent of Character features, rarely preclude conjoint therapy. In fact, if the problem is due to interference by close relatives, family therapy could be the treatment of choice. In our experience, one problem with Cultural and ethnic factors can be a difference between the couple and the therapist. Certainly, there are cases in which additional supervision or consultation is required to initiate and maintain a culturally sensitive process. Occasionally, referral to a more appropriate therapist is indicated. Cultural and ethnic factors may represent significant problems for some couples, although more likely these are contextual issues that are neither primary nor severe.

Contract problems, on the other hand, can be critical for a couple's relationship. Like the serious problems in the domains of Character features and Commitment, Contract problems can be "show-stoppers." That is, if a couple is attempting to maintain the relationship within the constraints of an unhealthy or unworkable contract, either explicitly or implicitly, the therapeutic process will become stuck. At best, progress in therapy will be very limited until the bad contract is renegotiated or redefined. On the one hand, due to ever-changing life circumstances or other life-cycle stages of development, many couples do enter therapy because of the need and desire to adjust or modify their respective expectations, roles, responsibilities, and future directions. These are good cases for brief couple therapy. On the other hand, some unfortunate partners have based their relationships on significantly unhealthy Contract features and to modify these connections is to set the stage for dissolution of the relationship. In these cases (e.g., domestic violence, rescuing and enabling substance abusers, a marital system where an overadequate partner requires an underadequate partner), separation or divorce may be seen as a constructive outcome.

As we begin considerations of what we have referred to as the "four core Cs" of a long-term marriage, that is, Commitment, Caring, Communication, and Conflict resolution, Commitment seems to be the most frequently encountered "show-stopper" among the four. That is, many unmarried, long-term, cohabiting couples who seek couples therapy have important Commitment issues regarding loyalty, trust, security, and permanence. Many chronically dissatisfied married and remarried couples also have problems believing that their partners have caring commitments to them or are committed to making changes that they desire. These latter couples may experience stability but can harbor long-term distrust about their own or their partners' willingness or abilities to establish a satisfying relationship. In working with many couples in which one or both partners have been significantly ambivalent regarding Commitment, we have found that they tend to be insecure and preoccupied with it until some sense of security is perceived. Therefore, when present, Commitment issues are best addressed very early in therapy as a prerequisite to other work in the four core Cs.

For most couples seeking marital therapy, the Caring domain requires attention. Also, while caring expressions might be temporarily withheld, dormant, or the exchange process has been somewhat damaged, the interventions associated with BCT can often help couples to recover and/or improve on the motivational and skill factors related to Caring. Of course, the prognosis for success in this area is best when the couple still has, or at least formerly had, a strong repertoire of caring behaviors that can be revitalized. Unfortunately, on the far end of the Caring continuum, we know that partners who have learned to disrespect, abuse, and even despise one another are very poor candidates for reconstructing a positive relationship. Brief conjoint therapy usually is not very successful in these cases.

Communication problems not only are the number one complaint of therapy-seeking couples, Communication also is the most likely domain of all the 7Cs to be dysfunctional. Fortunately, the area of Communication is traditionally the most responsive to the BCT approach. Clearly, it can be argued that dyadic communication effectiveness is the most critical skill set that a couple can develop. Effective verbal and nonverbal communication is a requirement for identifying, sharing, understanding, appreciating, and resolving most relationship issues. There are two basic client requisites to rapid improvement in couple communication under brief therapy conditions: motivation and competence. Difficulties associated with the previously discussed 7Cs can and often do interfere with partners' levels of motivation and competence. For example, if a person has mental or behavioral competence problems (i.e., due to substance abuse, low intelligence, psychosis, cognitive deficits associated with major depression) or if s/he has motivational problems (i.e., dislikes the partner, has a competing agenda, wants more distance rather than more closeness), then communication training in therapy tends to fail. The same conditions often hold true for work in the areas of problem-solving and Conflict resolution. Essentially, until the couple attains minimum levels of function in the other 7Cs, therapeutic achievements in these two psychoeducational areas of interpersonal function are more difficult to obtain. Alternatively, we have found that when there are no significant or serious problems in the Character features, Contract, Commitment, and Caring domains for a given couple, then rather rapid and enduring improvements can be made in the skills of Communication and Conflict resolution.

In most BCT approaches to marital dysfunction, problem-solving training, extending into conflict-resolution training, is a logical extension of the basic communication skills training module. At least one possible distinction between general communication and problem-solving training and work in the Conflict resolution domain of the 7Cs concerns anger management. Here partners' temperaments and (un)developed abilities to identify, express, and manage their anger come into play. In the context of marital conflict, heightened emotional arousal combined with limited verbal skills often can set the stage for regrettable interactions. One frequent outcome of dysfunction in this area is the fact that negative exchanges do not solve the problems at hand. Additionally, if the fighting either escalates into more destructive exchanges or causes partners to withdraw to avoid future aversive exchanges, then couples therapy may play a critical role in helping these couples regain or develop these important conflict-management skills.

In summary, in most instances our case formulations derive from an assessment and evaluation process that includes semistructured clinical interviews, paper-and-pencil questionnaires, and an observed sample of couple problem-solving. This information is organized into the framework of the 7Cs and serves as the basis for feedback and treatment planning prior to the intervention phase of therapy. Based on the problems and objectives of a given couple, variable emphasis is placed both concurrently and sequentially on improving 7C domains of marital function. Once again, in most brief treatment situations, work in the area of Caring, Communication, and Conflict resolution is included in the treatment package. Most couples also need work in one or more of the other 7Cs.

CONCURRENT DIAGNOSES AND TREATMENT

As suggested in the 7C conceptualization above, in the domain of Character features, either or both partners may present for marital therapy while suffering from individual psychiatric disorders. These concurrent diagnoses need to be identified, the severity evaluated, and treatments of choice prioritized and sequenced appropriately. Some concurrent psychiatric diagnoses are more prevalent than others when working with distressed couples. For example, in several studies the comorbidity between marital distress and clinical depression in one or both partners has been found to be about 50%. A chronically depressed person puts significant stress on a marriage, and a bad marriage depresses people. On the one hand, when either partner is severely depressed, most clinicians believe that the depression should be treated before outpatient couples therapy is initiated. Couples therapy has a much better prognosis when partners are stable psychiatrically and they can function on an interpersonal level. On the other hand, when depression and marital distress coexist, couples therapy may be the treatment of choice, especially when a poorly functioning relationship is a primary cause for partners' depression. Similarly, depending on the treatment setting, several other concurrent diagnoses may present with marital dysfunction. Typical among them are adjustment disorders, alcohol and drug abuse, anxiety disorders, bipolar disorder, borderline personality disorder, posttraumatic stress disorder, schizophrenia, and various sexual disorders. In all cases, the clinician must make a determination as to whether the individual partners' psychiatric problems are significant enough to be treated before, in lieu of, concurrent with, or after the treatment of marital dysfunction.

TREATMENT PLAN AND OUTCOME

Jeffrey and Linda endorsed the formulation that Contract issues were the primary cause of their problems. Preferred social, sexual, and domestic sex-roles had to be modified as a result of Linda's spinal cord injury. The failure of the couple to adjust well to Linda's disability had resulted in steady erosion of formerly strong Communication and Caring behaviors to the point where Commitment was shaken. The first two treatment sessions were designed to improve the couple's mutual support and understanding. The partners were helped to understand how and why their relationship had changed and the insidious process by which the demand/withdraw and escalating fighting and distancing behaviors had emerged as prevalent in their interactions. The next four sessions were devoted to enhancing the expression of Caring behaviors and eliminating the destructive and disrespectful aspects of their problem-solving interactions. In this domain, the couple was helped to negotiate a reduction of Jeffrey's drinking episodes (some of these were motivated by his desire to withdraw from and avoid anticipated aversive interactions with Linda). In addition, Linda was encouraged to be more selective regarding the domestic and child-care support behaviors that she expected from Jeffrey. She learned to reduce her vague complaints (e.g., character assassination) and to request specific assistance in areas that she was willing to let Jeffrey accomplish in his own way.

As the couple came to realize how they *both* were struggling with personal, family, and work-related stressors and that, out of frustration, they were working against instead of with one another, their abilities to collaborate and compromise were enhanced. As a result of the acceptance work and the short-term skill training regarding Caring, Communication, and Conflict-resolution behaviors, commitment and marital satisfaction improved. The final two sessions of an 8-week treatment course were devoted to specific discussion and development of a pleasurable sexual relationship in light of Linda's disability and to relapse prevention planning to help the couple maintain the gains of marital therapy. Overall, the therapist and couple assessed the outcome of therapy as much improved, with the following 7C pre- to post-ratings: Character: 4 to 6; Cultural and ethnic factors: 6 to 6 (no change); Contract: 2 to 5; Commitment: 4 to 6; Caring: 4 to 6; Communication: 5 to 6; and Conflict resolution: 2 to 5.

COMPLICATIONS AND TREATMENT IMPLICATIONS

Since the 1980s, various BCT groups have been developing models of theory and intervention to reduce recidivism that are meant to extend and improve on the effectiveness of BCT. Emphasis has been placed on integrating interventions that do not focus strictly on behavior change and the classic communication, problem-solving, and behavioral exchange treatments that are the hallmarks of BCT. Full discussion is beyond the scope of this chapter. Suffice it to say that approaches labeled "functional family therapy," "cognitive-behavioral," "behavioral-systems," and "acceptance and change" represent these efforts to deal with recidivism that may result from strict reliance on a behavioral approach.

The most recent effort to integrate distinctly nonbehavior-change interventions into the traditional BCT approach is represented in the work of Jacobson and Christensen (1996). Clinical experience and some research has suggested that couples who are severely distressed, older, emotionally disengaged, have significant areas of incompatibility, and are devoid of an affectionate/sexual relationship are not good candidates for a behavior change approach. The idea is that certain progress needs to be made toward helping partners to gain emotional acceptance of their mate and their relationship status in lieu of or before behavior change efforts can be effective. In this approach, and for these types of couples, acceptance therapy (i.e., acceptance interventions) is instituted at the very beginning of therapy. The therapist joins the couple in recognizing the mutual dilemma of their polarized positions, works to create empathic understanding for each partner's good intentions, and attempts to convert partners' chronic struggle to change their mate into acceptance of their partner and the relationship as they are. Therapists suggest that in certain areas change is not really possible and that emotional acceptance is the best way to reduce distress and dissatisfaction. For example, partners are taught that originally attractive individual differences are not behaviors likely to change, nor should the lack of partners' change in these areas be taken personally or be the cause for blame. Additional strategic interventions include helping the couple to understand their mutual problem from a rational versus an emotional perspective, building emotional tolerance of undesired behaviors, and resignation with self-care. For example, long-term repetitive arguments are reframed as validating the existence of a problem that will not go away, but the couple can learn not to invest energy into the chronic and futile struggle. Role-playing, faking bad behavior, and identifying the positive or protective functions of certain behaviors can lead to better tolerance. The last resort is to help partners "give up" on the change efforts, to accept the status quo via resignation, and to divert and devote personal resources into self-care activities (e.g., get your need for closeness satisfied by other people). Ironically, when acceptance interventions are successful, some couples are then ready to benefit from traditional behavior-change interventions (i.e., BCT).

An alternative strategy that we have employed to deal with complications while implementing BCT is to begin the intervention phase in traditional BCT fashion. If and when so-called "blocks to progress" are encountered, then we introduce either the acceptance interventions outlined above or other strategic interventions that are designed to deal with the "resistance" problem at hand. First, the therapist should be confident that whatever complication that is encountered is not due to therapist error in conceptualizing or implementing the BCT interventions (e.g., giving homework assignments that are beyond the partners' levels of competence or motivation). Thereafter, interventions such as interpreting the resistance, changing the context or reframing the motivation or purpose of a behavioral pattern, prescribing the symptom, or adding individual sessions to confront partners' self-, relationship-, or therapy-defeating behaviors may well be helpful. When the blocks to progress are addressed, a return to BCT interventions can be successful. Unfortunately, some couples are so immobilized that they are simply unwilling to change their attitudes, their behaviors, or their plan to stay together despite the chronic state of distress. These couples usually drop out of therapy on their own, or therapy may have to be terminated by the therapist as ineffective.

DEALING WITH MANAGED CARE
AND ACCOUNTABILITY

As mentioned above, BCT and related approaches to marital dysfunction are fairly well suited to a brief treatment model (i.e., 12–20 sessions). If managed care plans cover this amount of work, then couple evaluations can be fairly comprehensive and outcomes usually are positive. Typically, some requirement for meeting a "medical necessity" for care is involved in managed care plans, and this may require that one partner meet the criteria for a DSM-IV axis I diagnosis. While meeting these criteria may open the door for limited couple therapy, it also suggests that at least one of the partners is suffering from a major mental illness or psychiatric disorder. Such a condition may complicate and extend the need for couple treatment, while also requiring individual therapy or psychotropic medications. Many practitioners believe that this somewhat restrictive system is workable, as long as 8, 10, 12, or more conjoint sessions are approved. On the other hand, many managed care plans either do not cover conjoint therapy at all or they cover as few as three sessions. Attempting to evaluate and remediate usually longstanding marital dysfunction in three sessions requires more skill and magic than most therapists possess. Interestingly, Bagarozzi (1996) has proposed a model for providing assessment and treatment for distressed couples in 3–6 sessions. However, the approach seems to require procedures that focus on a single, most salient problem (i.e., symptom), and lasting success would require tremendous motivation and readiness to change on the part of the couple. To complete the necessary work, most couples have to pay extra for extended services or seek couple therapy outside the plan.

OUTCOME AND FOLLOW-UP

Research on the immediate outcomes and effectiveness of couple therapy across a number of theoretical approaches has indicated about a 70% improvement rate for a 12- to 20-session course of conjoint therapy. Follow-up at 1 year suggests that about half of all couples maintain their treatment gains. Some researchers have claimed to have achieved better results; however, controlled studies or replications of single studies that used small samples are needed before these outcomes can be confirmed. If we rely on currently available empirical data, the good news is that the majority of couples seeking and participating in relatively brief couple therapy increase their level of relationship satisfaction and dyadic function. The bad news is that almost half of the treated couples, no matter what approach is used, fail to improve on baseline levels of marital dysfunction or they relapse within 1 year.

One caveat, however, is in order when one interprets these outcome data. In terms of overall individual and family member health outcomes, some therapeutic efforts must be considered successful when separation or divorce is the result. Clearly, some dysfunctional marriages make people sick or keep people sick, both emotionally and physically. In certain cases, couple therapy cannot repair the damage and the health of individuals cannot be rehabilitated if partners remain together. Brief couple therapy may serve a good purpose in helping these partners to terminate bad marriages. Data on this point are sparse. However, in a study surveying hundreds of women 2 years after a first divorce, 70% claimed that they were better off out of the marriage than if they had remained in it. Undoubtedly, there is room for improvement in the success rate for marital therapy. However, it will never be the case that all couples will be helped to save a dysfunctional marriage. Despite the current overutilization of divorce, it will always be the best solution for some unfortunate couples.

DEALING WITH RECIDIVISM

Basically, this issue was addressed under the section entitled "Complications and Treatment Implications" above. Increasingly, it appears that the proper combination of acceptance and change interventions offers the couple with marital dysfunction the best chance of maintaining relationship improvement. Beyond that, given a brief therapy format, many clinicians encourage couples to develop an individualized "maintenance" program that takes into account the relationship's inherent strengths and vulnerabilities. Regular and semistructured marriage assessment reviews are suggested as a primary preventive measure. The couple also may be invited to return to the therapist for a tune-up or booster session either before or at the first signs of relapse.

SUMMARY

This chapter has been written with an emphasis on conceptual and clinical *considerations* for working with couples who present in an outpatient setting with marital dysfunction. Couple therapy may be indicated as the single treatment of choice or it may be applied either concurrently or sequentially as an adjunct to other individual and group psychotherapies. In the realm of brief conjoint treatments, an approach called behavioral couple therapy features a number of empirically validated interventions that work well in a short-term format. BCT emphasizes a multimethod assessment phase, typically including semistructured conjoint and individual interviews, paper-and-pencil questionnaires, and observed samples of couple problem-solving communication. Standard treatment modules include communication and problem-solving training as well as behavioral exchange interventions. The authors have developed a conceptual framework called the 7Cs that includes seven critical elements of a long-term intimate relationship: Character features, Cultural and ethnic factors, Contract, Commitment, Caring, Communication, and Conflict resolution. BCT assessment and intervention techniques are integrated with an analysis of each couple's functional level on the 7Cs to construct an individualized treatment plan. As needed, additional interventions based on acceptance theory and family systems theory may be considered in situations in which behavior change interventions do not seem to be appropriate or when the traditional BCT approach may not be sufficient to help certain couples reduce high levels of dissatisfaction and dysfunction. The vast majority of couples seeking therapy can be helped with a brief treatment approach featuring BCT and additional interventions described above. Certain marriages are fundamentally unhealthy and unworkable for its members; brief couple therapy may have an important role in helping these couples to terminate a growth-inhibiting or otherwise destructive relationship.

REFERENCES

Birchler, G. R. (1983). Marital dysfunction. In M. Hersen (Ed.), *Outpatient behavioral therapy: A clinical guide* (pp. 229–269). New York: Grune & Stratton.

Birchler, G. R., & Schwartz, L. (1994). Marital dyads. In M. Hersen & S. M. Turner (Eds.), *Diagnostic interviewing* (2nd ed., pp. 277–304). New York: Plenum.

Birchler, G. R., Doumas, D. M., & Fals-Stewart, W. (1999). The seven Cs: A behavioral-systems framework for evaluating marital distress. *The Family Journal, 7*(3), 253–264.

Bagarozzi, D. A. (1996). *The couple and family in managed care: Assessment, evaluation, and treatment*. New York: Brunner/Mazel.

Crits-Christoph, P., Frank, E., Chambliss, D. L., Brody, C., & Karp, J. F. (1995). Training in empirically validated treatments: What are clinical psychology students learning? *Professional Psychology: Research and Practice, 26*, 514–522.

Jacobson, N. S., & Christensen, A. (1996). *Integrative couple therapy: Promoting acceptance and change.* New York: Norton.

Jacobson, N. S., & Margolin, G. (1979). *Marital therapy: Strategies based on social learning and behavior-exchange principles.* New York: Brunner/Mazel.

Notarius, C. I., & Markman, H. (1993). *We can work it out: Making sense of marital conflict.* New York: Putnam's Sons.

Snyder, D. K. (1979). Multidimensional assessment of marital satisfaction. *Journal of Marriage and the Family, 41,* 813–823.

Spanier, G. B. (1976). Measuring dyadic adjustment: New scales for assessing the quality of marriage and similar dyads. *Journal of Marriage and the Family, 38,* 15–28.

CHAPTER

Considerations for Ethnically Diverse Clients

Daniel S. McKitrick and Sandra Y. Jenkins

School of Professional Psychology
Pacific University
Forest Grove, Oregon

Effective Brief Therapies: A Clinician's Guide

INTRODUCTION

More than one-third of the population of the United States consists of ethnic minorities, and ethnic minorities will become the majority of the population between the years 2030 and 2050 (Sue & Sue, 1999). The field of planned brief therapy also is growing impressively, and currently consists of more than 150 books and edited paper collections in the English language, about 2000 journal articles, and at least three journals (Bloom, 1997). Remarkably little attention has been devoted to considering ethnic minority clients in the brief therapy literature, however. Within the area of behavior therapy, for instance, which is perhaps more likely than the other major areas of therapy to operate briefly, Iwamasa (1997) laments that "over the past several decades, only 1.31% of the articles published in three leading behavioral journals, *Behavioral Assessment, Behavior Modification,* and *Behavior Therapy*, focused on ethnic minority groups" (p. 347).

Steenbarger (1993), unique in his efforts to comprehensively consider brief therapy treatment of ethnic minority clients, has developed a "multi-contextual model." While his bold efforts to marry brief and multicultural therapy yield some useful guidelines for practitioners, his model has limitations. Specifically, by basing his model primarily on the differences among only four "developmental assumptions" of these two complex therapy approaches, Steenbarger oversimplifies the approaches in order to create a manageable model. Multicultural therapy, especially, is characterized by a need to attend myriad variables that comprise the complexity of its varied clients and their cultural contexts (Sue & Sue, 1999).

In this chapter, we take a broader approach than Steenbarger does. We build on over two decades of work on "multicultural counseling competencies" carried out by countless scholars and practitioners through professional associations such as the American Psychological Association, the Association for Multicultural Counseling and Development, and the American Counseling Association. Working from a recently revised list of these competencies (Sue *et al.*, 1998), we identify issues to be considered when operationalizing competencies in the context of brief therapy. We are following the lead of those who developed the competencies and who intended them to serve as aspirational ideals that can be applied generically and can be further developed as they are operationalized across different contexts (Sue *et al.*, 1998).

Our operationalization incorporates consideration of the following foci that have been identified in the literature as characterizing brief therapy. Bloom (1997) lists 24 "shared beliefs" among brief therapists, ranging from the philosophical ("Where there is life there is change, with or without psychotherapy. The job of the psychotherapist is to guide and accelerate that change." p. 263) to the practical ("The leverage of the therapist, initially very high, decreases rapidly. Therapeutic efficiency and effectiveness can be maximized by keeping episodes as short as possible." p. 263). Steenbarger and Budman (1998, p. 285) label five "common principles": focus, activity, therapist values, client involvement, and novelty. Koss and Shiang (1994, p. 674) summarize eight "common elements" of brief therapy: prompt and early intervention, clients with good ability to relate, focused and limited goals within predetermined time limits, attainable therapy goals, focus on concrete here-and-now content, and active and directive therapists, experienced therapists who can conduct initial rapid assessment and who can track early-identified goals, and a flexible therapist role. Hoyt (1995, pp. 6–7, 27–30) identifies eight characteristics of brief therapy in managed care: "Specific problem solving"; "Rapid response and early intervention"; "Clear definition of patient and therapist responsibilities, with an emphasis on patient competencies, resources and involvement"; "Time is used flexibly and creatively"; "Interdisciplinary cooperation"; "Multiple formats and modalities"; "Intermittent treatment or a 'family practitioner' model"; and "Results orientation and accountability."

After competencies are operationalized, a case study with an African-American client is presented and discussed in light of the multicultural counseling competency implications for conducting brief therapy.

OPERATIONALIZING THE MULTICULTURAL COUNSELING COMPETENCIES IN BRIEF THERAPY

Note that, in operationalizing the multicultural counseling competencies specifically in the context of several foci that characterize brief therapy, we purposely are not addressing the general operationalization of the competencies within counseling and psychotherapy. We refer the reader to the excellent article by Arredondo *et al.* (1996) for an example of such a general operationalization. We believe that multiculturally competent brief therapists should consider both the general and the brief-therapy–specific operationalizations in their practices. Note also that, along with Arredondo *et al.* (1996), we assume sensitivity not only to ethnic differences but also to other significant diversity factors, such as age, gender, sexual orientation, disability, religion, and socioeconomic class. Finally, this is a first effort and not intended to be exhaustive. We encourage other people to contribute to this effort, providing their own perspectives on brief therapy and multicultural competencies. In our operationalizing, we follow the format of the multicultural counseling competencies (Sue *et al.*, 1998), addressing competencies related to beliefs and attitudes, knowledge, and skills in each of three dimensions: Dimension 1 considers counselor self-awareness, Dimension 2 considers counselor knowledge of diverse clients, and Dimension 3 considers counselor skills. We focus on the competencies we see as most pertinent to brief therapy.

Dimension 1: Counselor Self-Awareness

> The first dimension deals with counselors' attitudes and beliefs about race, culture, ethnicity, gender, and sexual orientation; the need to check biases and stereotypes; development of a positive orientation toward multiculturalism; and the way counselors' values and biases may hinder effective counseling and therapy. (Sue *et al.*, 1998, p. 37)

Beliefs

Multiculturally competent brief therapists (MCBTs) need to be aware of their brief therapy heritage. In other words, an important subset of their brief therapy worldviews is that which is shared with other brief therapists. "Worldview" can be defined as the lens through which one sees the world. Worldview is determined in large part by multiple factors which comprise one's cultural context. MCBTs also need to value, respect, and be comfortable with conflicts between their brief therapy worldviews and the worldviews of their diverse clients. Finally, brief therapists need to recognize how their worldviews might limit their competency in working with diverse clients.

Operationalization

1. MCBTs are aware of the impact on their brief therapy worldviews of the common brief therapy beliefs, principles, elements, and characteristics found in the literature (e.g., Bloom, 1997; Koss & Shiang, 1994; Steenbarger & Budman, 1998). As appropriate, this may include characteristics of brief therapy as practiced in managed care (e.g., Hoyt, 1995).

2. MCBTs are aware of how their brief therapy worldviews may conflict with their diverse clients' worldviews. For instance, contrary to common brief therapy beliefs (Bloom, 1997), there may be client cultural contexts in which it is not always the therapist's job to accelerate life

change, where psychotherapy is not always better than no psychotherapy, and where detours from focal issues may be appropriate.

3. MCBTs, on discovering potential conflicts with their diverse clients' worldviews, are comfortable with respectfully considering if it is appropriate to modify their brief therapy worldviews so as to accommodate the diverse clients. They also consider whether they are able to make such modifications, may need outside consultation or education, or may need to refer to another practitioner with necessary expertise. They can cite examples of discovering and resolving such conflicts.

Knowledge

In attending to their brief therapy worldviews, therapists also should attend to the specific areas of oppression, racism, discrimination, stereotyping, and negative communication styles within their brief therapy worldviews and the worldviews of the managed care organizations with which they are associated. Therapists may be unaware of some or all of these specific factors, and thereby may unintentionally incorporate some of them into their own behavior or otherwise expose clients to their effects.

Operationalization

1. MCBTs can identify possible oppression, racism, discrimination, stereotyping, and negative communication styles within their brief therapy and managed care worldviews.

2. MCBTs can and routinely do identify possible impacts of the above factors on themselves and their ethnically diverse clients. They can cite examples of how they have done this.

3. MCBTs can and routinely do assess to make sure they are not incorporating any of the above factors into their brief therapy worldviews. They can cite examples of how they have done this.

Skills

Given the previously mentioned dearth of literature on using brief therapies with ethnic minority clients, it may be challenging for counselors to find knowledgeable consultants, pertinent training and education, and knowledgeable professional resources for referral. Nonetheless, brief therapists must use available resources and resist the temptation to work beyond their competency limits. Also, they must consciously develop nonracist identities.

Operationalization

1. MCBTs routinely refer to and seek information, consultation, and training from professionals with expertise in brief treatment of ethnically diverse clients, as appropriate, even in the face of scarcity of resources.

2. MCBTs can describe in detail how they do the above, naming experts in the literature and their communities and giving examples of when they have referred and sought information.

3. MCBTs can describe in detail how they build and maintain nonracist identities.

Dimension 2: Counselor Knowledge of Diverse Clients' Worldviews

> The second dimension recognizes that the culturally skilled helping professional is knowledgeable and understanding of his or her own worldview, has specific knowledge of the cultural groups he or she works with, and understands sociopolitical influences. (Sue *et al.*, 1998, pp. 37–38)

Beliefs and Attitudes

Under Dimension 1, above, we considered how brief therapist worldviews may conflict with diverse client worldviews. Here, under Dimension 2, we further consider how brief therapist worldviews may actually interfere with their understanding of diverse client worldviews and their underlying cultural contexts. For example, the press for rapid therapeutic progress (Hoyt, 1995; Koss & Shiang, 1994; Steenbarger & Budman, 1998) makes brief therapists vulnerable to needing to simplify the brief therapy process. They may find it irritating and inefficient to expend extra time routinely considering how diverse clients' cultural contexts might affect therapy process. This leaves the therapists vulnerable to stereotyping ethnic minority clients. As another example, many ethnic clients drop out of therapy because therapy offers a poor fit for their needs (Sue & Sue, 1999). Therapists could consider how to modify brief therapy so as to suit diverse clients' needs. However, brief therapists' worldviews may influence them to judgmentally characterize the goodness-of-fit problems as being the diverse clients' problems. For instance, in the common cases where therapists are European-American, minority clients with histories of mixed experiences relating with European-Americans may be seen as having difficulty forming the necessary "rapid bonds with therapists that are needed for brief work" (Steenbarger & Budman, 1998, p. 284). They also may be seen as having difficulty in having the requisite ready "acceptance of the competence, authority, and benevolence of the therapist" (Koss & Shiang, 1994, p. 674).

Operationalization

1. MCBTs are aware of how their worldviews, as affected by common brief therapy beliefs, principles, elements, and characteristics, may negatively affect their ability to attend to and understand diverse clients' worldviews.

2. MCBTs use their awareness (see above) to routinely decide to attend to and understand diverse clients' worldviews from an unbiased perspective, rather than to be distracted by brief therapy worldviews that might lead them to be judgmental toward diverse clients. They can give examples of when and how they have done the above.

Knowledge

The multiple knowledge areas important to understanding ethnic minority clients' cultural contexts include sociopolitical influences (which, in turn, include impoverishment, lack of power, and racism), life experiences, historical factors, cultural heritage, and cultural identity development (Sue *et al.*, 1998). Many brief therapists do not understand how these knowledge areas affect diverse clients' personality development, emotional expression, symptom manifestation, help-seeking behavior, reactions to brief therapy, and the like. Therapists, then, may overestimate universal similarities among clients and may feel justified in using the same approaches with minority clients that they use with nonminority clients (Sue & Sue, 1999).

Recognizing these potential problems, brief therapists need to acquire adequate knowledge of their diverse clients' cultural contexts as a step toward determining if and how they should modify their counseling approaches for diverse clients (Sue & Sue, 1999).

Operationalization

1. MCBTs have knowledge of their diverse clients' worldviews, as found in such cultural contexts as sociopolitical influences, life experiences, historical factors, cultural heritage, cultural identity development,

and cultural impacts on therapy-related issues. They can describe the cultural context and worldview of any diverse client with whom they are working and some related implications for the brief therapy process.

2. MCBTs do not blindly follow brief therapy approaches that have not been developed with diverse clients' cultural contexts in mind.

Skills

In addition to simply knowing about their diverse clients' worldviews, brief therapists need to keep up with the literature and seek education on diverse clients' worldviews and implications for brief therapy practice. Standard professional ways of generating such information should be augmented with information gained from interaction with people from diverse backgrounds in the community, outside of professional settings. Since information on this topic has been sparse, brief therapists also should look for ways to generate relevant information.

Operationalization

1. MCBTs can describe in detail how they seek education on diverse clients' worldviews and the implications of diverse clients' worldviews for brief therapy practice (e.g., by naming pertinent journals and books they read, describing literature searches they do, identifying training they seek, and describing interactions they have outside of professional settings with people from diverse backgrounds).

2. MCBTs can describe ways in which they augment the above ways of seeking education by generating knowledge on the topic. For instance, they can ask trainers in brief therapy or in cross-cultural issues to comment on the topic. Also they can develop an informal approach of ongoing testing of hypotheses they generate from their clinical experiences of working with diverse clients in brief therapy. Additionally, they can do and encourage others to do formal research on the topic.

Dimension 3: Counselor Skills

The last dimension deals with specific skills (intervention techniques and strategies) needed in working with culturally different groups; it includes both individual and institutional competencies. (Sue *et al.*, 1998, p. 38)

Beliefs and Attitudes

Managed care has incentives to reach into the community for resources and to use multiple nontraditional intervention modes (Hoyt, 1995). These incentives can position managed care brief therapists to appreciate the benefit of attending to and respecting minority clients' religious and spiritual beliefs about healthy functioning, indigenous helping practices and networks, and languages of origin. In other words, they can appreciate that by incorporating their sensitivity to such factors into their interventions they can enhance effectiveness with minority clients (Sue & Sue, 1999). The same may be said of brief therapists in general, to the extent to which they abide by the common brief therapy principle of incorporating "novel skills, experiences, and understandings into treatment as ways of speeding up change processes" (Steenbarger & Budman, 1998, p. 285).

Operationalization

1. MCBTs attend to community resources and novel, nontraditional ways of intervening. They take advantage of brief therapy and managed care incentives to attend to minority clients' religious and spiritual beliefs about healthy functioning, indigenous helping practices and networks, and languages of origin. They are aware that attention to such factors can make their services more effective, and they can cite examples of incorporating such factors successfully into their brief therapy practice with specific diverse clients.

Knowledge

MCBTs need to learn in detail about how to incorporate their knowledge of minority clients' cultural contexts into their practices. Such learning should address how the common features of brief therapy practices and assessment instruments may not be inherently sensitive to minority clients' cultural backgrounds. For instance, the traditional emphasis on early, routinized client assessment in brief therapy is intended to help therapists focus on specific goal-oriented detail. Therapists are warned against getting sidetracked with detail that is "irrelevant to the agreed-on goals" (Koss & Shiang, 1994, p. 674). An unexamined incorporation of this traditional brief therapy assessment approach into work with minority clients could result in inattention to crucial cultural context variables. Similarly, the usual here-and-now focus in the brief therapy process (Koss & Shiang, 1994) could inappropriately preclude attention to minority clients' family traditions and other historical contexts that may be central to clients' conceptualizations of their problems (Sue & Sue, 1999).

MCBTs' learning also should address potentially discriminatory practices at organizational, community, and general social levels that may affect clients' psychological well-being. In the managed care setting, to the extent that traditional brief therapy characteristics become institutionalized (Hoyt, 1995), minority clients may be subjected to discrimination related to these characteristics. Managed care organizations, their business clients, and the public at large may be unaware of such discrimination or may prioritize cost-cutting efficiencies above monitoring potential discriminatory practices.

Operationalization

1. MCBTs consider the cultural details of minority clients' cultural backgrounds in relation to specific features of brief therapy and related assessment practices, and in relation to potentially discriminatory brief therapy and managed care practices at organizational, community, and social levels. They can cite examples of doing brief therapy with diverse clients where they have considered how common brief therapy and managed care features may affect their ability to adequately accommodate diverse clients' cultural contexts.

Skills

In order to develop and learn to practice culturally appropriate brief therapy skills and techniques, MCBTs need to be able to make modifications to common brief therapy practice when that practice conflicts with adequate attention to diverse clients' needs. Also, they need to be able to take advantage of the instances when common brief therapy practice can naturally enhance adequate attention to diverse clients' needs. Several examples, both positive and negative, of the interaction of common brief therapy features and minority client cultural contexts have been cited throughout this chapter. In this section, common brief therapy features that have not yet been mentioned are related to development of appropriate brief therapy strategies and techniques with diverse clients.

Operationalization

1. MCBTs recognize and take advantage of the fact that their abilities to work in varied ways, including out of the traditional brief therapy

setting, help them adapt to diverse clients' cultural contexts. These abilities to work in varied ways potentially are enhanced by several common beliefs of brief therapists (Bloom, 1997), and by the elements and principles of brief therapy (Koss & Shiang, 1994; Steenbarger & Budman, 1998). These beliefs, elements, and principles include: (a) the importance of collaboration between client and therapist, which sets the stage for communication about cultural context and highlights the importance of attending to clients' languages-of-origin; (b) the catalyst effect of therapy that potentiates client change within therapy and also between sessions and after therapy is over, which helps therapists recognize the multiple factors that can effect change, including inherent community networks, traditional and spiritual healers, and innumerable social services and novel interventions; (c) the conceptualization of therapy as involving intermittent sessions as needed, which can interact with the catalyst effect (see above) to help the therapist and client incorporate out-of-therapy change agents into the therapy process in a way that allows an ongoing therapeutic relationship; (d) the need to be comfortable with being teachers as well as therapists and the need to be flexible in the brief therapist role, which opens the door to considering other roles than therapist that may be appropriate for certain cultural contexts, such as advisor, consultant, networker for traditional/religious/spiritual healers, and advocate for systems interventions; (e) a developmental perspective where clients are seen as engaged in ongoing adaptive efforts, which can help brief therapists incorporate into their work attention to their own and their clients' cultural identity development; and (f) the importance of avoiding premature termination, which encourages the therapist to attend to the many potential brief therapy cross-cultural context conflicts that can lead to early termination, as mentioned under "Beliefs and Attitudes" in Dimension 2.

2. MCBTs recognize and take advantage of the fact that their openness to working in varied ways to adapt to diverse clients' cultural contexts also can be enhanced by common characteristics of brief therapy in managed care (Hoyt, 1995). Included are: (a) rapid response and early intervention, which can encourage therapists to use a variety of pretherapy interventions, such as educating clients about the therapy process and any number of community resources such as support and social services; (b) an emphasis on client competence, resources, and involvement, which can predispose therapists routinely to incorporate other-than-therapy resources from the clients' communities; (c) multiple formats and modalities, which can promote routine use of client community resources and of other-than-therapist roles; and (d) interdisciplinary cooperation, which, if

broadly considered, can include indigenous healers, religious and spiritual leaders, and other community and family leaders.

3. MCBTs anticipate and avoid potential discrimination and negative impacts on their ability to attend to diverse clients' cultural contexts, which might be caused by common brief therapist beliefs (Bloom, 1997) and elements and principles of brief therapy (Koss & Shiang, 1994; Steenbarger & Budman, 1998). They are concerned with: (a) the belief that virtually all clients, regardless of diagnosis and problem severity, can be helped quickly, which may encourage inappropriate efforts to treat culturally complex problems briefly; (b) the belief that some psychotherapy is better than no psychotherapy, which may interfere with the therapist considering roles, modes, and settings outside of the traditional ones; (c) the limitation of therapeutic goals to those that are readily attainable, which may cause therapists to miss some important goals, such as using social interventions to address problems in pertinent community systems; and (d) the active direction of the pace of therapy by therapists rather than clients, which can restrict the ability of therapists to flexibly adapt their helping styles to other than the common culture-bound brief therapy style.

4. MCBTs anticipate and avoid the potential negative impacts on their ability to attend to diverse clients' cultural contexts of some common managed care brief therapy characteristics (Hoyt, 1995): (a) a specific problem-solving focus, which in and of itself is not problematic, but which potentially could predispose therapists to see clients' cultural-context–based conflicts with social systems, including managed care, as being the clients', versus the systems', problems, and (b) results orientation and accountability, which, if conceptualized flexibly, are not problematic in and of themselves, but which, if conceptualized inflexibly as measuring only "efficacious relief of symptoms" (Hoyt, 1995, p. 7), could predispose therapists to missing complex culture-related issues.

CASE ILLUSTRATION

Our case illustration provides for a discussion of the strengths and weaknesses of brief therapy models in terms of multicultural counseling competencies. The client's name and some demographic and historical details have been changed to protect client privacy.

Clarice was a 32-year-old, married, African-American woman who was recently discharged from an inpatient mental health facility in a local hospital. She was hospitalized when she began to threaten the woman who was director of the catering school where she taught. She became suspicious that she would be fired when she received poor ratings in her annual evaluation. She threatened to "shoot anybody trying to mess with me," becoming irrational and agitated to the point where the police were called. She claimed that she had been forced to stand on her feet all day teaching in the school after she had an operation in which her "insides were cut open" and the wound in her side would not heal. She was certain that the school director was trying to kill her. She also claimed that she had been repeatedly raped by a man living in her neighborhood and that she had been sexually molested by one of the deacons in her church.

Her husband was totally dismayed by her claims, especially that she was being raped by someone in the neighborhood. He reported that she had undergone an operation in her abdominal area, but that the doctors had stated that the incision had healed properly. One of her adult sons had lived at home, but he had become so disturbed by his mother's behavior that he moved out of the house.

After consulting with the referring hospital staff psychologist, the therapist became concerned that Clarice might bring a gun to the session. The therapist also decided that marital therapy would probably be the best intervention, since Clarice's husband was becoming exhausted and exasperated by her behavior, and he would have to be responsible for her.

In the first session, Clarice arrived wearing a bright red dress, red hat with black feathers, and gold satin shoes, with brightly colored fingernails and heavily scented perfume. Even though bright clothing is appropriate in the African-American community, her clothing and makeup were extreme attire for a weekday meeting with a psychologist. She created the impression that she was depressed and attempting to cover her despondency with a colorful facade.

Clarice was somatically preoccupied, talking incessantly about her operations, injuries to her hip, and other illnesses. She stated that she had been followed to the therapy session by two white men who had been pursuing her on and off for several days. She could not describe the men or their car, and she became upset when she felt pressed to provide a clear description. At the end of the session the therapist stated, "I understand you don't feel safe. Do you think you will be safe here?" When Clarice replied that yes, she did feel safe, the therapist stated, "In that case, you will not need to bring a gun to the sessions, so please don't." Clarice threw back her head and smiled; then she shook her head and assured the therapist that she would not bring a gun with her to the following sessions.

In the next three sessions, Clarice continued to talk incessantly about physical traumas, operations, physical pain, and the white men following her. She thought that she was probably working too hard and needed to get some rest. Yet she insisted on working 15-hour days cooking because the family needed the money. She expressed her concerns about her son leaving home and his plans to marry. She clearly wanted him to remain at home with her.

Clarice did not respond well to empathic statements or requests to be specific or to clarify her beliefs. She did not respond at all when asked to say what she was feeling. Instead, she became silent or changed the subject. Each time she was evasive when asked to talk about her childhood, her marriage, or her friendships.

The therapist decided to try another approach. In the fourth session, Clarice was asked to focus on what she thought could be done to help her. She thought for awhile and said she wanted some ideas about how she could prevent another "breakdown." She was worried because this had been the second "breakdown" with a stay in the hospital. The therapist asked her what she wanted to do in the sessions, and she said that she thought talking to someone was helpful, but she also needed ideas. The therapist commented that it seemed hard for her to talk about herself. She smiled and said, "Yes, I don't know how you do this therapy thing. I've never done it before, but they say it will help me stay out of the hospital, so I think I will try it." Clarice expressed concerns about how long therapy would take, because she did not have much money and her insurance would only pay for a few sessions. She seemed confused about what to expect. She suggested that she come once a month to save money. The therapist asked if it would be helpful to include her husband in the sessions. Clarice replied she would like to "think that over and let you know."

In the next session, Clarice stated that the white men were no longer following her and she felt better. She had decided that she did not want her husband to attend the sessions, because she wanted this time for herself. She mostly wanted to talk about her son. Again she asked if she could come once a month.

The therapist told Clarice that once a month was not enough therapy time to be helpful to her, and suggested that they meet for 30 minutes twice a week for a short period and then switch to 30 minutes per week until she "got the hang of how to do the therapy thing." Then they could switch to an hour every other week. Clarice thought that would be fine. The therapist suggested that Clarice get a calendar and keep track of what she did each day. She could also use the calendar to write down what she wanted to talk about in the therapy sessions. It was also suggested that Clarice get a notebook to keep track of any suggestions that she found helpful.

In the next session, Clarice appeared in less colorful and formal clothing. She showed the therapist her notebook and her calendar, which she had started to fill in. She said that she now saw that she really was working too hard. She wanted to cut back on her teaching in the catering school and was not certain that she wanted to continue teaching there. She stated that she wanted to talk about her church and her fear and anger with one of the deacons. She stated that he was a friend of hers who had invited her to join the church and had entrusted her with many important church responsibilities. Alternately, she described him as someone who "came on to" her, and this had caused jealousy among other women and rumors of an affair. She did not seem to recall that at one point she had apparently accused him of sexually molesting her. She wanted some advice on what to do about this situation, since she was concerned that the animosity of the other women had resulted in some of them shunning her. The therapist suggested that perhaps there was someone in the church with whom she could talk. In the interim she could avoid contact with the deacon. Clarice thought these were good ideas.

Over the next several sessions, Clarice's outlook improved and the therapy time was switched to 30 minutes per week. During this period Clarice began to talk about her childhood, although in limited ways. She revealed that she had been born in the South and her family had moved when she was a small child. Her father was a laborer who was very strict with his children. Her mother fixed hair, did laundry, and was a devout church member. The family was devastated when an older sister got pregnant in her teens and was sent out of the home. Clarice remembered being sexually molested by a white man in the neighborhood and by older African-American boys. She never spoke about any of this to her family. She also remembered being sent to live with an aunt for several months, but she did not remember why. She speculated that her mother had been seriously ill at that time. Clarice had difficulties in high school because she did not know how to talk to people, but she was especially afraid to talk to boys. She got into a fight with a girl who "accused" her of having a boyfriend and was spreading rumors about her.

Her parents separated while Clarice was in high school. She recalled her mother saying that her father had "fooled around," which greatly upset her. She missed her father terribly. She tried to see him whenever possible. She said, "I never felt happy after Daddy left." Within a year, her father became involved with another lady, at which time Clarice left school, married her husband, and had two sons.

Clarice was now getting better, and her remaining sessions were scheduled for 1 hour every other week. One day she stated that she did not want to talk about her mental illness because she was "over that now." She did recall, however, that the first time she had begun to "get funny" was when her father died. She remembered shaving and dressing him for his funeral. Shortly after that, she never felt the same. Then she had problems in her side and in her hip and in her "insides." She cried slightly for the first time. At the end of this session, she wanted ideas about how to talk with her son, and she stated emphatically that she did not want to talk about sad things anymore. The therapist suggested that she needed more time with her friends and that she could make a list of things she wanted to talk to her son about so that the therapist could help her sort out her thoughts. Again she was asked if she wanted to include her husband in the sessions, and again she preferred to come in alone.

After another 2 months, Clarice stated that she was worried that therapy was costing too much, because she also had expensive psychiatric sessions and medications to buy. She also stated that she felt it had helped her. She seemed to suggest that she wanted to terminate. The impression of the therapist was that after 5 months of therapy Clarice had reached her limit of needing the therapist in her life. She did, in fact, feel much better physically and psychologically. She had cut back to half-time at the catering school and was no longer having problems there. She was getting along much better with the people in her church and was having much less contact with the deacon. She was looking forward to her son's wedding, and she talked about missing him. The therapist asked Clarice to continue for two more biweekly sessions, just to make sure that her feelings continued to be positive.

In the last session, Clarice reported that she felt the therapy had been helpful, but that she wanted to stop coming, since she no longer needed it. She stated that she would like to know that she could come back and see the therapist if she ever needed it again.

DISCUSSION

Clarice is representative of the type of client who is well suited for brief therapy. In some circumstances the therapy process will be brief out of necessity. Clarice was clearly suffering from delusions and she was, therefore, not inclined to define her problems in psychological terms. She sought therapy for a very critical and practical problem (i.e., she wanted to avoid the devastation and humiliation of another hospitalization). She had no reason to feel attached to the therapist except as a source of ideas and practical guidance. Her trust level was very low, and she wanted improvements with as little risk-taking on her part as possible. Deep levels of engagement would have been perceived as too invasive. A long dialogue on her feelings and childhood experiences would have had little functional meaning for her in any case. She had few financial resources, and she lacked experience talking about herself in an introspective way. Therefore, a brief model of therapy tightly focused on addressing her mental and social functioning issues was effective and appropriate in this instance.

Drawbacks associated with a brief model also were present. Items 1–4 hereunder reflect the types of issues that require MCBTs to have the skills to adapt brief therapy to diverse clients' cultural contexts (Dimension 3), and Item 5 reflects the importance of knowing about diverse clients' contexts (Dimension 2) and being wary of one's own potential bias (Dimension 1):

1. Her excessive, though understandable, lack of trust meant that a productive working alliance took considerable time to establish.

2. The client needed to feel empowered and respected. She also needed some acknowledgment of her strengths and assets. Insisting on a brief marital therapy that would have focused on her husband playing a "paternalistic" role would have not have served those purposes.

3. It was important to be realistic about what could be achieved in a brief therapy that might also have some lasting impact on her chronic mental health problems. Given that she might need ongoing mental health services, it seemed likely that the most important thing was establishment of a trusting and respectful environment.

4. Considering the developmental course of the client's ability to convey information about herself in a focused manner, her ability to trust the therapist, and her limited financial resources, negotiation of the most effective therapy process was difficult to achieve.

5. The therapist needed to be familiar with the cultural norms of her behavior to assess adequately her level of dangerousness, as well as the cultural appropriateness of her presentations and gestures, before determining effective and relevant treatment goals.

Real problems might have occurred when the therapist addressed concerns that Clarice might come to the sessions with a gun, when clearly she had no such intentions. The possibility that she might have been insulted by the therapist's lack of trust and lack of ability to accurately judge her intentions could have fractured the relationship beyond repair. Clarice's commitment to her own treatment goals allowed her take the therapist's mistake in stride and continue with the therapy work.

This client example addresses the complex aspects of psychotherapy with people whose psychological problems are compounded by imposed struggles with race, gender, and socioeconomic status. Herein lies the significance of Dimension 2. This client illustrates common features derived from cultural norms of African-American culture. She exhibits beliefs and values that are often present in the authors' clinical experience with African-American women. Major themes include strong family ties, an emphasis on the importance of relationships (including the therapeutic alliance), expectations of problem-focused therapy, excessive anxieties about trusting the therapist, a strong need to be self-reliant, an overemphasis on maintaining one's "pride," and a fear of the stigma of needing mental health services. Strong values concerning sexual modesty, religious beliefs, preoccupations with physical attractiveness, and unrealistically poor self-esteem are also major themes.

Gender-oriented conflicts surrounding balancing career pursuits and marital goals were also evident themes. Difficulties with self-affirmation, self-care, assertiveness, and how to form intimate bonds were persistent problems.

Any of these cultural, gender, and social worldview issues could clash with typical brief therapy worldviews (Dimension 1). In the African-American female client there is often a predominance of themes, values, and financial circumstances that clash with "normal" therapy relationships.

As directed by Dimension 1, these conflicting value positions must be kept in mind when we combine the competencies of multicultural therapy with the goals of brief therapy. Further, this case illustrates many skills that are not specifically mentioned in Dimension 3. In this case, the brief therapist needed to be knowledgeable enough about the cultural and gender/class contexts (Dimension 2) so as to be able to apply the following specific skills:

1. Accurately assess the client's potential for dangerousness.

2. Accurately assess client preparedness for therapy.

3. Accurately gauge clients' therapy skills (e.g., their ability to voice complex concepts, express their feelings and their conflicts, and their willingness to divulge personal information).

4. Accurately gauge the length of time necessary to establish sufficient trust to form a therapeutic alliance.

5. Respond properly to themes of victimization and fears of victimization.

6. Respond properly to themes of anger and resentment.

7. Respond properly to themes of low self-esteem by encouraging risk-taking and empowering the client to direct the treatment and life goals.

8. Offer flexible treatment approaches and therapy structures, such as making appropriate adjustments in session length and frequency and fee adjustments.

9. Maintain proper connectedness, while avoiding becoming overinvolved in the client's life.

10. Provide simple, easy to understand, honest, and straightforward responses to client questions and requests.

11. Provide suggestions, while avoiding becoming over-controlling or overdirecting or engaging in excessive advice-giving.

12. Accurately gauge the proper depth, intensity, and timing of confrontations and interpretations of clients psychological material.

13. Accurately distinguish between appropriate cultural expressions and behaviors and inappropriate defensive maneuvers.

14. Express a valuing of clients' strengths, while accurately confronting clients' weaknesses.

SUMMARY

In this chapter, we build on the work of scholars who have developed general multicultural counseling competencies (Sue *et al.*, 1998). We take some initial steps toward operationalizing these competencies in the context of brief therapy, as characterized by common brief therapy beliefs (Bloom, 1997), principles (Steenbarger & Budman, 1998), and elements (Koss & Shiang, 1994), as well as by common characteristics of brief therapy in the managed care setting (Hoyt, 1995). The specific guidelines generated by this operationalization then are augmented by a list of further guidelines generated by discussion of a case illustration. It is our hope that these guidelines will be used by brief therapists along with directions from other pertinent documents, such as the general multicultural counseling competencies (Sue *et al.*, 1998), the operationalization of these general competencies (Arredondo *et al.*, 1996), the American Psychological Association's (1993) "Guidelines for Providers of Psychological Services to Ethnic, Linguistic, and Culturally Diverse Populations," and the American Psychological Association's (1992) "Ethical Principles of Psychologists and Code of Conduct," in order to provide effective and relevant services to ethnically diverse clients.

REFERENCES

American Psychological Association (1992). Ethical principles of psychologists and code of conduct. *American Psychologist, 47*, 1597–1611.

American Psychological Association (1993). Guidelines for providers of psychological services to ethnic, linguistic, and culturally diverse populations. *American Psychologist, 48*, 45–48.

Arredondo, P., Toporek, R., Brown, S. P., Jones, J., Locke, D. C., Sanchez, J., & Stadler, H. (1996). Operationalization of the multicultural counseling competencies. *Journal of Multicultural Counseling and Development, 24*, 42–78.

Bloom, B. L. (1997). *Planned short-term psychotherapy: A clinical handbook* (2nd ed.). Boston: Allyn & Bacon.

Hoyt, M. F. (1995). *Brief therapy and managed care: Readings for contemporary practice.* San Francisco: Jossey Bass.

Iwamasa, G. Y. (1997). Behavior therapy and a culturally diverse society: Forging an alliance. *Behavior Therapy, 28*, 347–358.

Koss, M. P., & Shiang, J. (1994). Research on brief psychotherapy. In A. E. Bergin & S. L. Garfield (Eds.), *Handbook of psychotherapy and behavior change* (4th ed., pp. 664–700). New York: Wiley.

Steenbarger, B. N. (1993). A multicontextual model of counseling: Bridging brevity and diversity. *Journal of Counseling and Development, 72,* 8–15.

Steenbarger, B. N., & Budman, S. H. (1998). Principles of brief and time-effective therapies. In G. P. Koocher, J. C. Norcross, & S. S. Hill (Eds.), *Psychologists' desk reference* (pp. 283–287). New York: Oxford University Press.

Sue, D. W., & Sue, D. (1999). *Counseling the culturally different.* New York: Wiley.

Sue, D. W., Carter, R. T., Casas, J. M., Fouad, N. A., Ivey, A. E., Jensen, M., LaFromboise, T., Manese, J. E., Ponterotto, J. G., & Vaquez-Nutall, E. (Eds.) (1998). *Multicultural counseling competencies: Individual and organizational development.* Thousand Oaks, CA: Sage.

Considerations for Older Adults

Barry A. Edelstein, Ronald R. Martin,
and Jeffrey L. Goodie

Department of Psychology
West Virginia University
Morgantown, West Virginia

Effective Brief Therapies: A Clinician's Guide

INTRODUCTION

Currently, there are approximately 34 million people over the age of 65 in the United States. Of these individuals, it has been estimated that roughly one-quarter meet criteria for a DSM-IV diagnosis (Gatz *et al.*, 1996). In light of the foregoing, it is important that mental health professionals be aware of the basic characteristics of older adults, as they will increasingly consti-tute a significant portion of the adult population seen for mental health problems.

U.S. Census Bureau data (1992–94) reveal that, among older adults: (1) individuals aged 85 and over are the most rapidly growing population segment; (2) life expectancy has increased to approximately 76 years of age; (3) racial and ethnic diversity is increasing; (4) women outnumber men by approximately 3 to 2; (4) the majority of men are married, while most women are not; (5) approximately 30% live alone; (6) rises in chronic health problems and disabilities with advanced age may translate into greater needs for personal assistance with everyday activities; (7) the poverty range may vary from 11 to 16%; and (8) roughly 60% of these individuals have obtained a high school diploma.

The purpose of the present chapter is to acquaint the reader with some of the more important facts about older adults that can influence the expediency and effectiveness with which assessment and treatment are accomplished. This chapter describes the findings of research pertinent to normal aging across several domains (i.e., sensory, cognitive, social, and physiological functioning). Specifically, efforts will be made to discuss how mental health professionals can improve assessment and treatment of older adults by tailoring their approaches to compensate for normal corre-lates of aging. The normal correlates of aging may have an impact on the mental health professional's assessment and treatment of older adults.

AGING OF THE SENSORY SYSTEMS: VISION AND HEARING

Sensory deficits can affect both the physical and psychological integrity of the older adult. They can influence the assessment picture and the process and outcome of therapy via changes in information processing, mobility, independence, social behavior, and even self-concept. The interested reader is referred to Whitbourne (1996) for more detailed discussions of physiological changes accompanying the normal aging process and their psychological implications.

Vision

Several age-related changes occur in the visual system that can affect the behavior of older adult clients, which can potentially affect clinical presentation, assessment outcome, and therapy process. The density (thickness) of the lens of the eye increases with age, causing increased light absorption and light scattering within the lens. These changes can result in greater susceptibility to glare and problems associated with abrupt changes in light intensity. To minimize the effects of this problem, one can use antiglare computer monitor screens and avoid using high-gloss paper for self-report inventories, visual aids, and figure drawing tasks. Also, one should avoid having the client face a window, which can contribute to glare.

A reduction in light reaching the retina is experienced for a variety of reasons, including thickening of the lens, pigmentation of the vitreous humor, reduction in the number of photoreceptors (rods and cones), and reduction in the size of the pupil. To address such diminished light, one can increase the amount of available light in the room in general, and on the face of the clinician in particular. The light should be bright, but not glaring.

Thickening of the lens is also accompanied by a yellowing of the lens, which decreases one's ability to discriminate among colors within the green-blue-violet color spectrum. In addition, the vitreous humor becomes pigmented with age, resulting in a reduction in the amount of light reaching the retina and absorption of shorter wavelengths of light. These changes result in alterations of color perception. In general, the therapist should initially determine whether the client has visual difficulties involving color, contrast, or field deficits.

The capsule of the lens loses it elasticity with age, resulting in a loss of accommodation and visual acuity (usually presbyopia). Always ask the client whether he or she normally wears corrective lenses and encourage the client to wear them during the session. Since some older adults cannot focus closely, try not to bring objects too close to them for inspection. Self-report inventories can be printed in larger fonts (e.g., 14 to 16 points) to enable clients with accommodation problems to see the material more easily. One should be careful not to make the font size too large (e.g., >16 points), as this can impede reading. Magnifiers and reading glasses can be kept handy for those clients who have forgotten their reading glasses. For older adults with severe visual deficits, one can still be adaptive in one's approach. For example, one could limit nonverbal directions, relying more heavily on verbal or kinesthetic cueing. One can also use multimodal (say and do) directions when possible. Various diseases (e.g., diabetes mellitus, cataracts, glaucoma, macular degeneration, myotonic dystrophy, hypoparathyroidism, Wilson's disease) and medications (phenothiazines, corticosteroids, antibiotics, antimalarials) can also affect the visual system. Thus, it is important for the therapist to have a detailed medical history, including a list of the current medications being taken.

In general, changes in the visual system can result in diminished assessment performance when the assessment method requires adequate vision. Visual deficits can also result in changes in social behavior arising from a failure to recognize friends and acquaintances. Moreover, visual problems can also result in reluctance to participate in any activity requiring reasonable visual acuity. Other potential vision-related problems include falls resulting from poor visual acuity and insufficient lighting, automobile accidents resulting from glare and rapid changes in light intensity, decreased ability to perform tasks of daily living (e.g., driving, housekeeping, food preparation, shopping), a decrease in some leisure activities, difficulty reading lips (if hearing impaired), and diminished self-efficacy and self-esteem (Edelstein *et al.*, 1996).

Hearing

One in three individuals above the age of 60 suffers from significant hearing impairment (Zarit & Zarit, 1987). These hearing losses are due to a variety of factors, including age-related changes in the physiology of the auditory system, drugs (e.g., certain antibiotics, aspirin, quinine, alcohol, tobacco, carbon monoxide, certain diuretics), circulatory disorders, noise, and certain organic disorders (e.g., acoustic neuromas, syphilis, multiple sclerosis, cardiovascular accidents, Paget's disease; Vernon, 1989). Hearing impairment can have quite wide-ranging effects on a client's lifestyle and psychological well-being. One might see, for example, a reduction in the number of leisure activities (e.g., religious services, television, social gatherings) and an increase in suspiciousness, hostility, depression, and paranoia.

The ability to detect high-frequency tones decreases dramatically with age as a function of presbycusis, causing difficulties in understanding conversational speech. This is due primarily to the fact that consonant sounds are in the higher frequencies. Thus, clients may have greater difficulty understanding the speech of women and children. Clients may be able to hear speech but not be able to understand the specific words, hearing primarily the sounds of vowels (Heckheimer, 1989). The ability to accurately hear speech in the presence of background noise may also be impaired.

Signs that the client may not be able to hear or understand the clinician include failure of the client to respond when spoken to, inappropriate interpretations of clinician statements, inappropriate responses to clinician statements or requests, frequent requests to repeat statements, and tilting of the head or turning of one ear toward the clinician (Heckheimer, 1989). If the client appears to have difficulty understanding the clinician's speech, the clinician should consider reducing any background noise, using simpler sentences, and avoiding the use of words that are not being understood. One can also ask the client what can be done to make communication easier.

Hearing loss can also result in an impaired ability to understand broken or rapid speech. This problem can often be avoided by merely speaking slowly and distinctly. If communication continues to be impeded, one can write down key words or sentences.

Some clients will compensate for hearing loss by reading lips. Consequently, it is important to not overarticulate, which can distort speech and facial gestures. Be sure there is good lighting on your face, and avoid a situation in which you are seated with a window behind you. The latter can shadow your face and increase the likelihood of glare on assessment materials. Lip reading is a stressful and demanding task, so breaks should be considered during evaluations and therapy sessions.

In general, it is a good idea for the clinician to position him or herself close to the client. If assessing a hearing-impaired client, one might consider providing the test questions in oral and written form. Assistive devices such as audio listening aids and amplifiers can be helpful. These are inexpensive and can be kept handy for hearing-impaired clients. It is important to ask the client if a hearing aid is used. If so, the client should be encouraged to use it during sessions. Some of the drawbacks of hearing aid use are minimized by quiet environments with few auditory distractions. Clients who are reluctant to wear their hearing aids due to background noise can be reminded of this. Finally, it is important to be vigilant for selective (i.e., functional) hearing impairment characterized by hearing losses associated with task demands, poor motivation, and perhaps fear of performance failure.

COGNITION AND MEMORY

Certain declines may occur in memory and cognition over the adult lifespan that may have a substantial impact on assessment and treatment of older adults. These declines are not inevitable consequences of aging for all older adults. In general, older adults may have difficulty with therapeutic tasks that place significant demands on their ability to remember or mentally manipulate information in a very quick and accurate manner. However, not all aspects of cognition evidence decline over the adult life-span. Therefore, those areas that evidence maintenance or improvement may be utilized in order to maximize the effectiveness of assessment and treatment procedures.

Memory

Currently, age-related differences in memory are perhaps best conceptualized using resource theories. These theories operate on the premise that limitations exist in the cognitive resources of older adults (i.e., mental time, space, and energy). Given these limited resources, age differences in memory are likely to be found under several different conditions (Smith, 1996). A description of these conditions are provided in the following paragraphs.

Insufficient environmental support. Older clients may experience difficulty while attempting to recall information (e.g., relevant dates, names, faces, individuals, events, therapeutic instructions) in the absence of any environmental support (i.e., cues that facilitate recall). To manage this potential problem, therapists should arrange to maximize the amount of environmental support available to their clients when free recall of information is required. During assessment, therapists may encourage their clients to bring along relevant documentation or records (e.g., medical reports, diaries, photographs). During treatment, therapists may record the content of their therapy sessions (e.g., make written notes or audiotapes of sessions to give to their older clients) to facilitate later recall. Records of information and instructions may be especially useful in situations where the information must be recalled at a later point in time (e.g., when homework is assigned to clients).

Working memory difficulties. Situations that require individuals to hold and manipulate information in memory become more difficult for older adults. Therefore, any lengthy or complex information that is conveyed verbally during assessment or treatment may be difficult for some older clients to retain and act on. To address this issue, therapists should reduce the demands on the older client's working-memory capacities. For example, clients may be presented with summary notes or audiotapes that describe lengthy, complex information, or they may be encouraged to record such information for themselves. Another possibility for reducing the demands on working memory would involve taking the to-be-remembered information and breaking it down into smaller elements that may be addressed individually.

Inhibition of irrelevant information. Older adults may experience difficulty inhibiting task-irrelevant thoughts when memorizing and recalling information. Therapists may attempt to minimize the presence or influence of such task-irrelevant thoughts by avoiding the use of tangential or trivial information when explaining assessment procedures or therapeutic tasks. Along these lines, therapists may assist their older clients by giving them a bare-bones, concise summary of requests or information.

Reductions in perceptual speed. Older adults typically do not perform as well as younger adults on tasks that place demands on perceptual speed (i.e., ability to quickly process information). It is therefore important to minimize the salience of perceptual speed. This may be accomplished by presenting older clients with the to-be-remembered information at a slower pace that is comfortable for them, thus allowing them more time to process and digest the information. The therapist can also periodically check with the client to determine whether the information is being processed. To avoid an acquiescent yes response to the question of recall and understanding, which is common for older adults (Cooley *et al.*, 1998), therapists might periodically have the client summarize the information being presented. Therapists may provide the rationale that they merely want to ensure that the client is getting the most important information.

General comments and recommendations. Memory difficulties that occur within the context of therapy may cause the older client to become frustrated and irritated. These negative affective responses may be directed towards the self, the therapist, or the process of therapy in general. Regardless of the target of these negative affective responses, they are likely to have an adverse impact on the therapeutic process. Therefore, it is important for therapists to be vigilant in noting any trends in memory difficulties or complaints. Once particular difficulties are recognized (e.g., problems with working memory), therapists may then avoid taxing weaker aspects of their clients' memory capacities. Further, therapists may structure their assessment or treatment procedures to accommodate any memory difficulties. For example, older clients that experience difficulties with working memory may be offered a structured, concise, written summary of the information that is to be remembered and mentally manipulated.

Cognition

The findings from cross-sectional and longitudinal studies have indicated that older adults experience declines in several aspects of cognition. However, these studies also show that some aspects of cognition may be maintained, or even improved, well into adulthood.

Declines in information-processing speed. Given the slower information-processing speeds of older adults, therapists should be aware that cognitively demanding tasks (e.g., assessment devices, educational components, or instructions) may proceed at a slower pace. Therefore, therapists may need to repeat new information often, or budget more time to cover cognitively demanding tasks. Further, in preparation for future sessions, therapists may choose to send their older clients home with materials that might be studied in between sessions. Overall, the slower information-processing speed of older clients may even extend certain timelines associated with therapy (e.g., the projected number of expected sessions).

Declines in attention. Research has indicated that older adults do not perform well on tasks that demand sustained attention. Therefore, it follows that older adults are likely to have difficulty with assessment or treatment procedures that are relatively lengthy, and do not offer an opportunity for breaks. Scheduling rest periods between and within assessment and therapeutic tasks may therefore improve the performance of older adults.

As previously mentioned, older adults may experience greater difficulty than younger adults in their ability to selectively attend to a target stimulus, while filtering out extraneous stimuli. Therefore, therapists should manipulate the assessment and therapeutic environment to minimize or eliminate extraneous stimuli. Therapists might ensure that they provide quiet environments, featuring relatively silent electronic or mechanical equipment. Or, if it is not feasible to acquire such silent equipment, then the equipment should be stored or located elsewhere. Therapists may further choose to turn their telephone ringers down, use digital clocks, and arrange their offices to be uncluttered, with neutral furnishings and decorations.

Declines in mental flexibility and abstraction. Older adults may experience declines in their capacity for abstraction and mental flexibility (e.g., ability to quickly shift topics). Therefore, during assessment and treatment, therapists may need to adopt a more concrete speaking and writing style.

Declines in numeric ability. Longitudinal studies of age changes in cognition have indicated that declines occur by the mid-50s in numeric ability. Given this decline, all therapeutic tasks should be screened to ensure that they do not load heavily on this ability. Alternatively, therapists should allow their older clients extra time for mental calculations, or provide external devices (i.e., calculators with large number pads and display screens).

Declines in capacity for inductive reasoning. Longitudinal studies have shown decline in individuals in their late 60s on tasks that involve inductive reasoning (i.e., the ability to make inferences based on specific pieces of information). Other research has indicated that older adults may be less likely than younger adults to work from the "ground up" when problem-solving or making decisions (i.e., they are less likely to consider the individual pieces of information contained within a problem). Instead, older adults may be more likely to rely on heuristics or "rules of thumb" in order to simplify the problem-solving or decision-making process. For example, older adults may not be likely to consider the individual pros and cons of a particular therapeutic intervention. Instead, they may be more likely to apply the rule "whatever my therapist recommends, I do." Therefore, therapists may wish to ask their older clients to describe how they arrived at decisions that are especially important. As a result, ineffective or inefficient rules of thumb may be identified and replaced with more effective and efficient problem-solving or decision-making strategies.

Maintenance or improvements in crystallized intelligence and expertise. Maintenance or possibly improvement may occur in one's crystallized intelligence (i.e., procedural and factual knowledge base) or more specifically, one's expertise in a given area. Therefore, it may be possible for therapists to identify general or specific areas of knowledge that their clients may possess in order to determine if this knowledge may be used to facilitate therapy. For clients with good abstraction skills, therapists may even describe therapeutic processes metaphorically, using their clients' special areas of knowledge. For example, assuming that an older client has some expertise in gardening, the therapist may then describe the process of therapy as a way of weeding out maladaptive behaviors, while transplanting more adaptive ones.

Maintenance or improvements in wisdom. Wisdom (i.e., a deep understanding of life's contextual qualities) may develop well into old age. Given this premise, therapists may help their older clients access and utilize their wisdom. Specifically, therapists may ask clients about what they have learned from a situation in the past that is similar to the current situation in an effort to apply that knowledge to their current problems.

Maintenance or improvements in language ability. For the majority of the adult life-span, most aspects of language ability are maintained and may even be improved on (e.g., verbal comprehension and vocabulary). This implies that complex discussions with older adults are possible well into old age.

Declines in verbal abilities begin to occur as older adults approach their 80s, although the reader should understand that this does not necessarily occur with all individuals. At this point, therapists should begin to consider the use of assessment instruments and treatment stimuli that employ an appropriate reading level. If very old clients experience communication difficulties, therapists may choose to use instruments or stimuli that feature pictorial contents. For very old clients, communication should be straightforward, and free of complex, polysyllabic terms and phrases.

Maintenance or improvements in creativity. Research that involves creativity has shown that for some areas (e.g., philosophy, writing novels) creativity may be maintained well into old age. Within the context of therapy, therapists may access their older clients' creativity, in order to arrive at innovative and individualized solutions to their clients' problems. Specifically, the client's creative abilities may be employed in activities designed to brainstorm about possible solutions to identified problems.

SOCIAL RELATIONSHIPS

Social relationships are a particularly important aspect of an older adult's life. An evaluation of the social relationships of the older adult should include an assessment of the number and perceived quality of social relationships. Social relationships can have positive and negative effects. Thus, it is important to document not only positive and supportive relationships, but also sources of negative interactions (e.g., overprotective support, annoyance, violence, abuse). The presence of negative interactions and the lack of positive ones place the older adult at greater risk for developing mental and physical health problems (Lang & Carstensen, 1996).

Social Networks

As adults age, they become more selective of their friends, and manage social relationships to maximize the emotional benefits derived from those relationships (Lang & Carstensen, 1996). Older adults, compared to younger adults, often have fewer individuals with whom they regularly interact and consider important in their lives. However, when older adults lose someone in their social network, that loss may have a more significant psychological impact than that observed in younger adults. Therefore, older adults' social networks are traditionally smaller, and changes in the social network may have more detrimental effects on the individual compared to younger individuals.

The social network of the older adult may also be impacted by role changes that accompany increased age (e.g., retirement). For example, after retirement the individual may not have regular contact with former colleagues who provided frequent interactions and who may have contributed to the individual's sense of identity (e.g., coal miner, businessperson, professional) and purpose. The older adult may have difficulty adjusting to a new role (e.g., retiree) and not have the same level of contact with others or may be uncomfortable with establishing a new identity or purpose. Anxiety or depression may develop as a result of the adjustment difficulty. However, the older adult may have more time to engage in leisure pursuits and specific areas of interest. Traditionally, older adults will engage in more sedentary activities, such as reading, visiting with others, and watching television. Therefore, working with the older adult to establish new goals, discussing the issues associated with role changes, and developing coping mechanisms (e.g., developing hobbies, joining social groups) may help the older adult adapt more successfully to these new roles (Knight, 1996).

Social Interactions

The quality of the interactions that older adults have with others is another important aspect of social relationships. Positive interactions and high-quality social support are significant factors for predicting successful adaptation in later life. An assessment of the social interactions of the older adult may reveal strengths, weaknesses, or detrimental aspects of these interactions (e.g., abuse, social isolation). It is most important to determine how the individual *perceives* the interactions. Specifically, does the individual perceive the interactions as positive (i.e., supportive) or negative (i.e., aversive)? For example, although an individual's child might regularly visit, cook meals, and provide transportation, the older adult may experience a lack of control and a loss of self-esteem, particularly if he or she is capable of performing some of those functions. The child may be unwittingly contributing to the parent's dependency, and the loss of a sense of control and self-esteem, by attempting to assist the parent. An intervention may range from providing information to the child regarding the effects of his or her behavior, to the application of assertiveness training for the older adult.

Older adults are not only recipients of support but also important providers of support. This can be a very significant source of gratification for the older adult, particularly if there has been a shift in roles (e.g., retirement). It is important to determine whether the older adult is satisfied with the amount of support he or she provides to others (e.g., caring for a grandchild). There are often many opportunities for older adults to volunteer time and expertise in most communities.

AGE-RELATED HEALTH AND MEDICAL ISSUES

In addition to increasing cognitive, physical, and social challenges, older adults are more likely than younger adults to experience physical illnesses and require the use of medications. Approximately 80% of those 65 and older have at least one chronic disease (e.g., diabetes, hypertension, chronic obstructive pulmonary disease). Working with older adults necessitates an awareness of the biological changes and medical conditions faced by the older adult, and the impact that these changes and their treatments may have on daily functioning.

Age-Related Health Changes

Heart disease, chronic obstructive pulmonary disease, osteoporosis, and diabetes are among the many chronic diseases experienced by older adults. These diseases are often accompanied by chronic conditions (e.g., pain, difficulty breathing) that can be disabling. Because of the prominence of these medical disorders, an awareness of their influences on the older individual may help therapists to adapt assessment and therapy to better serve the older client. Whitbourne (1996) and Shaid and Huber (1996) provide more complete reviews of age-related biological and medical changes.

Cardiovascular system. As an individual ages, structural changes of the cardiovascular system may affect the individual's daily functioning. The heart's pumping capacity is reduced due to changes in the ventricles and cellular structures of the heart. The amount of blood ejected from the heart and the sensitivity of the heart to neural stimulation, which controls the timing and rate of heart contractions, are reduced. Arteries become thicker and less flexible with age. Consequently, the cardiovascular system's ability to distribute blood and oxygen throughout the body is diminished and older individuals become more susceptible to hypertension (i.e., high blood pressure) and cardiovascular diseases. Older adults may also tire more quickly during physical exertion and may find that they are no longer able to complete tasks or take part in activities in which they once engaged with ease. The inability to complete tasks may be frustrating to the client and may serve as a reminder of increasing age (Whitbourne, 1996). Consequently, symptoms of depression (e.g., negative evaluative thoughts) or anxiety (e.g., fear of disability or death) may be related to these decreased levels of functioning. Likewise, increased anxiety or stress responses may place more strain on the cardiovascular system, potentially increasing the risk of heart disease.

Respiratory system. Respiratory system changes also may have a significant impact on daily functioning. The lungs provide the mechanism for gas exchange to and from the bloodstream. Aging results in structural changes of the lungs (e.g., decreased elastic recoil and increased chest wall rigidity) that decrease lung capacity and the efficiency of this gas exchange. These increasing inefficiencies of the respiratory system may lead to increased fatigue and shortness of breath during exertion. Individuals may experience cognitive panic attack symptoms (e.g., fear of suffocation). Chronic obstructive pulmonary disease, which is the increased resistance to airflow due to some pathological process (e.g., emphysema, asthma, or chronic bronchitis), also limits the functioning of the respiratory system and exacerbates the age-related deficiencies of the respiratory system. Similar to cardiovascular changes, respiratory changes result in physical limitations for the individual that may be frustrating, distressing, and anxiety provoking. However, these changes may also serve as a cue for the individual to engage in more healthy behaviors (e.g., exercising, quitting smoking).

Immune system. Immunologic changes make older adults more susceptible to infections (e.g., pneumonia and influenza). The immune system responds more slowly to infections as the number of certain cells associated with fighting infection (e.g., helper T-cells, mature T-lymphocytes) diminish with age. In addition to an increased likelihood of developing infections, a compromised immune system has also been linked to an increased incidence of cancer. Psychological disorders may also compound problems associated with changes in the immune system. For example, depression has been associated with decreased immune functioning. Older adults, who already have decreased immune system responsiveness, may then be at even greater risk of developing an infection if they experience depressive symptoms.

Musculoskeletal system. Changes in the bones, joints, and muscles also may have significant impact on older individuals. Bones lose mineral content and thus become more brittle and susceptible to fractures. This can also increase the likelihood of falls resulting from fractures associated with ambulation. However, the rate at which mineral content is lost varies depending on hormonal influences and behavioral history (e.g., smoking, physical activity, diet). Increased muscle age results in decreased strength and flexibility, which may also contribute to an increased incidence of falls among the elderly. Individuals may also develop a fear of falling or even experience posttraumatic stress disorder symptoms following a fall (Edelstein & Drozdick, 1998).

Summary and recommendations. Considering the many biological and medical changes that accompany increased age, therapists working with older adults need to work in *conjunction* with medical staff to educate older clients about natural changes associated with age. Clients may become distressed about changes that occur with increased age (e.g., walking results in shortness of breath, tiredness, or soreness) or they may be diagnosed with a medical disorder that will seriously impact their quality of life. Additionally, presenting symptoms may be indicative of both psychological and medical problems. Shortness of breath and chest tightness may be related to anxiety, or may indicate serious cardiovascular or respiratory changes. Changes in sleep patterns, decreased energy, and a diminished appetite may be part of the natural aging process or a function of depression. Likewise, psychological changes, such as memory problems, increased agitation, or paranoia, may be due to psychological (e.g., depression) or medical causes (e.g., cancer, Alzheimer's disease). Consultation with physicians is essential to appropriate assessment of whether presenting symptoms are related to psychological problems, medical disease, or both.

Therapists working with older adults should also be prepared to assist clients with their adaptation to the physiological limitations of aging. Assessing concerns about health-related issues and biological changes may be important for improving overall functioning. For example, an individual who expresses a fear of falling may be less likely to engage in enjoyable activities away from home. Issues such as developing appropriate pacing for strenuous activities, pain management, and lifestyle and psychological changes associated with increasing age are important to consider when assisting clients in the successful adaptation of the older adult.

Medication Use

Medication use contributes additional complexities to assessment and treatment of older adults. The average ambulatory older adult is prescribed two to four different medications. The medications used to treat many of the medical disorders have side-effects that result in cognitive and behavioral changes. For example, antihypertensive medications may cause nightmares, insomnia, and fatigue. Insulin injections may yield temporary cognitive impairment. Medication taken in the morning may negatively influence the client's behavior (e.g., increase agitation, increase drowsiness, and decrease concentration). Therefore, assessment interviews and testing should be scheduled during a time of day when the potential impact of medical conditions and medications is as limited as possible.

Another problem associated with medication use is that 70% of older adults take only 50–75% of the prescribed doses of a medication. They therefore may not receive the full benefits from medical treatments. Thus, it is important to determine the extent to which medical regimens are followed before drawing conclusions regarding the efficacy of pharmacological treatment. When appropriate, medication compliance should be addressed in the context of overall treatment. Regular therapy sessions are also opportunities to develop strategies for and monitor compliance with medical regimens.

The problems with medication use, along with the physical changes of the cardiovascular, respiratory, immune, and musculoskeletal systems, as well as other natural physiological aging and disease processes, can have a significant impact on the older adult's daily physical and psychological functioning. By taking these factors into consideration, the clinician can maximize treatment efficacy.

SUMMARY

Older adults can be quite different from younger adults along a variety of physical and psychological dimensions. Consequently, they often present new and complex assessment and treatment challenges to the therapist. It is important for therapists to be knowledgeable of age-related changes, their potential psychological and physiological consequences, and the implications of these consequences on addressing the psychological problems of older adults. For a more comprehensive understanding of older adults and their assessment and treatment, the interested reader is referred to Carstensen *et al.* (1996).

REFERENCES

Carstensen, L., Edelstein, B., & Dornbrand, L. (1996). *Practical handbook of clinical gerontology.* Thousand Oaks, CA: Sage.

Cooley, S., Deitch, I. M., Harper, M. S., Hinrichsen, G., Lopez, M., & Molinari, V. A. (1998). What practitioners should know about working with older adults. *Professional Psychology: Research and Practice, 29*, 413–427.

Edelstein, R., & Drozdick, L. (1998). Falls among older adults. In B. Edelstein (Ed.), *Comprehensive clinical psychology*, Vol. 7: *Clinical geropsychology*. Oxford: Elsevier.

Edelstein, B., Staats, N., Kalish, K., & Northrop, L (1996). Assessment of older adults. In M. Hersen & V. B. Van Hasselt (Eds.), *Psychological treatment of older adults: An introductory text* (pp. 35–68). New York: Plenum.

Gatz, M., Kasl-Godley, J. E., & Karel, M. J. (1996). Aging and mental disorders. In J. Birren & K. W. Schaie (Eds.), *Handbook of the psychology of aging* (4th ed., pp. 365–382). New York: Academic Press.

Heckheimer, E. F. (1989). *Health promotion of the elderly in the community.* New York: Saunders.

Knight, B. G. (1996). *Psychotherapy with older adults.* Thousand Oaks, CA: Sage.

Lang, F. R., & Carstensen, L. L. (1996). Social relationships and adaptation in late life. In B. A. Edelstein (Ed.), *Clinical geropsychology* (Vol. 7, pp. 55–72). Oxford: Elsevier Science.

Shaid, E. C., & Huber, K. (1996). *Gerontology review guide for nurses.* New York: Springer.

Smith, A. D. (1996). Memory. In J. E. Birren & K. W. Schaie (Eds.), *Handbook of the psychology of aging* (pp. 236–250). New York: Academic Press.

Vernon, M. (1989). Assessment of persons with hearing disabilities. In T. Hunt & C. J. Lindley (Eds.), *Testing older adults: A reference guide for geropsychological assessments* (pp. 150–162). Austin, TX: Pro-Ed.

Whitbourne, S. K. (1996). *The aging individual: Physical and psychological perspectives.* New York: Springer.

Zarit, J., & Zarit, S. (1987). Molar aging: The physiology and psychology of normal aging. In L. Carstensen and B. Edelstein (Eds.), *Handbook of clinical gerontology* (pp. 18–32). New York: Pergamon.

Author Index

454   Author Index

Welkowitz, L. A., 104
Wells, A., 102–103, 112
Whitbourne, S. K., 434, 444
Whittal, M. L., 266
Wickramaserka, I., 233
Williams, D. A., 158
Williams, J. B. W., 122, 340
Wilson, G. T., 266
Wittchen, H. U., 101, 110
Wolpe, J., 80, 92
Wood, B. A., 85
Woody, S. R., 158

Yehuda, R., 153
Young, J., 377
Youngren, M. A., 22–24
Yutzy, S. H., 182

Zarit, J., 436
Zarit, S., 436
Zeiss, A. M., 23, 24
Zimering, R. T., 152
Zuellig, A. R., 163
Zweben, A., 45, 46

Subject Index